BLACK AMERICAN BIOGRAPHIES

THE JOURNEY OF ACHIEVEMENT

AFRICAN AMERICAN HISTORY AND CULTURE

BLACK AMERICAN BIOGRAPHIES

THE JOURNEY OF ACHIEVEMENT

EDITED BY JEFF WALLENFELDT, MANAGER, GEOGRAPHY AND HISTORY

Britannica®
Educational Publishing

IN ASSOCIATION WITH

ROSEN
EDUCATIONAL SERVICES

Published in 2011 by Britannica Educational Publishing
(a trademark of Encyclopædia Britannica, Inc.)
in association with Rosen Educational Services, LLC
29 East 21st Street, New York, NY 10010.

Distributed exclusively by Rosen Educational Services.
For a listing of additional Britannica Educational Publishing titles, call toll free (800) 237-9932.

First Edition

Britannica Educational Publishing
Michael I. Levy: Executive Editor
J.E. Luebering: Senior Manager
Marilyn L. Barton: Senior Coordinator, Production Control
Steven Bosco: Director, Editorial Technologies
Lisa S. Braucher: Senior Producer and Data Editor
Yvette Charboneau: Senior Copy Editor
Kathy Nakamura: Manager, Media Acquisition
Jeff Wallenfeldt, Manager, Geography and History

Rosen Educational Services
Hope Lourie Killcoyne: Senior Editor and Project Manager
Nelson Sá: Art Director
Cindy Reiman: Photography Manager
Matthew Cauli: Designer, Cover Design
Introduction by Laura Loria

Library of Congress Cataloging-in-Publication Data

Black American biographies : the journey of achievement / edited by Jeff Wallenfeldt.
-- 1st ed.
      p. cm. — (African American history and culture)
In association with Britannica Educational Publishing, Rosen Education Services
Includes bibliographical references and index.
ISBN 978-1-61530-137-9 (library binding)
1. African Americans—Biography--Dictionaries, Juvenile. I. Wallenfeldt, Jeffrey H.
E185.96.B523 2011
920.0092'96073—dc22

2010010373

Manufactured in the United States of America

On the cover: U.S. abolitionist, writer, and orator Frederick Douglass is among the brightest lights in the African American firmament, an august gathering most recently illuminated by the ascendancy of yet another eloquent and stirring leader, Pres. Barack Obama. *Getty Images (Obama); MPI/Hulton Archive/Getty Images (Douglass)*

On pages 21, 72, 117, 147, 180, 213, 324: Martin Luther King, Jr. was among the hundreds of thousands who came to the nation's capital in August of 1963 to demand equal rights for black Americans. *Hulton Archive/Getty Images*

CONTENTS

27

44

71

77

84

113

128

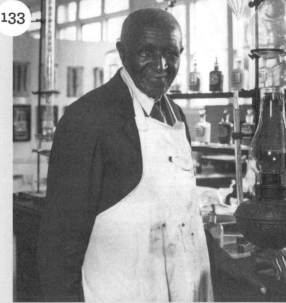

133

148

165

174

192

206

231

233

258

277

285

344

354

371

384

385

INTRODUCTION

For Americans, the pursuit of happiness has long been bound up with striving for excellence and achievement. But, although the Declaration of Independence found the fundamental equality of all people (or at least of men) to be self-evident and the right to liberty inalienable, for African Americans the pursuit of not just achievement and excellence but of liberty and equality was long obstructed by barriers of "race" and class and by the social and economic framework of life in the United States. As this book details, the black experience in America has been marked by hardship unlike that experienced by any other ethnic group in the country. Within these pages, readers will meet or rediscover a host of African Americans who have overcome these barriers to make important contributions to American political, religious, social, economic, and cultural life. In doing so, these men and women not only improved the lot of African Americans but that of all Americans.

Slavery is the scourge of American history, a source of national shame that dates from the arrival of the first African slaves in Jamestown colony in 1619. As this "peculiar institution" persisted into the 19th century, many African Americans fought for the emancipation of their people through methods varying from written protest to violent uprising. The most effective slave revolt in U.S. history was led by Nat Turner in 1831. Turner, the seven other slaves who were his initial followers, and those who joined them sustained their uprising for two days, killing his owners' family as well as 60 other white people before being stopped by the Virginia militia. After six weeks in hiding, Turner was tried and hanged. His rebellion led to a tightening of restrictions placed on slaves in regard to education and their ability to hold meetings precisely because it had served notice that slaves were capable of and willing to organize, arm themselves, and put life and limb on the line in order to escape bondage.

Risk came in many forms for abolitionists, who battled slavery with words as wells as deeds. Harriet Tubman, an escaped slave, was heralded as "the Moses of her people" for her courageous work as a conductor on the Underground Railroad. Risking her own liberty over the course of 19 separate expeditions into the slave state of Maryland, Tubman led more than 300 slaves to freedom in Canada. Skillful stealth of another sort was employed by David Walker. His pamphlet "*Appeal . . . to the Colored Citizens of the World*," published in 1829, called for a slave uprising to end bondage in the South. A Boston clothing storeowner, Walker cleverly slipped these pamphlets into the pockets of the garments he sold to white sailors or passed them on directly to black sailors, hoping his call

From the depths of slavery to the stewardship of a nation, the 400-year-long story of African Americans has arced from extreme adversity to the ultimate in achievement. On the facing page, Pres. Barack Obama and first lady Michelle Obama dance at the Neighborhood Inaugural Ball, their first official dance as first couple, Jan. 20, 2009. The Washington Post/Getty Images

to action would reach Southern ports. Reach the South the documents did, but not without consequences for Walker, as explained in this book.

Newspapers also played an important role in the struggle. From 1846 to 1849 the abolitionist weekly the *North Star*, published in Rochester, N.Y., benefited from the combined talents of two of the mid-19th century's most gifted African American writers and activists, Martin Delany and Frederick Douglass.

Activism thrived in the black community then, as it would for the generations to come. Foremost among the many African American activists who have worked to address civil rights issues was the Rev. Martin Luther King, Jr., who came to prominence as the leader of the Southern Christian Leadership Conference. Following the successful Montgomery Bus Boycott, which was sparked by Rosa Parks's famous refusal to give up her bus seat for a white man, King and the SCLC sought change through non-violent protest. Throughout the 1960s he travelled the country to lead demonstrations and deliver speeches, railing against segregation and injustice, the most famous of his orations being his "I Have a Dream" speech, delivered as part of the 1963 March on Washington. Five years later, while in Memphis supporting a sanitation workers' strike, he was assassinated.

Among the host of groundbreaking activists who preceded King was Booker T. Washington. Born shortly before the outbreak of the American Civil War,

Washington was convinced that the way for African Americans to improve their lives was through the mastery of manual trades and agricultural skills along with the acquisition of economic power. As president of the Tuskegee Normal and Industrial Institute from 1881 to 1915, Washington took two small converted buildings and grew them into the thriving learning community with a $2 million endowment at the time of his death. W.E.B. Du Bois and Ida Wells-Barnett, who were among the founders of the National Association for the Advancement of Colored People (NAACP) in 1909, considered Washington's pragmatic approach of acquiring vocational skills "accommodation." Instead, they called for an end to segregation and worked to ensure African Americans the rights guaranteed them by the Constitution. Winning workers' rights was the goal of African American trade unionist A. Philip Randolph, who was founding president of the Brotherhood of Sleeping Car Porters.

Some leaders of the Civil Rights movement of the 1950s, '60s, and '70s were more revolutionary in their approach, notably Malcolm X, a prominent figure in the Nation of Islam, who rejected King's non-violent philosophies, famously calling for blacks to defend their rights "by any means necessary." Malcolm's life ended violently when he was gunned down in 1965 by members of the Nation after he had left it to embrace a more orthodox Islamic philosophy. Much influenced by Malcolm, Eldridge

Cleaver, author of *Soul on Ice*, joined the Black Panther party and sought to spread its radical message.

At the same time, advances were made for and by African Americans within the system. In 1967, Pres. Lyndon B. Johnson appointed Thurgood Marshall to the Supreme Court, the first African American to hold the post. Famous for having successfully argued *Brown v. Board of Education* in 1954, the liberal-leaning Marshall rigorously continued his work of guaranteeing the constitutional rights of all citizens. More recently, Colin Powell served as the first African American chairman of the Joint Chiefs of Staff (1989-93). In 2001 he would go on to become the first African American secretary of state. When Condoleezza Rice replaced him in 2005, she became the first African American woman to hold that position.

But undoubtedly the culmination of years of struggle by African Americans to find true representation within government was the election as president in 2008 of Barack Obama, an African American senator from Illinois. A black man had become the leader of the free world.

Boundless talent and tremendous effort have been at the root of the accomplishments of many famous African Americans, not least those of George Washington Carver, whose pioneering agricultural science helped take the peanut from a footnote in America's ledger to the South's number two cash crop by 1940. Carver studied legumes, including peanuts, as a way to renew soil and provide a cheap, plentiful source of protein. His research revived the lagging Southern farm economy, upon which many African Americans depended. Far above the fields, in 1921, aviator Bessie Coleman became the first black woman to earn an international pilot's license. Soon after she began performing in aerial shows in the United States, though, she refused to fly for segregated audiences. Coleman used her fame to encourage other African Americans to follow her into the sky and to raise money to establish a school to train black aviators.

In the business world, black entrepreneurs made great strides, as well. From 1980 to 1991 Robert L. Johnson, the founder of Black Entertainment Television, oversaw the transformation of a small cable station into the first African American-controlled company to be traded on the New York Stock Exchange. In 2001, Johnson's sale of BET made him the first black American billionaire. He used his earnings to become the first African American majority owner of a franchise in the National Basketball Association, when he bought the Charlotte Bobcats. Another captain of industry, Kenneth Chenault, helped revive the sagging fortunes of American Express in the 1990s on the way to becoming its chief executive officer and the first African American CEO of a Fortune 500 company. He then steered the company through hard times after the September 11 attacks, which damaged its headquarters and in which 11 of its employees were killed.

It is hard to imagine American culture without the contributions of the multitude of gifted black artists who have helped shape it. Among the many African Americans who have left indelible marks on American literature are a pair of women, Toni Morrison, who earned a Pulitzer Prize for her novel *Beloved* (1987), based on the true story of a runaway slave, and the Nobel Prize for literature in 1993; and Maya Angelou, considered by many a national treasure for her poetry and prose, especially 1970's *I Know Why The Caged Bird Sings*. Broadway is home for the talents of choreographer Savion Glover, who developed the tap style known as "hitting," featured in his Tony Award-winning show *Bring in 'Da Noise, Bring in 'Da Funk*. In print journalism, Gordon Parks bore witness to the civil rights movement and ghetto life with memorable images during his tenure (1948-72) as the first African American staff photographer for *Life* magazine. On the air, in 1978 Max Robinson became the first African American to anchor a nightly network news program, a major feat at a time when most Americans looking for television news turned to the three networks—ABC, NBC, and CBS.

The 2001 Academy Awards ceremony was an important moment in black history. That night, Halle Berry and Denzel Washington won the awards for best actress and actor, becoming, the second and third African Americans to receive best-acting honours in leading roles. Sidney Poitier, who had been the first African American to take the top acting Oscar, for his performance in *Lilies of the Field* (1963), made a point of choosing characters that defied black stereotypes throughout his long career. Another Oscar winner, Whoopi Goldberg (best supporting actress in 1990 for her role in *Ghost*), is also well known as a comedian. Other African American comedians such as Richard Pryor, Bill Cosby, and Eddie Murphy have enjoyed tremendous success on both the big and small screens.

American music has been much defined and frequently dominated by African American artists. Most genres of popular music from rock to soul to pop have been greatly influenced by black musicians. Jazz, an original American style of music has both European and African roots, but was the exclusive domain of black artists in its early days. The long list of African Americans who pushed the boundaries of the genre has to include Charlie Parker, Louis Armstrong, Dizzy Gillespie, and Miles Davis. Similarly vital to the development of the blues were the legendary B.B. King and Muddy Waters, who, among others, added electric guitar to the acoustic blues of the South.

In the 1950s, rhythm and blues caught the imagination of both young blacks and whites, leading to development of both rock and roll and soul music, the latter of which, in effect, was a secularized version of the deeply emotional gospel music. During the 1960s and '70s, in the hands of a stable of immensely talented writers, producers, and performers at Detroit's Motown Record Corporation (among them Smokey Robinson, Stevie

Wonder, the Supremes, the Temptations, the Jackson 5), soul, too, crossed over to become the "Sound of Young America." Soul begat disco, but it also led the way to funk. By the 1980s, the dominant form of music in the African American community was hip-hop, popularized by artists such as Public Enemy and Run-D.M.C. As hip-hop moved into the new century, popular performers Jay-Z and Diddy were nearly as renowned as music executives and entrepreneurs as they were as rappers.

On the baseball diamond, basketball court, football field, and beyond, the contributions of African American athletes have been game changing. Most famously, Jackie Robinson spectacularly broke major league baseball's colour barrier as the National League's Rookie of the Year in 1947. Two years later he won the League's batting championship with .342 average and its Most Valuable Player award. In 1966, Willie Mays, widely regarded as the best all-around player in baseball history, became the game's highest paid player to that date. Barry Bonds broke the record for career home runs with his 756th in 2007, surpassing the total amassed by Hank Aaron in the 1950s, '60s, and '70s. In basketball, although Michael Jordan is generally recognized as the greatest player in NBA history, the efforts of Wilt Chamberlain, Bill Russell, and Magic Johnson kept many a sports fan in spectator heaven. As for the gridiron, dozens of African American players have been enshrined in the Pro Football Hall of Fame in Canton, Ohio, including a pantheon of great running backs headed by Jim Brown and Walter Payton.

In the boxing ring, Muhammad Ali, who proclaimed himself to be "the Greatest," was the first fighter to win the world heavyweight championship on three separate occasions over his 20-year career. George Foreman was the heavyweight champion twice and, at age 45 in 1994, the division's oldest title holder. In track and field, Jesse Owens triumphed in the Olympics of 1936 in Berlin, winning four gold medals and embarrassing Adolf Hitler, for whom the Olympics were meant to prove Aryan superiority. Sprinter Florence Griffith Joyner—"FloJo"—who won three gold medals and one silver medal at the 1988 Olympic Games in Seoul, also set records for the 100-meter and 200-meter dashes that have lasted for decades. Among the world's best-known athletes at the beginning of the 21st century were tennis superstar sisters Venus and Serena Williams, and Tiger Woods, who, at age 21 in 1997, was the first black golfer to win the Masters Tournament, and in 2001 became the first player to win all four major professional golf tournaments in one year.

In this book, readers will find the often dramatic, heroic, inspiring, and human stories of hundreds of African Americans who have made history. From popular artists to politicians, athletes to activists, these men and women from all over America have contributed to the legacy of the black American experience—and the American experience as a whole.

CHAPTER 1

ABOLITIONISM AND ACTIVISM

The African American struggle for freedom has had many faces and taken many forms. Often, in the beginning, it was a whisper, a secret lesson in reading and writing performed out of the sight of masters who forbade slave literacy, or it took the form of coded language—the forerunner of hip slang—that allowed slaves to communicate in the presence of unknowing slave owners. Before long it was a clarion call to action sounded with force and eloquence from the pulpit, the podium, the pavement, and in print. This chapter examines the lives and work of some of those who led the way toward fulfilling the promise the Declaration of Independence and the Constitution of the United States held for African Americans, keeping their eyes—and those of the people they led—on the prize of freedom and equality.

ABOLITIONISTS

One response to slavery was outright rebellion. Beginning early in the history of the republic, revolts led by slaves such as Gabriel and Nat Turner ultimately failed, but nevertheless shook the foundation of Southern society, prompting ever more repressive reactions by slave owners fearful that their way of life was threatened from inside and outside. Beyond the South the abolition movement gained force in the early

19th century, advanced partly by scores of sympathetic whites. Prominent among them were William Lloyd Garrison, who helped organize the American Anti-Slavery Society and was the publisher of the influential abolitionist periodical *The Liberator*; novelist Harriet Beecher Stowe, whose *Uncle Tom's Cabin* (1852) opened the eyes of millions to the inhumanity of slavery; and John Brown, who led an assault by black and white abolitionists on the federal arsenal in Harpers Ferry, Va. (now West Virginia), in 1859 in an attempt to spark a slave revolt, and whose biographer David S. Reynolds characterized as "the *least* racist white person" among those pre-Civil War figures he had investigated.

Notwithstanding the courage and commitment of these white fellow travelers, it was African American abolitionists who most forcefully and evocatively conveyed the urgency of the plight of their people, including David Walker, author of the incendiary pamphlet *Appeal . . . to the Colored Citizens of the World* . . . (1829); physician, army officer, and writer Martin R. Delany, whose righteous indignation was couched in an early form of black nationalism; and Frederick Douglass, the preeminent African American spokesman of his day, an organizer, journalist, and author who had the ear of Abraham Lincoln. Harriet Tubman not only provided an impassioned female voice but also risked her life again and again as a conductor on the Underground Railroad.

Martin R. Delany

(b. May 6, 1812, Charles Town, Va., U.S.—d. Jan. 24, 1885, Xenia, Ohio)

Abolitionist, physician, and editor Martin Robison Delany espoused black nationalism and racial pride even before the Civil War period, anticipating expressions of such views a century later.

In search of quality education for their children, the Delanys moved to Pennsylvania when Martin was a child. At 19, while studying nights at an African American church, he worked days in Pittsburgh. Embarking on a course of militant opposition to slavery, he became involved in several racial improvement groups. Under the tutelage of two sympathetic physicians he achieved competence as a doctor's assistant as well as in dental care, working in this capacity in the South and Southwest (1839).

Returning to Pittsburgh, Delany started a weekly newspaper, the *Mystery*, which publicized grievances of blacks in the United States and also championed women's rights. The paper won an excellent reputation, and its articles were often reprinted in the white press. From 1846 to 1849 Delany worked in partnership with the abolitionist leader Frederick Douglass in Rochester, N.Y., where they published another weekly, the *North Star*. After three years Delany decided to pursue formal medical studies; he was one of the first blacks to be admitted to Harvard Medical School and became a leading Pittsburgh physician.

In the 1850s Delany developed an overriding interest in foreign colonization opportunities for African Americans, and in 1859–60 he led an exploration party to West Africa to investigate the Niger Delta as a location for settlement.

In protest against oppressive conditions in the United States, Delany moved in 1856 to Canada, where he continued his medical practice. At the beginning of the Civil War (1861–65) he returned to the United States and helped recruit troops for the famous 54th Massachusetts Volunteers, for which he served as a surgeon. To counter a desperate Southern scheme to impress its slaves into the military forces late in the war, in February 1865, Delany was made a major (the first black man to receive a regular army commission) and was assigned to Hilton Head Island, S.C., to recruit and organize former slaves for the North. When peace came in April he became an official in the Freedmen's Bureau, serving for the next two years.

In 1874 Delany ran unsuccessfully for lieutenant governor as an Independent Republican in South Carolina; thereafter his fortunes declined. He was the author of *The Condition, Elevation, Emigration, and Destiny of the Colored People of the United States Politically Considered* (1852).

FREDERICK DOUGLASS

(b. February 1818?, Tuckahoe, Md., U.S.—d. Feb. 20, 1895, Washington, D.C.)

Frederick Douglass was one of the most eminent human-rights leaders of the 19th century. His oratorical and literary brilliance thrust him into the forefront of the U.S. abolition movement, and he became the first black citizen to hold high rank in the U.S. government.

Separated as an infant from his slave mother (he never knew his white father), Frederick (born Frederick Augustus Washington Bailey) lived with his grandmother on a Maryland plantation until, at age eight, his owner sent him to Baltimore to live as a house servant with the family of Hugh Auld, whose wife defied state law by teaching young Frederick to read. Auld, however, declared that learning would make him unfit for slavery, and Frederick was forced to continue his education surreptitiously with the aid of schoolboys in the street. Upon the death of his master, Frederick was returned to the plantation as a field hand at 16. Later, he was hired out in Baltimore as a ship caulker. Frederick tried to escape with three others in 1833, but the plot was discovered before they could get away. Five years later, however, he fled to New York City and then to New Bedford, Mass., where he worked as a labourer for three years, eluding slave hunters by changing his surname to Douglass.

At a Nantucket, Mass., antislavery convention in 1841, Douglass was invited to describe his feelings and experiences under slavery. These extemporaneous remarks were so poignant and naturally eloquent that he was unexpectedly catapulted into a new career as agent for the Massachusetts Anti-Slavery Society. From then on, despite heckling and mockery, insult, and violent personal

Frederick Douglass. Library of Congress, Washington, D.C.

attack, Douglass never flagged in his devotion to the abolitionist cause.

To counter skeptics who doubted that such an articulate spokesman could ever have been a slave, Douglass felt compelled to write his autobiography in 1845, revised and completed in 1882 as *Life and Times of Frederick Douglass*. Douglass's account became a classic in American literature as well as a primary source about slavery from the bondsman's viewpoint. To avoid recapture by his former owner, whose name and location he had given in the narrative, in 1845 Douglass left on a two-year speaking tour of Great Britain and Ireland. Abroad, Douglass helped to win many new friends for the abolition movement and to cement the bonds of humanitarian reform between the continents.

Douglass returned with funds to purchase his freedom and also to start his own antislavery newspaper, the *North Star* (later *Frederick Douglass's Paper*), which he published from 1847 to 1860 in Rochester, N.Y. The abolition leader William Lloyd Garrison disagreed with the need for a separate, black-oriented press, and the two men broke over this issue as well as over Douglass's support of political action to supplement moral suasion. Thus, after 1851 Douglass allied himself with the faction of the movement led by James G. Birney. He did not countenance violence, however, and specifically counseled against the raid on Harpers Ferry, Va. (October 1859).

During the Civil War (1861–65) Douglass became a consultant to Pres. Abraham Lincoln, advocating that former slaves be armed for the North and that the war be made a direct confrontation against slavery. Throughout Reconstruction (1865–77), Douglass fought for full civil rights for freedmen and vigorously supported the women's rights movement.

After Reconstruction, Douglass served as assistant secretary of the Santo Domingo Commission (1871), and in the District of Columbia he was marshal (1877–81) and recorder of deeds (1881–86); finally, he was appointed U.S. minister and consul general to Haiti (1889–91).

GABRIEL

(b. *c.* 1775, near Richmond, Va., U.S.—d. September 1800, Richmond)

Bondsman Gabriel Prosser, better known simply as Gabriel, planned the first major slave rebellion in U.S. history (Aug. 30, 1800). His abortive revolt greatly increased the whites' fear of the slave population throughout the South.

The son of an African-born mother, Gabriel grew up as the slave of Thomas H. Prosser. Gabriel became a deeply religious man, strongly influenced by biblical example. In the spring and summer of 1800, he laid plans for a slave insurrection aimed at creating an independent black state in Virginia with himself as king. He planned a three-pronged attack on Richmond, Va., that would seize the arsenal, take the powder house, and kill all whites except Frenchmen, Methodists, and Quakers. Some historians believe that Gabriel's army of 1,000 slaves (other estimates range from 2,000 to 50,000), assembled 6 miles (9.5 km) outside the city on the appointed night, might have succeeded had it not been for a violent rainstorm that washed out bridges and inundated roads. Before the rebel forces could be reassembled, Governor James Monroe, already informed of the plot, ordered out the state militia. Gabriel and about 34 of his companions were subsequently arrested, tried, and hanged.

Harriet Tubman

(b. c. 1820, Dorchester county, Md., U.S.—d. March 10, 1913, Auburn, N.Y.)

Bondwoman Harriet Tubman escaped from slavery in the South to become a leading abolitionist before the Civil War. She led hundreds of bondsmen to freedom in the North along the route of the Underground Railroad—an elaborate secret network of safe houses organized for that purpose.

Born a slave, Araminta Ross later adopted her mother's first name, Harriet. From early childhood she worked variously as a maid, a nurse, a field hand, a cook, and a woodcutter. About 1844 she married John Tubman, a free black.

In 1849, on the strength of rumours that she was about to be sold, Tubman fled to Philadelphia, leaving behind her husband, parents, and siblings. In December 1850 she made her way to Baltimore, Md., whence she led her sister and two children to freedom. That journey was the first of some 19 increasingly dangerous forays into Maryland in which, over the next decade, she conducted upward of 300 fugitive slaves along the Underground Railroad to Canada. By her extraordinary courage, ingenuity, persistence, and iron discipline, which she enforced upon her charges, Tubman became the railroad's most famous conductor and was known as the "Moses of her people." It has been said that she never lost a fugitive she was leading to freedom.

Rewards offered by slaveholders for Tubman's capture eventually totaled $40,000. Abolitionists, however, celebrated her courage. John Brown, who consulted her about his own plans to organize an antislavery raid of a federal armoury in Harpers Ferry, Va. (now in West Virginia), referred to her as "General" Tubman. About 1858 she bought a small farm near Auburn, New York, where she placed her aged parents (she had brought them out of Maryland in June 1857), where she herself would come to live after the Civil War. From 1862 to 1865 she served as a scout, as well as nurse and laundress, for Union forces in South Carolina. For the Second Carolina Volunteers, under the command of Colonel James Montgomery, Tubman spied on Confederate territory. When she returned with information about the locations of warehouses and ammunition, Montgomery's troops were able to make

Harriet Tubman, c. *1890.* MPI/Hulton Archive/Getty Images

carefully planned attacks. For her wartime service Tubman was paid so little that she had to support herself by selling homemade baked goods.

After the Civil War Tubman settled in Auburn and began taking in orphans and the elderly, a practice that eventuated in the Harriet Tubman Home for Indigent Aged Negroes. The home later attracted the support of former abolitionist comrades and of the citizens of Auburn, continuing in existence for some years after her death. In the late 1860s and again in the late 1890s Tubman applied for a federal pension for her Civil War services. Some 30 years after her service, a private bill providing for $20 monthly was passed by Congress.

NAT TURNER

(b. Oct. 2, 1800, Southampton county, Va., U.S.—d. Nov. 11, 1831, Jerusalem, Va.)

Bondsman Nat Turner led the only effective, sustained slave rebellion (August 1831) in U.S. history. Spreading terror throughout the white South, his action set off a new wave of oppressive legislation prohibiting the education, movement, and assembly of slaves and stiffened proslavery, antiabolitionist convictions that persisted in that region until the Civil War (1861–65).

Turner was born the property of a prosperous small-plantation owner in a remote area of Virginia. His mother was an African native who transmitted a passionate hatred of slavery to her son. He learned to read from one of his master's sons, and he eagerly absorbed intensive religious training. In the early 1820s he was sold to a neighbouring farmer of small means. During the following decade Turner's religious ardour tended to approach fanaticism, and he saw himself called upon by God to lead his people out of bondage. He began to exert a powerful influence on many of the nearby slaves, who called him "the Prophet."

In 1831, shortly after he had been sold again—this time to a craftsman named Joseph Travis—a sign in the form of an eclipse of the Sun caused Turner to believe that the hour to strike was near. His plan was to capture the armoury at the county seat, Jerusalem, and, having gathered many recruits, to press on to the Dismal Swamp, 30 miles (48 km) to the east, where capture would be difficult. On the night of August 21, together with seven fellow slaves in whom he had put his trust, he launched a campaign of total annihilation, murdering Travis and his family in their sleep and then setting forth on a bloody march toward Jerusalem. In two days and nights about 60 white people were ruthlessly slain. Doomed from the start, Turner's insurrection was handicapped by lack of discipline among his followers and by the fact that only 75 blacks rallied to his cause. Armed resistance from the local whites and the arrival of the state militia—a total force of 3,000 men—provided the final crushing blow. Only a few miles from the county seat the insurgents were dispersed and either killed or captured, and many innocent slaves were massacred in the hysteria that followed. Turner eluded his pursuers for six weeks but was finally captured, tried, and hanged.

Nat Turner's rebellion put an end to the white Southern myth that slaves were either contented with their lot or too servile to mount an armed revolt. In Southampton county black people came to measure time from "Nat's Fray," or "Old Nat's War." For many years in black churches throughout the country, the name Jerusalem referred not only to the Bible but also covertly to the place where the rebel slave had met his death.

Turner has been most widely popularized by William Styron in his novel *The Confessions of Nat Turner* (1967).

DAVID WALKER

(b. Sept. 28, 1785, Wilmington, N.C., U.S.—d. June 28, 1830, Boston, Mass.)

Abolitionist David Walker was the author of one of the most radical documents of the antislavery movement, the pamphlet *Appeal . . . to the Colored Citizens of the World . . .* (1829), in which he urged slaves to fight for their freedom.

Born of a slave father and a free mother, Walker grew up free, obtained an education, and traveled throughout the country, settling in Boston. There he became involved in the abolition movement and was a frequent contributor to *Freedom's Journal*, an antislavery weekly.

Sometime in the 1820s he opened a secondhand clothing store on the Boston waterfront. Through this business he could purchase clothes taken from sailors in barter for drink and then resell them to seamen about to embark. In the copious pockets of these garments he concealed copies of his *Appeal*, which he reasoned would reach Southern ports and pass through the hands of other used-clothes dealers who would know what to do with them. He also used sympathetic black seamen to distribute pamphlets directly.

When the smuggled pamphlets began to appear in the South, the states reacted with legislation prohibiting circulation of abolitionist literature and forbidding slaves to learn to read and write. Warned that his life was in danger, Walker refused to flee to Canada. His body was found soon afterward near his shop; many believed he had been poisoned.

Walker's *Appeal* for a slave revolt, widely reprinted after his death, was accepted by a small minority of abolitionists, but most antislavery leaders and free blacks rejected his call for violence at the time.

Walker's only son, Edwin G. Walker, was elected to the Massachusetts legislature in 1866.

ACTIVISTS

The Civil War and its aftermath brought emancipation, citizenship, and suffrage to African Americans, at least in the amendments to the Constitution of the United States that guaranteed the same (the Thirteenth, Fourteenth, and Fifteenth Amendments, respectively). Yet the de facto fulfillment of those civil rights was just beginning. African Americans joined together in a call for change, but the chorus was not always harmonious; indeed, the goals and methods of those at the forefront of the movement were often polarized— whether it was the focus on economic self-empowerment at the expense of the pursuit of civil rights advocated by Booker T. Washington, whom his rival for influence W.E.B. Du Bois saw as accomodationist, or the nonviolent resistance of Martin Luther King that came to be seen as too timid by black nationalists and radicals such as Malcolm X, Stokely Carmichael, and Eldridge Cleaver. Moreover, in addition to those whose speeches have been anthologized, there were countless others who rallied smaller audiences or brought solace and hope to friends and family and who undertook actions of civil disobedience both unplanned—such as Rosa Parks's refusal to yield her seat on a segregated bus—and planned, such as the students who undertook sit-ins at "whites only" lunch counters and those who marched and met police baton charges. The following are portraits of some of the principal players in a revolution that was both "live," as poet Gil Scott Heron promised it would be, and "televised," as he predicted, tongue in cheek, that it would not be.

Ralph David Abernathy

(b. March 11, 1926, Linden, Ala., U.S.—d. April 17, 1990, Atlanta, Ga.)

Pastor and civil-rights leader Ralph David Abernathy was Martin Luther King's chief aide and closest associate during the civil rights movement of the 1950s and '60s.

The son of a successful farmer, Abernathy was ordained as a Baptist minister in 1948 and graduated with a B.S. degree from Alabama State University in 1950. His interest then shifted from mathematics to sociology, and he earned an M.A. degree in the latter from Atlanta University in 1951. That same year he became pastor of the First Baptist Church in Montgomery, Ala., meeting King a few years later when the latter became pastor of another Baptist church in the same city. In 1955–56 the two men organized a boycott by black citizens of the Montgomery bus system that forced the system's racial desegregation in 1956. This nonviolent boycott marked the beginning of the civil rights movement that was to desegregate American society during the following two decades.

King and Abernathy continued their close collaboration as the civil rights movement gathered momentum, and in 1957 they founded the Southern Christian Leadership Conference (SCLC; with King as president and Abernathy as secretary-treasurer) to organize the nonviolent struggle against segregation throughout the South. In 1961 Abernathy relocated his pastoral activities to Atlanta, and that year he was named vice president at large of the SCLC and King's designated successor there. He continued as King's chief aide and closest adviser until King's assassination in 1968, at which time Abernathy succeeded him as president of the SCLC. He headed that organization until his resignation in 1977, after which he resumed his work as the pastor of a Baptist church in Atlanta. His autobiography, *And the Walls Came Tumbling Down,* appeared in 1989.

ELLA BAKER

(b. Dec. 13, 1903, Norfolk, Va., U.S.—d. Dec. 13, 1986, New York, N.Y.)

Community organizer and political activist Ella Baker brought her skills and principles to bear in the major civil rights organizations of the mid-20th century.

Baker was reared in Littleton, N.C. In 1918 she began attending the high school academy of Shaw University in Raleigh, N.C. Baker continued her college education at Shaw, graduating as valedictorian in 1927. She then moved to New York City in search of employment. There she found people suffering from poverty and hardship caused by the Great Depression and was introduced to the radical political activism that became her life's work. In the early 1930s, in one of her first efforts at implementing social improvement, she helped organize the Young Negroes Cooperative League, which was created to form cooperative groups that would pool community resources and thus provide less-expensive goods and services to members.

Baker married T.J. Roberts in the late 1930s and then joined the staff of the National Association for the Advancement of Colored People (NAACP), first as a field secretary and later as national director of the NAACP's various branches. Unhappy with the bureaucratic nature of the NAACP and newly responsible for the care of her young niece, she resigned from her director position in 1946, but worked with the New York branch to integrate local schools and improve the quality of education for black children.

Inspired by the historic bus boycott in Montgomery, Ala., in 1955, Baker cofounded the organization In Friendship to raise money for the civil rights movement in the South. In 1957 she met with a group of Southern black ministers and helped form the Southern Christian Leadership Conference (SCLC) to coordinate reform efforts throughout the South. Martin Luther King, Jr., served as the SCLC's first president and Baker as its director. She left the SCLC in 1960 to help student leaders of college activist groups organize the Student Nonviolent Coordinating Committee (SNCC). With her guidance and encouragement, SNCC became one of the foremost advocates for human rights in the country. Her influence was reflected in the nickname she acquired: "Fundi," a Swahili word meaning a person who teaches a craft to the next generation.

Baker continued to be a respected and influential leader in the fight for human and civil rights until her death on her 83rd birthday.

JULIAN BOND

(b. Jan. 14, 1940, Nashville, Tenn., U.S.)

Legislator and civil rights leader Julian Bond is best known for his fight to take his duly elected seat in the Georgia House of Representatives.

The son of prominent educators, Bond attended Morehouse College in Atlanta, Ga., where he helped found a civil rights group and led a sit-in movement intended to desegregate Atlanta lunch counters. In 1960 he joined in creating the Student Nonviolent Coordinating Committee (SNCC), and he later served as communications director for the group. In 1965 he won a seat in the Georgia state legislature, but his endorsement of a SNCC statement accusing the United States of violating international law in Vietnam prompted the legislature to refuse to admit him. The voters in his district twice reelected him, but the legislature barred him each time. Finally, in December 1966, the U.S. Supreme Court ruled the exclusion unconstitutional, and Bond was sworn in on Jan. 9, 1967.

At the Democratic National Convention in 1968, Bond led an insurgent group of delegates that won half of Georgia's seats. He seconded the nomination of Eugene McCarthy and became the first black man to have his name placed in nomination for the vice presidential candidacy of a major party. Younger than the minimum age required for the position under the Constitution, however, Bond withdrew his name.

Bond served in the Georgia House of Representatives from 1967 to 1975 and in the Georgia Senate from 1975 to 1987. In 1986 he ran unsuccessfully for a seat in the U.S. House of Representatives. In addition to his legislative activities, Bond served as president of the Southern Poverty Law Center and as executive chairman of the National Association for the Advancement of Colored People (NAACP).

STOKELY CARMICHAEL

(b. June 29, 1941, Port of Spain, Trin.—d. Nov. 15, 1998, Conakry, Guinea)

Born in the West Indies, civil rights activist and black nationalist Stokely Carmichael was the originator of the rallying slogan "black power."

Carmichael immigrated to New York City in 1952, attended high school in the Bronx, and enrolled at Howard University in 1960. There he joined the Student Nonviolent Coordinating Committee (SNCC) and the Nonviolent Action Group. In 1961 Carmichael was one of several Freedom Riders who traveled through the South challenging segregation laws in interstate transportation. For his participation he was arrested and jailed for about 50 days in Jackson, Miss.

Carmichael continued his involvement with the civil rights movement and SNCC after his graduation with honours from Howard University in 1964. That summer he joined SNCC in Lowndes county, Alabama, for an African American voter registration drive and helped to organize the Lowndes County Freedom Organization, an independent political party. A black panther was chosen as the party's emblem, a powerful image later adopted in homage by the Black Panther Party.

During this period Carmichael and others associated with SNCC supported the nonviolence approach to desegregation espoused by Martin Luther King, Jr., but Carmichael was becoming increasingly frustrated, having witnessed beatings and murders of several civil-rights activists. In 1966 he became the chairman of SNCC, and during a march

Stokely Carmichael. Hulton Archive/Getty Images

in Mississippi he rallied demonstrators in founding the "black power" movement, which espoused self-defense tactics, self-determination, political and economic power, and racial pride. This controversial split from King's ideology of nonviolence and racial integration was seen by moderate blacks as detrimental to the civil-rights cause and was viewed with apprehension by many whites.

Before leaving SNCC in 1968, Carmichael traveled abroad speaking out against political and economic repression and denouncing U.S. involvement in the Vietnam War. Upon his return, Carmichael's passport was confiscated and held for 10 months. He left the United States in 1969 and moved with his first wife (1968–79), South African singer Miriam Makeba, to Guinea, West Africa. He also changed his name to Kwame Ture in honour of two early proponents of Pan-Africanism, Ghanaian Kwame Nkrumah and Guinean Sékou Touré. Carmichael helped to establish the All-African People's Revolutionary Party, an international political party dedicated to Pan-Africanism and the plight of Africans worldwide. In 1971 he wrote *Stokely Speaks: Black Power Back to Pan-Africanism.*

ELDRIDGE CLEAVER

(b. 1935, Wabbaseka, near Little Rock, Ark., U.S.—d. May 1, 1998, Pomona, Calif.)

Activist Eldridge Cleaver earned a lasting place in African American history with his autobiographical volume *Soul on Ice* (1968), a classic statement of black alienation in the United States.

Cleaver was an inmate of correctional institutions in California almost constantly from his junior high school days until 1966 for crimes ranging from possession of marijuana to assault with intent to murder. While in prison, he supplemented his incomplete education with wide reading and became a follower of the Black Muslim separatist Malcolm X. He also began writing the essays that would eventually be collected in *Soul on Ice*, and whose publication in *Ramparts* magazine helped him win parole in 1966.

After being paroled, Cleaver met Huey Newton and Bobby Seale, who had just founded the Black Panther Party in Oakland, Calif. Cleaver soon became the party's minister of information. The publication in 1968 of *Soul on Ice*, a collection of angry memoirs in which Cleaver traced his political evolution while denouncing American racism, made him a leading black radical spokesman. In April 1968, however, he was involved in a shoot-out in Oakland between Black Panthers and police that left one Panther dead and Cleaver and two police officers wounded. Faced with reimprisonment after the shoot-out, Cleaver jumped bail in November 1968 and fled first to Cuba and then to Algeria.

Having broken with the Panthers in 1971 and grown disillusioned with communism, Cleaver returned voluntarily to the United States in 1975. The charges against him were dropped in 1979 when he pled guilty to assault in connection with the 1968 shoot-out and was put on five years' probation. In his later years Cleaver proclaimed himself a born-again Christian and a Republican, engaged in various business ventures, and struggled with an addiction to cocaine.

W.E.B. Du Bois

(b. Feb. 23, 1868, Great Barrington, Mass., U.S.—d. Aug. 27, 1963, Accra, Ghana)

Sociologist W.E.B. (William Edward Burghardt) Du Bois was the most important black protest leader in the United States during the first half of the 20th century. He shared in the creation of the National Association for the Advancement of Colored People (NAACP) in 1909 and edited *The Crisis*, its magazine, from 1910 to 1934. Late in life he became identified with communist causes.

Early Career

Du Bois graduated from Fisk University, a black institution at Nashville, Tenn., in 1888. He received a Ph.D. from Harvard University in 1895. His doctoral dissertation, *The Suppression of the African Slave-Trade to the United States of America, 1638–1870*, was published in 1896. Although Du Bois took an advanced degree in history, he was broadly trained in the social sciences; and, at a time when sociologists were theorizing about race relations, he was conducting empirical inquiries into the condition of blacks. For more than a decade he devoted himself to sociological investigations of blacks in America, producing 16 research monographs published between 1897 and 1914 at Atlanta University, where he was a professor, as well as *The Philadelphia Negro; A Social Study* (1899), the first case study of a black community in the United States.

Although Du Bois had originally believed that social science could provide the knowledge to solve the race problem, he gradually came to the conclusion that in a climate of virulent racism, expressed in such evils as lynching, peonage, disfranchisement, Jim Crow segregation laws, and race riots, social change could be accomplished only through agitation and protest. In this view, he clashed with the most influential black leader of the period, Booker T. Washington, who, preaching a philosophy of accommodation, urged blacks to accept discrimination for the time being and elevate themselves through hard work and economic gain, thus winning the respect of the whites. In 1903, in his famous book *The Souls of Black Folk*, Du Bois charged that Washington's strategy, rather than freeing the black man from oppression, would serve only to perpetuate it. This attack crystallized the opposition to Booker T. Washington among many black intellectuals, polarizing the leaders of the black community into two wings—the "conservative" supporters of Washington and his "radical" critics.

Two years later, in 1905, Du Bois took the lead in founding the Niagara Movement, which was dedicated chiefly to attacking the platform of Booker T. Washington. The small organization, which met annually until 1909, was seriously weakened by internal squabbles and Washington's opposition. But it was significant as an ideological forerunner and direct inspiration for the interracial NAACP, founded in 1909. Du Bois played a prominent part in the creation of the NAACP and became the association's director of research and editor of its magazine, *The Crisis*. In this role he wielded an unequaled influence among middle-class blacks and progressive whites as the propagandist for the black protest from 1910 until 1934.

Both in the Niagara Movement and in the NAACP, Du Bois acted mainly as an integrationist, but his thinking always exhibited, to varying degrees, separatist-nationalist tendencies. In *The Souls of Black Folk* he had expressed the characteristic dualism of black Americans:

> *One ever feels his twoness—an American, a Negro; two souls, two thoughts, two unreconciled strivings; two warring ideals in one dark body, whose dogged strength alone keeps it from being torn asunder . . . He simply wishes to make it possible for a man to be both a Negro and an American, without being cursed and spit upon by his fellows, without having the doors of Opportunity closed roughly in his face.*

BLACK NATIONALISM AND SOCIALISM

Du Bois's black nationalism took several forms—the most influential being his pioneering advocacy of Pan-Africanism, the belief that all people of African descent had common interests and should work together in the struggle for their freedom. Du Bois was a leader of the first Pan-African Conference in London in 1900 and the architect of four Pan-African Congresses held between 1919 and 1927. Second, he articulated a cultural nationalism. As the editor of *The Crisis*, he encouraged the development of black literature and art and urged his readers to see "Beauty in Black." Third, Du Bois's black nationalism is seen in his belief that blacks should develop a separate "group economy" of producers' and consumers' cooperatives as a weapon for fighting economic discrimination and black poverty. This doctrine became especially important during the economic catastrophe of the 1930s and precipitated an ideological struggle within the NAACP.

Du Bois resigned from the editorship of *The Crisis* and the NAACP in 1934, yielding his influence as a race leader and charging that the organization was dedicated to the interests of the black bourgeoisie and ignored the problems of the masses. His interest in cooperatives was a part of his nationalism that developed out of his Marxist leanings. At the turn of the century, Du Bois had been an advocate of black capitalism and black support of black business, but by about

1905 he had been drawn toward socialist doctrines. Although he joined the Socialist Party only briefly in 1912, he remained sympathetic to Marxist ideas throughout the rest of his life.

Upon leaving the NAACP, Du Bois returned to Atlanta University, where he devoted the next 10 years to teaching and scholarship. In 1940 he founded the magazine *Phylon*, Atlanta University's "Review of Race and Culture." In 1945 he published the "Preparatory Volume" of a projected encyclopaedia of the black, for which he had been appointed editor in chief. He also produced two major books during this period. *Black Reconstruction: An Essay Toward a History of the Part Which Black Folk Played in the Attempt to Reconstruct Democracy in America, 1860–1880* (1935) was an important Marxist interpretation of the Reconstruction era (the period following the American Civil War during which the seceded Southern states were reorganized according to the wishes of Congress), and, more significantly, it

W.E.B. Du Bois, c. 1950. Keystone/Hulton Archive/Getty Images

provided the first synthesis of existing knowledge of the role of blacks in that critical period of American history. In 1940 appeared *Dusk of Dawn*, subtitled *An Essay Toward an Autobiography of a Race Concept*. In this brilliant book, Du Bois explained his role in both the African and the African American struggles for freedom, viewing his career as an ideological case study illuminating the complexity of the black-white conflict.

Following this fruitful decade at Atlanta University, he returned once more to a research position at the NAACP (1944–48). This brief connection ended in a second bitter quarrel, and thereafter Du Bois moved steadily leftward politically. Identified with pro-Russian causes, he was indicted in 1951 as an unregistered agent for a foreign power. Although a federal judge directed his acquittal, Du Bois had become completely disillusioned with the United States. In 1961 he joined the Communist Party and, moving to Ghana, renounced his American citizenship more than a year later. *The Autobiography of W.E.B. Du Bois* was published in 1968.

MEDGAR EVERS

(b. July 2, 1925, Decatur, Miss., U.S.—d. June 12, 1963, Jackson, Miss.)

Activist Medgar Evers became a martyr to the cause of the civil rights movement when his murder received national attention.

Evers served in the U.S. Army in Europe during World War II. Afterward he and his elder brother, Charles Evers, both graduated from Alcorn Agricultural and Mechanical College (now Alcorn State University, Lorman, Miss.) in 1950. They settled in Philadelphia, Miss., and engaged in various business pursuits—Medgar was an insurance salesman, and Charles operated a restaurant, a gas station, and other enterprises—and at the same time began organizing local affiliates of the National Association for the Advancement of Colored People (NAACP). They worked quietly at first, slowly building a base of support; in 1954 Medgar moved to Jackson to become the NAACP's first field secretary in Mississippi. He traveled throughout the state recruiting members and organizing voter-registration drives and economic boycotts.

During the early 1960s the increased tempo of civil-rights activities in the South created high and constant tensions, and in Mississippi conditions were often at the breaking point. On June 12, 1963, a few hours after Pres. John F. Kennedy had made an extraordinary broadcast to the nation on the subject of civil rights, Medgar Evers was shot and killed in an ambush in front of his home. The murder made Evers, until then a hardworking and effective but relatively obscure figure outside Mississippi, a nationally known figure. He was buried with full military honours in Arlington National Cemetery and awarded the 1963 Spingarn Medal of the NAACP.

Charles Evers immediately requested and was granted appointment by the

NAACP to his brother's position in Mississippi, and afterward he became a major political figure in the state. Evers's widow, Myrlie Evers-Williams, was the first woman to head the NAACP (1995–98).

Byron de La Beckwith, a white segregationist, was charged with the murder. He was set free in 1964 after two trials resulted in hung juries but was convicted in a third trial held in 1994. Beckwith was given a life sentence, and in 2001 he died in prison.

JAMES FARMER

(b. Jan. 12, 1920, Marshall, Texas, U.S.—d. July 9, 1999, Fredericksburg, Va.)

As a leader of the Congress of Racial Equality (CORE), James Farmer helped shape the civil rights movement through his nonviolent activism and organizing of sit-ins and Freedom Rides, which broadened popular support for passage of the Civil Rights and Voting Rights acts in the mid-1960s.

Farmer was educated at Wiley College in Marshall, Texas (1938), and at Howard University in Washington, D.C. (1941), where his father taught divinity. A conscientious objector on religious grounds, Farmer received a military deferral in World War II, and he joined the pacifist Fellowship of Reconciliation (FOR). In 1942 he cofounded CORE, which originated integrated bus trips through the South, called Freedom Rides, to challenge local efforts to block

James Farmer, 1964. U.S. News and World Report Magazine Photograph Collection, Library of Congress, Washington, D.C. (digital file no. LC-DIG-ppmsc-01266)

the desegregation of interstate busing. Farmer, who sought racial justice by means of nonviolence, was often a target of racial violence himself.

He resigned from the leadership of CORE in 1965, and in 1968 he lost a run for a seat in the U.S. House of Representatives to Shirley Chisholm. In 1969–70 he served as assistant secretary of health, education and welfare under

Pres. Richard M. Nixon. In 1985 Farmer published his autobiography, *Lay Bare the Heart*, and in 1998 he was awarded the Presidential Medal of Freedom.

MARCUS GARVEY

(b. Aug. 17, 1887, St. Ann's Bay, Jamaica—d. June 10, 1940, London, Eng.)

Charismatic leader Marcus Garvey organized the first important American black nationalist movement (1919–26), based in New York City's Harlem.

Marcus Garvey, 1922. UPI

Largely self-taught, Garvey attended school in Jamaica until he was 14. After traveling in Central America and living in London from 1912 to 1914, he returned to Jamaica, where, with a group of friends, he founded (Aug. 1, 1914) the Universal Negro Improvement and Conservation Association and African Communities League, usually called the Universal Negro Improvement Association (UNIA), which sought, among other things, to build in Africa a black-governed nation.

Failing to attract a following in Jamaica, Garvey went to the United States (1916) and soon established branches of the UNIA in Harlem and the other principal ghettos of the North. By 1919 the rising "Black Moses" claimed a following of about two million, though the exact number of association members was never clear. From the platform of the Association's Liberty Hall in Harlem, Garvey spoke of a "new Negro," proud of being black. His newspaper, *Negro World,* told of the exploits of heroes of the race and of the splendours of African culture. He taught that blacks would be respected only when they were economically strong, and he preached an independent black economy within the framework of white capitalism. To forward these ends, he established the Negro Factories Corporation and the Black Star Line (1919), as well as a chain of restaurants and grocery stores, laundries, a hotel, and a printing press.

He reached the height of his power in 1920, when he presided at an international convention in Liberty Hall, with delegates present from 25 countries. The affair was climaxed by a parade of 50,000 through the streets of Harlem, led by Garvey in flamboyant array.

His slipshod business methods, however, and his doctrine of racial purity and separatism (he even approved of the white racist Ku Klux Klan because it sought to separate the races) brought him bitter enemies among established black leaders, including labour leader A. Philip Randolph and W.E.B. Du Bois. Garvey's influence declined rapidly when he and other UNIA members were indicted for mail fraud in 1922 in connection with the sale of stock for the Black Star Line. He served two years of a five-year prison term, but in 1927 his sentence was commuted by Pres. Calvin Coolidge, and he was deported as an undesirable alien. Garvey was never able to revive the movement abroad, and he died in virtual obscurity.

FANNIE LOU HAMER

(b. Oct. 6, 1917, Ruleville, Miss., U.S.—d. March 14, 1977, Mound Bayou, Miss.)

Civil rights activist Fannie Lou Hamer (née Fannie Lou Townsend) is remembered for her efforts to desegregate the Mississippi Democratic Party.

The youngest of 20 children, Fannie Lou was working the fields with her sharecropper parents at the age of six. Amid poverty and racial exploitation, she received only a sixth-grade education. In 1942 she married Perry ("Pap") Hamer.

Her civil rights activism began in August 1962, when she answered a call by the Student Nonviolent Coordinating Committee (SNCC) for volunteers to challenge voter registration procedures that excluded African Americans. Fired from her job for her activism, she became a field secretary for SNCC and a registered voter in 1963.

In 1964 Hamer became vice-chairperson of the Mississippi Freedom Democratic Party (MFDP), established

Fannie Lou Hamer, 1964. Library of Congress Prints and Photographs Division

after unsuccessful attempts by African Americans to work with the all-white Mississippi Democratic Party. As a leader of the MFDP she gave a nationally televised address to the Credentials Committee at the 1964 Democratic National Convention in which she described incidents of violence and injustice suffered by civil rights activists, including her own experience of a jailhouse beating that left her crippled.

In 1967 Hamer published *To Praise Our Bridges: An Autobiography*. As a member of the Democratic National Committee for Mississippi (1968–71) and the Policy Council of the National Women's Political Caucus (1971–77), she actively opposed the Vietnam War and worked to improve economic conditions in Mississippi.

BENJAMIN L. HOOKS

(b. Jan. 31, 1925, Memphis, Tenn., U.S. —d. Apr. 15, 2010, Memphis)

Jurist, minister, and government official Benjamin L. Hooks was executive director of the National Association for the Advancement of Colored People (NAACP) from 1977 to 1993.

Hooks attended Le Moyne College in Memphis (1941–43) and Howard University, Washington, D.C. (1943–44; B.A., 1944), served in the U.S. Army during World War II, and later studied law at De Paul University in Chicago (J.D., 1948); no law school in Tennessee was admitting blacks at that time. From 1949 until 1965 he practiced law in Memphis. He participated in restaurant sit-ins of the late 1950s and early '60s and joined the Board of Directors of the Southern Christian Leadership Conference, among many other civil-rights and public-service organizations. Ordained a Baptist minister in the mid-1950s, Hooks preached regularly at churches in both Memphis and Detroit, and he won a wide following for his eloquence as a public speaker.

Assistant public defender of Shelby County (Memphis) from 1961, he was appointed judge of Shelby County Criminal Court in 1965, the first black to hold that position. He was elected for a full eight-year term in 1966, but he resigned in 1968. In July 1972 Hooks was appointed to the U.S. Federal Communications Commission and became the first black FCC commissioner. He resigned to become executive director of the NAACP on Aug. 1, 1977, succeeding Roy Wilkins. Hooks stressed the need for affirmative action and pressed for increased minority voter registration. He deplored underrepresentation of minorities in media ownership. He was awarded the Presidential Medal of Freedom in 2007.

JESSE JACKSON

(b. Oct. 8, 1941, Greenville, S.C., U.S.)

Civil rights leader, Baptist minister, and politician Jesse Jackson's bids for the U.S. presidency (in the Democratic Party's nomination races in 1983–84 and

1987–88) were the most successful by an African American until 2008, when Barack Obama captured the Democratic presidential nomination. Jackson's life and career have been marked by both accomplishment and controversy.

Jesse Louis Burns adopted the name of his stepfather, Charles Jackson, at about age 15. A good student in high school, Jesse was elected class president and later attended the University of Illinois (1959–60) on a football scholarship. He then transferred to the predominantly black Agricultural and Technical College of North Carolina in Greensboro and received a B.A. in sociology (1964). He moved to Chicago in 1966, did graduate work at the Chicago Theological Seminary, and was ordained a Baptist minister in 1968.

While an undergraduate, Jackson became involved in the civil rights movement. In 1965 he went to Selma, Ala., to march with Martin Luther King, Jr., and became a worker in King's Southern Christian Leadership Conference (SCLC). Jackson helped found the Chicago branch of Operation Breadbasket, the economic arm of the SCLC, in 1966 and served as the organization's national director from 1967 to 1971. He was in Memphis, Tenn., with King when the civil rights leader was assassinated on April 4, 1968, though his exact location at the moment King was shot has long been a matter of controversy. Accused of using the SCLC for personal gain, Jackson was suspended by the organization, whereupon he formally resigned in 1971 and founded Operation PUSH (People United to Save Humanity), a Chicago-based organization in which he advocated black self-help and achieved a broad audience for his liberal views. In 1984 he established the National Rainbow Coalition, which sought equal rights for African Americans, women, and homosexuals. These two organizations merged in 1996 to form the Rainbow/PUSH Coalition.

Jackson began traveling widely in the late 1970s to mediate or spotlight international problems and disputes. In 1979 he visited South Africa, where he spoke out against apartheid, and he later journeyed to the strife-ridden Middle East and campaigned to give Palestinians their own state. While some observers and government officials frowned on his diplomatic missions as meddlesome and self-aggrandizing, Jackson nonetheless won praise for negotiating the release of U.S. soldiers and civilians around the world, including in Syria (1984), Iraq (1990), and Yugoslavia (1999).

In the 1980s Jackson became a leading national spokesman and advocate for African Americans. His voter-registration drive was a key factor in the election of Chicago's first African American mayor, Harold Washington, in April 1983. The following year Jackson ran for the Democratic presidential nomination. During the campaign he drew criticism for his relationship with Louis Farrakhan of the Nation of Islam and for making a disparaging remark about New York's Jewish community; Jackson later apologized for his comments and distanced

Jesse Jackson at the Democratic National Convention, July 28, 2004. Jim Rogash/ WireImage/Getty Images

himself from Farrakhan. In what was then the strongest showing ever by an African American candidate, Jackson placed third in the primary voting. In 1988 he staged another bid for the Democratic nomination and came in second to the party's eventual nominee, Michael Dukakis. Jackson's increasing influence within the Democratic Party ensured that African American issues were an important part of the party's platform. Jackson, a dynamic orator, made memorable speeches at later Democratic conventions but declined to run again for the presidency.

In 1989 Jackson took residency in Washington, D.C., and in 1990, when the Washington City Council created two unpaid offices of "statehood senator"—popularly called "shadow senator"—to lobby the U.S. Congress for statehood for the District of Columbia, Jackson won election to one of the posts, his first elective office. In 1997 Pres. Bill Clinton named him a special envoy to Africa, where he traveled to promote human rights and democracy. That year Jackson also founded the Wall Street Project, which sought to increase minority opportunities in corporate America.

During the impeachment hearings against Clinton in 1998, Jackson counseled the president, and in 2000 Clinton awarded him the Presidential Medal of Freedom. That year Jackson also received a Master of Divinity degree from the Chicago Theological Seminary. Jackson continued his social activism, giving lectures and leading protests. His books

include *Straight from the Heart* (1987; ed. by Roger D. Hatch and Frank E. Watkins) and *Legal Lynching: Racism, Injustice, and the Death Penalty* (1995). His son Jesse Jackson, Jr., was elected to the U.S. Congress in 1995.

VERNON E. JORDAN, JR.

(b. Aug. 15, 1935, Atlanta, Ga., U.S.)

Attorney, civil rights leader, business consultant, and influential power broker Vernon E. Jordan, Jr., never held political office but served as a key adviser in the 1990s to Pres. Bill Clinton, having befriended him and his wife, Hillary Rodham Clinton, decades earlier.

Jordan grew up in Georgia and studied political science at DePauw University (B.A., 1957), where he distinguished himself as a compelling public speaker. After studying law at Howard University (J.D., 1960), Jordan joined the effort to desegregate colleges and universities and helped lead black student Charlayne Hunter through a group of whites protesting the University of Georgia's integration policy in 1961. He was named field secretary for the National Association for the Advancement of Colored People (NAACP) in Georgia (1961–63) and then became director of the Southern Regional Council for the Voter Education Project (1964–68). By 1966 Jordan's political influence was evident through his participation in Pres. Lyndon B. Johnson's civil rights conference. As director of the United Negro College Fund in 1970, he raised $10 million in contributions that benefited African American institutions. While serving as president of the National Urban League (1972–81), Jordan joined corporate boards such as American Express and Dow Jones, thereby using business connections to press the case for minority hiring and advancement. He survived a white supremacist's assassination attempt in 1980 but was wounded by gunshot. In 1981 Jordan moved into private law practice, joining the Washington, D.C., office of a Texas law firm in 1982 and quietly exerting his influence in corporate and political affairs for an increasingly elite clientele. After advising Bill Clinton's 1992 presidential campaign, Jordan helped guide the new president's transition into office but never took any political appointment, preferring instead to remain behind the scenes as one of Clinton's closest friends and a powerful political force in and beyond the nation's capital. He published an autobiography, *Vernon Can Read!* (written with Annette Gordon-Reed), in 2001.

CORETTA SCOTT KING

(b. April 27, 1927, Marion, Ala., U.S.—d. Jan. 30, 2006, Rosarito, Mex.)

Coretta Scott King, the wife of Martin Luther King, Jr., was an important civil rights activist in her own right.

Coretta Scott graduated from Antioch College in Yellow Springs, Ohio, and in 1951 enrolled at the New England Conservatory of Music in Boston. While working toward a degree in voice, she met Martin Luther King, Jr., then a graduate theology student at Boston University. They were married in 1953 and had four children.

After both had completed their studies, the Kings moved to Montgomery, Ala., where Martin Luther King had accepted a position as pastor of the Dexter Avenue Baptist Church. Coretta Scott King joined her husband in civil rights activism in the 1950s and '60s, taking part in the Montgomery bus boycott (1955) and efforts to pass the 1964 Civil Rights Act.

Following the assassination of her husband in 1968 and the conviction of James Earl Ray for the murder, she continued to be active in the civil rights movement. She founded in Atlanta, Georgia, the Martin Luther King, Jr., Center for Nonviolent Social Change (commonly known as the King Center), which was led at the turn of the 21st century by her son Dexter. The family's attempt to sell portions of King's papers brought her criticism in the late 1990s. She wrote a memoir, *My Life with Martin Luther King, Jr.* (1969), and edited, with her son Dexter, *The Martin Luther King, Jr., Companion: Quotations from the Speeches, Essays, and Books of Martin Luther King, Jr.* (1998). In 1969 she established an annual Coretta Scott King Award to honour an African American author of an outstanding text for children, and in 1979 a similar award was added to honour an outstanding African American illustrator.

MARTIN LUTHER KING, JR.

(b. Jan. 15, 1929, Atlanta, Ga.,
U.S.—d. April 4, 1968, Memphis, Tenn.)

Baptist minister and social activist Martin Luther King, Jr. led the civil rights movement in the United States from the mid-1950s until his death by assassination in 1968. His leadership was fundamental to that movement's success in ending the legal segregation of African Americans in the South and other parts of the United States. King rose to national prominence as head of the Southern Christian Leadership Conference, which promoted nonviolent tactics, such as the massive March on Washington (1963), to achieve civil rights. He was awarded the Nobel Peace Prize in 1964.

EARLY YEARS

King (born Michael King, Jr.) came from a comfortable middle-class family steeped in the tradition of the Southern

Martin Luther King, Jr. Julian Wasser

black ministry: both his father and maternal grandfather were Baptist preachers. His parents were college-educated, and King's father had succeeded his father-in-law as pastor of the prestigious Ebenezer Baptist Church in Atlanta. The family lived on Auburn Avenue, otherwise known as "Sweet Auburn," the bustling "black Wall Street," home to some of the country's largest and most prosperous black businesses and black churches in the years before the civil rights movement. Young Martin received a solid education and grew up in a loving extended family.

This secure upbringing, however, did not prevent King from experiencing the prejudices then common in the South. He never forgot the time when, at about age six, one of his white playmates announced that his parents would no longer allow him to play with King, because the children were now attending segregated schools. Dearest to King in these early years was his maternal grandmother, whose death in 1941 left him shaken and unstable. Upset because he had learned of her fatal heart attack while attending a parade without his parents' permission, the 12-year-old King attempted suicide by jumping from a second-story window.

In 1944, at age 15, King entered Morehouse College in Atlanta under a special wartime program intended to boost enrollment by admitting promising high-school students such as himself. Before beginning college, however, King spent the summer on a tobacco farm in Connecticut; it was his first extended stay away from home and his first substantial experience of race relations outside the segregated South. He was shocked by how peacefully the races mixed in the North. "Negroes and whites go [to] the same church," he noted in a letter to his parents. "I never [thought] that a person of my race could eat anywhere." This summer experience in the North only deepened King's growing hatred of racial segregation.

At Morehouse, King favoured studies in medicine and law, but these were eclipsed in his senior year by a decision to enter the ministry, as his father had urged. King's mentor at Morehouse was the college president, Benjamin Mays, a social gospel activist whose rich oratory and progressive ideas had left an indelible imprint on King's father. Committed to fighting racial inequality, Mays accused the African American community of complacency in the face of oppression, and he prodded the black church into social action by criticizing its emphasis on the hereafter instead of the here and now; it was a call to service that was not lost on the teenage King. He graduated from Morehouse in 1948.

King spent the next three years at Crozer Theological Seminary in Chester, Pa., where he became acquainted with Mohandas Gandhi's philosophy of nonviolence as well as with the thought of contemporary Protestant theologians. He earned a bachelor of divinity degree in 1951. Renowned for his oratorical skills, King was elected president of Crozer's student body, which was composed almost exclusively of white students. As a professor at Crozer wrote in a letter of recommendation for King, "The fact that with our student body largely Southern in constitution a colored man should be elected to and be popular [in] such a position is in itself no mean recommendation." From Crozer, King went to Boston University, where, in seeking a firm foundation for his own theological and ethical inclinations, he studied man's relationship to God and received a doctorate (1955) for a dissertation titled "A Comparison of the Conceptions of God in the Thinking of Paul Tillich and Henry Nelson Wieman."

THE MONTGOMERY BUS BOYCOTT

While in Boston, King met Coretta Scott, a native Alabamian who was studying at the New England Conservatory of Music. They were married in 1953 and had four children. King had been pastor of the Dexter Avenue Baptist Church in Montgomery, Ala., slightly more than a year when the city's small group of civil rights advocates decided to contest racial segregation on that city's public bus system following the incident on Dec. 1, 1955, in which Rosa Parks, an African American woman, had refused to surrender her bus seat to a white passenger and as a consequence was arrested for violating the city's segregation law. Activists formed the Montgomery Improvement Association to boycott the transit system and chose King as their leader. He had the advantage of being a young,

well-trained man who was too new in town to have made enemies; he was generally respected, and it was thought that his family connections and professional standing would enable him to find another pastorate should the boycott fail.

In his first speech to the group as its president, King declared:

We have no alternative but to protest. For many years we have shown an amazing patience. We have sometimes given our white brothers the feeling that we liked the way we were being treated. But we come here tonight to be saved from that patience that makes us patient with anything less than freedom and justice.

These words introduced to the country a fresh voice, a skillful rhetoric, an inspiring personality, and in time a dynamic new doctrine of civil struggle. Although King's home was dynamited and his family's safety threatened, he continued to lead the boycott until, one year and a few weeks later, the city's buses were desegregated.

THE SOUTHERN CHRISTIAN LEADERSHIP CONFERENCE

Recognizing the need for a mass movement to capitalize on the successful Montgomery action, King set about organizing the Southern Christian Leadership Conference (SCLC), which gave him a base of operation throughout the South, as well as a national platform from which to speak. King lectured in all parts of the country and discussed race-related issues with religious and civil rights leaders at home and abroad. In February 1959 he and his party were warmly received by India's Prime Minister Jawaharlal Nehru and others; as the result of a brief discussion with followers of Gandhi about the Gandhian concepts of peaceful noncompliance (satyagraha), King became increasingly convinced that nonviolent resistance was the most potent weapon available to oppressed people in their struggle for freedom. King also looked to Africa for inspiration. "The liberation struggle in Africa has been the greatest single international influence on American Negro students," he wrote. "Frequently I hear them say that if their African brothers can break the bonds of colonialism, surely the American Negro can break Jim Crow."

In 1960 King and his family moved to his native city of Atlanta, where he

U.S. Pres. Lyndon B. Johnson talking with Martin Luther King, Jr., in the Oval Office at the White House, Washington, D.C., 1963. Yoichi Okamoto/Lyndon B. Johnson Library Photo

became co-pastor with his father of the Ebenezer Baptist Church. At this post he devoted most of his time to the SCLC and the civil rights movement, declaring that the "psychological moment has come when a concentrated drive against injustice can bring great, tangible gains." His thesis was soon tested as he agreed to support the sit-in demonstrations undertaken by local black college students. In late October he was arrested with 33 young people protesting segregation at the lunch counter in an Atlanta department store. Charges were dropped, but King was sentenced to Reidsville State Prison Farm on the pretext that he had violated his probation on a minor traffic offense committed several months earlier. The case assumed national proportions, with widespread concern over his safety, outrage at Georgia's flouting of legal forms, and the failure of Pres. Dwight D. Eisenhower to intervene. King was released only upon the intercession of Democratic presidential candidate John F. Kennedy—an action so widely publicized that it was felt to have contributed substantially to Kennedy's slender election victory eight days later.

In the years from 1960 to 1965, King's influence reached its zenith. Handsome, eloquent, and doggedly determined, King quickly caught the attention of the news media, particularly of the producers of that budding medium of social change—television. He understood the power of television to nationalize and internationalize the struggle for civil rights, and his well-publicized tactics of active nonviolence (sit-ins, protest marches) aroused the devoted allegiance of many African Americans and liberal whites in all parts of the country, as well as support from the administrations of Presidents Kennedy and Lyndon B. Johnson. But there were also notable failures, as in Albany, Ga. (1961–62), when King and his colleagues failed to achieve their desegregation goals for public parks and other facilities.

THE LETTER FROM THE BIRMINGHAM JAIL

In Birmingham, Ala., in the spring of 1963, King's campaign to end segregation at lunch counters and in hiring practices drew nationwide attention when police turned dogs and fire hoses on the demonstrators. King was jailed along with large numbers of his supporters, including hundreds of schoolchildren. His supporters did not, however, include all the black clergy of Birmingham, and he was strongly opposed by some of the white clergy who had issued a statement urging African Americans not to support the demonstrations. From the Birmingham jail, King wrote a letter of great eloquence in which he spelled out his philosophy of nonviolence:

You may well ask: "Why direct action? Why sit-ins, marches and so forth? Isn't negotiation a better path?" You are quite right in calling for negotiation. Indeed, this is the very purpose of direct action.

Nonviolent direct action seeks to create such a crisis and foster such a tension that a community which has constantly refused to negotiate is forced to confront the issue.

Near the end of the Birmingham campaign, in an effort to draw together the multiple forces for peaceful change and to dramatize to the country and to the world the importance of solving the U.S. racial problem, King joined other civil rights leaders in organizing the historic March on Washington. On Aug. 28, 1963, an interracial assembly of more than 200,000 gathered peaceably in the shadow of the Lincoln Memorial to demand equal justice for all citizens under the law. Here the crowds were uplifted by the emotional strength and prophetic quality of King's famous "I Have a Dream" speech, in which he emphasized his faith that all men, someday, would be brothers.

The rising tide of civil rights agitation produced, as King had hoped, a strong effect on national opinion and resulted in the passage of the Civil Rights Act of 1964, authorizing the federal government to enforce desegregation of public accommodations and outlawing discrimination in publicly owned facilities, as well as in employment. That eventful year was climaxed by the award to King of the Nobel Peace Prize in Oslo in December. "I accept this award today with an abiding faith in America and an audacious faith in the future of mankind," said King in his acceptance speech.

"I refuse to accept the idea that the 'isness' of man's present nature makes him morally incapable of reaching up for the eternal 'oughtness' that forever confronts him."

CHALLENGES OF THE FINAL YEARS

The first signs of opposition to King's tactics from within the civil rights movement surfaced during the March 1965 demonstrations in Selma, Ala., which were aimed at dramatizing the need for a federal voting-rights law that would provide legal support for the enfranchisement of African Americans in the South. King organized an initial march from Selma to the state capitol building in Montgomery but did not lead it himself. The marchers were turned back by state troopers with nightsticks and tear gas. He was determined to lead a second march, despite an injunction by a federal court and efforts from Washington to persuade him to cancel it. Heading a procession of 1,500 marchers, black and white, he set out across Pettus Bridge outside Selma until the group came to a barricade of state troopers. But, instead of going on and forcing a confrontation, he led his followers to kneel in prayer and then unexpectedly turned back. This decision cost King the support of many young radicals who were already faulting him for being too cautious. The suspicion of an "arrangement" with federal and local authorities—vigorously but not entirely convincingly denied—clung to the Selma affair. The country was nevertheless aroused, resulting in the passage of the Voting Rights Act of 1965.

Throughout the nation, impatience with the lack of greater substantive progress encouraged the growth of black militancy. Especially in the slums of the large Northern cities, King's religious philosophy of nonviolence was increasingly questioned. The rioting in the Watts district of Los Angeles in August 1965 demonstrated the depth of unrest among urban African Americans. In an effort to meet the challenge of the ghetto, King

and his forces initiated a drive against racial discrimination in Chicago at the beginning of the following year. The chief target was to be segregation in housing. After a spring and summer of rallies, marches, and demonstrations, an agreement was signed between the city and a coalition of African Americans, liberals, and labour organizations, calling for various measures to enforce the existing laws and regulations with respect to housing. But this agreement was to have little effect; the impression remained that

Martin Luther King, Jr. (centre), *and Malcolm X* (right), *1964.* Library of Congress, Washington, D.C. (digital file no. 3d01847u)

King's Chicago campaign was nullified partly because of the opposition of that city's powerful mayor, Richard J. Daley, and partly because of the unexpected complexities of Northern racism.

In Illinois and Mississippi alike, King was now being challenged and even publicly derided by young black-power enthusiasts. Whereas King stood for patience, middle-class respectability, and a measured approach to social change, the sharp-tongued, blue jean-clad young urban radicals stood for confrontation and immediate change. In the latter's eyes, the suit-wearing, calm-spoken civil rights leader was irresponsibly passive and old beyond his years (King was in his 30s)—more a member of the other side of the generation gap than their revolutionary leader. Malcolm X went so far as to call King's tactics "criminal": "Concerning nonviolence, it is criminal to teach a man not to defend himself when he is the constant victim of brutal attacks."

In the face of mounting criticism, King broadened his approach to include concerns other than racism. On April 4, 1967, at Riverside Church in New York City and again on the 15th at a mammoth peace rally in that city, he committed himself irrevocably to opposing U.S. involvement in the Vietnam War. Once before, in early January 1966, he had condemned the war, but official outrage from Washington and strenuous opposition within the black community itself had caused him to relent. He next sought to widen his base by forming a coalition of the poor of all races that would address itself to economic problems such as poverty and unemployment. It was a version of populism—seeking to enroll janitors, hospital workers, seasonal labourers, and the destitute of Appalachia, along with the student militants and pacifist intellectuals. His endeavours along these lines, however, did not engender much support in any segment of the population.

Meanwhile, the strain and changing dynamics of the civil rights movement had taken a toll on King, especially in the final months of his life. "I'm frankly tired of marching. I'm tired of going to jail," he admitted in 1968. "Living every day under the threat of death, I feel discouraged every now and then and feel my work's in vain, but then the Holy Spirit revives my soul again."

King's plans for a Poor People's March to Washington were interrupted in the spring of 1968 by a trip to Memphis, Tenn., in support of a strike by that city's sanitation workers. In the opinion of many of his followers and biographers, King seemed to sense his end was near. As King prophetically told a crowd at the Mason Temple Church in Memphis on April 3, the night before he died, "I've seen the promised land. I may not get there with you. But I want you to know tonight that we, as a people, will get to the promised land." The next day, while standing on the second-story balcony of the Lorraine Motel, where he and his associates were staying, King was killed by a sniper's bullet. The killing

Building in Washington, D.C., destroyed during the riots that followed the assassination of Martin Luther King, Jr., April 1968. Library of Congress, Washington, D.C. (digital file no. 03132u)

sparked riots and disturbances in over 100 cities across the country. On March 10, 1969, the accused assassin, a white man, James Earl Ray, pleaded guilty to the murder and was sentenced to 99 years in prison.

Ray later recanted his confession, claiming lawyers had coerced him into confessing and that he was the victim of a conspiracy. In a surprising turn of events, members of the King family eventually came to Ray's defense. King's son Dexter met with the reputed assassin in March 1997 and then publicly joined Ray's plea for a reopening of his case. When Ray died on April 23, 1998, Coretta Scott King declared, "America will never have the benefit of Mr. Ray's trial, which would have produced new revelations about the assassination . . . as well as establish the facts concerning Mr. Ray's innocence." Although the U.S. government conducted several investigations into the murder of King and each time concluded that Ray was the sole assassin, the killing remains a matter of controversy.

HISTORICAL SIGNIFICANCE AND LEGACY

In the years after his death, King remained the most widely known African American leader of his era. His stature as a major historical figure was confirmed by the successful campaign to establish a national holiday in his honour in the United States and by the building of a King memorial on the Mall in Washington, D.C., near the Lincoln Memorial, the site of his famous "I Have a Dream" speech in 1963. Many states and municipalities have enacted King holidays, authorized public statues and paintings of him, and named streets, schools, and other entities for him. These efforts to honour King have focused more on his role as a civil rights advocate than on his controversial speeches, during his final year, condemning American intervention in Vietnam and calling for the Poor People's Campaign.

The King holiday campaign overcame forceful opposition, with critics citing FBI surveillance files suggesting that King was an adulterous radical influenced by communists. Although the release of these files during the 1970s under the Freedom of Information Act fueled the public debate over King's legacy, the extensive archives that now exist document King's life and thought and have informed numerous serious studies offering balanced and comprehensive perspectives. Two major books featuring King—David J. Garrow's *Bearing the Cross* (1986) and Taylor Branch's *Parting the Waters* (1988)—won Pulitzer Prizes. Subsequent books and articles reaffirmed King's historical significance while portraying him as a complex figure: flawed, fallible, and limited in his control over the mass movements with which he was associated, yet also a visionary leader who was deeply committed to achieving social justice through nonviolent means.

Although the idea of a King national holiday did not gain significant congressional support until the late 1970s, efforts to commemorate King's life began almost immediately after his assassination. In 1968 Rep. John Conyers, Jr., of Michigan introduced a King holiday bill. The idea gradually began to attract political support once the newly formed Congressional Black Caucus included the holiday in its reform agenda. Coretta Scott King also played a central role in building popular support for the King holiday campaign while serving as founding president of the Atlanta-based Martin Luther King, Jr., Center for Nonviolent Social Change (later renamed the King Center), which became one of the major archives of King's papers.

Despite the overall conservative trend in American politics in the 1980s, which might have been expected to work against recognition of the efforts of a controversial activist, King holiday advocates gained political support by portraying him as a symbol of the country's progress in race relations. Musician Stevie Wonder contributed to the campaign by writing and recording "Happy Birthday," a popular tribute to King. In 1983 Coretta Scott King and Stevie Wonder participated in the 20th Anniversary March on Washington, which drew a bigger crowd than the original march.

After the House and the Senate voted overwhelmingly in favour of the King holiday bill sponsored by Sen. Ted Kennedy, Pres. Ronald Reagan put aside his initial doubts and signed the legislation on Nov. 3, 1983, establishing Martin Luther King, Jr., Day, to be celebrated annually on the third Monday in January. Coretta Scott King also succeeded in gaining congressional approval to establish a King Federal Holiday Commission to plan annual celebrations, beginning Jan. 20, 1986, that would encourage "Americans to reflect on the principles of racial equality and nonviolent social change espoused by Dr. King."

Celebration of the King national holiday did not end contention over King's legacy, but his status as an American icon became more widely accepted over time. The revelation during the early 1990s that King had plagiarized some of his academic writings and the occasional controversies involving his heirs did little to undermine recognition of King's enduring impact on the country. Even before the first King national holiday, members of King's fraternity, Alpha Phi Alpha, had proposed a permanent memorial in Washington, D.C. By the end of the

20th century, that proposal had secured governmental approval for the site on the Tidal Basin, near the Mall. In 2000 an international design competition ended with the selection of a proposal by ROMA Design Group. To build and maintain the memorial, the Martin Luther King, Jr. National Memorial Project Foundation eventually raised more than $100 million. Commemorations of King's life were also held in other countries, and in 2009 a congressional delegation traveled to India to mark the 50th anniversary of King's pilgrimage to what he called the "Land of Gandhi."

ASSESSMENT

As with the lives of other major historical figures, King's life has been interpreted in new ways by successive generations of scholars, many of whom have drawn attention to the crucial role of local black leaders in the African American protest movements of the 1950s and '60s. Recognizing that grassroots activists such as Rosa Parks, Fred Shuttlesworth, and others prepared the way for King's rise to national prominence, biographers and historians have questioned the view that Southern black protest movements relied on King's charismatic guidance. Nonetheless, studies of King continue to acknowledge his distinctive leadership role. For example, though he often downplayed his contribution to the Montgomery bus boycott, King's inspirational leadership and his speeches helped to transform a local protest over bus seating into a historically important event. More generally, studies of King have suggested that his most significant contribution to the modern African American freedom struggle was to link black aspirations to transcendent, widely shared democratic and Christian ideals. While helping grassroots leaders mobilize African Americans for sustained mass struggles, he inspired participants to believe that their cause was just and consistent with traditional American egalitarian values. King also appealed to the consciences of all Americans, thus building popular support for civil rights reform. His strategy of emphasizing nonviolent protest and interracial cooperation enabled him to fight effectively against the Southern system of legalized racial segregation and discrimination, but it also proved inadequate during his final years as he sought to overcome racial and economic problems that were national in scope.

MALCOLM X

(b. May 19, 1925, Omaha, Neb., U.S.—d. Feb. 21, 1965, New York, N.Y.)

A prominent figure in the Nation of Islam, Malcolm X articulated concepts of "race" pride and black nationalism in the early 1960s, and after his assassination, the widespread distribution of his life story—The Autobiography of Malcolm X (1965)—made him an ideological hero, especially among black youth.

EARLY YEARS AND CONVERSION

Born in Nebraska, Malcolm Little moved with his family to Lansing, Mich., while an infant. When Malcolm was six years old, his father, the Rev. Earl Little, a Baptist minister and former supporter of the early black nationalist leader Marcus Garvey, died after being hit by a streetcar, quite possibly the victim of murder by whites. The surviving family was so poor that Malcolm's mother, Louise Little, resorted to cooking dandelion greens from the street to feed her children. After she was committed to an insane asylum in 1939, Malcolm and his siblings were sent to foster homes or to live with family members.

Malcolm attended school in Lansing, Mich., but dropped out in the eighth grade when one of his teachers told him that he should become a carpenter instead of a lawyer. As a rebellious youngster Malcolm moved from the Michigan State Detention Home, a juvenile home in Mason, Mich., to the Roxbury section of Boston to live with an older half sister from his father's first marriage. There he became involved in petty criminal activities in his teenage years. Known as "Detroit Red" for the reddish tinge in his hair, he developed into a street hustler, drug dealer, and leader of a gang of thieves in Roxbury and Harlem, New York City.

While in prison for robbery from 1946 to 1952, Malcolm underwent a conversion that eventually led him to join the Nation of Islam, an African American movement that combined elements of Islam with black nationalism. His decision to join the Nation also was influenced by discussions with his brother Reginald, who had become a member in Detroit and who was incarcerated with Malcolm in the Norfolk Prison Colony in Massachusetts in 1948. Malcolm quit smoking and gambling and refused to eat pork in keeping with the Nation's dietary restrictions. In order to educate himself, he spent long hours reading books in the prison library, even memorizing a dictionary. He also sharpened his forensic skills by participating in debate classes. Following Nation tradition, he replaced his surname, "Little," with an "X," a custom among Nation of Islam followers who considered their family names to have originated with white slaveholders.

MALCOLM X AND THE NATION OF ISLAM

After his release from prison Malcolm helped to lead the Nation of Islam during the period of its greatest growth and influence. He met Elijah Muhammad in Chicago in 1952 and then began organizing temples for the Nation in New York, Philadelphia, and Boston as well as cities in the South. He founded the Nation's newspaper, *Muhammad Speaks*, which he printed in the basement of his home, and initiated the practice of requiring every male member of the Nation to sell an assigned number of newspapers on the street as a recruiting and fund-raising technique. He also articulated the Nation's racial doctrines on the inherent evil of whites and the natural superiority of blacks.

Malcolm rose rapidly to become the minister of Boston Temple No. 11, which he founded; he was later rewarded with the post of minister of Temple No. 7 in Harlem, the largest and most prestigious temple in the Nation after the Chicago headquarters. Recognizing his talent and ability, Elijah Muhammad, who had a special affection for Malcolm, named him the National Representative of the Nation of Islam, second in rank to Muhammad himself. Under Malcolm's lieutenancy, the Nation claimed a membership of 500,000. The actual number of members fluctuated, however, and the influence of the organization, refracted through the public persona of Malcolm X, always greatly exceeded its size.

An articulate public speaker, a charismatic personality, and an indefatigable organizer, Malcolm X expressed the pent-up anger, frustration, and bitterness of African Americans during the major phase of the civil rights movement from 1955 to 1965. He preached on the streets of Harlem and spoke at major universities such as Harvard University and the University of Oxford. His keen intellect, incisive wit, and ardent radicalism made him a formidable critic of American society. He also criticized the mainstream civil rights movement, challenging Martin Luther King, Jr.'s central notions of integration and nonviolence. Malcolm argued that more was at stake than the civil right to sit in a restaurant or even to vote. Rather, he argued that the most important issues were black identity, integrity, and independence. In contrast

Malcolm X, c. 1962. Richard Saunders/Hulton Archive/Getty Images

to King's strategy of nonviolence, civil disobedience, and redemptive suffering, Malcolm urged his followers to defend themselves "by any means necessary." His biting critique of the "so-called Negro" provided the intellectual foundations for the Black Power and black consciousness movements in the United States in the late 1960s and '70s. Through the influence of the Nation of Islam, Malcolm X helped to change the terms used to refer to African Americans from "Negro" and "coloured" to "black" and "Afro-American."

FINAL YEARS

In 1963 there were deep tensions between Malcolm and Eiljah Muhammad over the political direction of the Nation. Malcolm urged that the Nation become more active in the widespread civil rights protests instead of just being a critic on the sidelines. Muhammad's violations of the moral code of the Nation further worsened his relations with Malcolm, who was devastated when he learned that Muhammad had fathered children by six of his personal secretaries, two of whom filed paternity suits and made the issue public. Malcolm brought additional bad publicity to the Nation when he declared publicly that Pres. John F. Kennedy's assassination was an example of "chickens coming home to roost"—a violent society suffering the consequences of violence. In response to the outrage this statement provoked, Elijah Muhammad ordered Malcolm to observe a 90-day

period of silence, and the break between the two leaders became permanent.

Malcolm left the Nation in March 1964 and in the next month founded Muslim Mosque, Inc. During his pilgrimage to Mecca that same year, he experienced a second conversion and embraced Sunni Islam, adopting the Muslim name el-Hajj Malik el-Shabazz. Renouncing the separatist beliefs of the Nation, he claimed that the solution to racial problems in the United States lay in orthodox Islam. On the second of two visits to Africa in 1964, he addressed the Organization of African Unity (known as the African Union since 2002), an intergovernmental group established to promote African unity, international cooperation, and economic development. In 1965 he founded the Organization of Afro-American Unity as a secular vehicle to internationalize the plight of black Americans and to make common cause with the people of the developing world—to move from civil rights to human rights.

The growing hostility between Malcolm and the Nation led to death threats and open violence against him. On Feb. 21, 1965, Malcolm was assassinated while delivering a lecture at the Audubon Ballroom in Harlem; three members of the Nation of Islam were convicted of the murder. He was survived by his wife, Betty Shabazz, whom he had married in 1958, and six daughters. His martyrdom, ideas, and speeches contributed to the development of black nationalist ideology and the Black Power movement and helped to popularize the values of autonomy and independence among African Americans in the 1960s and '70s.

JAMES MEREDITH

(b. June 25, 1933, Kosciusko, Miss., U.S.)

Activist James Meredith gained national renown at a key juncture in the civil rights movement in 1962, when he became the first African American student at the University of Mississippi. State officials, initially refusing a U.S. Supreme Court order to integrate the school, blocked Meredith's entrance, but, following large campus riots that left two people dead, Meredith was admitted to the university under the protection of federal marshals.

Meredith served in the U.S. Air Force (1951–60) before attending an all-black school, Jackson State College (1960–62). His repeated applications to the University of Mississippi were denied solely on the basis of his race, according to the verdict of his 1961–62 court battle, which was won on appeal with the legal assistance of the National Association for the Advancement of Colored People (NAACP). In the fall of 1962, as mob violence seemed imminent, U.S. Attorney General Robert F. Kennedy called in federal protection so that Meredith could register for classes. Meredith's tenure at Mississippi was brief; he graduated in 1963 and wrote a memoir about the experience, called *Three Years in Mississippi* (1966).

Meredith continued to balance education and activism throughout the rest of the decade, attending the University of Ibadan in Nigeria (1964–65) and Columbia University (1966–68). In June 1966 he began a solitary protest march, which he called the March Against Fear, from Memphis, Tenn., to Jackson, Miss., when he was shot by a sniper. The crime mobilized many civil rights leaders to resume the march, which Meredith was able to rejoin after a period of hospitalization.

ROSA PARKS

(b. Feb. 4, 1913, Tuskegee, Ala., U.S.—d. Oct. 24, 2005, Detroit, Mich.)

Civil rights activist Rosa Parks, who refused to relinquish her seat on a public bus to a white man, precipitating the 1955–56 Montgomery bus boycott in Alabama, is recognized as the spark that ignited the U.S. civil rights movement.

In 1932 Rosa Louise McCauley married Raymond Parks, who encouraged her to return to high school and earn a diploma. She later made her living as a seamstress. In 1943 Parks became a member of the Montgomery chapter of the National Association for the Advancement of Colored People (NAACP), and she served as its secretary until 1956. On Dec. 1, 1955, she was arrested for refusing to give her bus seat to a white man, a violation of the city's racial segregation ordinances. Under the aegis of the Montgomery Improvement Association and the leadership of the young pastor of the Dexter Avenue Baptist Church, Martin Luther King, Jr., a boycott of the municipal bus company was begun on December 5. (African Americans constituted some 70 percent of the ridership.) On Nov. 13, 1956, the U.S. Supreme Court upheld a lower court's decision declaring Montgomery's segregated seating unconstitutional, and the court order was served on December 20; the boycott ended the following day. For her role in starting the successful campaign, which brought King to national prominence, Parks became known as the "mother of the civil rights movement."

In 1957 Parks moved with her husband and mother to Detroit, where from 1965 to 1988 she was a member of the staff of Michigan Congressman John Conyers, Jr. She remained active in the NAACP, and the Southern Christian Leadership Conference established the annual Rosa Parks Freedom Award in her honour. In 1987 she cofounded the Rosa and Raymond Parks Institute for Self Development to provide career training for young people. She was the recipient of numerous awards, including the Presidential Medal of Freedom (1996) and the Congressional Gold Medal (1999). Her autobiography, *Rosa Parks: My Story* (1992), was written with Jim Haskins.

A. PHILIP RANDOLPH

(b. April 15, 1889, Crescent City, Fla., U.S.—d. May 16, 1979, New York, N.Y.)

Trade unionist A. Philip Randolph was a dedicated and persistent leader in the struggle for justice and parity for African Americans.

The son of a Methodist minister, Randolph moved to the Harlem district of New York City in 1911. He attended City College at night and, with Chandler Owen, founded an employment agency in 1912, attempting, through it, to organize black workers. In 1917, following the entry of the United States in World War I, the two men founded a magazine, *The Messenger* (after 1929, *Black Worker*), that called for more positions in the war industry and the armed forces for blacks. After the war, Randolph lectured at New York's Rand School of Social Science and ran unsuccessfully for offices on the Socialist Party ticket.

In 1925, as founding president of the Brotherhood of Sleeping Car Porters, Randolph began organizing that group of black workers and, at a time when half the affiliates of the American Federation of Labor (AFL) barred blacks from membership, took his union into the AFL. Despite opposition, he built the first successful black trade union; the brotherhood won its first major contract with the Pullman Company in 1937. The following year, Randolph removed his union from the AFL in protest against its failure to fight discrimination in its ranks and took the brotherhood into the newly formed Congress of Industrial Organizations (CIO). He then returned to the question of black employment in the federal government and in industries with federal contracts. He warned Pres. Franklin D. Roosevelt that he would lead thousands of blacks in a protest march on

Washington, D.C.; Roosevelt, on June 25, 1941, issued Executive Order 8802, barring discrimination in defense industries and federal bureaus and creating the Fair Employment Practices Committee. After World War II, Randolph founded the League for Nonviolent Civil Disobedience Against Military Segregation, resulting in the issue by Pres. Harry S. Truman on July 26, 1948, of Executive Order 9981, banning segregation in the armed forces.

When the AFL merged with the CIO in 1955, Randolph was made a vice president and member of the executive council of the combined organization. He was the first president (1960–66) of the Negro American Labor Council, formed by Randolph and others to fight discrimination within the AFL-CIO.

In an echo of his activities of 1941, Randolph was a director of the March on Washington for Jobs and Freedom, which brought more than 200,000 persons to the capital on Aug. 28, 1963, to demonstrate support for civil-rights policies for blacks. Two years later, he formed the A. Philip Randolph Institute for community leaders to study the causes of poverty. Suffering chronic illness, he resigned his presidency of the Brotherhood of Sleeping Car Porters in 1968 and retired from public life.

BOBBY SEALE

(b. Oct. 22, 1936, Dallas, Texas, U.S.)

Political activist Bobby Seale founded the Black Panther Party with Huey Newton and was its national chairman. Seale was one of a generation of young African American radicals who broke away from the traditionally nonviolent civil rights movement to preach a doctrine of militant black empowerment. Following the dismissal of murder charges against him in 1971, Seale somewhat moderated his more militant views and devoted his time to effecting change from within the system.

Seale grew up in Dallas and in California. Following service in the U.S. Air Force, he entered Merritt College, in Oakland, Calif. There his radicalism took root in 1962, when he first heard Malcolm X speak. Seale helped found the Black Panthers in 1966. Noted for their violent views, they also ran medical clinics and served free breakfasts to school children, among other programs.

In 1969 Seale was indicted in Chicago for conspiracy to incite riots during the Democratic national convention the previous year. The court refused to allow him to have his choice of lawyer. When Seale repeatedly rose to insist that he was being denied his constitutional right to counsel, the judge ordered him bound and gagged. He was convicted of 16 counts of contempt and sentenced to four years in prison. In 1970–71 he and a codefendant were tried for the 1969 murder of a Black Panther suspected of being a police informant. The six-month-long trial ended with a hung jury.

Following his release from prison, Seale renounced violence as a means to an end and announced his intention to work within the political process. He ran for mayor of Oakland in 1973, finishing second. As the Black Panther Party faded from public view, Seale took on a quieter role, working to improve social services in black neighbourhoods and to improve the environment. Seale's writings include such diverse works as *Seize the Time* (1970), a history of the Black Panther movement and *Barbeque'n with Bobby* (1988), a cookbook.

AL SHARPTON

(b. Oct. 3, 1954, Brooklyn, N.Y., U.S.)

Civil rights activist and minister Al Sharpton began preaching at age four, becoming an ordained Pentecostal minister at age 10. In 1971 he founded a national youth organization that promoted social and economic justice for African Americans. He graduated from Tilden High School in Brooklyn in 1972 and briefly attended Brooklyn College. A colourful and popular figure in the African American community, Sharpton embarked upon controversial protests that gained wide coverage in the national media and sometimes precipitated confrontations with police. In 1991 Sharpton formed the National Action Network, a civil rights organization that promoted progressive policies, including affirmative action and reparations for African Americans for the enslavement of their ancestors. In the 1990s he entered the political arena, unsuccessfully seeking the Democratic Party nominations

for mayor of New York City and for U.S. senator from New York state. In 2004 Sharpton campaigned unsuccessfully for the Democratic nomination for the U.S. presidency.

EMMETT TILL

(b. July 25, 1941, Chicago, Ill., U.S.—d. Aug. 28, 1955, Money, Miss.)

The murder of teenager Emmett Till in 1955 was a catalyst for the emerging civil rights movement.

Till was born to working-class parents on the South Side of Chicago. When he was barely 14 years old, Till took a trip to rural Mississippi to spend the summer with relatives. He had been warned by his mother (who knew him to be a jokester accustomed to being the centre of attention) that whites in the South could react violently to behaviour that was tolerated in the North. This animosity was exacerbated by the U.S. Supreme Court's 1954 decision (in *Brown* v. *Board of Education of Topeka*), which overturned the "separate but equal" doctrine established in *Plessy* v. *Ferguson* (1896) that had allowed racial segregation in public facilities.

Till arrived in Money, Miss., on Aug. 21, 1955. He stayed with his great-uncle, Moses Wright, who was a sharecropper, and he spent his days helping with the cotton harvest. On August 24, Till and a group of other teens went to a local grocery store after a day of working in the fields. Accounts of what transpired thereafter vary. Some witnesses stated that one of the other boys dared Till to talk to the store's cashier, Carolyn Bryant, a white woman. It was reported that Till then whistled at, touched the hand or waist of, or flirted with the woman as he was leaving the store. Whatever the truth, Till did not mention the incident to his great-uncle. In the early morning hours of August 28, Roy Bryant, the cashier's husband, and J.W. Milam, Bryant's half brother, forced their way into Wright's home and abducted Till at gunpoint. Bryant and Milam severely beat the boy, gouging out one of his eyes. They then took him to the banks of the Tallahatchie River, where they killed him with a single gunshot to the head. The two men tied the teen's body to a large metal fan with a length of barbed wire before dumping the corpse into the river.

Wright reported the kidnapping to the police, and Bryant and Milam were arrested the following day. On Aug. 31, 1955, Till's corpse was discovered in the river. His face was unrecognizable as a result of the assault, and positive identification was possible only because Till was wearing a monogrammed ring that had belonged to his father. On September 2, less than two weeks after Till had embarked on his journey south, the train bearing his remains arrived in Chicago. Till's mother kept her son's casket open, choosing to reveal to the tens of thousands who attended the funeral the brutality that had been visited on her son. The appalling images of Till's body in the casket appeared in the pages of *Jet* magazine and the *Chicago Defender*, and his murder became a rallying point for the civil rights movement.

The trial of Till's killers began on Sept. 19, 1955, and from the witness stand Wright identified the men who had kidnapped Till. After four days of testimony and a little more than an hour of deliberation an all-white, all-male jury (at the time, blacks and women were not allowed to serve as jurors in Mississippi) acquitted Bryant and Milam of all charges. Protected from further prosecution by double jeopardy statutes, the pair was paid for the story and interviewed by their lawyer and a journalist in a 1956 article for *Look* magazine in which they related the circumstances of Till's kidnapping and murder. In 2004 the Federal Bureau of Investigation reopened the case. Although Bryant and Milam were long dead, agents sought to obtain a conclusive account of Till's final hours. The three-year investigation, during which Till's body was exhumed for a complete autopsy, did not lead to the filing of criminal charges, but it did uncover a deathbed confession by Milam's brother Leslie, who admitted his own involvement in the kidnapping and murder.

BOOKER T. WASHINGTON

(b. April 5, 1856, Franklin County, Va., U.S.—d. Nov. 14, 1915, Tuskegee, Ala.)

Booker Taliaferro Washington was the most influential spokesman for African

Booker T. Washington. Library of Congress, Washington, D.C.

Americans between 1895 and 1915. An educator and reformer, he was also the first president and principal developer of Tuskegee Normal and Industrial Institute (now Tuskegee University).

Washington was born in a slave hut but, after emancipation, moved with his family to Malden, W. Va. Dire poverty ruled out regular schooling; at age nine he began working, first in a salt furnace and later in a coal mine. Determined to get an education, he enrolled at the Hampton Normal and Agricultural Institute in Virginia (1872), working as a janitor to help pay expenses. He

graduated in 1875 and returned to Malden, where for two years he taught children in a day school and adults at night. Following studies at Wayland Seminary, Washington, D.C. (1878–79), he joined the staff of Hampton.

In 1881 Washington was selected to head a newly established normal school for blacks at Tuskegee, an institution with two small, converted buildings, no equipment, and very little money. Tuskegee Normal and Industrial Institute became a monument to his life's work. At his death 34 years later, it had more than 100 well-equipped buildings, some 1,500 students, a faculty of nearly 200 teaching 38 trades and professions, and an endowment of approximately $2 million.

Washington believed that the best interests of black people in the post-Reconstruction era could be realized through education in the crafts and industrial skills and the cultivation of the virtues of patience, enterprise, and thrift. He urged his fellow blacks, most of whom were impoverished and illiterate farm labourers, to temporarily abandon their efforts to win full civil rights and political power and instead to cultivate their industrial and farming skills so as to attain economic security. Blacks would thus accept segregation and discrimination, but their eventual acquisition of wealth and culture would gradually win for them the respect and acceptance of the white community. This would break down the divisions between the two races and lead to equal citizenship for blacks in the end. In his epochal speech (Sept. 18, 1895) to a racially mixed audience at the Atlanta Exposition, Washington summed up his pragmatic approach in the famous phrase: "In all things that are purely social we can be separate as the fingers, yet one as the hand in all things essential to mutual progress."

These sentiments were called the Atlanta Compromise by such critics as W.E.B. Du Bois, who deplored Washington's emphasis on vocational skills to the detriment of academic development and civil rights. And indeed, it is true that during the period of Washington's ascendancy as national spokesman of U.S. blacks his race was systematically excluded both from the franchise and from any effective participation in national political life, and rigid patterns of segregation and discrimination became institutionalized in the Southern states. Even Washington's visit to the Roosevelt White House in 1901 was greeted with a storm of protest as a "breach of racial etiquette."

Most blacks felt comfortable with Washington's approach, however, and his influence among whites was such that he became an unofficial arbiter determining which black individuals and institutions were deemed worthy to benefit from government patronage and white philanthropic support. He went on to receive honorary degrees from Harvard University (1896) and Dartmouth College (1901). Among his dozen books is his autobiography, *Up from Slavery* (1901), translated into many languages.

IDA B. WELLS-BARNETT

(b. July 16, 1862, Holly Springs, Miss., U.S.—d. March 25, 1931, Chicago, Ill.)

No one was more determined to bring an end to lynching in the United States in the 1890s than Ida B. Wells-Barnett.

Ida Bell Wells was the daughter of slaves. Educated at Rust University, a freedmen's school in her native Holly Springs, Miss., at age 14 Wells began teaching in a country school. She continued to teach after moving to Memphis, Tenn., in 1884 and attended Fisk University in Nashville during several summer sessions. In 1887 the Tennessee Supreme Court, reversing a Circuit Court decision, ruled against Wells in a suit she had brought against the Chesapeake & Ohio Railroad for having been forcibly removed from her seat after she had refused to give it up for one in a "colored only" car. Using the pen name Iola, Wells in 1891 wrote some newspaper articles critical of the education available to African American children. Her teaching contract was not renewed. She thereupon turned to journalism, buying an interest in the *Memphis Free Speech*.

In 1892, after three friends of hers had been lynched by a mob, Wells began an editorial campaign against lynching that quickly led to the violent destruction of her newspaper's office. She continued her antilynching crusade, first as a staff writer for the *New York Age* and then as a lecturer and organizer of antilynching societies. She traveled to speak in a number of major U.S. cities and twice visited Great Britain for the cause. In 1895 she married Ferdinand L. Barnett, a Chicago lawyer, editor, and public official, and adopted the name Wells-Barnett. From that time she restricted her travels, but she was very active in Chicago affairs. Wells-Barnett contributed to the *Chicago Conservator*, her husband's newspaper, and to other local journals; published a detailed look at lynching in *A Red Record* (1895); and was active in organizing local African American women in various causes, from the antilynching campaign to the suffrage movement. She founded what may have been the first black woman suffrage group, Chicago's Alpha Suffrage Club.

From 1898 to 1902 Wells-Barnett served as secretary of the National Afro-American Council, and in 1910 she founded and became first president of the Negro Fellowship League, which aided newly arrived migrants from the South. From 1913 to 1916 she served as a probation officer of the Chicago municipal court. She was militant in her demand for justice for African Americans and in her insistence that it was to be won by their own efforts. While she took part in the 1909 meeting of the Niagara Movement, she would have nothing to do with the less radical National Association for the Advancement of Colored People that sprang from it. Her autobiography, *Crusade for Justice*, was published posthumously in 1970.

ROY WILKINS

(b. Aug. 30, 1901, St. Louis, Mo., U.S.—d. Sept. 8, 1981, New York, N.Y.)

Civil-rights leader Roy Wilkins served as the executive director (1955–77) of the National Association for the Advancement of Colored People (NAACP) and was often referred to as the senior statesman of the civil rights movement.

After graduation from the University of Minnesota, Minneapolis (1923), Wilkins became a reporter and later managing editor of the *Kansas City Call*, a newspaper serving the black community. Joining the staff of the NAACP in 1931, he edited its official publication, *The Crisis*, between 1934 and 1949 and simultaneously directed the NAACP antidiscrimination program across the United States. In 1949–50 he was chairman of the National Emergency Civil Rights Mobilization, an organization composed of more than 100 local and national groups.

Appointed to the NAACP's highest administrative post during the early stage of the civil rights movement, Wilkins directed the organization on a course that sought equal rights for blacks through legal redress. In August 1963 he helped organize and later addressed the historic civil rights March on Washington. Devoted to the principle of nonviolence, he rejected racism in all its forms, including black separatism. Nevertheless, the pressure of black activist groups prompted the NAACP, under his leadership, to diversify its activities to include nonviolent direct action and to extend legal aid to other, frequently more militant, groups.

In 1968 Wilkins served as chairman of the U.S. delegation to the International Conference on Human Rights. He was made director emeritus of the NAACP in 1977.

WHITNEY M. YOUNG, JR.

(b. July 31, 1921, Lincoln Ridge, Ky., U.S.—d. March 11, 1971, Lagos, Nigeria)

An articulate civil rights leader, Whitney M. Young, Jr., spearheaded the drive for equal opportunity for African Americans in U.S. industry and government service during his 10 years as head of the National Urban League (1961–71), the world's largest social-civil rights organization. His advocacy of a "Domestic Marshall Plan"— massive funds to help solve America's racial problems—was felt to have strongly influenced federal poverty programs sponsored by Democratic Party administrations in Washington (1963–69).

After army service in World War II, Young switched his career interest from medicine to social work, in which he took his M.A. from the University of Minnesota (1947). Starting as director of industrial relations for the Urban League at St. Paul, Minn. (1947–50), he moved to Omaha, Neb., where he served as executive secretary (1950–54). Becoming dean of the School of Social Work of Atlanta University in 1954, he was instrumental in improving relations between city and university.

Appointed executive director of the National Urban League in 1961, Young won an impressive reputation as a national black activist who helped bridge the gap between white political and business leaders and poor blacks and militants. Under his direction the organization grew from 60 to 98 chapters and shifted its focus from middle-class concerns to the needs of the urban poor. Young was particularly credited with almost singlehandedly persuading corporate America and major foundations to aid the civil rights movement through financial contributions in support of self-help programs for jobs, housing, education, and family rehabilitation.

Young, who had been a consultant on racial matters to both Pres. John F. Kennedy and Pres. Lyndon B. Johnson, was in Nigeria at a conference sponsored by the Ford Foundation to enhance Afro-American understanding when he died.

Notwithstanding the fact that individuals such as Douglass, Washington, and King had dialogued with U.S. presidents, the foregoing portraits have mostly depicted political work done from the outside. The chapter that follows considers the contributions of African Americans inside the government complex.

W.E.B Du Bois, c. 1900. MPI/Hulton Archive/Getty Images

Booker T. Washington. Hulton Archive/Getty Images

TALENTED TENTH

W.E.B. Du Bois was one of a number of black intellectuals who feared that what they saw as the overemphasis on industrial training (as evidenced, for example, by the plan proposed by Booker T. Washington in the 1895 Atlanta Compromise) would confine African Americans permanently to the ranks of second-class citizenship. In order to achieve political and civil equality, Du Bois emphasized the necessity for higher education to develop the leadership capacity among the most able 10 percent of black Americans. He stressed the importance of educating African American teachers, professional men, ministers, and spokesmen, who would earn their special privileges by dedicating themselves to "leavening the lump" and "inspiring the masses." The phrase Talented Tenth first appeared in Du Bois's The Negro Problem *(1903).*

CHAPTER 2

PROTECT AND SERVE

As the barriers of segregated society began to fall, African Americans ascended to positions of power and responsibility at all levels and in all branches of government. African Americans made crucial contributions not just in elected office but also as civil servants, diplomats, and government officials, as well as in the judiciary and the military. This chapter looks at some of those African Americans who pushed back the barriers in American political and civil life so that they might protect and serve all Americans.

POLITICIANS

The adoption of the Fourteenth and Fifteenth Amendments and imposition of Radical Reconstruction in the states of the former Confederacy initiated a brief period of widespread involvement of African Americans in legislative and administrative government in the South. Hundreds of African Americans were elected to state legislatures and positions in local government. In 1870 Joseph Hayne Rainey of South Carolina, a former slave, became the first African American to serve in the U.S. House of Representatives. He was joined by an increasing number of African Americans until the 48th Congress convened with eight African American representatives. During Reconstruction, Hiram R. Revels, Blanche Kelso Bruce, and P.B.S. Pinchback were all elected to the U.S. Senate (though the last was barred from serving). With the demise of Reconstruction, the rise of Jim Crow, and the introduction of exclusionary voting laws, black representation in state government and in Congress dwindled and quickly became negligible. When Bruce left the Senate in 1881, no African American would again serve in the body until Edward Brooke of Massachusetts took office in 1967. The small African American presence in the House of Representatives increased following the success of the Voting Rights Act of 1965, and in the last decades of the 20th century the Congressional Black Caucus, formed in 1969, grew significantly in size and influence.

In a number of cases, civil rights activists became politicians, notably Georgia state legislator Julian Bond, U.S. Representative John Lewis of Georgia, and Jesse Jackson, who made landmark runs for the presidential nomination of the Democratic Party in 1984 and 1988. But during the 1960s, '70s, and '80s African American influence on electoral politics was most keenly felt in city government as African American representation on city councils swelled and a growing number of mayorships were assumed by African Americans. By 1990, the three largest U.S. cities—New York City, Los Angeles, and Chicago—were or had been led by a black mayor. In 1992 Carol Moseley Braun became the second African American since the end of Reconstruction to serve in the U.S. Senate. The third, Barack Obama, who, like Braun, represented Illinois, would ascend to the country's highest office as the 44th president of the United States in 2009.

MARION BARRY

(b. March 6, 1936, Itta Bena, Miss., U.S.)

Civil rights activist and politician Marion Barry served four terms as mayor of Washington, D.C. He received a bachelor's degree from LeMoyne College (1958) and a master's degree from Fisk University (1960). He was a founding member of the Student Nonviolent Coordinating Committee and was selected as its first national chairman. In 1971 Barry was elected to the Washington, D.C., city school board and in 1974 won a seat on the city council. He was elected mayor in 1978 and twice won reelection, serving as a strong advocate of statehood for the District of Columbia. In 1990 Barry was convicted of a misdemeanour drug charge and sentenced to six months in prison. Following his release from prison, Barry reentered politics in Washington, D.C., winning a seat on the city council in 1992. In 1994 he was once again elected mayor; he left office after his term expired. In 2004 he was elected to the Washington, D.C., city council.

TOM BRADLEY

(b. Dec. 29, 1917, Calvert, Texas, U.S.—d. Sept. 29, 1998, Los Angeles, Calif.)

The first African American mayor of a predominantly white city, Tom Bradley served an unprecedented five terms as mayor of Los Angeles (1973–93).

The son of sharecroppers and the grandson of slaves, Bradley grew up in poverty. When he was seven years old, his parents moved to Los Angeles. Excelling at track and football, Bradley entered the University of California, Los Angeles, on an athletic scholarship but left without a degree in 1940 to join the Los Angeles police department. While an officer, Bradley took a law degree at Southwestern University in 1956. Over 21 years he rose through the ranks to become a lieutenant, the highest rank achieved to that time by an African American. He became active in the Democratic Party and in 1963 reached another milestone when he became the first African American member to be elected to the Los Angeles city council, representing a racially mixed district.

His first mayoral campaign was in 1969; the city was still recovering from the Watts riots of 1965, and his defeat was attributed to a perception of him, fostered by his rival the incumbent Sam Yorty, as a militant radical. In 1973, however, he defeated Yorty after establishing the support of a coalition with white voters. Bradley was reelected four times. He attempted to run for governor twice without success.

Bradley's achievements included securing the 1984 Summer Olympic Games for Los Angeles and presiding over two decades of expansion and civic growth. In 1989 questions were raised about the consulting fees he accepted from firms doing business with the city. Although he avoided criminal indictment, civil charges were filed against him, and he was fined. The biggest crisis of Bradley's career came in 1992 in the wake of the acquittal of four white police officers who had been indicted for the beating of Rodney King, a black motorist, in an incident caught on videotape. Five days of rioting ensued in which more than 50 persons were killed, thousands injured, and widespread arson and looting occurred. Bradley was widely criticized for his failure to contain the crisis and did not seek a further term.

EDWARD BROOKE

(b. Oct. 26, 1919, Washington, D.C., U.S.)

Edward Brooke was the first African American popularly elected to the U.S. Senate, where he served two terms (1967–79).

Brooke earned his undergraduate degree at Howard University (Washington, D.C.) in 1941 and served as an infantry officer during World War II, achieving the rank of captain. After being discharged, he earned two law degrees at Boston University and was editor of the *Boston University Law Review.*

Brooke began practicing law in 1948 and became a successful Boston attorney. Entering politics, he was defeated in attempts to win a seat in the Massachusetts legislature in 1950 and 1952. He also failed in his 1960 bid to become the Massachusetts secretary of state. From 1961 to 1962 he served as chairman of the Boston Finance Commission, seeking evidence of corruption in city politics.

In 1962 Brooke, a Republican in an overwhelmingly Democratic state, was elected attorney general of Massachusetts. A vigorous prosecutor of official corruption, he was reelected in 1964 by a large margin, despite the success of Democrats that year (Democratic Pres. Lyndon Johnson captured more than 75 percent of the vote in Massachusetts against Republican Barry Goldwater).

In 1966 Brooke ran for a seat in the U.S. Senate and won by nearly half a million votes. That year he also published *The Challenge of Change: Crisis in Our Two-Party System*, which focused on self-help as a way to address the social issues facing the United States during the 1960s. He established a reputation as a soft-spoken moderate on civil rights and a leader of the progressive wing of his party. In 1972 he was overwhelmingly reelected. In 1978, however, beset by personal problems including accusations of financial misdeeds and a divorce, Brooke lost his bid for a third term. In 2008 journalist Barbara Walters revealed that she and Brooke had engaged in an affair for several years prior to his divorce.

After leaving the Senate in 1979, Brooke became chairman of the National Low-Income Housing Coalition and resumed the practice of law. The recipient of numerous honours, he was awarded the Presidential Medal of Freedom in 2004 and the Congressional Gold Medal in 2009. His memoir, *Bridging the Divide* (2007), explores issues of race and class as viewed from his experiences as an African American Republican politician from a largely Democratic state.

BLANCHE K. BRUCE

(b. March 1, 1841, Prince Edward county, Va., U.S.—d. March 17, 1898, Washington, D.C.)

Blanche K. Bruce represented Mississippi in the U.S. Senate during the Reconstruction era.

The son of a slave mother and white planter father, Bruce was well educated as a youth. After the Civil War, he moved to Mississippi, where in 1869 he became a supervisor of elections. By 1870 he was an emerging figure in state politics. After serving as sergeant at arms in the state senate, Bruce held the posts of county assessor, sheriff, and member of the Board of Levee Commissioners of the Mississippi River. Through these positions he amassed enough wealth to purchase a plantation in Floreyville, Miss.

In 1874 Mississippi's Republican-dominated state legislature elected Bruce, a Republican, to a seat in the U.S. Senate. He served from 1875 to 1881, advocating just treatment for both blacks and Indians and opposing the policy excluding Chinese immigrants. He sought improvement of navigation on the Mississippi and advocated better

Blanche K. Bruce. Library of Congress, Washington, D.C.

relations between the races. Much of his time and energy he devoted to fighting fraud and corruption in federal elections.

Bruce lost his political base in Mississippi with the end of Reconstruction governments in the South. He remained in Washington when, at the conclusion of his Senate term, he was appointed register of the Treasury. He served in that post from 1881 to 1885 and again from 1895 to 1898. He was also recorder of deeds in the District of Columbia (1889–95) and a trustee of Howard University.

SHIRLEY CHISHOLM

(b. Nov. 30, 1924, Brooklyn, N.Y, U.S.—d. Jan. 1, 2005, Ormond Beach, Fla.)

Shirley Chisholm (née Shirley St. Hill) was the first African American woman to be elected to the U.S. Congress.

Chisholm was the daughter of immigrants; her father was from British Guiana (now Guyana) and her mother from Barbados. She grew up in Barbados and in her native Brooklyn, New York, and graduated from Brooklyn College (B.A., 1946). While teaching nursery school and serving as director of the Friends Day Nursery in Brooklyn, she studied elementary education at Columbia University (M.A., 1952) and married Conrad Q. Chisholm in 1949 (divorced 1977). An education consultant for New York City's day-care division, Chisholm was also active with community and political groups, including the National Association for the Advancement of Colored People (NAACP) and her district's Unity Democratic Club. In 1964–68 she represented her Brooklyn district in the New York state legislature.

In 1968 Chisholm was elected to the U.S. House of Representatives, defeating the civil rights leader James Farmer. In Congress she quickly became known as a strong liberal who opposed weapons development and the war in Vietnam and favoured full-employment proposals. As a candidate for the Democratic nomination for U.S. president in 1972, Chisholm

Shirley Chisholm. Hulton Archive/Getty Images

won 152 delegates before withdrawing from the race.

Chisholm, a founder of the National Women's Political Caucus, supported the Equal Rights Amendment and legalized abortions throughout her congressional career, which lasted from 1969 to 1983. She wrote the autobiographical works *Unbought and Unbossed* (1970, an expanded 40th anniversary edition of which was released in 2010) and *The Good Fight* (1973).

After her retirement from Congress, Chisholm remained active on the lecture circuit. She held the position of Purington Professor at Mount Holyoke College (1983–87) and was a visiting scholar at Spelman College (1985). In 1993 she was invited by President Bill Clinton to serve as ambassador to Jamaica but declined because of poor health.

MAYNARD JACKSON

(b. March 23, 1938, Dallas, Texas, U.S.—d. June 23, 2003, Arlington, Va.)

Maynard Jackson was the first African American mayor of Atlanta, serving three terms (1974–82 and 1990–94).

Jackson's father was a Baptist minister, his mother a professor of French. He entered Morehouse College through a special-entry program and received a bachelor's degree in political science and history in 1956. He then attempted law school but was forced to drop out. Later he enrolled in North Carolina Central University School of Law, received a J.D. degree in 1964, and found work as an attorney for the National Labor Relations Board in Atlanta. Jackson, a member of the Democratic Party, made his first attempt at elective office in 1968 with a run for the U.S. Senate; although he was unsuccessful, he caught the public's eye and gained the office of vice mayor of Atlanta in 1969.

Jackson's runoff victory in 1973 over the white incumbent under whom he had served as vice mayor was widely seen as a turning point for the "New South." Atlanta's population was nearly 50 percent black, and Jackson implemented an affirmative action program to ensure that minorities shared in the prosperity of the expanding city through municipal contracts. One of his major achievements was the expansion of Hartsfield Atlanta International Airport into a major transportation hub, "ahead of schedule and under budget." (It was renamed Hartsfield-Jackson Atlanta International Airport after his death.) He reformed the police force and worked to maintain calm when the city was terrorized by a string of child murders. After his reelection in 1977, he was barred from a third consecutive term and supported the successful candidacy of Andrew Young. Jackson then worked as a municipal bond attorney while staying active in politics. In his third bid for the mayoralty, he was swept into office with nearly 80 percent of the vote. He counted among his triumphs the securing of Atlanta as the site of the 1996

Olympic Summer Games. Ill health led him to decline seeking a further term, and he returned to the bond business, founding his own firm.

David Dinkins

(b. July 10, 1927, Trenton, N.J., U.S.)

David Dinkins served as the first African American mayor of New York City (1990–94).

After graduating from high school in 1945, Dinkins attempted to enlist in the U.S. Marine Corps but was told that the "Negro quota" had already been met. He eventually was drafted and served with the Marines. He went to Howard University on the GI Bill of Rights, studying mathematics (B.S., 1950). In 1953 Dinkins entered Brooklyn Law School and was introduced to politics when he married Joyce Burrows, the daughter of a New York state assemblyman. He joined a law firm and became increasingly involved with the Democratic Party.

Elected to a term in the state assembly in 1965, he later served as president of elections for New York City, as city clerk, and as Manhattan borough president before his successful bid for the mayor's office in 1989. Dinkins took office at a time when New York City was racked by racial discord. Both ethnic tensions and crime statistics increased during his term, and he became the first black mayor of a major U.S. city to be denied reelection.

Barbara C. Jordan

(b. Feb. 21, 1936, Houston, Texas, U.S.—d. Jan. 17, 1996, Austin, Texas)

Lawyer, educator, and politician Barbara C. Jordan served as a member of the U.S. House of Representatives from Texas (1972–78). She was the first African American congresswoman to come from the Deep South.

Jordan was the youngest of three daughters in a close-knit family. As a high school student, she became a skilled public speaker, winning a national debate contest in 1952. She attended Texas Southern University in Houston, becoming a member of the debate team that tied Harvard University in a debate—one of her proudest college moments. Following graduation (magna cum laude in 1956), she attended Boston University Law School, where she was one of only two women—both African Americans from Houston—to graduate. She passed the Massachusetts bar exam but moved to Tuskegee Institute (later renamed Tuskegee University) in Alabama and taught there for one year before returning to Texas and gaining admittance to the bar there.

Jordan was an effective campaigner for the Democrats during the 1960 presidential election, and this experience propelled her into politics. In 1962 and 1964 she was an unsuccessful candidate for the Texas House of Representatives, but she was elected in 1966 to the Texas

Senate, the first African American member since 1883 and the first woman ever elected to that legislative body.

Jordan's success in Texas politics came from her knowledge of and adherence to the rules of the political process. She went to great lengths to fit in and sought advice on committee assignments. Her own legislative work focused on the environment, antidiscrimination clauses in state business contracts, and urban legislation, the last being a political challenge in a state dominated by rural interests. She captured the attention of President Lyndon Johnson, who invited her to the White House for a preview of his 1967 civil rights message.

Jordan remained in the Texas Senate until 1972, when she was elected to U.S. House of Representatives from Texas' 18th district. In the House, Jordan advocated legislation to improve the lives of minorities, the poor, and the disenfranchised and sponsored bills that expanded workers' compensation and strengthened the Voting Rights Act of 1965 to cover Mexican Americans in the Southwest.

Although she acquired a reputation as an effective legislator, Jordan did not become a national figure until 1974, when her participation in the hearings held by the House Judiciary Committee on the impeachment of Pres. Richard M. Nixon was televised nationwide. Her keynote address at the 1976 Democratic National Convention confirmed her reputation as one of the most commanding and articulate public speakers of her era.

Jordan decided not to seek a fourth term and retired from Congress in 1979. In that year also she published *Barbara Jordan, a Self-Portrait*. She then accepted a position at the University of Texas, Austin, where she taught at the Lyndon B. Johnson School of Public Affairs until her death. Despite her absence from Washington, D.C., she remained influential in political affairs. In the 1990s she served as an adviser on ethics in government for Texas governor Ann Richards and also was chairman for the U.S. Commission on Immigration Reform. In 1992 she again gave the keynote address at the Democratic National Convention.

JOHN R. LYNCH

(b. Sept. 10, 1847, Concordia Parish, La., U.S.—d. Nov. 2, 1939, Chicago, Ill.)

Following the Civil War, John R. Lynch served in the Mississippi state legislature and U.S. House of Representatives and was prominent in Republican Party affairs of the 1870s and '80s.

Born a slave, Lynch was freed during the Civil War and settled in Natchez, Miss. There he learned the photography business, attended night school, and in 1869 entered public life as justice of the peace for Natchez county.

In November 1869 Lynch was elected to the Mississippi House of Representatives, and he was reelected in 1871. Although blacks never were in the majority in the Mississippi legislature, Lynch was chosen speaker of the House in 1872. That same year he was elected to Congress, and he was reelected in 1874. But by 1876 Reconstruction was over, and Lynch was defeated for a third term. In 1880 he ran again and was declared the loser, but he contested the decision and eventually was returned to his congressional seat. In the House he backed civil-rights legislation.

Lynch retired to his plantation in Adams county, Miss., in 1883. In 1889 he returned to public office when President Benjamin Harrison appointed him fourth auditor of the U.S. Treasury for the Navy Department. Always active in the Republican Party, Lynch served as a delegate to the national Republican conventions of 1872, 1884, 1888, 1892, and 1900. He was temporary chairman in 1884—the first black to preside over a national convention of a major U.S. political party.

In his book *The Facts of Reconstruction* (1913), Lynch attempted to dispel the erroneous notion that Southern state governments after the Civil War were under the control of blacks.

Carol Moseley Braun

(b. Aug. 16, 1947, Chicago, Ill., U.S.)

In 1992, Carol Moseley Braun, a Democrat from Illinois, became the first African American woman elected to the U.S. Senate.

Carol Moseley attended the University of Illinois at Chicago (B.A., 1969) and received a law degree from the University of Chicago (1972). She married Michael Braun in 1973 (divorced 1986) and worked as an assistant U.S. attorney before her election to the Illinois House of Representatives in 1978. During her 10 years there she became known for her advocacy of health-care and education reform and gun control. She was named assistant leader for the Democratic majority.

From 1988 to 1992 Moseley Braun served as Cook county (Illinois) recorder of deeds. Displeased with U.S. Sen. Alan Dixon's support of U.S. Supreme Court nominee Clarence Thomas, she ran against Dixon in the 1992 Democratic primary. Though poorly financed, she won an upset victory over Dixon on her way to capturing a seat in the Senate.

Shortly after becoming senator, Moseley Braun won clashes with Southern senators over a patent for a Confederate insignia. She was noted for her support of individual retirement accounts for homemakers and for filibustering to restore budget monies for youth job training and for senior citizens. Her record was tarnished, however, by her helping to ease legal restrictions on the sale of two television broadcasting companies, by lavish personal spending of campaign money, and by her favouring legislation to benefit a corporate campaign donor. She also was criticized for associating with two Nigerian military dictators.

In 1998 Moseley Braun lost her seat to her Republican challenger, Peter Fitzgerald. From 1999 to 2001 she served as U.S. ambassador to New Zealand. She unsuccessfully sought the Democratic Party presidential nomination in 2004.

BARACK OBAMA

(b. Aug. 4, 1961, Honolulu, Hawaii, U.S.)

Barack Hussein Obama, the 44th president of the United States (2009–), is the first African American to hold the office. Before winning the presidency, Obama represented Illinois in the U.S. Senate (2005–08). He was the third African American to be elected to that body since the end of Reconstruction (1877). In 2009 he was awarded the Nobel Peace Prize "for his extraordinary efforts to strengthen international diplomacy and cooperation between peoples."

EARLY LIFE

Obama's father, Barack Obama, Sr., was a teenage goatherd in rural Kenya; he won

Barack Obama is sworn in as the 44th U.S. president. His wife, Michelle, and daughters Malia and Sasha look on. Timothy A. Clary/AFP/Getty Images

a scholarship to study in the United States and eventually became a senior economist in the Kenyan government. Obama's mother, S. Ann Dunham, grew up in Kansas, Texas, and Washington state before her family settled in Honolulu. In 1961 she and Barack Sr. met in a Russian language class at the University of Hawaii and married less than a year later.

When Obama was age two, Barack Sr. left to study at Harvard University; shortly thereafter, in 1964, Ann and Barack Sr. divorced. (Obama saw his father only one more time, during a brief visit when Obama was 10.) Later Ann remarried, this time to another foreign student, Lolo Soetoro from Indonesia, with whom she had a second child, Maya. Obama lived for several years in Jakarta with his half sister, mother, and step-father. While there, Obama attended both a government-run school where he received some instruction in Islam and a Catholic private school where he took part in Christian schooling.

He returned to Hawaii in 1971 and lived in a modest apartment, sometimes with his grandparents and sometimes with his mother. (She remained for a time in Indonesia, returned to Hawaii, and then went abroad again—partly to pursue work on a Ph.D.—before divorcing Soetoro in 1980.) For a brief period his mother was aided by government food stamps, but the family mostly lived a middle-class existence. In 1979 Obama graduated from Punahou School, an elite college preparatory academy in Honolulu.

Obama attended Occidental College in suburban Los Angeles for two years and then transferred to Columbia University in New York City, where in 1983 he received a bachelor's degree in political science. Influenced by professors who pushed him to take his studies more seriously, Obama experienced great intellectual growth during college and for a couple of years thereafter. He led a rather ascetic life and read works of literature and philosophy by William Shakespeare, Friedrich Nietzsche, Toni Morrison, and others. After serving for a couple of years as a writer and editor for Business International Corp., a research, publishing, and consulting firm in Manhattan, he took a position in 1985 as a community organizer on Chicago's largely impoverished Far South Side. He returned to school three years later and graduated magna cum laude in 1991 from Harvard University's law school, where he was the first African American to serve as president of the *Harvard Law Review*. While a summer associate in 1989 at the Chicago law firm of Sidley Austin, Obama met Chicago native Michelle Robinson, a young lawyer at the firm. The two married in 1992.

After receiving his law degree, Obama moved to Chicago and became active in the Democratic Party. He organized Project Vote, a drive that registered tens of thousands of African Americans on voting rolls and that is credited with having helped Democrat Bill Clinton win Illinois and capture the presidency in 1992. The effort also helped make Carol

U.S. Pres. Barack Obama at a town hall meeting in Henderson, Nev., Feb. 19, 2010. Mandel Ngan/AFP/Getty Images

Moseley Braun, an Illinois state legislator, the first African American woman elected to the U.S. Senate. During this period, Obama wrote his first book and saw it published. The memoir, *Dreams from My Father* (1995), is the story of Obama's search for his biracial identity by tracing the lives of his now-deceased father and his extended family in Kenya. Obama lectured on constitutional law at the University of Chicago and worked as an attorney on civil rights issues.

POLITICS AND THE PRESIDENCY

In 1996 Obama was elected to the Illinois Senate, where, most notably, he helped pass legislation that tightened campaign finance regulations, expanded health care to poor families, and reformed criminal justice and welfare laws. In 2004 he was elected to the U.S. Senate, defeating Republican Alan Keyes in the first U.S. Senate race in which the two leading candidates were African Americans. While campaigning for the U.S. Senate, Obama gained national recognition by delivering the keynote address at the Democratic National Convention in July 2004. The speech wove a personal narrative of Obama's biography with the theme that all Americans are connected in ways that transcend political, cultural, and geographical differences. The address lifted Obama's once obscure memoir onto best-seller lists, and, after taking office the following year, Obama quickly became a major figure in his party. A trip to visit his father's home in Kenya in August 2006

gained international media attention, and Obama's star continued ascending. His second book, *The Audacity of Hope* (2006), a mainstream polemic on his vision for the United States, was published weeks later, instantly becoming a major best seller. In February 2007 he announced at the Old State Capitol in Springfield, Ill., where Abraham Lincoln had served as a state legislator, that he would seek the Democratic Party's presidential nomination in 2008.

Obama's personal charisma, stirring oratory, and his campaign promise to bring change to the established political system resonated with many Democrats, especially young and minority voters. On Jan. 3, 2008, Obama won a surprise victory in the first major nominating contest, the Iowa caucus, over Sen. Hillary Clinton, who was the overwhelming favourite to win the nomination. Five days later, however, Obama finished second to Clinton in the New Hampshire primary, and a bruising—and sometimes bitter—primary race ensued. Obama won more than a dozen states—including Illinois, his home state, and Missouri, a traditional political bellwether—on Super Tuesday, February 5. No clear front-runner for the nomination emerged, however, as Clinton won many states with large populations, such as California and New York. Obama produced an impressive string of victories later in the month, handily winning the 11 primaries and caucuses that immediately followed Super Tuesday, which gave him a significant lead in pledged delegates. His momentum slowed in early March when Clinton won significant victories in Ohio and Texas. Though still maintaining his edge in delegates, Obama lost the key Pennsylvania primary on April 22. Two weeks later he lost a close contest in Indiana but won the North Carolina primary by a large margin, widening his delegate lead over Clinton. She initially had a big lead in so-called superdelegates (Democratic Party officials allocated votes at the convention that were unaffiliated with state primary results), but, with Obama winning more states and actual delegates, many peeled away from her and went to Obama. On June 3, following the final primaries in Montana and South Dakota, the number of delegates pledged to Obama surpassed the total necessary to claim the Democratic nomination.

On August 27 Obama became the first African American to be nominated for the presidency by either major party and went on to challenge Republican Sen. John McCain for the country's

Michelle and Barack Obama and Jill and Joe Biden at Invesco Field on the final night of the Democratic National Convention in Denver, Aug. 28, 2008. Carol M. Highsmith/Library of Congress, Washington, D.C.

highest office. McCain criticized Obama, still a first-term senator, as being too inexperienced for the job. To counter, Obama selected Joe Biden, a veteran senator from Delaware who had a long resume of foreign policy expertise, to be his vice-presidential running mate. Obama and McCain waged a fierce and expensive contest. Obama, still bolstered by a fever of popular support, eschewed federal financing of his campaign and raised hundreds of millions of dollars, much of it coming in small donations and over the Internet from a record number of donors. Obama's fund-raising advantage helped him buy massive amounts of television advertising and organize deep grassroots organizations in key battleground states and in states that had voted Republican in previous presidential cycles.

The two candidates offered a stark ideological choice for voters. Obama called for a swift withdrawal of most combat forces from Iraq and a restructuring of tax policy that would bring more relief

Results of the American presidential election, 2008.

to lower- and middle-class voters, while McCain said the United States must wait for full victory in Iraq and charged that Obama's rhetoric was long on eloquence but short on substance. Just weeks before election day, Obama's campaign seized on the economic meltdown that had resulted from the catastrophic failure of U.S. banks and financial institutions in September, calling it a result of the Republican free-market-driven policies of the eight-year administration of George W. Bush.

Obama won the election, capturing nearly 53 percent of the popular vote and 365 electoral votes. Not only did he hold all the states that John Kerry had won in the 2004 election, but he also captured a number of states (e.g., Colorado, Florida, Nevada, Ohio, and Virginia) that the Republicans had carried in the previous two presidential elections. On election night tens of thousands gathered in Chicago's Grant Park to see Obama claim victory. Shortly after his win, Obama resigned from the Senate. On Jan. 20, 2009, hundreds of thousands turned out in Washington, D.C., to witness Obama taking the oath of office as president. Later that year he was awarded the Nobel Peace Prize.

MICHELLE OBAMA

(b. Jan. 17, 1964, Chicago, Ill., U.S.)

Michelle Obama, the wife of Barack Obama, 44th president of the United States, is the first African American first lady.

Michelle Robinson grew up on Chicago's South Side, the daughter of Marian Robinson (née Marian Shields), a homemaker, and Fraser Robinson, a worker in the city's water-purification plant. She studied sociology and African American studies at Princeton University (B.A., 1985) in New Jersey before attending Harvard Law School (J.D., 1988). Returning to Chicago, she took a job as a junior associate at Sidley Austin LLP, where she specialized in intellectual property law. In 1989, while at the firm, she met Barack Obama, who had been hired as a summer associate. Seeking a more public-service-oriented career path, in 1991 she became an assistant to Chicago Mayor Richard M. Daley. The following year she and Barack, then a community organizer, were married. From 1992 to 1993 Michelle was the assistant commissioner for the Chicago Department of Planning and Development, and in 1993 she founded the Chicago branch of Public Allies, a leadership-training program for young adults; she served as the branch's executive director until 1996.

Barack was elected to the Illinois Senate in 1996, and that year Michelle became the associate dean of student services at the University of Chicago, where she helped organize the school's community outreach programs. In 2002 she became the executive director of community and external affairs for the University of Chicago. Two years later Barack was elected to the U.S. Senate and came to national prominence with a speech he

Michelle Obama on the cover of Newsweek, *Feb. 25, 2008.* PRNewsFoto/Newsweek/AP Images

gave on the final night of the 2004 Democratic National Convention. In 2005 she became vice president of community and external affairs for the University of Chicago Medical Center.

When her husband announced his candidacy for the 2008 Democratic presidential nomination, Michelle took a prominent role in his campaign. She took leave from her position at the University of Chicago to devote herself more fully to campaigning while still maintaining time to care for her and Barack's two young daughters. An adept speaker, she stumped extensively for her husband during the long Democratic primary race, and in June 2008 Barack became the party's presumptive nominee. Michelle's openness on the campaign trail and in interviews—she often humanized her husband by discussing his faults and implored observers not to "deify him"— endeared her to many. However, critics of her husband's campaign took issue with some of her comments—such as when she remarked, while campaigning in

U.S. Pres. Barack Obama and First Lady Michelle Obama waving to the crowds during the Inaugural Parade, Jan. 20, 2009, Washington, D.C. MC1 Chad J. McNeeley/U.S. Department of Defense

Wisconsin in February 2008, that "for the first time in my adult lifetime, I am really proud of my country." Michelle later clarified her statement—saying that she meant to say that she was proud that Americans were eagerly engaging in the political process during the 2008 election—and she continued to have an active role in her husband's campaign. Indeed, campaign aides referred to her as "the closer," for her persuasiveness on the stump among uncommitted voters who attended rallies.

On Nov. 4, 2008, Barack was elected 44th president of the United States, defeating Arizona Sen. John McCain; he took office on Jan. 20, 2009.

PINCKNEY BENTON STEWART PINCHBACK

(b. May 10, 1837, Macon, Ga., U.S.—d. Dec. 21, 1921, Washington, D.C.)

Pinckney Benton Stewart Pinchback served as a Union officer in the Civil War

Barack and Michelle Obama with their daughters, Sasha (in white dress) *and Malia, in the Green Room of the White House, Washington, D.C., 2009.* Photo by Annie Leibovitz/Official White House Photo

and was a leading figure in Louisiana politics during Reconstruction.

Pinchback was one of 10 children born to a white Mississippi planter and a former slave mother—whom the father had freed before the boy's birth. When the father died in 1848, the family fled to Ohio, fearing that white relatives might attempt to re-enslave them.

Pinchback found work as a cabin boy on a canal boat and worked his way up to steward on the steamboats plying the Mississippi, Missouri, and Red rivers. After war broke out between the states in 1861, he ran the Confederate blockade on the Mississippi to reach Federal-held New Orleans; there he raised a company of black volunteers for the North, called the Corps d'Afrique. When he encountered racial discrimination in the service, however, he resigned his captain's commission.

Returning to New Orleans after the war, Pinchback organized the Fourth Ward Republican Club and served as a delegate to the convention that established a new constitution for Louisiana. He was elected to the state senate in 1868 and then was named its president pro tempore; as such he became lieutenant governor upon the death of the incumbent in 1871. From Dec. 9, 1872, to Jan. 13, 1873, he served as acting governor while impeachment proceedings were in progress against Henry Clay Warmoth. In the meantime he went into business and acquired control of a Republican paper, the New Orleans *Louisianian*.

In 1872 Pinchback was elected to Congress, but his Democratic opponent contested the election and won the seat. A year later Pinchback was elected to the U.S. Senate, but he was again refused the seat amid charges and countercharges of fraud and election irregularities—although some observers said it was the colour of his skin that counted against him. He was appointed to his last office in 1882 as surveyor of customs in New Orleans.

At the age of 50 Pinchback decided to take up a new profession and entered Straight College, New Orleans, to study law; he was subsequently admitted to the bar. Disillusioned with the outcome of Reconstruction and the return to power of the traditional white hierarchy, he moved to Washington, D.C., where he remained active in politics.

HIRAM R. REVELS

(b. Sept. 1, 1822, Fayetteville, N.C., U.S.—d. Jan. 16, 1901, Aberdeen, Miss.)

During Reconstruction clergyman and educator Hiram R. Revels became the first African American to be elected to the U.S. Senate (1870–71).

Born of free parents, young Revels traveled to Indiana and Illinois to receive the education that was denied him in the South. He was ordained a minister in the African Methodist Episcopal Church in 1845 and eventually settled in Baltimore, Md., where he served as a church pastor and principal of a school for blacks. Soon after the Civil War began (1861), he helped organize two volunteer regiments of blacks for service in the Union Army. Two years later he joined the Federal forces to serve as a chaplain to a black regiment stationed in Mississippi.

After the war Revels settled in Natchez, Miss., to preach to a large congregation. Despite some misgivings about entering politics, he accepted appointment by the military governor as alderman (1868) and was later (1869) elected to the state senate. Although Revels was a Republican, he was anxious not to encourage race friction with white Southerners; he therefore supported legislation that would have restored the power to vote and to hold office to disenfranchised members of the former Confederacy. In January 1870 he was elected to the U.S. Senate to fill the unexpired term of the former Confederate president, Jefferson Davis. He performed competently in office, advocating desegregation in the schools and on the railroads.

On leaving the Senate, Revels became president of Alcorn Agricultural and Mechanical College, a recently opened institution of higher education for blacks, near Lorman, Miss. In 1874, however, he was dismissed from the college presidency. In 1875 he helped overturn the Republican (Carpetbag) government of Mississippi, defending his action on the grounds that too many politicians in that party were corrupt. He was rewarded by the Democratic administration, which returned him to the chief post at Alcorn in 1876, where he remained until his retirement.

ADAM CLAYTON POWELL, JR.

(b. Nov. 29, 1908, New Haven, Conn., U.S.—d. April 4, 1972, Miami, Fla.)

Adam Clayton Powell, Jr., was a prominent pastor, liberal legislator, and civil-rights leader.

Powell was the son of the pastor of the Abyssinian Baptist Church in Harlem, New York City. Brought up in a middle-class home, he received his B.A. from Colgate University (Hamilton, N.Y.) in 1930 and his M.A. from Columbia University in 1932. He succeeded his father as pastor of the Abyssinian Baptist Church in 1937 and eventually built up its membership to 13,000 people. With the church as his power base, Powell was able to build a formidable public following in Harlem through his crusades for jobs and housing for the poor. He won election to the New York City Council in 1941, becoming the first black man to serve on that body. In 1945 he won election to the U.S. House of Representatives as a Democrat from Harlem. There he began a long fight against racial segregation. He served 11 successive terms in the House and became chairman of its Education and Labor Committee in 1960. In that capacity he played a leading role in the passage of a minimum wage act, antipoverty acts, and bills supporting manpower training and federal aid to education, about 50 major pieces of social legislation in all.

Powell's outspoken opposition to racism and his flamboyant lifestyle made him enemies, however, and in the early 1960s he became involved in a lawsuit with a woman who claimed he had wrongly accused her of collecting police graft. He was cited for contempt of court in 1966 for refusing to pay damages, and in 1967 the House voted to deprive him of his seat. He was nevertheless reelected in his district in 1968 but was then deprived by his colleagues in the House of his committee chairmanship and his seniority. In 1969 the U.S. Supreme Court decided that the action of the House in depriving him of his seat had been unconstitutional, but by that time Powell's health was failing. After his defeat in the Democratic primary election of 1970, he resigned as pastor of the Abyssinian Baptist Church in 1971 and retired to the island of Bimini in The Bahamas.

ROBERT SMALLS

(b. April 5, 1839, Beaufort, S.C., U.S.—d. Feb. 23, 1915, Beaufort)

Born into slavery, Robert Smalls became a Union naval hero in the Civil War and went on to serve as a congressman from South Carolina during Reconstruction.

His mother was a house slave and his father an unknown white man. Smalls was taken by his master in 1851 to Charleston, S.C., where he worked as a hotel waiter, hack driver, and rigger. In 1861, at the outbreak of the war, he was hired to work aboard the steamship *Planter*, which operated as an armed transport and dispatch vessel, carrying guns and ammunition for the Confederate army. On May 13, 1862, he and the other blacks on board seized control of the ship in Charleston Harbor, succeeded in passing through Confederate checkpoints, and turned the ship, its cargo of weapons, and several important documents over to a Union naval squadron blockading the city. This exploit brought Smalls great fame throughout the North. In 1863, when he was piloting the ironclad *Keokuk* in the battle for Fort Sumter, the vessel took many hits and was eventually sunk. Smalls's bravery was rewarded with command of the *Planter* later that year. He was the first African American captain of a vessel in U.S. service.

After the war, Smalls rose rapidly in politics, despite his limited education. From 1868 to 1870 he served in the South Carolina House of Representatives and from 1870 to 1874 in the state Senate. He was elected to the U.S. House of Representatives (1875–79, 1882–83, 1884–87), where his outstanding political action was support of a bill that would have required equal accommodations for both races on interstate conveyances. In 1877, however, he was convicted of having taken a $5,000 bribe while in the state Senate; sentenced to three years in prison, he was pardoned by the governor. The case against him was clearly politically motivated. In 1895 he delivered a moving speech before the South Carolina constitutional convention in a gallant but futile attempt to prevent the virtual disfranchisement of blacks.

A political moderate, Smalls spent his last years in Beaufort, where he served as port collector (1889–93, 1897–1913).

CARL STOKES

(b. June 21, 1927, Cleveland, Ohio, U.S.—d. April 3, 1996, Cleveland)

In 1967 Carl Stokes became the first African American to serve as mayor of a major American city, when he was elected to that office in Cleveland, Ohio.

A young child when his father died, Stokes held a number of odd jobs to help support his family. He dropped out of high school to work in a foundry and later served (1945–46) in the U.S. Army during World War II. After earning his high school diploma, he studied law at the University of Minnesota (B.S., 1954) and Cleveland-Marshall Law School (LL.B., 1956). In 1957 he passed the bar and the following year was appointed assistant city prosecutor in Cleveland. During this time Stokes became increasingly involved in civil rights activities and the Democratic Party.

In 1962 Stokes was elected to the Ohio General Assembly, where he developed a reputation as a moderate. Narrowly defeated in his 1965 bid for Cleveland's mayorship, he won the post in 1967. As mayor, Stokes sought to improve Cleveland's declining economy and to create racial unity. His efforts were undermined in 1968 by the Glenville riots, in which a shoot-out between police officers and African Americans led to several deaths and sparked looting and arson. He was reelected in 1969 but retired from politics in 1971.

Stokes then moved to New York City to become a television news anchor and later won an Emmy Award for his broadcast work. After returning to Cleveland, he served as general counsel (1980–83) to the United Automobile Workers before being elected a municipal court judge in 1983. From 1994 to 1995 Stokes served as U.S. ambassador to the Republic of Seychelles. His autobiography, *Promises of Power*, was published in 1973.

HAROLD WASHINGTON

(b. April 15, 1922, Chicago, Ill., U.S.—d. Nov. 25, 1987, Chicago)

Harold Washington gained national prominence as the first African American mayor of Chicago (1983–87).

During World War II, Washington joined the army and served as an engineer in the South Pacific. After returning home in 1946, he graduated from Roosevelt University (B.A., 1949), earned a law degree from Northwestern University (1952), and established a private law practice in Chicago. He succeeded his father, a part-time Methodist minister, as Democratic precinct captain before working as a city attorney (1954–58) and a state labour arbitrator (1960–64). He then served in the Illinois House of Representatives (1965–76), the Illinois State Senate (1976–80), and the U.S. House of Representatives (1980–83).

During his second term in Congress, Washington was persuaded by black leaders to enter the 1983 mayoral race in Chicago. Overcoming negative publicity—in 1970 his law license was suspended for failure to perform paid legal work and in 1972 he spent more than a month in jail for failing to file his federal income tax return for four years—and campaigning for reform and an end to city patronage, he won the Democratic nomination by upsetting incumbent Mayor Jane Byrne and Richard M. Daley, the son of four-term mayor Richard J. Daley. In the general election Washington narrowly defeated Bernard Epton, a virtually unknown white Republican, in a record voter turnout tinged with racial overtones.

Washington was often unable to implement his programs during his first term in office because the opposition in City Council controlled a majority of the 50 council seats. After a court ruled that several ward boundaries violated the law by disfranchising minority voters, new elections in those wards finally gave him control of the council in 1986. The following year he was easily reelected to a second term even though he had pushed through an unpopular $70 million property tax increase. Washington died in office seven months later.

DOUGLAS WILDER

(b. Jan. 17, 1931, Richmond, Va., U.S.)

Douglas Wilder became the first popularly elected African American governor in the United States when he assumed the leadership of Virginia.

Wilder received a bachelor's degree in chemistry from Virginia Union University (1951) and a law degree from Howard University (1959). He pursued a legal and political career in Richmond, Va., and served as a director of the Richmond chapter of the National Urban League. In 1969 he became the first African American since Reconstruction to win a seat in the Virginia Senate. Wilder, a Democrat, acquired a reputation as a moderate, and in 1985 he was elected state lieutenant governor, the first African American to win statewide office in Virginia. Nominated by the Democratic Party for governor in 1989, he narrowly defeated the Republican candidate with 50.2 percent of the vote. He declared his candidacy for the 1992 Democratic Party nomination for the presidency of the United States, but he withdrew before the primaries began. Constitutionally barred from running for a second consecutive term as governor, Wilder left office in 1994. In 2004 he was elected mayor of Richmond. Wilder decided not to seek reelection in 2008, and he was succeeded by Dwight C. Jones later that year.

COLEMAN YOUNG

(b. May 24, 1918, Tuscaloosa, Ala., U.S.—d. Nov. 29, 1997, Detroit, Mich.)

Coleman Young was the first African American mayor of Detroit (1974–93).

In 1923 Young moved with his family from the South to Detroit. Unable to obtain a scholarship to attend college, he began working on an assembly line at the Ford Motor Company, where he became involved in union activities and civil rights issues. He was drafted during World War II and served with the Tuskegee Airmen, the first African American flying unit in the U.S. military. Near the end of his service, he was briefly imprisoned for trying to desegregate an officers' club. After returning to Detroit, he helped found in 1951 the National Negro Labor Council (NNLC), which sought jobs for African Americans. In 1952 Young, who had developed a reputation as a radical, was called before the House Committee on Un-American Activities. His pugnacious testimony earned him widespread publicity, and he later disbanded the NNLC so that he would not have to turn over its membership list. Blacklisted by labour organizations, he was forced to take a series of odd jobs before becoming an insurance salesman.

In 1964 Young was elected to the Michigan Senate, and four years later he became the Democratic National Committee's first African American member. In 1973 he ran for mayor of Detroit and won a close election. At the time, the city was struggling with unemployment, crime, and suburban flight. As mayor, Young sought to revitalize Detroit, attracting new businesses, reforming the police department, and overseeing major construction projects. Outspoken and often controversial, Young proved popular with African American voters—he was reelected an unprecedented four times—but alienated many in the white community. Faced with failing health, he decided not to run for reelection in 1993. His autobiography, *Hard Stuff* (written with Lonnie Wheeler), was published in 1994.

GOVERNMENT OFFICIALS, DIPLOMATS, AND SOLDIERS

African Americans began shedding blood for American causes as early as the death of Crispus Attucks during the Boston Massacre in 1770. They have served in every war waged by the United States, including fighting on both sides of the American Revolution and making a massive contribution to the Union effort in the Civil War. Although the U.S. military would not be desegregated until after World War II, black cavalrymen, called "buffalo soldiers" by Native Americans, were a ubiquitous presence in the frontier West, and the contributions of a squadron of African American flyers, the Tuskegee Airmen, are the stuff of legend. Colin Powell played a special role in U.S. history as not only the first African American to serve as the chairman of the Joint Chiefs of Staff but also as the first African American to serve as the secretary of state. He is but one of many African Americans who played important roles in the military and as government officials and diplomats.

CRISPUS ATTUCKS

(b. 1723?—d. March 5, 1770, Boston, Mass., U.S.)

Crispus Attucks, martyr of the Boston Massacre, was one of the first American heroes.

Attucks's life prior to the day of his death is still shrouded in mystery. Most historians say that he was black; others argue that his ancestry was both African and Natick Indian. In any event, in the fall of 1750, a resident of Framingham, Mass., advertised for the recovery of a runaway slave named Crispus—usually thought to be the Crispus in question. In the 20-year interval between his escape from slavery and his death at the hands of British soldiers, Attucks probably spent a good deal of time aboard whaling ships.

All that is definitely known about him concerns the Boston Massacre on March 5, 1770. Toward evening that day, a crowd of colonists gathered and began taunting a small group of British soldiers. Tension mounted rapidly, and when one of the soldiers was struck the others fired their muskets, killing three of the Americans instantly and mortally wounding two others. Attucks was the first to fall, thus becoming one of the first men to lose his life in the cause of American independence. His body was carried to Faneuil Hall, where it lay in state until March 8, when all five victims were buried in a common grave. Attucks was the only victim of the Boston Massacre whose name was widely remembered. In 1888 the Crispus Attucks monument was unveiled in the Boston Common.

RALPH BUNCHE

(b. Aug. 7, 1904, Detroit, Mich., U.S.—d. Dec. 9, 1971, New York, N.Y.)

Diplomat Ralph Bunche was a key member of the United Nations for more than two decades and the winner of the 1950 Nobel Prize for Peace for his successful negotiation of an Arab-Israeli truce in Palestine the previous year.

Bunche worked his way through the University of California at Los Angeles and graduated in 1927. He also earned graduate degrees in government and international relations at Harvard University (1928, 1934) and studied in England and South Africa. In 1928 he joined the faculty of Howard University, Washington, D.C., where he set up a department of political science. Meanwhile, he traveled through French West Africa on a Rosenwald field fellowship, studying the administration of French Togoland, a mandated area, and Dahomey, a colony. He later did

Ralph Bunche, 1951. Carl Van Vechten Collection/Library of Congress, Washington, D.C. (neg. no. LC-USZ62-54231)

postdoctoral research at Northwestern University, Evanston, Ill., and at the London School of Economics before returning to Africa for further studies in colonial policy. Between 1938 and 1940 he collaborated with Gunnar Myrdal, the Swedish sociologist, in the monumental study of U.S. race relations, published as *An American Dilemma* in 1944.

During World War II Bunche served in the U.S. War Department, the Office of Strategic Services, and the State Department. He was active in the preliminary planning for the United Nations at the San Francisco Conference of 1945 and in 1947 joined the permanent UN Secretariat in New York as director of the new Trusteeship Department.

Asked by Secretary General Trygve Lie to aid a UN special committee appointed to negotiate a settlement between warring Palestinian Arabs and Jews, he was thrust unexpectedly into the principal role when the chief mediator, Count Folke Bernadotte, was assassinated in 1948. Bunche finally negotiated armistices between February and May 1949.

Elevated in 1955 to the post of undersecretary and two years later to undersecretary for special political affairs, Bunche became chief troubleshooter for Secretary General Dag Hammarskjöld. One task he undertook was the UN program concerning peaceful uses of atomic energy. In 1956 he supervised the deployment of a 6,000-man UN neutral force in the area of the Suez Canal following the invasion of that area by British, French, and Israeli troops. In 1960 he again found himself in charge of UN peacekeeping machinery—this time in the Congo region. Finally, in 1964 he went to Cyprus to direct the 6,000 neutral troops that intervened between hostile Greek Cypriots and Turks.

Attracting some criticism for seeming to neglect the civil rights movement at home during the 1950s and '60s, Bunche began to speak out more directly on U.S. racial discrimination. In addition, though not in the best of health, he participated in the 1965 civil rights marches in both Selma and Montgomery, Ala., and also served as a board member for the National Association for the Advancement of Colored People for 22 years. *Ralph J. Bunche: Selected Speeches and Writings* was published in 1995.

Benjamin O. Davis, Sr.

(b. July 1, 1877, Washington, D.C., U.S.—d. Nov. 26, 1970, North Chicago, Ill.)

Benjamin O. Davis, Sr., was the first African American general in the U.S. Army.

After serving as a volunteer in the Spanish-American War (1898), Davis enlisted as a private in the 9th Cavalry of the U.S. Army. He rose to sergeant major within two years and earned a commission as a second lieutenant in 1901. In the next four decades he served in Liberia and the Philippines and taught military science at the Tuskegee Institute and at Wilberforce University. All of his duty assignments were designed to avoid a situation in which Davis might be put in command of white troops or officers. He rose slowly through the ranks, becoming the first black colonel in the army in 1930. In 1940 he was promoted to brigadier general by Pres. Franklin D. Roosevelt. After commanding the 2nd Cavalry Division in 1941, he was assigned to the office of the inspector general of the army. During World War II he headed a special unit charged with safeguarding the status and morale of black soldiers in the army, and he served in the European theatre as a special adviser on race relations. He retired in 1948 after 50 years of service.

PATRICIA ROBERTS HARRIS

(b. May 31, 1924, Mattoon, Ill., U.S.—d. March 23, 1985, Washington, D.C.)

Patricia Roberts Harris (née Patricia Roberts) was the first African American woman named to a U.S. ambassadorship and the first as well to serve in a presidential cabinet.

Harris grew up in Mattoon and in Chicago. She graduated from Howard University, Washington, D.C., in 1945, pursued graduate studies for two years at the University of Chicago, and from 1946 to 1949 was a program director for the Young Women's Christian Association in Chicago. In 1949 she returned to Washington, D.C., where she did further graduate work at American University and worked as assistant director of the American Council on Human Rights (1949–53). For six years thereafter she was executive director of the national headquarters of Delta Sigma Theta sorority. In 1960 she graduated from the law school at George Washington University and was admitted to the District of Columbia bar. After a year in the criminal division of the U.S. Department of Justice, she became associate dean of students and lecturer in law at Howard University. During 1962–65 she worked with the National Capital Area Civil Liberties Union. Although she relinquished her administrative post at Howard in 1963, she remained on the Howard faculty.

In 1963 Harris was named cochair, with Mildred McAfee Horton, of the National Women's Committee for Civil Rights. Serving as U.S. ambassador to Luxembourg from 1965 to 1967, she was the first African American woman to hold ambassadorial rank. She rejoined the Howard law faculty from 1967 to 1969. From January 1977 to August 1979, she was U.S. secretary of housing and urban development, and she thereafter was secretary of health, education and welfare (later health and human services). She was the first African American woman to be a member of a presidential cabinet.

In 1981 she returned to George Washington University as a full-time professor of law, and in 1982 she made an unsuccessful bid for mayor of Washington, D.C.

Colin Powell, 2001. U.S. Department of State

COLIN POWELL

(b. April 5, 1937, New York, N.Y., U.S.)

Colin Powell served as the chairman of the Joint Chiefs of Staff (1989–93) and secretary of state (2001–05), the first African American to hold either position.

The son of Jamaican immigrants, Powell grew up in the Harlem and South Bronx sections of New York City and attended the City College of New York (B.S., 1958), serving in the Reserve Officers' Training Corps (ROTC). He entered the army upon graduation, served in Vietnam in 1962–63 and 1968–69, and then studied at George Washington University in Washington, D.C. In 1972 he took his first political position, as a White House fellow, and soon became an assistant to Frank Carlucci, then deputy director of the Office of Management and Budget (OMB). Powell held various posts over the next few years, in the Pentagon and elsewhere, and in 1983 became senior military assistant to Secretary of Defense Caspar Weinberger. In 1987 he joined the staff of the National Security Council as deputy to Carlucci, then assistant to the president for national security affairs. Late in 1987 Pres. Ronald Reagan appointed Powell to succeed Carlucci. Early in 1989 Powell took over the Army Forces Command.

In April 1989 Powell became a four-star general, and in August Pres. George Bush nominated him chairman of the Joint Chiefs of Staff. As chairman, he played a leading role in planning the invasion of Panama (1989) and the Desert Shield and Desert Storm operations of the Persian Gulf crisis and war (August 1990–March 1991). He retired from the military in 1993, sparking speculation that he would enter politics. Although he decided not to run for president in 1996, he joined the Republican Party and spoke out on national issues. In 2001 he was appointed secretary of state by Pres. George W. Bush. Powell unsuccessfully sought broader international support for the Iraq War. His controversial speech before the United Nations (February 2003) was later revealed to be based on faulty intelligence. Considered a political moderate in an administration dominated by hard-liners, Powell saw his influence in the White House wane, and he announced his resignation in 2004, shortly after Bush's reelection; he was succeeded by Condoleezza Rice in 2005. *My American Journey*, his autobiography (written with Joseph E. Persico), was published in 1995.

CONDOLEEZZA RICE

(b. Nov. 14, 1954, Birmingham, Ala., U.S.)

Educator and politician Condoleezza Rice served as national security adviser (2001–05) and secretary of state (2005–09) to Pres. George W. Bush.

At age 15 Rice entered the University of Denver. Although she had earlier

Condoleezza Rice. U.S. Department of State

considered a career as a concert pianist, she turned to the study of international relations, earning a bachelor's degree in the field in 1974. She later obtained a master's degree (1975) in economics from the University of Notre Dame and a doctorate (1981) in international studies from the University of Denver, where her specialty was eastern and central Europe and the Soviet Union, including military and security affairs. Rice joined the faculty of Stanford University in 1981. In 1986 she served as an assistant to the Joint Chiefs of Staff on nuclear strategy, and during the administration of Pres. George Bush she was director for Soviet and eastern European affairs for the National Security Council (NSC) and a special assistant to the president. In 1991 Rice returned to Stanford and in 1993 began a six-year tenure as provost, during which time she balanced the university's budget and revamped the curriculum for undergraduates.

In 1999 Rice left Stanford to become foreign policy adviser to the presidential

U.S. Vice President Dick Cheney talking on the phone with U.S. Pres. George W. Bush as National Security Adviser Condoleezza Rice (seated) and other senior staff listen at the Presidential Emergency Operations Center, Sept. 11, 2001. Eric Draper/The White House

campaign of George W. Bush, and upon his election she was named head of the NSC, the first woman to hold this position. Following the September 11 attacks in 2001, she proved to be an important and influential adviser to Bush. She supported the U.S.-led attacks on terrorist and Taliban targets in Afghanistan (2001) and aligned herself with hard-liners who advocated the overthrow of Iraqi Pres. Ṣaddām Ḥussein. When the administration drew criticism for the Iraq War (2003) and the handling of terrorist threats prior to Sept. 11, 2001, Rice vigorously defended the president's policy.

In 2005 she succeeded Colin Powell as secretary of state, becoming the first African American woman to have the position. In her post, Rice helped negotiate an end to Israel's occupation of the Gaza Strip. She also persuaded North Korea to return to talks aimed at dismantling that country's nuclear weapons program. Rice led an intense effort to promote democracy and broker a U.S.-friendly peace in the Middle East. After fighting broke out in July 2006 between Israel and Lebanon-based Hezbollah forces, Rice initially defended the decision by the United States not to seek an immediate cease-fire, but the following month she urged the United Nations Security Council to adopt such a resolution. She also joined European foreign ministers in calling for sanctions against Iran, after that country failed to halt its nuclear program or allow inspections of its nuclear facilities.

Rice's writings include *The Soviet Union and the Czechoslovak Army, 1948–1983: Uncertain Allegiance* (1984) and *Germany Unified and Europe Transformed: A Study in Statecraft* (1995, with Philip Zelikow).

ROBERT C. WEAVER

(b. Dec. 29, 1907, Washington, D.C., U.S.—d. July 17, 1997, New York, N.Y.)

Noted economist Robert C. Weaver was the first African American to serve in the U.S. cabinet.

Weaver, the great-grandson of a slave, was educated (B.S., 1929; M.A., 1931; and Ph.D., 1934) at Harvard University. He held several positions in various agencies of the U.S. government for the next 10 years, starting as the first African American adviser on racial problems in the Department of the Interior. After World War II he served for a time in Chicago as executive director of the Mayor's Committee on Race Relations, taught briefly at several universities, and wrote *Negro Labor, a National Problem* (1946) and *The Negro Ghetto* (1948). From 1949 to 1955 he directed the fellowship program of the John Hay Whitney Foundation, after which he became rent commissioner in New York state and, as such, a member of the governor's cabinet. He was active in the civil rights movement and served for a year as national chairman of the National Association for the Advancement of Colored People. In 1960 Pres. John F. Kennedy appointed

BUFFALO SOLDIER

Buffalo soldiers of the 25th Infantry at Fort Keogh, Mont., 1890. Gladstone Collection/Library of Congress, Washington, D.C. (digital file number: cph 3g06161)

An 1866 law authorized the U.S. Army to form cavalry and infantry regiments made up of African American soldiers; the resulting units were the 9th and 10th cavalries and the 38th through 41st infantries (these four were later reduced to the 24th and 25th infantries, which often fought alongside the cavalry regiments). The law required their officers to be white.

The 10th Cavalry, originally head-quartered at Fort Leavenworth, Ks., was commanded by Col. Benjamin Grierson; his men were provided with aged horses, deteriorating equipment, and inadequate supplies of ammunition. Their duties included escorting stagecoaches, trains, and work parties and policing cattle rustlers and illegal traders who sold guns and liquor to Native Americans, but their principal mission was to control the Indians of the Plains and Southwest, who called the black troops buffalo soldiers, though the significance of the nickname is uncertain. After the Red River Indian War (1874–75) the 10th Cavalry was transferred to Texas, where the 9th Cavalry, commanded by Col. Edward Hatch, had long been based.

The combined forces fought outlaws and Native Americans who often conducted raids and robberies from sanctuaries in Mexico. They carried out a campaign against the Apache, who were resisting relocation and confinement on reservations. After numerous battles with Victorio and his Apache band, the soldiers managed to subdue them in 1880. While the 10th Cavalry continued in action against the remaining Apache for another decade, the 9th was sent to Indian Territory (later Oklahoma) to deal with whites who were illegally settling on Indian lands. In 1892–96, after Grierson's retirement, the 10th Cavalry relocated to Montana Territory with orders to round up and deport the Cree Indians to Canada.

The buffalo soldiers were noted for their courage and discipline. Drunkenness, an especially widespread problem in the army, was rare among them; in a period when nearly a third of white army enlistees deserted, the black soldiers had the U.S. Army's lowest desertion and court-martial rates. In nearly 30 years of frontier service buffalo soldiers took part in almost 200 major and minor engagements. From 1870 to 1890, 14 buffalo soldiers were awarded medals of honour, the army's highest award for bravery. The 9th and 10th cavalries later distinguished themselves by their fighting in the Spanish-American War and in the 1916 Mexican campaign. One of the 10th Cavalry's officers was John J. Pershing, whose nickname Black Jack reflected his advocacy of black troops.

Weaver to head the federal Housing and Home Finance Agency. In 1966 Pres. Lyndon B. Johnson named him head of the new Department of Housing and Urban Development.

Weaver left the government in 1969 to become president of Bernard Baruch College of the City University of New York and from 1970 to 1978 was professor of urban affairs at Hunter College. His other publications include *The Urban Complex* (1964) and *Dilemmas of Urban America* (1965).

ANDREW YOUNG

(b. March 12, 1932, New Orleans, La., U.S.)

Politician, civil-rights leader, and clergyman Andrew Young served as the U.S. ambassador to the United Nations and as the mayor of Atlanta.

Young was reared in a middle-class black family, attended segregated Southern schools, and later entered Howard University (Washington, D.C.) as

TUSKEGEE AIRMEN

In response to pressure from the National Association for the Advancement of Colored People (NAACP), the black press, and others, the War Department in January 1941 formed the all-black 99th Pursuit Squadron of the U.S. Army Air Corps (later the U.S. Army Air Forces), to be trained using single-engine planes at the segregated Tuskegee Army Air Field at Tuskegee, Ala. The base opened on July 19, and the first class graduated the following March. Lieutenant Colonel Benjamin Oliver Davis, Jr., became the squadron's commander.

The squadron, which became known as the Tuskegee Airmen, received further training in French Morocco, before their first mission, on June 2, 1943, a strafing attack on Pantelleria Island, an Italian island in the Mediterranean Sea. Later that year the Army activated three more squadrons that, joined in 1944 by the 99th, constituted the 332nd Fighter Group. It fought in the European theatre and was noted as the Army Air Forces' only escort group that did not lose a bomber to enemy planes.

The Tuskegee airfield program expanded to train pilots and crew to operate two-engine B-25 medium bombers. These men became part of the second black flying group, the 477th Bombardment Group. Shortages of crew members, technicians, and equipment troubled the 477th, and before it could be deployed overseas, World War II ended. Altogether 992 pilots graduated from the Tuskegee airfield courses; they flew 1,578 missions and 15,533 sorties, destroyed 261 enemy aircraft, and won over 850 medals.

a premed student. But he turned to the ministry and graduated in 1955 from the Hartford Theological Seminary (Hartford, Conn.) with a divinity degree.

A pastor at several black churches in the South, Young became active in the civil-rights movement—especially in voter registration drives. His work brought him in contact with Dr. Martin Luther King, Jr., and Young joined with King in leading the Southern Christian Leadership Conference (SCLC). Following King's assassination in 1968, Young worked with Ralph Abernathy until he resigned from the SCLC in 1970.

Defeated that year in his first bid for a seat in Congress, Young ran again in 1972 and won. He was reelected in 1974 and 1976. In the House he opposed cuts in funds for social programs while trying to block additional funding for the war in Vietnam. He was an early supporter of Jimmy Carter, and, after Carter's victory in the 1976 presidential elections, Andrew Young was made the United States ambassador to the United Nations. His apparent sympathy with the Third World made him very controversial, and he was finally forced to resign in 1979 after it became known that he had met with a representative of the Palestine Liberation Organization. In 1981 Young was elected mayor of Atlanta, and he was reelected to that post in 1985, serving through 1989.

LAWYERS AND JURISTS

The use and abuse of the U.S. legal system have been at the centre of the African American struggle for freedom and civil rights, so it is perhaps not surprising that the efforts of black lawyers and legal scholars have been pivotal to American history. The profiles of the two African Americans who have risen to serve on the U.S. Supreme Court point to the changes those efforts have wrought but also to obstacles yet to be surmounted. Thurgood Marshall, who as a lawyer successfully argued perhaps the most important civil rights case, *Brown* v. *Board of Education of Topeka*, before the Supreme Court, became the first African American Supreme Court justice and a prominent liberal voice on the Court for decades. The second African American justice, Clarence Thomas, has proved to be among the court's most conservative members. Thomas's ascent to the Court occurred in post-*Brown* America, yet the spectre of racism attended his televised Senate confirmation hearings, which Thomas called a "high-tech lynching" when accusations of sexual harassment (allegedly during his service in the Department of Justice) were raised against him.

MARIAN WRIGHT EDELMAN

(b. June 6, 1939, Bennettsville, S.C., U.S.)

Lawyer and civil rights activist Marian Wright Edelman (née Marian Wright) founded the Children's Defense Fund in 1973.

Edelman attended Spelman College in Atlanta (B.A., 1960) and Yale University

Law School (LL.B., 1963). After work registering African American voters in Mississippi, she moved to New York City as a staff attorney for the Legal Defense and Educational Fund of the National Association for the Advancement of Colored People (NAACP).

In 1964 Edelman returned to the South and became the first African American woman to pass the bar in Mississippi. In private practice, she took on civil rights cases and fought for funding of one of the largest Head Start programs in the country. She served as director of the Legal Defense and Educational Fund in Jackson, Miss.

Marian Wright Edelman. Charley Gallay/Getty Images

(1964–68), and then moved to Washington, D.C., to start the Washington Research Project of the Southern Center for Public Policy, a public interest law firm. From 1971 to 1973 Edelman was the director of Harvard University's Center for Law and Education, and in 1973 she founded and became president of the Children's Defense Fund (CDF) in Washington, D.C. The CDF became a highly effective organization in advocating children's rights. In 1996 she founded a similar organization, Stand for Children.

Edelman's publications include *Children Out of School in America: A Report* (1974), *Portrait of Inequality: Black and White Children in America* (1980), *Families in Peril: An Agenda for Social Change* (1987), *The Measure of Our Success: A Letter to My Children and Yours* (1992), and *Guide My Feet: Meditations and Prayers on Loving and Working for Children* (1995). Her honours include a MacArthur Foundation Fellowship (1985) and several humanitarian awards. In 2000 Edelman received the Presidential Medal of Freedom, the country's highest civilian award, and the Robert F. Kennedy Lifetime Achievement Award for her writings. In 2002 she published *I'm Your Child, God: Prayers for Children and Teenagers.* That same year, Edelman received the National Mental Health Association Tipper Gore Remember the Children Volunteer Award. In 2005 she published *I Can Make a Difference: A Treasury to Inspire Our Children*, and in 2008 she published *The Sea Is So Wide and My*

Boat Is So Small: Charting a Course for the Next Generation.

CHARLES HAMILTON HOUSTON

(b. Sept. 3, 1895, Washington, D.C., U.S.—d. April 22, 1950, Washington, D.C.)

Lawyer and educator Charles Hamilton Houston was instrumental in laying the legal groundwork that led to U.S. Supreme Court rulings outlawing racial segregation in public schools.

Houston graduated as one of six valedictorians from Amherst College (B.A., 1915). After teaching for two years at Howard University in Washington, D.C., he enlisted in the U.S. Army and was commissioned a second lieutenant in field artillery and served in France and Germany during World War I.

Following his discharge in 1919, Houston enrolled at Harvard Law School (LL.B., 1922; D.J.S., 1923), where he was the first black editor of the *Harvard Law Review*. He went on to study civil law at the University of Madrid. After being admitted to the bar in the United States in 1924, he practiced law with his father until 1950.

As vice-dean of Howard University Law School (1929–35), Houston shaped it into a significant institution. The school trained almost one-fourth of the nation's black law students, among them Thurgood Marshall. During Houston's tenure the school became accredited by the Association of American Law Schools and the American Bar Association.

Houston made significant contributions in the battle against racial discrimination, challenging many of the Jim Crow laws. In 1935–40 he served as special counsel for the National Association for the Advancement of Colored People (NAACP), arguing several important civil rights cases before the U.S. Supreme Court. In *State ex rel. Gaines* v. *Canada* (1938), Houston argued that it was unconstitutional for Missouri to exclude blacks from the state's university law school when, under the "separate but equal" provision, no comparable facility for blacks existed within the state. Houston's efforts to dismantle the legal theory of "separate but equal" came to fruition after his death, with the historic *Brown* v. *Board of Education* (1954) decision, which prohibited segregation in public schools.

Houston's contributions to the abolition of legal discrimination went largely unrecognized until after his death. He was posthumously awarded the NAACP's Spingarn Medal in 1950. Several public schools bear his name, as does the main building of the Howard Law School, which was dedicated in 1958. A law professorship and several student organizations also honour Houston.

THURGOOD MARSHALL

(b. July 2, 1908, Baltimore, Md., U.S.—d. Jan. 24, 1993, Bethesda, Md.)

Thurgood Marshall was the first African American member of the Supreme Court of the United States (1967–91). As an attorney, he successfully argued before the U.S. Supreme Court the case of *Brown v. Board of Education of Topeka* (1954), which declared unconstitutional racial segregation in American public schools.

Marshall was the son of William Canfield Marshall, a railroad porter and a steward at an all-white country club, and Norma Williams Marshall, an elementary school teacher. He graduated with honours from Lincoln University (Pennsylvania) in 1930. After being rejected by the University of Maryland Law School because he was not white, Marshall attended Howard University Law School; he received his degree in 1933, ranking first in his class. At Howard he was the protégé of Charles Hamilton Houston, who encouraged Marshall and other law students to view the law as a vehicle for social change.

Upon his graduation from Howard, Marshall began the private practice of law in Baltimore. Among his first legal victories was *Murray v. Pearson* (1935), in which Marshall successfully sued the University of Maryland for denying an African American applicant admission to its law school simply on the basis of race. In 1936 Marshall became a staff lawyer under Houston for the National Association for the Advancement of Colored People (NAACP); in 1938 he became the lead chair in the legal office of the NAACP, and two years later he was named chief of the NAACP Legal Defense and Educational Fund.

Throughout the 1940s and '50s Marshall distinguished himself as one of the country's top lawyers, winning 29 of the 32 cases that he argued before the U.S. Supreme Court. Among them were cases in which the court declared unconstitutional a Southern state's exclusion of African American voters from primary elections (*Smith v. Allwright* [1944]), state judicial enforcement of racial "restrictive covenants" in housing (*Shelley v. Kraemer* [1948]), and "separate but equal" facilities for African American professionals and graduate students in state universities (*Sweatt v. Painter* and *McLaurin v. Oklahoma State Regents* [both 1950]). Without a doubt, however, it was his victory before the Supreme Court in *Brown v. Board of Education of Topeka* that established his reputation as a formidable and creative legal opponent and an advocate of social change. Indeed, students of constitutional law still examine the oral arguments of the case and the ultimate decision of the court from both a legal and a political perspective; legally, Marshall argued that segregation in public education produced unequal schools for African Americans and whites (a key element in the strategy to have the court overrule the "separate but equal" doctrine established in *Plessy v. Ferguson* [1896]), but it was Marshall's reliance on psychological, sociological, and historical data that presumably sensitized the court to the deleterious effects of institutionalized segregation on the self-image, social worth, and social progress of African American children.

Thurgood Marshall. Library of Congress, Washington, D.C. (neg. no. LC-USZC6-26)

In September 1961 Marshall was nominated to the U.S. Court of Appeals for the Second Circuit by Pres. John F. Kennedy, but opposition from Southern senators delayed his confirmation for several months. Pres. Lyndon B. Johnson named Marshall U.S. solicitor general in July 1965 and nominated him to the Supreme Court on June 13, 1967; Marshall's appointment to the Supreme Court was confirmed (69–11) by the U.S. Senate on Aug. 30, 1967.

During Marshall's tenure on the Supreme Court, he was a steadfast liberal, stressing the need for equitable and just treatment of the country's minorities by the state and federal governments. A pragmatic judicial activist, he was committed to making the U.S. Constitution work; most illustrative of his approach was his attempt to fashion a "sliding scale" interpretation of the Fourteenth Amendment's equal protection clause that would weigh the objectives of the government against the nature and interests of the groups affected by the law. Marshall's sliding scale was never adopted by the Supreme Court, though in several major civil rights cases of the 1970s the court echoed Marshall's views. He was also adamantly opposed to capital punishment and generally favoured the rights of the national government over the rights of the states.

Marshall served on the Supreme Court as it underwent a period of major ideological change. In his early years on the bench, he fit comfortably among a liberal majority under the leadership of Chief Justice Earl Warren. As the years passed, however, many of his closest allies, including Warren, either retired or died in office, creating opportunities for Republican presidents to swing the pendulum of activism in a conservative direction. By the time he retired in 1991, he was known as "the Great Dissenter," one of the last remaining liberal members of a Supreme Court dominated by a conservative majority.

CHARLOTTE E. RAY

(b. Jan. 13, 1850, New York, N.Y., U.S.—d. Jan. 4, 1911, Woodside, Queens, N.Y.)

Charlotte E. Ray was the first female African American lawyer in the United States.

Ray studied at the Institution for the Education of Colored Youth in Washington, D.C., and by 1869 she was teaching at Howard University. There she studied law, receiving her degree in 1872. Her admission that year to the District of Columbia bar made her the first woman admitted to practice in the District of Columbia and the first black woman certified as a lawyer in the United States.

Ray opened a law office in Washington, D.C., but racial prejudices proved too strong, and she could not obtain enough legal business to maintain an active practice. By 1879 she had returned to New York City, where she taught in the public schools. In the late 1880s she married a man with the surname of Fraim; little is known of her later life.

CLARENCE THOMAS

(b. June 23, 1948, Pinpoint, near Savannah, Ga., U.S.)

In 1991, Clarence Thomas became the second African American to serve on the Supreme Court of the United States. Appointed to replace Thurgood Marshall, Thomas gave the court a decisive conservative cast.

Thomas's father abandoned the family when Thomas was two years old. After the family house was destroyed by fire, Thomas's mother, a maid, remarried, and Thomas, then age seven, and his brother were sent to live with their grandfather. Clarence was educated in Savannah, Ga., at an all-African American Roman Catholic primary school run by white nuns and then at a boarding-school seminary, where he graduated as the only African American in his class. He attended Immaculate Conception Abbey in his freshman year of college and then transferred to Holy Cross College in Worcester, Mass., where he graduated with a bachelor's degree in 1971. He received a law degree from Yale University in 1974.

Thomas was successively assistant attorney general in Missouri (1974–77), a lawyer with the Monsanto Company (1977–79), and a legislative assistant to Republican Sen. John C. Danforth of Missouri (1979–81). In the Republican presidential administrations of Ronald Reagan and George Bush, Thomas served as assistant secretary in the U.S. Department of Education (1981–82), chairman of the Equal Employment Opportunity Commission (EEOC; 1982–90), and judge on the U.S. Court of Appeals for the Federal District in Washington, D.C. (1990–91), a post to which he was appointed by Bush.

Marshall's retirement gave Bush the opportunity to replace one of the court's most liberal members with a conservative. The president was under significant political pressure to appoint another African American, and Thomas's service under Republican senators and presidents made him an obvious choice. Despite his appeal to Republican partisans, however, his nomination engendered controversy for several reasons: he had little experience as a judge; he had produced little judicial scholarship; and he refused to answer questions about his position on abortion (he claimed during his confirmation hearings that he had never discussed the issue). Nevertheless, Thomas seemed headed for easy confirmation until a former aide stepped forward to accuse him of sexual harassment, a subject that dominated the latter stages of the hearings. The aide, Anita Hill, an African American law professor at the University of Oklahoma who had worked for Thomas at the EEOC and the Department of Education, alleged in televised hearings that Thomas had made sexually offensive comments to her in an apparent campaign of seduction. Thomas denied the charge and accused the Senate Judiciary Committee of engineering a "high-tech lynching." A deeply divided Senate only narrowly confirmed Thomas's nomination by a vote of 52 to 48.

On the Supreme Court, Thomas maintained a relatively quiet presence but evidenced a strong conservatism in his votes and decisions, frequently siding with fellow conservative Antonin Scalia. This alliance was forged in Thomas's first major case, *Planned Parenthood of Southeastern Pennsylvania* v. *Casey* (1992), in which he joined Scalia's dissent, which argued that *Roe* v. *Wade* (1973), the ruling that established the legal right to abortion, should be reversed. Thomas's conservative ideology also was apparent in his opinions on the issue of school desegregation; in *Missouri* v. *Jenkins* (1995), for example, he wrote a 27-page concurring opinion that condemned the extension of federal power into the states and tried to establish a legal justification for reversing the desegregation that had begun in 1954 with *Brown* v. *Board of Education of Topeka*. Because "desegregation has not produced the predicted leaps forward in black educational achievement," Thomas argued, "there is no reason to think that black students cannot learn as well when surrounded by members of their own race as when they are in an integrated environment."

Although the controversy surrounding his appointment dissolved shortly after he joined the bench, Thomas will perhaps always be measured against the justice he succeeded. Ideologically, Thomas and Marshall were stark contrasts, and throughout his career Thomas worked against many of the causes championed by his predecessor. As one of the most reliable conservatives appointed by Republican presidents, Thomas generally followed a predictable pattern in his opinions—conservative, restrained, and suspicious of the reach of the federal government into the realm of state and local politics.

Whether elected or appointed, the public servants presented here were engaged in government work, but, as the following chapter will show, African Americans did not have to hold office to make important contributions to society.

CHAPTER 3

EXPLORATION, EDUCATION, EXPERIMENTATION, AND ECUMENISM

By the early 21st century, the list of firsts by African Americans was long and distinguished, yet perhaps more significant was the proliferation of contributions of African Americans who followed these pioneers in fields from exploration and aviation to education and from science to business and religion. This chapter explores the lives and contributions of some of the most influential of these pioneers.

EXPLORERS, AVIATORS, AND ASTRONAUTS

The post-World War II electric blues that were created in Chicago by African American musicians might not have occurred—or at least might have happened somewhere else—were it not for Jean-Baptist-Point Du Sable, who in 1799 established the settlement that became Chicago. Matthew Alexander Henson, who traveled to North Pole with William Peary, was an explorer of a different type, as were early aviator Bessie Coleman and astronauts Guion S. Bluford, Jr., and Mae Jemison.

GUION S. BLUFORD, JR.

(b. Nov. 22, 1942, Philadelphia, Pa., U.S.)

Astronaut Guion S. Bluford, Jr., was the first African American to travel into space.

Guion S. Bluford, Jr., 1992. NASA/Johnson Space Center

Bluford received an undergraduate degree in aerospace engineering from Pennsylvania State University in 1964 and was commissioned as an officer in the U.S. Air Force, where he trained as a fighter pilot. He flew 144 combat missions during the Vietnam War. In 1978 he earned a doctorate in aerospace engineering from the Air Force Institute of Technology.

Bluford was one of 35 individuals selected in 1978 from 10,000 applicants in NASA's first competition to become space shuttle astronauts. On Aug. 30, 1983, he rode into Earth orbit on the shuttle orbiter *Challenger*; he subsequently flew on three additional shuttle missions between 1985 and 1992. Bluford served as a mission specialist on all four flights, with responsibility for a variety of in-orbit tasks, including the deployment of an Indian communications satellite as well as the operation and deployment of scientific and classified military experiments and payloads.

In 1987 Bluford received a graduate degree in business administration from the University of Houston, Clear Lake. He left NASA in July 1993 for a private-sector career in the information technology and engineering services field.

Guion S. Bluford, Jr., exercising on a treadmill aboard the U.S. space shuttle Challenger *in Earth orbit, 1983.* NASA

BESSIE COLEMAN

(b. Jan. 26, 1893, Atlanta, Texas, U.S.—d. April 30, 1926, Jacksonville, Fla.)

Aviator Bessie Coleman was a star of early aviation exhibitions and air shows.

One of 13 children, Coleman grew up in Waxahachie, Texas, where her mathematical aptitude freed her from working in the cotton fields. She attended college in Langston, Okla., briefly, then moved to Chicago, where she worked as a manicurist and restaurant manager and became interested in the then-new profession of aviation.

Discrimination thwarted Coleman's attempts to enter aviation schools in the United States. Undaunted, she learned

Bessie Coleman. NASA

French and at age 27 was accepted at the Caudron Brothers School of Aviation in Le Crotoy, France. Black philanthropists Robert Abbott, founder of the *Chicago Defender*, and Jesse Binga, a banker, assisted with her tuition. On June 15, 1921, she became the first American woman to obtain an international pilot's license from the Fédération Aéronitique Internationale. In further training in France, she specialized in stunt flying and parachuting; her exploits were captured on newsreel films. She returned to the United States, where racial and gender biases precluded her becoming a commercial pilot. Stunt flying, or barnstorming, was her only career option.

Coleman staged the first public flight by an African American woman in America on Labor Day, Sept. 3, 1922. She became a popular flier at aerial shows, though she refused to perform before segregated audiences in the South. Speaking at schools and churches, she encouraged blacks' interest in aviation; she also raised money to found a school to train black aviators. Before she could found her school, however, during a rehearsal for an aerial show, the plane carrying Coleman spun out of control, catapulting her 2,000 feet to her death.

JEAN-BAPTIST-POINT DU SABLE

(b. 1750?, St. Marc, Saint-Domingue [now Haiti]—d. Aug. 28, 1818, St. Charles, Mo., U.S.)

Pioneer trader Jean-Baptist-Point Du Sable founded the settlement that later became the city of Chicago.

Du Sable, whose French father had moved to Haiti and married a black woman there, is believed to have been a freeborn. At some time in the 1770s he went to the Great Lakes area of North America, settling on the shore of Lake Michigan at the mouth of the Chicago River, with his Potawatomi wife, Kittihawa (Catherine). His loyalty to the French and the Americans led to his arrest in 1779 by the British, who took him to Fort Mackinac. From 1780 to 1783 or 1784 he managed for his captors a trading post called the Pinery on the St. Clair River in present-day Michigan, after which he returned to the site of Chicago. By 1790 Du Sable's establishment there had become an important link in the region's fur and grain trade.

In 1800 Du Sable sold out and moved to Missouri, where he continued as a farmer and trader until his death. But his 20-year residence on the shores of Lake Michigan had established his title as Father of Chicago.

MATTHEW ALEXANDER HENSON

(b. Aug. 8, 1866, Charles County, Md., U.S.—d. March 9, 1955, New York, N.Y.)

Explorer Matthew Alexander Henson accompanied Robert E. Peary on most of his expeditions, including that to the North Pole in 1909.

Orphaned as a youth, Henson went to sea at the age of 12 as a cabin boy on the sailing ship *Katie Hines.* Later, while working in a store in Washington, D.C., he met Peary, who hired him as a valet for

his next expedition to Nicaragua (1888). Peary, impressed with Henson's ability and resourcefulness, employed him as an attendant on his seven subsequent expeditions to the Arctic (1891–92; 1893–95; 1896; 1897; 1898–1902; 1905–06; 1908–09). In 1909 Peary and Henson, accompanied by four Eskimos, became the first men to reach the North Pole, the rest of the crew having turned back earlier. Henson's account of the journey, *A Negro Explorer at the North Pole,* appeared in 1912. The following year, by order of Pres. William Howard Taft, Henson was appointed a clerk in the U.S. Customs House in New York City, a post he held until his retirement in 1936. Henson received the Congressional medal awarded all members of the Peary expedition (1944).

MAE JEMISON

(b. Oct. 17, 1956, Decatur, Ala., U.S.)

Physician Mae Jemison was the first African American woman to become an astronaut. In 1992 she spent more than a week orbiting Earth in the space shuttle *Endeavour.*

Jemison moved with her family to Chicago at the age of three. There she was introduced to science by her uncle and developed interests throughout her childhood in anthropology, archaeology, evolution, and astronomy. While still a high school student, she became interested in biomedical engineering, and after graduating in 1973, at the age of 16, she entered Stanford University. There she

Mae Jemison aboard the space shuttle **Endeavour.** NASA Marshall Space Flight Center

received degrees in chemical engineering and African American studies (1977).

In 1977 Jemison entered medical school at Cornell University in Ithaca, N.Y., where she pursued an interest in international medicine. After volunteering for a summer in a Cambodian refugee camp in Thailand, she studied in Kenya in 1979. She graduated from medical school in 1981, and, after a short time as a general practitioner with a Los Angeles medical group, she became a medical officer with the Peace Corps in West Africa. There she managed health care for Peace Corps and U.S. embassy personnel and worked in conjunction with the National Institutes of Health and the Centers for Disease Control on several research projects, including development of a hepatitis B vaccine.

After returning to the United States, Jemison applied to the National Aeronautics and Space Administration (NASA) to be an astronaut. In October 1986, she was 1 of 15 accepted out of 2,000 applicants. Jemison completed her training as a mission specialist with NASA in 1988. She became an astronaut office representative with the Kennedy Space Center at Cape Canaveral, Fla., working to process space shuttles for launching and to verify shuttle software. Next, she was assigned to support a cooperative mission between the United States and Japan designed to conduct experiments in materials processing and the life sciences. In September 1992, STS-47 Spacelab J became the first successful joint U.S.-Japan space mission.

Jemison's maiden space flight came with the week-long September 1992 mission of the shuttle *Endeavour*. At that time she was the only African American woman astronaut. After completing her NASA mission, she formed the Jemison Group, to develop and market advanced technologies.

EDUCATORS AND ACADEMICS

African American educators have made contributions to all realms of knowledge and study (including science and medicine, examined below), but the academics presented here are particularly notable for their work in understanding the black experience and in deepening the knowledge of African American history and culture. Indeed, the idea for an African American History Month was first conceived by one of the educators profiled here, historian Carter G. Woodson, in concert with members of his Association for the Study of Negro Life and History (now the Association for the Study of African American Life and History). Having begun in February 1926 as Negro History Week, it became African American History Month in 1976 and is a time when schools focus on the history and achievements of African Americans.

JOHN HOPE FRANKLIN

(b. Jan. 2, 1915, Rentiesville, Okla., U.S.—d. March 25, 2009, Durham, N.C.)

Historian and educator John Hope Franklin is noted for his scholarly reappraisal of the Civil War era and the importance of the black struggle in shaping modern American identity. He also helped fashion the legal brief that led to the historic Supreme Court decision outlawing public school segregation, *Brown v. Board of Education of Topeka* (1954) and was instrumental in the development of African American Studies programs at colleges and universities.

Franklin was the son of a lawyer. After attending Fisk University, Nashville, Tenn. (A.B., 1935), and Harvard University (A.M., 1936; Ph.D., 1941), he continued his career in education with teaching positions at a number of schools, among them Howard University, Washington, D.C. (1947–56), Brooklyn (N.Y.) College (1956–64), the University of Chicago (1964–82; emeritus thereafter), and Duke University, Durham, N.C. (1982–92).

Franklin first gained international attention with the publication of *From Slavery to Freedom* (1947; 9th. ed., 2009). His other works treating aspects of the

American Civil War include *The Militant South, 1800–1861* (1956), *Reconstruction: After the Civil War* (1961), and *The Emancipation Proclamation* (1963). He also edited three books of the Civil War period, as well as several other books, including *Color and Race* (1968) and *Black Leaders of the Twentieth Century* (1982). *George Washington Williams: A Biography* (1985), *Race and History: Selected Essays, 1938–1988* (1989), and *The Color Line: Legacy for the Twenty-First Century* (1993) are among his later publications.

In 1995 U.S. Pres. Bill Clinton honoured Franklin with the Presidential Medal of Freedom; two years later Clinton appointed the scholar to the seven-member Race Initiative Advisory Board.

HENRY LOUIS GATES, JR.

(b. Sept. 16, 1950, Keyser, W.Va., U.S.)

Literary critic and scholar Henry Louis Gates, Jr., is known for his pioneering theories of African literature and African American literature. He introduced the notion of *signifyin'* to represent African and African American literary and musical history as a continuing reflection and reinterpretation of what has come before.

Gates's father, Henry Louis Gates, Sr., worked in a paper mill and moonlighted as a janitor; his mother, Pauline Coleman Gates, cleaned houses. Gates graduated as valedictorian of his high school class in 1968 and attended a local junior college before enrolling at Yale University, where he received a bachelor's degree in history in 1973. After receiving two fellowships in 1970, he took a leave of absence from Yale to visit Africa, working as an anesthetist in a hospital in Tanzania and then traveling through other African nations. In 1973 he entered Clare College at the University of Cambridge, where one of his tutors was the Nigerian writer Wole Soyinka. Soyinka persuaded Gates to study literature instead of history; he also taught him much about the culture of the Yoruba, one of the largest Nigerian ethnic groups. After receiving his doctoral degree in English language and literature in 1979, Gates taught literature and African American studies at Yale University, Cornell University, Duke University, and Harvard University, where he was appointed W.E.B. Du Bois Professor of the Humanities in 1991.

In 1980 Gates became codirector of the Black Periodical Literature Project at Yale. In the years that followed he earned a reputation as a "literary archaeologist" by recovering and collecting thousands of lost literary works (short stories, poems, reviews, and notices) by African American authors dating from the early 19th to the mid-20th century. In the early 1980s Gates rediscovered the earliest novel by an African American, Harriet E. Wilson's *Our Nig* (1859), by proving that the work was in fact written by an African American woman and not, as had been widely assumed, by a white man from the North. From the 1980s Gates edited a number of critical anthologies of African American literature, including

Henry Louis Gates, Jr. Jemal Countess/Getty Images

Black Literature and Literary Theory (1984), *Bearing Witness: Selections from African American Autobiography in the Twentieth Century* (1991), and (with Nellie Y. McKay) *The Norton Anthology of African American Literature* (1997).

Gates developed the notion of signifyin' in *Figures in Black: Words, Signs, and the "Racial" Self* (1987) and *The Signifying Monkey: A Theory of Afro-American Literary Criticism* (1988). Signifyin' is the practice of representing an idea indirectly, through a commentary that is often humourous, boastful, insulting, or provocative. Gates argued that the pervasiveness and centrality of signifyin' in African and African American literature and music means that all such expression is essentially a kind of dialogue with the literature and music of the past. Gates traced the practice of signifyin' to Esu, the trickster figure of Yoruba mythology, and to the figure of the "signifying monkey," with which Esu is closely associated. He applied the notion to the interpretation of slave narratives and showed how it informs the works of Phillis Wheatley, Zora Neale Hurston, Frederick Douglass, the early African American writers of periodical fiction, Ralph Ellison, Ishmael Reed, Alice Walker, and Wole Soyinka.

In *Loose Canons: Notes on the Culture Wars* (1992) and elsewhere Gates argued for the inclusion of African American literature in the Western canon. Other works by Gates include *Speaking of Race, Speaking of Sex: Hate Speech, Civil Rights, and Civil Liberties* (1994), *Colored People: A Memoir* (1994), *The Future of the Race* (1996; with Cornel West), *Thirteen Ways of Looking at a Black Man* (1997), *The Trials of Phillis Wheatley: America's First Black Poet and Her Encounters with the Founding Fathers* (2003), *America Behind the Color Line: Dialogues with African Americans* (2004), and *In Search of Our Roots* (2009). Gates was much in the news in 2009 after a controversial encounter with a policeman outside his home in Cambridge, Mass., that led to his arrest, charges of racism against the policeman, and finally to a much-publicized meeting at the White House between Gates and the arresting officer that was hosted by Pres. Barack Obama.

CORNEL WEST

(b. June 2, 1953, Tulsa, Okla., U.S.)

Philosopher, African American studies scholar, and political activist Cornel West is best known as the author of the influential book *Race Matters* (1993). In it he lamented what he saw as the spiritual impoverishment of the African American underclass and critically examined the "crisis of black leadership" in the United States.

West's father was a civilian U.S. Air Force administrator and his mother an elementary school teacher and eventually a principal. During West's childhood the family settled in an African American working-class neighbourhood in Sacramento, Calif. There

West regularly attended services at the local Baptist church, where he listened to moving testimonials of privation, struggle, and faith from parishioners whose grandparents had been slaves. Another influence on West during this time was the Black Panther Party, whose Sacramento offices were near the church he attended. The Panthers impressed upon him the importance of political activism at the local level and introduced him to the writings of Karl Marx.

In 1970, at age 17, West entered Harvard University on a scholarship. He graduated magna cum laude three years later with a bachelor's degree in Middle Eastern languages and literature. He attended graduate school in philosophy at Princeton University, where he was influenced by the American pragmatist philosopher Richard Rorty. (West briefly abandoned work on his dissertation to write a novel, which was never published.) After receiving his doctoral degree in 1980, West taught philosophy, religion, and African American studies at several colleges and universities, including Union Theological Seminary, Yale University (including the Yale Divinity School), the University of Paris, Princeton University, and Harvard University, where he was appointed Alphonse Fletcher, Jr., University Professor in 1998. He returned to Princeton in 2002.

West's work was characteristically wide-ranging, eclectic, original, and provocative. His several books analyzing issues of race, class, and justice or tracing the history of philosophy typically combined a political perspective based on democratic socialism (*see* social democracy), a Christian moral sensibility, and a philosophical orientation informed by the tradition of American pragmatism. His best-known work, *Race Matters*, a collection of essays, was published exactly one year after the start of riots in Los Angeles that were sparked by the acquittal of four white policemen on charges of aggravated assault in the beating of Rodney King, an African American motorist. The book discussed the pervasive despair and "nihilism" of African Americans in poverty and criticized African American leaders for pursuing strategies that West believed were shortsighted, narrow-minded, or self-serving. West also considered issues such as black-Jewish relations, the renewed popularity of Malcolm X, and the significance of the Los Angeles riots themselves.

West was always a political activist as well as an academic, and he did not hesitate to participate in demonstrations or to lend his name or presence to causes he felt were just. At times his activism created tensions with the administrations of the universities where he taught. In 2001 the new Harvard University president, Lawrence Summers, reportedly admonished West in private for devoting too much time to political activity and other extracurricular pursuits. Their dispute was soon joined by supporters and detractors of West both inside and outside the academy, who debated not only the merits of West's scholarship but also the commitment of Summers and Harvard to affirmative action programs. Eventually West resigned his position at Harvard and moved to Princeton.

West's other works include *The American Evasion of Philosophy: A Genealogy of Pragmatism* (1989), *The Ethical Dimensions of Marxist Thought* (1991), *Beyond Eurocentrism and Multiculturalism* (1993), and *Democracy Matters: Winning the Fight Against Imperialism* (2004). In 2001 he recorded a raplike spoken-word CD entitled *Sketches of My Culture*. In 2003 he appeared as the character Councillor West in the popular movies *The Matrix Reloaded* and *The Matrix Revolutions*.

WILLIAM JULIUS WILSON

(b. Dec. 20, 1935, Derry township, Pa, U.S.)

Sociologist William Julius Wilson's views on race and urban poverty helped

Cornel West. Lawrence Lucier/Getty Images

shape U.S. public policy and academic discourse.

Wilson was educated at Wilberforce University (B.A., 1958) and Bowling Green State University (M.A., 1961) in Ohio, as well as at Washington State University (Ph.D., 1966). He joined the faculty of the University of Massachusetts (Amherst) as an assistant professor of sociology in 1965. In 1972 he moved to the University of Chicago, becoming a full professor in 1975 and gaining a chaired university professorship in 1990. Wilson conducted research, taught, wrote on inner-city poverty, and led the Center for the Study of Urban Inequality at the University of Chicago until 1996, when he joined Harvard University as a university professor in sociology and became the director of Harvard's Joblessness and Urban Poverty Research Program.

In two seminal works, *The Declining Significance of Race: Blacks and Changing American Institutions* (1978) and *The Truly Disadvantaged: The Inner City, the Underclass, and Public Policy* (1987), Wilson maintained that class divisions and global economic changes, more than racism, created a large black underclass. In *When Work Disappears: The World of the New Urban Poor* (1996), he showed how chronic joblessness deprived those in the inner city of skills necessary to obtain and keep jobs.

Wilson disputed the liberal stance that the "black underclass" (a term he later abandoned) owed its existence to entrenched racial discrimination; he also disagreed with the conservative view that African American poverty was due to cultural deficiencies and welfare dependency. Instead, Wilson implicated sweeping changes in the global economy that pulled low-skilled manufacturing jobs out of the inner city, the flight from the ghetto of its most successful residents, and the lingering effects of past discrimination. He believed the problems of the underclass could be alleviated only by "race neutral" programs such as universal health care and government-financed jobs. Wilson was a MacArthur Prize fellow from 1987 to 1992, and he was awarded the National Medal of Science in 1998.

CARTER G. WOODSON

(b. Dec. 19, 1875, New Canton, Va., U.S.—d. April 3, 1950, Washington, D.C.)

Historian Carter G. Woodson is credited with opening the long-neglected field of African American studies.

Of a poor family, Woodson supported himself by working in the coal mines of Kentucky and was thus unable to enroll in high school until he was 20. After graduating in less than two years, he taught high school, wrote articles, studied at home and abroad, and received his Ph.D. from Harvard University (1912). In 1915 he founded the Association for the Study of Negro Life and History to encourage scholars to engage in the intensive study of the black past. Prior to this work, the field had been largely neglected or distorted in the hands of historians who accepted the traditionally biased picture of blacks in American and world affairs. In 1916 Woodson edited the first issue of the association's principal scholarly publication, *The Journal of Negro History,* which, under his direction, remained an important historical periodical for more than 30 years.

Woodson was dean of the College of Liberal Arts and head of the graduate faculty at Howard University, Washington, D.C. (1919–20), and dean at West Virginia State College, Institute, W. Va. (1920–22). While there, he founded and became president of Associated Publishers to bring out books on black life and culture, since experience had shown him that the usual publishing outlets were rarely interested in scholarly works on blacks.

Important works by Woodson include the widely consulted college text *The Negro in Our History* (1922; 10th ed., 1962); *The Education of the Negro Prior to 1861* (1915); and *A Century of Negro Migration* (1918). He was at work on a projected six-volume *Encyclopaedia Africana* at the time of his death.

SCIENCE AND MEDICINE

Though probably best remembered for his work with peanuts, George Washington Carver was more than just an agricultural scientist; he was a legend who devoted his life to bringing practical knowledge to those in need. While he is arguably the most famous black scientist, African American contributions to science and medicine stretch back from the 18th century efforts of polymath Benjamin Banneker through those of Carver and his contemporary behavioral scientist Charles Henry Turner to the present.

BENJAMIN BANNEKER

(b. Nov. 9, 1731, Ellicott's Mills, Md., U.S.—d. Oct. 25, 1806, Baltimore, Md.)

Mathematician, astronomer, compiler of almanacs, inventor, and writer Benjamin Banneker was one of the first important African American intellectuals.

A free man who owned a farm near Baltimore, Banneker was largely self-educated in astronomy by watching the stars, and in mathematics by reading borrowed textbooks. In 1761 he attracted attention by building a wooden clock that kept precise time. Encouraged in his studies by a Maryland industrialist, Joseph Ellicott, he began astronomical calculations about 1773, accurately predicted a solar eclipse in 1789, and published annually from 1791 to 1802 the *Pennsylvania, Delaware, Maryland, and Virginia Almanac and Ephemeris.* Appointed to the District of Columbia Commission by Pres. George Washington in 1790, he worked with Andrew Ellicott and others in surveying Washington, D.C.

As an essayist and pamphleteer, Banneker opposed slavery and war. He sent a copy of his first almanac to Thomas Jefferson, then U.S. secretary of state, along with a letter asking Jefferson's aid in bringing about better conditions for

American blacks. Banneker's almanacs were acclaimed by European scientists to whom Jefferson made them known.

GEORGE WASHINGTON CARVER

(b. 1861?, near Diamond Grove, Mo., U.S.—d. Jan. 5, 1943, Tuskegee, Ala.)

Agricultural chemist, agronomist, and experimenter George Washington Carver developed new products derived from peanuts, sweet potatoes, and soybeans that helped revolutionize the agricultural economy of the South. For most of his career he taught and conducted research at the Tuskegee Normal and Industrial Institute (now Tuskegee University) in Tuskegee, Ala.

Carver was the son of a slave woman owned by Moses Carver. During the Civil War, slave owners found it difficult to hold slaves in the border state of Missouri, and Moses Carver therefore sent his slaves, including the young child and his mother, to Arkansas. After the war, Moses Carver learned that all his former slaves had disappeared except for a child named George. Frail and sick, the motherless child was returned to his former master's home and nursed back to health. The boy had a delicate sense of colour and form and learned to draw; later in life he devoted considerable time to painting flowers, plants, and landscapes. Though the Carvers told him he was no longer a slave, he remained on their plantation until he was about 10 or 12 years old, when he left to acquire an education. He spent some time wandering about, working with his hands and developing his keen interest in plants and animals.

By both books and experience, George acquired a fragmentary education while doing whatever work came to hand in order to subsist. He supported himself by varied occupations that included general household worker, hotel cook, laundry-man, farm labourer, and homesteader. In his late 20s he managed to obtain a high school education in Minneapolis, Kan., while working as a farmhand. After a university in Kansas refused to admit him because he was black, Carver matriculated at Simpson College, Indianola, Iowa, where he studied piano and art, subsequently transferring to Iowa State Agricultural College (Ames, Iowa), where he received a bachelor's degree in agricultural science in 1894 and a master of science degree in 1896.

Carver left Iowa for Alabama in the fall of 1896 to direct the newly organized department of agriculture at the Tuskegee Normal and Industrial Institute, a school headed by the noted black American educator Booker T. Washington. At Tuskegee, Washington was trying to improve the lot of black Americans through education and the acquisition of useful skills rather than through political agitation; he stressed conciliation, compromise, and economic development as the paths for black advancement in American society. Despite many offers elsewhere, Carver would remain at Tuskegee for the rest of his life.

After becoming the institute's director of agricultural research in 1896, Carver devoted his time to research projects aimed at helping Southern agriculture, demonstrating ways in which farmers could improve their economic situation. He conducted experiments in soil management and crop production and directed an experimental farm. At this time agriculture in the Deep South was in serious trouble because the unremitting single-crop cultivation of cotton had left the soil of many fields exhausted and worthless, and erosion had then taken its toll on areas that could no longer sustain any plant cover. As a remedy, Carver urged Southern farmers to plant peanuts and soybeans, which, since they belong to the legume family, could restore nitrogen to the soil while also providing the protein so badly needed in the diet of many Southerners. Carver found that Alabama's soils were particularly well-suited to growing peanuts and sweet potatoes, but when the state's farmers began cultivating these crops instead of cotton, they found little demand for them on the market. In response to this problem, Carver set about enlarging the commercial possibilities of the peanut and sweet potato through a long and ingenious program of laboratory research. He ultimately developed 300 derivative products from peanuts—among them cheese, milk, coffee, flour, ink, dyes, plastics, wood stains, soap, linoleum, medicinal oils, and cosmetics—and 118 from sweet potatoes, including flour, vinegar, molasses, rubber, ink, a synthetic rubber, and postage stamp glue.

In 1914, at a time when the boll weevil had almost ruined cotton growers, Carver revealed his experiments to the public, and increasing numbers of the South's farmers began to turn to peanuts, sweet potatoes, and their derivatives for income. Much exhausted land was renewed, and the South became a major new supplier of agricultural products. When Carver arrived at Tuskegee in 1896, the peanut had not even been recognized as a crop, but within the next half century it became one of the six leading crops throughout the United States and, in the South, the second cash crop (after cotton) by 1940. In 1942 the U.S. government allotted five million acres of peanuts to farmers. Carver's efforts had finally helped liberate the South from its excessive dependence on cotton.

Among Carver's many honours were his election to Britain's Society for the Encouragement of Arts, Manufactures, and Commerce (London) in 1916 and his receipt of the Spingarn Medal in 1923. Late in his career he declined an invitation to work for Thomas A. Edison at a salary of more than $100,000 a year. Presidents Calvin Coolidge and Franklin D. Roosevelt visited him, and his friends included Henry Ford and Mohandas K. Gandhi. Foreign governments requested his counsel on agricultural matters: Joseph Stalin, for example, in 1931 invited him to superintend cotton plantations in southern Russia and to make a tour of the Soviet Union, but Carver refused.

George Washington Carver, c. 1935. Hulton Archive/Getty Images

In 1940 Carver donated his life savings to the establishment of the Carver Research Foundation at Tuskegee for continuing research in agriculture. During World War II he worked to replace the textile dyes formerly imported from Europe, and in all he produced dyes of 500 different shades.

Many scientists thought of Carver more as a concoctionist than as a contributor to scientific knowledge. Many of his fellow blacks were critical of what they regarded as his subservience. Certainly, this small, mild, soft-spoken, innately modest man, eccentric in dress and mannerism, seemed unbelievably heedless of the conventional pleasures and rewards of this life. But these qualities endeared Carver to many whites, who were almost invariably charmed by his humble demeanour and his quiet work in self-imposed segregation at Tuskegee. As a result of his accommodation to the mores of the South, whites came to regard him with a sort of patronizing adulation.

Carver thus increasingly came to stand for much of white America as a kind of saintly and comfortable symbol of the intellectual achievements of black Americans. Carver was evidently uninterested in the role his image played in the racial politics of the time. His great desire in later life was simply to serve humanity; and his work, which began for the sake of the poorest of the black sharecroppers, paved the way for a better life for the entire South. His efforts brought about a significant advance in agricultural training in an era when agriculture was the largest single occupation of Americans, and he extended Tuskegee's influence throughout the South by encouraging improved farm methods, crop diversification, and soil conservation.

Joycelyn Elders

(b. Aug. 13, 1933, Schaal, Ark., U.S.)

Physician and public health official Joycelyn Elders (née Minnie Lee Jones) served (1993–94) as U.S. surgeon general, the first African American and the second woman to hold that post.

Elders was the first of eight children in a family of sharecroppers. At age 15 she entered Philander Smith College, a historically black liberal arts college in Little Rock, Ark., on a scholarship from the United Methodist Church. That year she saw a doctor for the first time in her life and subsequently determined to become a physician herself. In 1952 she graduated from college after only three years. The following year she joined the army; she was trained as a physical therapist in Texas and served at army hospitals in San Francisco and Denver, Colo. In 1956 she entered the University of Arkansas Medical School in Little Rock on the GI Bill, and in 1960 she was the only woman to graduate from that institution. Also in 1960, she married Oliver Elders. Following an internship in pediatrics at the University of Minnesota Hospital in Minneapolis (1960–61), she returned to Arkansas for a residency at the University of Arkansas Medical Center, where she rose to chief pediatric resident in 1963 and pediatric research fellow in 1964. She earned a degree in biochemistry from the university (M.S., 1967) and joined the faculty at the medical school in 1967, rising to full professor by 1976.

Arkansas Gov. Bill Clinton appointed Elders to the office of director of public health in 1987. In that position she initiated a project to reduce the level of teen pregnancy through availability of birth control, counseling, and sex education at school-based clinics; achieved a 10-fold increase in early childhood screenings from 1988 to 1992 and a 24 percent rise in the immunization rate for two-year-olds; and expanded the availability of HIV testing and counseling services, breast cancer screenings, and around-the-clock care for elderly and terminally ill patients.

On the strength of these achievements, Elders in 1993 was nominated by Pres. Bill Clinton for the post of U.S. surgeon general. Although her confirmation process was lengthy and controversial—involving criticisms of

Joycelyn Elders during her confirmation hearings as U.S. surgeon general, July 23, 1993. Kort Duce/AFP/Getty Images

her financial dealings and her outspokenness on sex education—she was eventually confirmed. As chief U.S. medical officer, she played an important role in Clinton's early efforts to reorganize the health care system, and she regularly urged the public to consider unorthodox solutions to public health problems. Some of her suggestions concerning sex education in the public schools, however, caused great controversy, and in December 1994 Clinton asked her to resign.

In 1995 she returned to the University of Arkansas, teaching and practicing pediatric endocrinology. Following her retirement in 1999, she lectured widely on public health issues. Her autobiography, *Joycelyn Elders, MD*, written with David Chanoff, was published in 1996.

MARY MAHONEY

(b. May 7, 1845, Dorchester, Mass., U.S.—d. Jan. 4, 1926, Boston, Mass.)

Mary Mahoney was the first African American woman to complete the course of professional study in nursing.

Mahoney apparently worked as a maid at the New England Hospital for Women and Children in Boston before being admitted to its nursing school in 1878. She received her diploma in 1879, becoming the first black woman to complete nurse's training. At the time of her graduation, seriously ill patients were routinely treated at home rather than in a hospital, and Mahoney was employed for many years as a private-duty nurse. One of the first black members of the Nurses Associated Alumnae of the United States and Canada (subsequently renamed the American Nurses Association, or ANA), she later joined the National Association of Colored Graduate Nurses (NACGN) and addressed its first annual convention in Boston (1909). The association awarded her life membership in 1911 and elected her its national chaplain.

From 1911 to 1912 Mahoney served as supervisor of the Howard Orphan Asylum for Black Children in Kings Park, Long Island, N.Y. Returning to Boston, she is reputed to have been one of the first women in that city to register to vote after the ratification of the Nineteenth Amendment in 1920. Ten years after her death in 1926, the NACGN honoured her memory by establishing the Mary Mahoney Medal, an award to a member for distinguished service to the profession. After the NACGN merged with the ANA in 1951, the award was continued. It is now conferred biennially on an individual who has made a significant contribution to opening up opportunities in nursing to minorities.

Mahoney was named to the Nursing Hall of Fame in 1976 and to the National Women's Hall of Fame in 1993.

CHARLES HENRY TURNER

(b. Feb. 3, 1867, Cincinnati, Ohio, U.S.—d. Feb. 14, 1923, Chicago, Ill.)

Behavioral scientist Charles Henry Turner is best known for his work showing that social insects can modify their behaviour as a result of experience. Turner is also well known for his commitment to civil rights and for his attempts to overcome racial barriers in American academia.

Turner's birthplace of Cincinnati had established a progressive reputation for African American opportunity and advancement. In 1886, after his graduation as class valedictorian from Gaines High School, he enrolled in the University of Cincinnati to pursue a B.S. degree in biology. Turner graduated in 1891; he remained at the University of Cincinnati and earned an M.S. degree, also in biology, the following year. In 1887 he married Leontine Troy.

Despite having an advanced degree and more than 20 publications to his credit, Turner found it difficult to find employment at a major American university, possibly as a result of racism or his preference to work with young African American students. He held teaching positions at various schools, including Clark College (now Clark Atlanta University), a historically black college in Atlanta, from 1893 to 1905. He returned to school to earn a Ph.D. in zoology (magna cum laude) in 1907 from the University of Chicago. After Leontine died in 1895, Turner married Lillian Porter. In 1908 Turner finally settled in St. Louis, Mo., as a science teacher at Sumner High School. He remained there until his retirement in 1922.

During his 33-year career, Turner published more than 70 papers, many of them written while he confronted numerous challenges, including restrictions on his access to laboratories and research libraries and restrictions on his time due to a heavy teaching load at Sumner. Furthermore, Turner received meagre pay and was not given the opportunity to train research students at either the undergraduate or the graduate level. Despite these challenges, he published several morphological studies of vertebrates and invertebrates.

Turner also designed apparatuses (such as mazes for ants and cockroaches and coloured disks and boxes for testing the visual abilities of honeybees), conducted naturalistic observations, and performed experiments on insect navigation, death feigning, and basic problems in invertebrate learning. Turner may have been the first to investigate Pavlovian conditioning in an invertebrate. In addition, he developed novel procedures to study pattern and colour recognition in honeybees (*Apis*), and he discovered that cockroaches trained to avoid a dark chamber in one apparatus retained the behaviour when transferred to a differently shaped apparatus. At the time, the study of insect behaviour was dominated by 19th-century concepts of taxis and kinesis, in which social insects are seen to alter their behaviour in specific responses to specific stimuli. Through his observations Turner was able to establish that insects can modify their behaviour as a result of experience.

Turner was one of the first behavioral scientists to pay close attention to the use of controls and variables in experiments. In particular, he was aware of the importance of variables called training variables, which influence performance. One such example of a training variable is the "intertrial interval," which is the time that occurs between learning experiences. Reviews by Turner on invertebrate behaviour appeared in such important publications as *Psychological Bulletin* and the *Journal of Animal Behavior*. In 1910 Turner was elected a member of the Academy of Sciences of St. Louis. The French naturalist Victor Cornetz later named the circling movements of ants returning to their nest *tournoiement de Turner* ("Turner circling"), a phenomenon based on one of Turner's previous discoveries.

Turner maintained a lifelong commitment to civil rights, first publishing on this issue in 1897. As a leader of the civil rights movement in St. Louis, he passionately argued that only through education can the behaviour of both black and white racists be changed. He suggested that racism could be studied within the framework of comparative psychology, and his animal research intimated the existence of two forms of racism. One form is based on an unconditioned response to the unfamiliar, whereas the other is based on principles of learning such as imitation.

BUSINESSPEOPLE

The African American entrepreneurial tradition stretches all the way from the commercial savvy of the West African merchants who were the forebears of American slaves, through the early business efforts of free blacks and even slaves, to the start-up real estate, banking, and insurance concerns of the last quarter of the 19th century. By the early 20th century, black capitalists were involved in the manufacture of automobiles, dolls, embalming fluid, haircare products, and toothpaste, to mention but a few of the business endeavours undertaken in spite of race-based difficulties in establishing credit. The entrepreneurs and businesspeople profiled here are generally more recent inheritors of that tradition of business ingenuity, ability, and pluck.

KENNETH CHENAULT

(b. June 2, 1951, Mineola, N.Y., U.S.)

Businessman Kenneth Chenault was one of the first African Americans to become the chief executive officer (CEO) of a Fortune 500 firm, the American Express Company.

The son of a dentist and a dental hygienist, Chenault grew up on Long Island and attended the Waldorf School, an alternative school, where he developed his first leadership skills as senior class president and as a captain of sports teams. He studied history at Bowdoin College (B.A., 1973) and attended Harvard University Law School (J.D., 1976). After working for a law firm and a management consultancy, Chenault eventually accepted a job in 1981 with American Express.

In his early years with American Express, Chenault revived the company's Merchandise Services division by replacing cheap goods with finer offerings such as durable luggage and personal accessories. He rose through American Express's ranks at a time when employee diversity was of negligible concern. As a firm with more than 100 years of history, American Express risked relying too heavily on its past success and was slow to engage its competitors, but Chenault implemented strategies that revived the firm in an era of cutthroat competition among credit- and charge-card issuers. By the time of his appointment as chief operating officer and president in 1997, it was evident that Chenault would likely be chosen as American Express's next CEO, which he was, in 2001.

One of his first challenges as CEO involved guiding the company through a recovery from the attacks of Sept. 11, 2001, when American Express lost 11 employees and suffered damage to its headquarters. The company's travel business slowed in the aftermath, causing American Express to respond with new offerings such as small business services—evidence that, under Chenault's direction, a company formerly known for patrician operating principles was now innovating and building competitive strongholds in new and established markets.

JOHN H. JOHNSON

(b. Jan. 19, 1918, Arkansas City, Ark., U.S.—d. Aug. 8, 2005, Chicago, Ill.)

Magazine and book publisher John H. Johnson was the first African American to attain major success in those fields.

Johnson and his family settled in Chicago after visiting that city during the 1933 World's Fair. He later became an honour student at Du Sable High School in Chicago, where he was managing editor of the school paper and business manager of the yearbook. Those experiences influenced his choice of journalism as a career. While studying at the University of Chicago and Northwestern University, Johnson worked for a life insurance company that marketed to African American customers. There he conceived the idea of a magazine for blacks; in 1942 he began publication of *Negro Digest*. Its first issue sold some 3,000 copies, and within a year the monthly circulation was 50,000. From that beginning, Johnson launched *Ebony*, a general-interest magazine catering to an African American audience, in 1945. *Ebony*'s initial pressrun of 25,000 copies was completely sold out. By the early 21st century it had a circulation of some 1.7 million.

Johnson went on to create other black publications, including *Jet* magazine in 1951. His firm, Johnson Publishing Company, later diversified into book publishing, radio broadcasting, insurance, and cosmetics manufacturing. In the 1980s Linda Johnson Rice, his daughter, began assuming management of the company. Johnson was awarded the Presidential Medal of Freedom in 1996.

ROBERT L. JOHNSON

(b. April 8, 1946, Hickory, Miss., U.S.)

Businessman Robert L. Johnson founded Black Entertainment Television (BET) and was the first African American majority owner of a major professional sports team in the United States.

Johnson grew up in Freeport, Ill., as the 9th of 10 children. He majored in history at the University of Illinois (B.A., 1968) and, after studying public affairs at Princeton University (M.A., 1972), moved to Washington, D.C., where he worked for the Corporation for Public Broadcasting and the National Urban League. He began cultivating valuable political and business connections that later helped him bankroll his vision of creating a black-owned cable television company. As a lobbyist for the nascent cable industry from 1976 to 1979, he noticed that the large African American TV audience was going unrecognized and untapped. Johnson built BET from a tiny cable outlet, airing only two hours of programming a week in 1980, to a broadcasting giant that claimed an audience of more than 70 million households.

In 1991 BET became the first black-controlled company to be listed on the New York Stock Exchange. BET thrived in the 1990s, adding more cable channels and expanding its reach through new film and publishing divisions, music channels, and a Web site. Viewership expanded along with the product line, while major media companies began to invest in the growing network. After taking BET private again in 1998, Johnson and his partners sold BET Holdings to the giant media group Viacom in 2001 for some $3 billion, though he remained at BET as its chief executive officer. The sale made him the first African American billionaire. Johnson then formed the umbrella group RLJ Companies, which operated widely in the media, sports, gaming, real estate, and hospitality industries.

After attempting to purchase a National Basketball Association franchise throughout the 1990s, Johnson was approved as the owner of an expansion team in Charlotte, N.C., in 2003 (the city's former team, the Hornets, had just moved to New Orleans, La.). The new team, called the Bobcats, began competition in 2004. Johnson's purchase of the franchise, estimated at $300 million, also included the Sting, the Women's National Basketball Association team in Charlotte. Johnson launched C-SET (Carolinas Sports Entertainment Network), a regional sports and entertainment cable TV network, in October 2004. In 2006 Johnson, along with the film producers Harvey Weinstein and Bob Weinstein, created the company Our Stories Films to develop family oriented movies aimed at African American audiences.

CHARLES CLINTON SPAULDING

(b. Aug. 1, 1874, Columbus county, N.C., U.S.—d. Aug. 1, 1952, Durham, N.C.)

Charles Clinton Spaulding built the North Carolina Mutual Life Insurance Company into the country's largest black-owned business by the time of his death, when it was worth about $40 million.

At the age of 20, Spaulding left his father's farm and moved to Durham, N.C., where in 1898 he completed what was equivalent to a high school education and became the manager of a black-owned grocery store. In 1899 he was hired as a part-time agent by the recently established North Carolina Mutual and Provident Association; the following year he was promoted to full-time general manager, the company's only full-time position. Spaulding was an early proponent of saturation advertising, inundating local businesses with promotional items bearing his company's name.

In the first decade of the century the company prospered, establishing subsidiaries and supporting a variety of local businesses. Spaulding was elevated to vice president in 1908, and then to secretary-treasurer in 1919, when the firm officially changed its name to the North Carolina Mutual Life Insurance Company. By 1920 the company had over 1,000 employees and several offices along the East Coast. In 1923 Spaulding became president, a position he held until his death in 1952. North Carolina Mutual continued to grow and to establish more black-operated subsidiaries in the 1920s. Spaulding's financial reorganization of the company insured its survival during the economic depression of the 1930s.

Although he was best noted for his business leadership, Spaulding was also involved in political and educational issues. As national chairman of the Urban League's Emergency Advisory Council in the 1930s, he campaigned to secure New Deal jobs for African Americans. As chairman of the Durham Committee on Negro Affairs, he engaged in voter registration efforts and convinced city officials to hire black police officers. Spaulding also supported education for blacks while serving as a trustee for Howard University, Shaw University, and North Carolina College.

RELIGIOUS LEADERS

The first institution in the United States in which African Americans were able to experience real self-direction was the church, which became the fulcrum of black community-building, education, business, and politics. Because of this and because of the limited opportunities for African American involvement in political life not just in the Jim Crow South but in the more tacitly segregated North, black political leaders and activists were often clerics. As a result some of the most important religious leaders in African American history are profiled elsewhere in this book, including the Rev. Martin

Luther King, Jr., the Rev. Ralph Abernathy, the Rev. Jesse Jackson, and Malcolm X.

RICHARD ALLEN

(b. Feb. 14, 1760, Philadelphia, Pa. U.S.—d. March 26, 1831, Philadelphia)

Richard Allen was the founder and first bishop of the African Methodist Episcopal Church, a major American denomination.

Soon after Allen was born, to slave parents, the family was sold to a Delaware farmer. At age 17 he became a Methodist convert and at 22 was permitted to preach. Two years later (1784), at the first general conference of the Methodist Episcopal Church at Baltimore, Allen was considered a talented candidate for the new denomination's ministry. In 1786 he bought his freedom and went to Philadelphia, where he joined St. George's Methodist Episcopal Church. Occasionally he was asked to preach to the congregation. He also conducted prayer meetings for blacks. Restrictions were placed on the number permitted to attend these meetings, and Allen, dissatisfied, withdrew in 1787 to help organize an independent Methodist church. In 1787 he turned an old blacksmith shop into the first church for blacks in the United States. His followers were known as Allenites.

In 1799 Allen became the first African American to be officially ordained in the ministry of the Methodist Episcopal Church. The organization of the Bethel Society led in 1816 to the founding of the African Methodist Episcopal Church, which elected Allen its first bishop.

FATHER DIVINE

(b. 1880?, Georgia?, U.S.—d. Sept. 10, 1965, Philadelphia, Pa.)

One of the most colourful African American figures of the 1930s was prominent religious leader Father Divine. The Depression-era movement he founded, the Peace Mission, was originally dismissed as a cult but is now generally hailed as an important precursor of the civil rights movement.

Father Divine's real given name is unknown, but at one point early in his life he was called George Baker, Jr. Reportedly born on a plantation in Georgia, Baker began his career in 1899 as an assistant to Father Jehovia (Samuel Morris), the founder of an independent religious group. During his early adult years, Baker was influenced by Christian Science and New Thought. In 1912 he left Father Jehovia and emerged several years later as the leader of what would become the Peace Mission movement. He settled first in the New York City borough of Brooklyn and then in Sayville, N.Y., an all-white community on Long Island, where he lived quietly during the 1920s. His following grew, and in 1931, when his Sayville neighbors complained about the growing attendance at meetings in his home, Father Divine was arrested and incarcerated for 30 days. When the judge who sentenced him died two days after the sentencing, Father Divine attributed the event to super natural intervention. His movement commemorates this event by annually publishing accounts of "divine retribution" visited on wrongdoers.

In 1933 Father Divine and his followers left Sayville for Harlem, where he became one of the most flamboyant leaders of the Depression era. There he opened the first of his Heavens, the residential hotels where his teachings were practiced and where his followers could obtain food, shelter, and job opportunities, as well as spiritual and physical healing.

The movement, whose membership numbered in the tens of thousands at its height during the Great Depression, builds on the principles of Americanism, brotherhood, Christianity, democracy, and Judaism, with the understanding that all "true" religions teach the same basic truths. Members are taught not to discriminate by race, religion, or colour, and they live communally as brothers and sisters. Father Divine's teachings were codified in 1936 in the "Righteous Government Platform," which called for an end to segregation, lynching, and capital punishment. Movement members refrain from using tobacco, alcohol, narcotics, and vulgar language, and they are celibate. Moreover, members attempt to embody virtue, honesty, and truth. The movement's teachings also demand "a righteous wage in exchange for a full

day's work." Members refuse to accumulate debt, and they possess neither credit nor life insurance.

During the Depression residents of the Heavens paid the minimal fee of 15 cents for meals and a dollar per week for sleeping quarters, a practice that allowed them to maintain their sense of dignity. In the opinion of many, Father Divine affirmed, amid the poverty of the Depression, the abundance of God with the free lavish banquets he held daily.

Heavens were opened across North America as well as in Europe, and, although most of its adherents were African Americans, the movement also attracted many whites (approximately one-fourth of its membership). The Heavens and related businesses brought in millions of dollars in revenue for the Peace Mission. Their success, however, also brought accusations of racketeering against Father Divine that, like the allegations of child abuse that were made against the movement, proved to be unfounded.

In 1942 Father Divine moved to suburban Philadelphia, in part to avoid paying a financial judgment in a suit brought by a former movement member. Four years later he married Edna Rose Ritchings, a Canadian member who, as Mother Divine, succeeded her husband as the movement's leader in 1965. The movement's membership has declined dramatically, however, not least because of the movement's strict dedication to celibacy.

Once dismissed as another cult leader, Father Divine was recognized in the late 20th century as an important social reformer. In the 1930s he was a champion of racial equality and an advocate of the economic self-sufficiency for African Americans that found broad acceptance only with the civil rights movement.

WALLACE D. FARD

(b. c. 1877, Mecca—d. 1934?)

Born in Mecca, Wallace D. Fard was the founder of the Nation of Islam (sometimes called Black Muslim) movement in the United States.

Fard immigrated to the United States sometime before 1930. In that year, he established in Detroit the Temple of Islam as well as the University of Islam, which was the temple's school, and the Fruit of Islam, a corps of male guards. Fard preached that blacks (who were not to be called Negroes) must prepare for an inevitable race war and that Christianity was the religion of slave owners. Accordingly, he gave his followers Arabic names to replace those that had originated in slavery. Fard offered blacks a credo of moral and cultural superiority to their white oppressors. In 1934 he disappeared without a trace. Members of the movement believe Fard to be the incarnation of Allah, and his birthday, February 26, is observed as Saviour's Day.

LOUIS FARRAKHAN

(b. May 11, 1933, Bronx, N.Y., N.Y., U.S.)

Louis Farrakhan served as the leader of the Nation of Islam from 1978 until 2007.

He was raised in Boston as Louis Eugene Walcott by his mother, Sarah Mae Manning, an immigrant from St. Kitts and Nevis, West Indies. Deeply religious as a boy, he became active in the St. Cyprian's Episcopal Church in his Roxbury neighbourhood. He graduated with honours from the prestigious Boston English High School, where he also played the violin and was a member of the track team. He attended the Winston-Salem Teachers College from 1951 to 1953 but dropped out to pursue a career in music. Known as "The Charmer," he performed professionally on the Boston nightclub circuit as a singer of calypso and country songs. In 1953 he married Khadijah (née Betsy Ross), with whom he would have nine children.

In 1955 Walcott joined the Nation of Islam. Following the custom of the Nation, he replaced his surname with an "X," a custom among Nation of Islam followers who considered their family names to have originated with white slaveholders. Louis X first proved himself at Temple No. 7 in Harlem, where he emerged as the protégé of Malcolm X, the minister of the temple and one of the most prominent members of the Nation of Islam. Louis X was given his Muslim name, Abdul Haleem Farrakhan, by Elijah

Muhammad, the leader of the Nation of Islam. Farrakhan was appointed head minister of Boston Temple No. 11, which Malcolm had established earlier.

After Malcolm X's break with the Nation in 1964 over political and personal differences with Elijah Muhammad, Farrakhan replaced Malcolm as head minister of Harlem's Temple No. 7 and as the National Representative of the Nation, the second in command of the organization. Like his predecessor, Farrakhan was a dynamic, charismatic leader and a powerful speaker with the ability to appeal to the African American masses.

When Elijah Muhammad died in February 1975, the Nation of Islam fragmented. Surprisingly, the Nation's leadership chose Wallace Muhammad (now known as Warith Deen Mohammed), the fifth of Elijah's six sons, as the new Supreme Minister. Disappointed that he was not named Elijah's successor, Farrakhan led a breakaway group in 1978, which he also called the Nation of Islam and which preserved the original teachings of Elijah Muhammad. Farrakhan disagreed with Wallace Muhammad's attempts to move the Nation to orthodox Sunni Islam and to rid it of Elijah Muhammad's radical black nationalism and separatist teachings, which stressed the inherent wickedness of whites.

Farrakhan became known to the American public through a series of controversies that began during the 1984 presidential campaign of the Rev. Jesse

Louis Farrakhan, 2004. Tim Sloan/AFP/ Getty Images

Jackson, whom Farrakhan supported. Farrakhan withdrew his support after Jewish voters protested his praise of Adolf Hitler, and he has been embroiled in a continuing conflict with the American Jewish community because of his making allegedly anti-Semitic statements; Farrakhan has denied being anti-Semitic. In later speeches he blamed the U.S. government for what he claimed was a conspiracy to destroy black people with AIDS and addictive drugs.

In 1995 the Nation sponsored the Million Man March in Washington, D.C., to promote African American unity and family values. Estimates of the number of marchers, most of whom were men, ranged from 400,000 to nearly 1.1 million, making it the largest gathering of its kind in American history. Under Farrakhan's leadership, the Nation of Islam established a clinic for AIDS patients in Washington, D.C., and helped to force drug dealers out of public housing projects and private apartment buildings in the city. It also worked with gang members in Los Angeles. Meanwhile, the Nation continued to promote social reform in African American communities in accordance with its traditional goals of self-reliance and economic independence.

In the early 21st century, the core membership of Farrakhan's Nation of Islam was estimated at between 10,000 and 50,000—though in the same period Farrakhan was delivering speeches in large cities across the United States that regularly attracted crowds of more than 30,000. Under Farrakhan's leadership, the Nation was one of the fastest growing of the various Muslim movements in the country. Foreign branches of the Nation were formed in Ghana, London, Paris, and the Caribbean islands. In order to strengthen the international influence of the Nation, Farrakhan established relations with Muslim countries, and in the late 1980s he cultivated a relationship with the Libyan dictator Muammar al-Qaddafi. After a near-death experience in 2000 resulting from complications from prostate cancer (he was diagnosed with cancer in 1991), Farrakhan toned down his racial rhetoric and attempted to strengthen relations with other minority communities, including Native Americans, Hispanics, and Asians. Farrakhan also moved his group closer to orthodox Sunni Islam in 2000, when he and Imam Warith Deen Mohammed, the leading American orthodox Muslim, recognized each other as fellow Muslims.

From the no-longer ivory towers of academia to the laboratory, from the banks of the Chicago River to the top of the globe, and from the sanctified reverie of Sunday to the bustling weekday world of the marketplace have come the preceding portraits of notable African Americans. Those that follow in the next chapter owe their significance to the printed word, pixels on screens, the plastic arts, and poetry in motion.

CHAPTER 4

ARTS AND LETTERS

Supporting evidence for Edward Bulwer-Lytton's truism "The pen is mightier than the sword" is abundant in African American literature and journalism. Indeed, the soul-stirring power of slave narratives, the imaginative evocations and provocations of African American poets and fiction writers, and the investigative reporting and opinion-making of black print and broadcast journalists have been among the most effective weapons of nonviolent protest wielded by the civil rights and freedom movement. This chapter examines some of the most influential and accomplished of those who have used language in the service of change and truth, as well as to tell the story of their people and stories of people in general.

WRITERS AND POETS

The rich tradition of African American literature that includes slave narratives, abolitionist polemics, trickster tales, the literary fruits of the Harlem Renaissance, the impassioned, incisive poems and novels of the later 20th century and early 21st century, and talents as immense as Langston Hughes, Richard Wright, James Baldwin, Ralph Ellison, and Toni Morrison can only be hinted at in these profiles of writers and poets.

MAYA ANGELOU

(b. April 4, 1928, St. Louis, Mo., U.S.)

Poet Maya Angelou earned much acclaim for her several volumes of autobiography that explore the themes of economic, racial, and sexual oppression.

Born Marguerite Johnson in St. Louis, Angelou spent much of her childhood in the care of her paternal grandmother in rural Stamps, Ark. Raped at the age of eight by her mother's boyfriend, she went through an extended period of muteness. This early life is the focus of Angelou's first autobiographical work, *I Know Why the Caged Bird Sings* (1970). Subsequent volumes of autobiography include *Gather Together in My Name* (1974), *Singin' and Swingin' and Gettin' Merry Like Christmas* (1976), *The Heart of a Woman* (1981), *All God's Children Need Traveling Shoes* (1986), and *A Song Flung Up to Heaven* (2002).

In 1940 Angelou moved with her mother to San Francisco and worked intermittently as a cocktail waitress, a prostitute and madam, a cook, and a dancer. It was as a dancer that she assumed her professional name. Moving to New York City in the late 1950s, Angelou found encouragement for her literary talents at the Harlem Writers' Guild. About the same time, Angelou landed a featured role in a State Department-sponsored production of George Gershwin's opera *Porgy and Bess*; with this troupe she toured 22 countries in Europe and Africa. She also studied dance with Martha Graham and Pearl Primus. In 1961 she performed in Jean Genet's *The Blacks*. That same year, she was persuaded by a South African dissident to whom she was briefly married to move to Cairo, Egypt, where she worked for the *Arab Observer*. She later moved to Ghana and worked on *The African Review*.

Angelou returned to California in 1966 and wrote *Black, Blues, Black* (aired 1968), a 10-part television series about the role of African culture in American life. When her screenplay *Georgia, Georgia* was produced in 1972, Angelou became the first African American woman to

Maya Angelou, 2003. Getty Images

have a feature film adapted from one of her own stories. She also acted in such movies as *Poetic Justice* (1993) and *How to Make an American Quilt* (1995) and appeared in several television productions, including the miniseries *Roots* (1977). In 1998 she made her directorial debut with *Down in the Delta* (1998).

Angelou's poetry, collected in such volumes as *Just Give Me a Cool Drink of Water 'fore I Diiie* (1971), *And Still I Rise* (1978), *Now Sheba Sings the Song* (1987), and *I Shall Not Be Moved* (1990), draws heavily on her personal history but employs the points of view of various personae. She also wrote a book of meditations, *Wouldn't Take Nothing for My Journey Now* (1993), and children's books that include *My Painted House, My Friendly Chicken and Me* (1994), *Life Doesn't Frighten Me* (1998), and the *Maya's World* series, which began publication in 2004 and featured stories of children from various parts of the world.

In 1981 Angelou became a professor of American studies at Wake Forest University, Winston-Salem, N.C. Among numerous other honours was her invitation to compose and deliver a poem for the inauguration of Pres. Bill Clinton in 1993.

JAMES BALDWIN

(b. Aug. 2, 1924, New York, N.Y., U.S.—d. Dec. 1, 1987, Saint-Paul, France)

The eloquence and passion of essayist, novelist, and playwright James Baldwin on the subject of race in America made him an important voice, particularly in the late 1950s and early 1960s, in the United States and, later, through much of western Europe.

The eldest of nine children, Baldwin grew up in poverty in the black ghetto of Harlem in New York City. From 14 to 16 he was active during out-of-school hours as a preacher in a small revivalist church, a period he wrote about in his semiautobiographical first and finest novel, *Go Tell It on the Mountain* (1953), and in his play about a woman evangelist, *The Amen Corner* (performed in New York City, 1965).

After graduation from high school, Baldwin began a restless period of ill-paid jobs, self-study, and literary apprenticeship in Greenwich Village, the then-bohemian quarter of New York City. He left in 1948 for Paris, where he lived for the next eight years. (In later years, from 1969, he became a self-styled "transatlantic commuter," living alternatively in the south of France and in New York and New England.) His second novel, *Giovanni's Room* (1956), deals with the white world and concerns an American in Paris torn between his love for a man and his love for a woman. Between the two novels came a collection of essays, *Notes of a Native Son* (1955).

In 1957 Baldwin returned to the United States and became an active participant in the civil-rights struggle that swept the nation. His book of essays, *Nobody Knows My Name* (1961), explores black–white relations in the United States. This theme also was central to

James Baldwin, 1964. Jenkins/Hulton Archive/Getty Images

his novel *Another Country* (1962), which examines sexual as well as racial issues.

The New Yorker magazine gave over almost all of its Nov. 17, 1962, issue to a long article by Baldwin on the Black Muslim separatist movement and other aspects of the civil-rights struggle. The article became a best-seller in book form as *The Fire Next Time* (1963). His bitter play about racist oppression, *Blues for Mister Charlie* ("Mister Charlie" being a black term for a white man), played on Broadway to mixed reviews in 1964.

Though Baldwin continued to write until his death—publishing works including *Going to Meet the Man* (1965), a collection of short stories; and the novels *Tell Me How Long the Train's Been Gone* (1968), *If Beale Street Could Talk* (1974), and *Just Above My Head* (1979); and *The Price of the Ticket* (1985), a collection of autobiographical writings—none of his later works achieved the popular and critical success of his early work.

OCTAVIA E. BUTLER

(b. June 22, 1947, Pasadena, Calif., U.S.—d. Feb. 24, 2006, Seattle, Wash.)

Author Octavia E. Butler is chiefly noted for her science fiction novels about future societies and superhuman powers. They are noteworthy for their unique synthesis of science fiction, mysticism, mythology, and African American spiritualism.

Butler was educated at Pasadena City College (A.A., 1968), California State University, and the University of California at Los Angeles. Encouraged by Harlan Ellison, she began her writing career in 1970. The first of her novels, *Patternmaster* (1976), was the beginning of her five-volume Patternist series about an elite group of mentally linked telepaths ruled by Doro, a 4,000-year-old immortal African. Other novels in the series are *Mind of My Mind* (1977), *Survivor* (1978), *Wild Seed* (1980), and *Clay's Ark* (1984).

In *Kindred* (1979) a contemporary black woman is sent back in time to a pre-Civil War plantation, becomes a slave, and rescues her white, slave-owning ancestor. Her later novels include the Xenogenesis trilogy—*Dawn: Xenogenesis* (1987), *Adulthood Rites* (1988), and *Imago* (1989)—and *The Parable of the Sower* (1993), *The Parable of the Talents* (1998), and *Fledgling* (2005). Butler's short story *Speech Sounds* won a Hugo Award in 1984, and her story *Bloodchild,* about

human male slaves who incubate their alien masters' eggs, won both Hugo and Nebula awards. Her collection *Bloodchild and Other Stories* was published in 1995. That same year Butler became the first science fiction writer to be awarded a MacArthur Foundation fellowship, and in 2000 she received a PEN Award for lifetime achievement.

CHARLES W. CHESNUTT

(b. June 20, 1858, Cleveland, Ohio, U.S.—d. Nov. 15, 1932, Cleveland)

Charles W. Chesnutt was the first important African American novelist.

Chesnutt was the son of free blacks who had left their native city of Fayetteville, N.C., prior to the Civil War. Following the war his parents moved back to Fayetteville, where Chesnutt completed his education and began teaching. He was named assistant principal (1877–80) and then principal (1880–83) of State Colored Normal School (now Fayetteville State University), but he became so distressed about the treatment of blacks in the South that he moved his wife and children to Cleveland. There he worked as a clerk-stenographer while becoming a practicing attorney and establishing a profitable legal stenography firm. In his spare moments he wrote stories.

Between 1885 and 1905 Chesnutt published more than 50 tales, short stories, and essays, as well as two collections of short stories, a biography of the antislavery leader Frederick Douglass, and three novels. His "The Goophered Grapevine," the first work by a black accepted by *The Atlantic Monthly* (August 1887), was so subtle in its refutation of the plantation school of Thomas Nelson Page that most readers missed the irony. This and similarly authentic stories of folk life among the North Carolina blacks were collected in *The Conjure Woman* (1899). *The Wife of His Youth and Other Stories of the Color Line* (1899) examines colour prejudice among blacks as well as between the races in a manner reminiscent of George W. Cable. *The Colonel's Dream* (1905) dealt trenchantly with problems of the freed slave. A psychological realist, Chesnutt made use of familiar scenes of North Carolina folk life to protest social injustice.

His works outranked any fiction written by blacks until the 1930s. Chesnutt's thematic use of the humanity of blacks and the contemporary inhumanity of man to man, black and white alike, anticipates the work of later writers as diverse as William Faulkner, Richard Wright, and James Baldwin.

COUNTEE CULLEN

(b. May 30, 1903, Louisville, Ky, U.S.—d. Jan. 9, 1946, New York, N.Y.)

Countee Cullen was one of the finest poets of the Harlem Renaissance.

Reared by a woman who was probably his paternal grandmother, Countee at age 15 was unofficially adopted by the Reverend F.A. Cullen, minister of Salem M.E. Church, one of Harlem's largest congregations. Countee won a citywide poetry contest as a schoolboy and saw his winning stanzas widely reprinted. At New York University (B.A., 1925) he won the Witter Bynner Poetry Prize and was elected to Phi Beta Kappa. Major American literary magazines accepted his poems regularly, and his first collection of poems, *Color* (1925), was published to critical acclaim before he had finished college.

Cullen received an M.A. degree from Harvard University in 1926 and worked as an assistant editor for *Opportunity* magazine. In 1928, just before leaving the United States for France (where he would study on a Guggenheim Fellowship), Cullen married Yolande Du Bois, daughter of W.E.B. Du Bois (divorced 1930). After publication of *The Black Christ and Other Poems* (1929), Cullen's reputation as a poet waned. From 1934 until the end of his life he taught in New York City public schools. Most notable among his other works are *Copper Sun* (1927), *The Ballad of the Brown Girl* (1928), and *The Medea and Some Poems* (1935). His novel *One Way to Heaven* (1932) depicts life in Harlem.

Cullen's use of racial themes in his verse was striking at the time, his material always fresh and sensitively treated. He drew some criticism, however, because he was heavily influenced by the Romanticism of John Keats and preferred to use classical verse forms rather than rely on the rhythms and idioms of his black American heritage.

PAUL LAURENCE DUNBAR

(b. June 27, 1872, Dayton, Ohio, U.S.—d. Feb. 9, 1906, Dayton)

Author Paul Laurence Dunbar's reputation rests upon his verse and short stories written in black dialect. He was the first African American writer to make a concerted attempt to live by his writings and one of the first to attain national prominence.

Both of Dunbar's parents were former slaves; his father escaped to freedom in Canada and then returned to the U.S. to fight in the Civil War. The young Dunbar was the only black student in his Dayton high school, where he was the popular editor of the school paper. He published his first volume of poetry, *Oak and Ivy* (1893), at his own expense while working as an elevator operator and sold copies to his passengers to pay for the printing. His second volume, *Majors and Minors* (1895), attracted the favourable notice of the novelist and critic William Dean Howells, who also introduced Dunbar's next book, *Lyrics of Lowly Life* (1896), which contained some of the finest verses of the first two volumes.

A vogue sprang up for Dunbar's poems; he read them to audiences in the U.S. and England, and when he returned from abroad he was given a job in the reading room of the Library of Congress in Washington, D.C. (1897–98). He turned to fiction as well as verse, publishing four collections of short stories and four novels before his early death. Writing for a largely white readership, Dunbar made use of the then current plantation tradition in both his stories and his poems, depicting the pre-Civil War South in pastoral, idyllic tones. Only in a few of his later stories did a suggestion of racial disquiet appear.

His first three novels—including *The Uncalled* (1898), which reflected his own spiritual problems—were about white characters. His last, sometimes considered his best, was *The Sport of the Gods* (1902), concerning an uprooted black family in the urban North.

RALPH ELLISON

(b. March 1, 1914, Oklahoma City, Okla., U.S.—d. April 16, 1994, New York, N.Y.)

Writer Ralph Ellison won eminence with his first novel (and the only one published during his lifetime), *Invisible Man* (1952).

Ellison left Tuskegee Normal and Industrial Institute (now Tuskegee University) in 1936 after three years' study of music and moved to New York City. There he befriended Richard Wright, who encouraged Ellison to try his hand at writing. In 1937 Ellison began contributing short stories, reviews, and essays to various periodicals. He worked on the Federal Writers' Project from 1938 to 1942, which he followed with a stint as the managing editor of *The Negro Quarterly* for just under a year.

Following service in World War II, he produced *Invisible Man*, which won the

Ralph Ellison in his New York City home, 1963. Ben Martin/Time & Life Pictures/ Getty Images

1953 National Book Award for fiction. The story is a bildungsroman that tells of a naive and idealistic (and, significantly, nameless) Southern black youth who goes to Harlem, joins the fight against white oppression, and ends up ignored by his fellow blacks as well as by whites. The novel won praise for its stylistic innovations in infusing classic literary motifs with modern black speech and culture, while providing a thoroughly unique take on the construction of contemporary African American identity. However, Ellison's treatment of his novel as first and foremost a work of art—as opposed to a primarily polemical work—led to some complaints from his fellow black novelists at the time that he was not sufficiently devoted to social change.

After *Invisible Man* appeared, Ellison published only two collections of essays: *Shadow and Act* (1964) and *Going to the Territory* (1986). He lectured widely on black culture, folklore, and creative writing and taught at various American colleges and universities. *Flying Home and Other Stories* was published posthumously in 1996. He left a second novel unfinished at his death; it was published, in a much-shortened form, as *Juneteenth* in 1999.

ERNEST J. GAINES

(b. Jan. 15, 1933, Oscar, La., U.S.)

Ernest J. Gaines's fiction, as exemplified by *The Autobiography of Miss Jane Pittman* (1971), his most acclaimed work, reflects African American experience and the oral tradition of his rural Louisiana childhood.

When Gaines was 15, his family moved to California. He graduated from San Francisco State College (now San Francisco State University) in 1957 and attended graduate school at Stanford University. He taught or was writer-in-residence at several schools, including Denison and Stanford universities.

Gaines's novels are peopled with well-drawn, recognizable characters who live in rural Louisiana, often in a fictional plantation area named Bayonne that some critics have compared to William Faulkner's mythical Yoknapatawpha County. In addition to *The Autobiography of Miss Jane Pittman,* a fictional personal history spanning the period from the Civil War to the freedom struggle of the 1960s, Gaines's novels include *Catherine Carmier* (1964), *Of Love and Dust* (1967), *In My Father's House* (1978), and *A Gathering of Old Men* (1983). In 1994 he received the National Book Critics Circle Award for *A Lesson Before Dying* (1993), the story of two African Americans—an intellectually disabled man wrongly accused of murder and a teacher who visits him in prison—living in Bayonne. In 2005 Gaines published *Mozart and Leadbelly*, a collection of stories and autobiographical essays about his childhood and his writing career.

NIKKI GIOVANNI

(b. June 7, 1943, Knoxville, Tenn., U.S.)

Poet Nikki Giovanni's writings range from calls for violent revolution to poems for children and intimate personal statements.

Giovanni grew up in Cincinnati, Ohio, and Knoxville, Tenn., and in 1960 she entered Nashville's Fisk University. By 1967, when she received her B.A., she was firmly committed to the civil rights movement and the concept of black power. In her first three collections of poems, *Black Feeling, Black Talk* (1968), *Black Judgement* (1968), and *Re: Creation* (1970), her content was urgently revolutionary and suffused with deliberate interpretation of experience through a black consciousness.

Giovanni's experiences as a single mother then began to influence her poetry. *Spin a Soft Black Song* (1971), *Ego-Tripping* (1973), and *Vacation Time* (1980) were collections of poems for children. Loneliness, thwarted hopes, and the theme of family affection became

Nikki Giovanni, 1973. Hulton Archive/Getty Images

increasingly important in her poetry during the 1970s. She returned to political concerns in *Those Who Ride the Night Winds* (1983), with dedications to black American heroes and heroines. From the late 1960s Giovanni was a popular reader of her own poetry, with performances issued on several recordings, and a respected speaker as well. In *Gemini* (1971) she presented autobiographical reminiscences, and *Sacred Cows . . . and Other Edibles* (1988) was a collection of her essays.

ALEX HALEY

(b. Aug. 11, 1921, Ithaca, N.Y., U.S.—d. Feb. 10, 1992, Seattle, Wash.)

Writer Alex Haley's works of historical fiction and reportage are grounded in the depiction of the struggles of African Americans.

Although his parents were teachers, Haley was an indifferent student. He began writing to avoid boredom during voyages while serving in the U.S. Coast Guard (1939–59). His first major work, *The Autobiography of Malcolm X* (1965), was an authoritative and widely read narrative based on Haley's interviews with the Black Muslim spokesman. The work is recognized as a classic of African American literature.

Haley's greatest success was *Roots: The Saga of an American Family* (1976). This saga covers seven American generations, from the enslavement of Haley's African ancestors to his own genealogical quest. The work forcefully shows relationships between generations and between races. *Roots* was adapted as a multi-episode television program, which, when first broadcast in January 1977, became one of the most popular shows in the history of American television and galvanized attention on African American issues and history. That same year Haley won a special Pulitzer Prize. A successful sequel was first broadcast in February 1979 as *Roots: The Next Generations.*

Roots spurred much interest in family history, and Haley created the Kinte Foundation (1972) to store records that aid in tracing black genealogy. Haley later admitted that his saga was partly fictional; the book was also the subject of a plagiarism suit, which Haley settled out of court.

CHESTER HIMES

(b. July 29, 1909, Jefferson City, Mo., U.S.—d. Nov. 12, 1984, Moraira, Spain)

Writer Chester Himes's novels reflect his encounters with racism. As an expatriate in Paris, he published a series of black detective novels.

The domination of his dark skinned father by his light-skinned mother was a source of deep resentment that shaped Himes's racial outlook. The family's frequent relocations, as well as the accidental blinding of his brother, further disrupted his childhood. Himes attended Ohio State University. From 1929 to 1936 he was jailed at the Ohio State Penitentiary for armed robbery, and while there he began to write fiction. A number of his stories appeared in *Esquire* and other American magazines. After his release from prison, he worked at numerous odd jobs and joined the Works Progress Administration, eventually serving as a writer with the Ohio Writers' Project.

Himes's first novel, *If He Hollers Let Him Go* (1945), details the fear, anger, and humiliation of a black employee of a racist defense plant during World War II. *Lonely Crusade* (1947) concerns racism in the labour movement. *Cast the First Stone* (1952) portrays prison life, and *The Third Generation* (1954) examines family life.

In the mid-1950s Himes moved to Paris. There he wrote chiefly murder mysteries set in New York City's Harlem. These include *The Crazy Kill* (1959), *Cotton Comes to Harlem* (1965; film, 1970), and *Blind Man with a Pistol* (1969; later retitled *Hot Day, Hot Night*). Among his other works are *Run Man, Run* (1966), a thriller; *Pinktoes* (1961), a satirical work of interracial erotica; and *Black on Black* (1973), a collection of stories. He also published two volumes of autobiography, *The Quality of Hurt* (1972) and *My Life As Absurdity* (1976).

LANGSTON HUGHES

(b. Feb. 1, 1902, Joplin, Mo., U.S.—d. May 22, 1967, New York, N.Y.),

Poet and writer Langston Hughes became, through numerous translations, one of the foremost interpreters to the world of the black experience in the United States.

Hughes's parents separated soon after his birth, and young Hughes was raised by his mother and grandmother. After his grandmother's death, he and his mother moved to half a dozen cities before reaching Cleveland, where they settled. His poem *The Negro Speaks of Rivers,* written the summer after his graduation from high school in Cleveland, was published in *The Crisis* (1921) and brought him considerable attention.

After attending Columbia University (1921–22), Hughes explored Harlem, forming a permanent attachment to what he called the "great dark city." He worked as a steward on a freighter bound for Africa. Back from seafaring and sojourning in Europe, he won an *Opportunity* magazine poetry prize in 1925. He received the Witter Bynner Undergraduate Poetry Award in 1926.

While working as a busboy in a hotel in Washington, D.C., Hughes put three of his own poems beside the plate of Vachel Lindsay in the dining room. The next day, newspapers around the country reported that Lindsay had discovered an African American busboy poet. A scholarship to Lincoln University in Pennsylvania followed, and before Hughes received his degree in 1929, his first two books had been published.

The Weary Blues (1926) was warmly received. *Fine Clothes to the Jew* (1927) was criticized harshly for its title and for its frankness, but Hughes himself felt it represented a step forward. A few months after graduation *Not Without Laughter* (1930), his first prose work, had a cordial

Langston Hughes in front of his home in Harlem, 1958. Robert W. Kelley/Time & Life Pictures/Getty Images

reception. In the '30s his poetry became preoccupied with political militancy; he traveled widely in the Soviet Union, Haiti, and Japan and served as a newspaper correspondent (1937) in the Spanish Civil War. He published a collection of short stories, *The Ways of White Folks* (1934), and *The Big Sea* (1940), his autobiography up to age 28.

Hughes wrote *A Pictorial History of the Negro in America* (1956), and the anthologies *The Poetry of the Negro* (1949) and *The Book of Negro Folklore* (1958; with Arna Bontemps). He also wrote numerous works for the stage, including the lyrics for *Street Scene*, an opera with music by Kurt Weill. A posthumous book of poems, *The Panther and the Lash* (1967), reflected the black anger and militancy of the 1960s. Hughes translated the poetry of Federico García Lorca and Gabriela Mistral. He was also widely known for his comic character Jesse B. Semple, familiarly called Simple, who appeared in Hughes's columns in the *Chicago Defender* and the *New York Post* and later in book form and on the stage. *The Collected Poems of Langston Hughes*, ed. by Arnold Rampersad and David Roessel, appeared in 1994.

AUDRE LORDE

(b. Feb. 18, 1934, New York, N.Y., U.S.—d. Nov. 17, 1992, St. Croix, U.S. Virgin Islands)

Poet, essayist, and autobiographer Audre Lorde is known for her passionate writings on lesbian feminism and racial issues.

The daughter of Grenadan parents, Lorde attended Hunter College and received a B.A. in 1959 and a master's degree in library science in 1961. She married in 1962 and wrote poetry while working as a librarian at Town School in New York; she also taught English at Hunter College. In 1968 her first volume of poetry, *The First Cities*, was published, and Lorde briefly left New York to become poet-in-residence at Tougaloo College in Mississippi.

Cables to Rage (1970) explored her anger at social and personal injustice and contained the first poetic expression of her lesbianism. Her next volumes, *From a Land Where Other People Live* (1973) and *New York Head Shop and Museum* (1974), were more rhetorical and political.

Coal (1976), a compilation of earlier works, was Lorde's first release by a major publisher, and it earned critical notice. Most critics consider *The Black Unicorn* (1978) to be her finest poetic work. In it she turned from the urban themes of her early work, looking instead to Africa, and wrote on her role as mother and daughter, using rich imagery and mythology.

The poet's 14-year battle with cancer is examined in *The Cancer Journals* (1980), in which she recorded her early battle with the disease and gave a feminist critique of the medical profession. In 1980 Lorde and African American writer and activist Barbara Smith created a new publishing house, Kitchen Table: Women of Color Press. Lorde's volume *A Burst of*

Light (1988), which further detailed her struggle with cancer, won a National Book Award in 1989. She also wrote the novel *Zami: A New Spelling of My Name* (1982), noted for its clear, evocative imagery and its treatment of a mother-daughter relationship. Her poetry collection, *Undersong: Chosen Poems Old and New*, was published in 1992. Her last volume of poetry, *The Marvelous Arithmetics of Distance*, was published posthumously, in 1993.

CLAUDE MCKAY

(b. Sept. 15, 1890, Jamaica, British West Indies—d. May 22, 1948, Chicago, Ill., U.S.)

Published in 1928, *Home to Harlem*, by Jamaican-born poet and novelist Claude McKay, was the most popular novel written by a black American to that time. Before going to the U.S. in 1912, he wrote two volumes of Jamaican dialect verse, *Songs of Jamaica* and *Constab Ballads* (1912).

After attending Tuskegee Institute (1912) and Kansas State Teachers College (1912–14), McKay went to New York in 1914, where he contributed regularly to *The Liberator*, then a leading journal of avant-garde politics and art. The shock of American racism turned him from the conservatism of his youth. With the publication of two volumes of poetry, *Spring in New Hampshire* (1920) and *Harlem Shadows* (1922), McKay emerged as the first and most militant voice of the Harlem Renaissance (*q.v.*). After 1922 McKay lived successively in the Soviet Union, France, Spain, and Morocco. In both *Home to Harlem* and *Banjo* (1929), he attempted to capture the vitality and essential health of the uprooted black vagabonds of urban America and Europe. There followed a collection of short stories, *Gingertown* (1932), and another novel, *Banana Bottom* (1933). In all these works McKay searched among the common folk for a distinctive black identity.

After returning to America in 1934, McKay was attacked by the Communists for repudiating their dogmas and by liberal whites and blacks for his criticism of integrationist-oriented civil rights groups. McKay advocated full civil liberties and racial solidarity. In 1940 he became a U.S. citizen; in 1942 he was converted to Roman Catholicism and worked with a Catholic youth organization until his death. He wrote for various magazines and newspapers, including the *New Leader* and the New York *Amsterdam News*. He also wrote an autobiography, *A Long Way from Home* (1937), and a study, *Harlem: Negro Metropolis* (1940). His *Selected Poems* (1953) was issued posthumously.

TONI MORRISON

(b. Feb. 18, 1931, Lorain, Ohio, U.S.)

Writer Toni Morrison is noted for her examination of black experience (particularly black female experience) within the black community. She received the Nobel Prize for Literature in 1993.

Born Chloe Anthony Wofford, Morrison grew up in the American Midwest in a family that possessed an intense love of and appreciation for black culture. Storytelling, songs, and folktales were a deeply formative part of her childhood. She attended Howard University (B.A., 1953) and Cornell University (M.A., 1955). After teaching at Texas Southern University for two years, she taught at Howard from 1957 to 1964. In 1965 she became a fiction editor. From 1984 she taught writing at the State University of New York at Albany, leaving in 1989 to join the faculty of Princeton University.

Morrison's first book, *The Bluest Eye* (1970), is a novel of initiation concerning a victimized adolescent black girl who is obsessed by white standards of beauty and longs to have blue eyes. In 1973 a second novel, *Sula*, was published; it examines (among other issues) the dynamics of friendship and the expectations for conformity within

Toni Morrison. Francois Guillot/AFP/Getty Images

the community. *Song of Solomon* (1977) is told by a male narrator in search of his identity; its publication brought Morrison to national attention. *Tar Baby* (1981), set on a Caribbean island, explores conflicts of race, class, and sex. The critically acclaimed *Beloved* (1987), which won a Pulitzer Prize for fiction, is based on the true story of a runaway slave who, at the point of recapture, kills her infant daughter in order to spare her a life of slavery. *Jazz* (1992) is a story of violence and passion set in New York City's Harlem during the 1920s. Subsequent novels are *Paradise* (1998), a richly detailed portrait of a black utopian community in Oklahoma, and *Love* (2003), an intricate family story that reveals the myriad facets of love and its ostensible opposite. *A Mercy* (2008) deals with slavery in 17th-century America.

A work of criticism, *Playing in the Dark: Whiteness and the Literary Imagination*, was published in 1992. Many of her essays and speeches were collected in *What Moves at the Margin: Selected Nonfiction* (edited by Carolyn C. Denard), published in 2008. Additionally, Morrison released several children's books, including *Who's Got Game?: The Ant or the Grasshopper?* and *Who's Got Game?: The Lion or the Mouse?*, both written with her son and published in 2003. *Remember* (2004) chronicles the hardships of black students during the integration of the American public school system; aimed at children, it uses archival photographs juxtaposed with captions speculating on the thoughts of their subjects. She also wrote the libretto for *Margaret Garner* (2005), an opera about the same story that inspired *Beloved*.

The central theme of Morrison's novels is the black American experience; in an unjust society her characters struggle to find themselves and their cultural identity. Her use of fantasy, her sinuous poetic style, and her rich interweaving of the mythic give her stories great strength and texture.

WALTER MOSLEY

(b. Jan. 12, 1952, Los Angeles, Calif., U.S.)

Mystery writer Walter Mosley is noted for his realistic portrayals of segregated inner-city life.

Mosley attended Goddard College and Johnson State College, and he became a computer programmer before publishing his first novel, *Devil in a Blue Dress* (1990; film 1995). Set in 1948, the novel introduces Ezekiel ("Easy") Rawlins, an unwilling amateur detective from the Watts section of Los Angeles. It presents period issues of race relations and mores as the unemployed Rawlins is hired to find a white woman who frequents jazz clubs in black districts.

In all his Easy Rawlins novels, Mosley used period detail and slang to create authentic settings and characters, especially the earnest, complex main character, who continually is faced with personal, social, and moral dilemmas. In *A Red Death* (1991), set during the

McCarthy era, Rawlins is blackmailed by the FBI into spying on a labour union organizer. In *White Butterfly* (1992) the police call on Rawlins to help investigate the vicious murders of four young women—three black and one white. Other novels featuring Rawlins include *Black Betty* (1994) and *A Little Yellow Dog* (1996). For the publication of *Gone Fishin'* (1997), a prequel to *Devil in a Blue Dress*, Mosley chose a small independent black publisher, Black Classic Press, over his longtime publisher W.W. Norton. The series continued with *Bad Boy Brawly Brown* (2002), *Little Scarlet* (2004), *Cinnamon Kiss* (2005), and *Blonde Faith* (2007).

Mosley's other novels include *RL's Dream* (1995), the story of a dying former blues guitarist (based on Robert Johnson) who is befriended by a young woman, and *The Man in My Basement* (2004), an examination of wealth, power, manipulation, and shifting relationships. *Always Outnumbered, Always Outgunned* (1997; filmed as *Always Outnumbered* for television, 1998), a collection of stories set in contemporary Watts, features the ex-convict Socrates Fortlow. Mosley returned to the Fortlow character in the stories of *Walkin' the Dog* (1999). In 2001 he returned to the mystery genre with the publication of *Fearless Jones*, introducing the title character and bookseller Paris Minton. In this book and its sequel, *Fear Itself* (2003), Mosley revisited the setting of Los Angeles in the 1950s. In 2008 he published *Diablerie*, a novel about a reformed alcoholic who confronts a violent secret from his past.

Mosley also tried his hand at other genres. He essayed science fiction in *Blue Light* (1998) and *Futureland* (2001), a group of interlocking stories, and nonfiction in *Workin' on the Chain Gang: Shaking Off the Dead Hand of History* (2000) and *What Next: A Memoir Toward World Peace* (2003).

ALICE WALKER

(b. Feb. 9, 1944, Eatonton, Ga., U.S.)

Novelist, short-story writer, and poet Alice Walker is a writer of tremendous insight. Her novels, most notably *The Color Purple* (1982), focus particularly on women.

Walker was the eighth child of sharecroppers. While growing up she was accidentally blinded in one eye, and her mother gave her a typewriter, allowing her to write instead of doing chores. She received a scholarship to attend Spelman College, where she studied for two years before transferring to Sarah Lawrence College. After graduating in 1965, Walker moved to Mississippi and became involved in the civil rights movement. She also began teaching and publishing short stories and essays. She married in 1967, but the couple divorced in 1976.

Walker's first book of poetry, *Once*, appeared in 1968, and her first novel, *The Third Life of Grange Copeland* (1970), a narrative that spans 60 years and three generations, followed two years later. A

Alice Walker. Peter Kramer/Getty Images

second volume of poetry, *Revolutionary Petunias and Other Poems*, and her first collection of short stories, *In Love and Trouble: Stories of Black Women*, both appeared in 1973. The latter bears witness to sexist violence and abuse in the African American community. After moving to New York, Walker completed *Meridian* (1976), a novel describing the coming of age of several civil rights workers in the 1960s.

Walker later moved to California, where she wrote her most popular novel, *The Color Purple* (1982). An epistolary novel, it depicts the growing up and self-realization of an African American woman between 1909 and 1947 in a town in Georgia. The book won a Pulitzer Prize and was adapted into a film by Steven Spielberg in 1985. A musical version produced by Oprah Winfrey and Quincy Jones premiered in 2004.

Walker's later fiction includes *The Temple of My Familiar*, an ambitious examination of racial and sexual tensions (1989); *Possessing the Secret of Joy* (1992), a narrative centred on female genital mutilation; *By the Light of My Father's Smile* (1998), the story of a family of anthropologists posing as missionaries in order to gain access to a Mexican tribe; and *Now Is the Time to Open Your Heart* (2005), about an older woman's quest for identity. Reviewers complained that these novels employed New Age abstractions and poorly conceived characters, though Walker continued to draw praise for championing racial and gender equality in her work. She also released the

volume of short stories *The Way Forward Is with a Broken Heart* (2000) and several other volumes of poetry, including *Absolute Trust in the Goodness of the Earth* (2003) and *A Poem Traveled Down My Arm* (2003). *Her Blue Body Everything We Know: Earthling Poems* (1991) collects poetry from 1965 to 1990.

Her essays were compiled in *In Search of Our Mother's Gardens: Womanist Prose* (1983), *Sent by Earth: A Message from the Grandmother Spirit After the Bombing of the World Trade Center and Pentagon* (2001), and *We Are the Ones We Have Been Waiting For* (2006). Walker also wrote juvenile fiction and critical essays on such female writers as Flannery O'Connor and Zora Neale Hurston. She cofounded a short-lived press in 1984.

PHILLIS WHEATLEY

(b. *c.* 1753, present-day Senegal?, West Africa—d. Dec. 5, 1784, Boston, Mass., U.S.)

Phillis Wheatley was the first black woman poet of note in the United States.

The young girl who was to become Phillis Wheatley was kidnapped and taken to Boston on a slave ship in 1761 and purchased by a tailor, John Wheatley, as a personal servant for his wife. She was treated kindly in the Wheatley household, almost as a third child. The Wheatleys soon recognized her talents and gave her privileges unusual for a slave, allowing her to learn to read and write. In less than two years, under the tutelage of Mrs. Wheatley and her daughter, Phillis had mastered English; she went on to learn Greek and Latin and caused a stir among Boston scholars by translating a tale from Ovid. From age 14 she wrote exceptionally mature, if conventional, poetry that was largely concerned with morality and piety.

Wheatley's better-known pieces include "To the University of Cambridge in New England," "To the King's Most Excellent Majesty," "On the Death of Rev. Dr. Sewell," and "An Elegiac Poem, on the Death of the Celebrated Divine … George Whitefield," the last of which was the first of her poems to be published, in 1770. She was escorted by Mr. Wheatley's son to London in 1773, and there her first book, *Poems on Various Subjects, Religious and Moral*, was published. Her personal qualities, even more than her literary talent, contributed to her great social success in London. She returned to Boston shortly thereafter because of the illness of her mistress. Both Mr. and Mrs. Wheatley died soon thereafter, and Phillis was freed. In 1778 she married John Peters, an intelligent but irresponsible free black man who eventually abandoned her. At the end of her life Wheatley was working as a servant, and she died in poverty.

Two books issued posthumously were *Memoir* and *Poems of Phillis Wheatley* (1834) and *Letters of Phillis Wheatley, the Negro Slave-Poet of Boston* (1864). Wheatley's work was frequently cited by abolitionists to combat the charge of innate intellectual inferiority among blacks and to promote educational opportunities for African Americans.

RICHARD WRIGHT

(b. Sept. 4, 1908, near Natchez, Miss., U.S.—d. Nov. 28, 1960, Paris, France)

Novelist and short-story writer Richard Wright was among the first African American writers to protest white treatment of blacks, notably in his novel *Native Son* (1940) and his autobiography, *Black Boy* (1945). He inaugurated the tradition of protest explored by other black writers after World War II.

Wright's grandparents had been slaves. His father left home when he was five, and the boy, who grew up in poverty, was often shifted from one relative to another. He worked at a number of jobs before joining the northward migration, first to Memphis, Tenn., and then to Chicago. There, after working in unskilled jobs, he got an opportunity to write through the Federal Writers' Project. In 1932 he became a member of the Communist Party, and in 1937 he went to New York City, where he became Harlem editor of the Communist *Daily Worker*.

He first came to the general public's attention with a volume of novellas, *Uncle Tom's Children* (1938), based on the question: How may a black man live in a country that denies his humanity? In each story but one the hero's quest ends in death.

His fictional scene shifted to Chicago in *Native Son*. Its protagonist, a poor black youth named Bigger Thomas, accidentally kills a white girl, and in the course of his ensuing flight his hitherto meaningless awareness of antagonism from a white world becomes intelligible. The book was a best-seller and was staged successfully as a play on Broadway (1941) by Orson Welles. Wright himself played Bigger Thomas in a motion-picture version made in Argentina in 1951.

In 1944 he left the Communist Party because of political and personal differences. Wright's *Black Boy* is a moving account of his childhood and young manhood in the South. The book chronicles the extreme poverty of his childhood, his experience of white prejudice and violence against blacks, and his growing awareness of his interest in literature.

After World War II, Wright settled in Paris as a permanent expatriate. *The Outsider* (1953), acclaimed as the first American existential novel, warned that the black man had awakened in a disintegrating society not ready to include him. Three later novels were not well-received. Among his polemical writings of that period was *White Man, Listen!* (1957), which was originally a series of lectures given in Europe. *Eight Men*, a collection of short stories, appeared in 1961.

The autobiographical *American Hunger*, which narrates Wright's experiences after moving to the North, was published posthumously in 1977. Some of the more candid passages dealing with race, sex, and politics in Wright's

books had been cut or omitted before original publication. Unexpurgated versions of *Native Son, Black Boy*, and his other works were published in 1991, however. A novella, *Rite of Passage* (1994), and an unfinished crime novel, *A Father's Law* (2008), were also published posthumously.

JOURNALISTS

The tremendous role played by television news in shaping public opinion in the 20th century is reflected in the fact that three of the four African American journalists profiled here made their names on TV and the fourth, columnist Carl Rowan, became a widely visible talking head in his own right at the end of his career. So influential and prestigious was the TV news desk that Carl Stokes, the first African American elected mayor of a major U.S. city, moved on to anchor local newscasts in New York City after leaving his post as Cleveland's highest elected official.

ED BRADLEY

(b. June 22, 1941, Philadelphia, Pa., U.S.—d. Nov. 9, 2006, New York, N.Y.)

For 25 years journalist Ed Bradley was associated with the televised newsmagazine *60 Minutes*.

As a student at Cheyney State College (now Cheyney University of Pennsylvania), Bradley worked his way into broadcasting by volunteering at

Philadelphia radio station WDAS-FM. After graduating with a degree in education (B.S., 1964), Bradley became an elementary schoolteacher but continued to work evenings in radio jobs that ranged from disc jockey to reporter. The station finally began paying Bradley a small hourly wage after he spent two days covering a Philadelphia race riot; however, he did not leave his teaching job until 1967, when he joined WCBS radio in New York City as a reporter.

Bradley held many other positions with CBS. He worked briefly in Paris in 1971, was stationed in Saigon, Viet., and Phnom Penh, Camb., in the early 1970s, and was injured by shrapnel while reporting in Cambodia. He moved to Washington, D.C., and began covering presidential campaigns in 1976, eventually becoming a White House correspondent. His feature stories, however, drew on topics from around the world. In 1980 he won awards for two CBS Special Reports: *The Boat People* (1979), exploring the plight of Southeast Asian refugees, and *Blacks in America: With All Deliberate Speed?* (1979), his in-depth examination of African American progress since the *Brown* v. *Board of Education* decision. He joined the staff of the long-running *60 Minutes* in 1981. Bradley received numerous honours during his career, including 4 George Foster Peabody Awards and 19 Emmys.

MAX ROBINSON

(b. May 1, 1939, Richmond, Va., U.S.—d. Dec. 20, 1988, Washington, D.C.)

Max Robinson was the first African American to anchor a nightly network newscast.

Robinson's first journalism job began and ended in 1959, when he was hired to read news at a Portsmouth, Va., television station. Although the station selected him over an otherwise all-white group of applicants, it still enforced a colour barrier by projecting an image of the station's logo to conceal Robinson as he read the news. He was fired the day after

Ed Bradley, 2006. Ray Tamarra/Getty Images

he presented the news without the logo obscuring his face. In 1965 he joined WTOP-TV in Washington, D.C., as a correspondent and camera operator, but he moved quickly to nearby WRC-TV, where he won awards for coverage of race riots and a documentary on life in poor urban neighbourhoods. He was hired back by WTOP as its first African American news anchor in 1969 and stayed there until 1978. Robinson moved to Chicago when ABC News chose him as one of three coanchors for ABC's *World News Tonight*. The anchor arrangement ended with the death of coanchor Frank Reynolds in 1983. Robinson left ABC News shortly thereafter and joined Chicago's WMAQ-TV as a news anchor (1984–87).

CARL ROWAN

(b. Aug. 11, 1925, Ravenscroft, Tenn. U.S.—d. Sept. 23, 2000, Washington, D.C.)

Journalist, writer, and radio and television commentator, Carl Rowan was one of the first African American officers in the U.S. Navy during World War II.

After serving as a communications officer in the navy, Rowan earned a degree in mathematics from Oberlin (Ohio) College (B.A., 1947) and studied journalism at the University of Minnesota (M.A., 1948). He next joined the staff of the *Minneapolis Tribune*, where he worked as a copy editor and in 1950 became one of the country's first African American reporters at a major daily newspaper. In 1954 he participated in an educational exchange program sponsored by the U.S. Department of State, delivering lectures in India, Pakistan, and Southeast Asia. Rowan broke colour barriers at the U.S. Department of State when he served as a deputy assistant secretary of state (1961–63) in the administration of President John F. Kennedy and as ambassador to Finland (1963–64) and director of the U.S. Information Agency (1964–65). From 1965 Rowan wrote newspaper columns, usually concerned with race relations, that were syndicated to 60 newspapers thrice weekly.

He was also a panelist on the weekly television show *Inside Washington* (originally *Agronsky and Company*). Between 1967 to 1996 Rowan authored eight books, including *South of Freedom* (1952), his reflections on life in the southern United States in the years leading up to the civil rights movement; *Wait Till Next Year: The Life Story of Jackie Robinson* (1960); and *Dream Makers, Dream Breakers: The World of Justice Thurgood Marshall* (1993), a biography of the first African American U.S. Supreme Court justice.

BERNARD SHAW

(b. May 22, 1940, Chicago, Ill., U.S.)

Bernard Shaw was first chief anchor for the Cable News Network (CNN). Shaw's childhood heroes included newsman Edward R. Murrow, whose television broadcasts inspired Shaw to pursue a career in journalism. He became an avid reader of newspapers in his hometown of Chicago, contributed to his high school paper, and read announcements for the school through its public-address system.

While serving in the U.S. Marine Corps (1959–63), Shaw introduced himself to CBS News correspondent Walter Cronkite, declaring his intention to join Cronkite at CBS in the future. While studying at the University of Illinois, Shaw began work as a radio news reporter and TV news writer (1964–68), and the Westinghouse Broadcast Corporation offered him an assignment covering the White House. By 1971 he had joined CBS as a reporter. He received a promotion to correspondent in 1974 but eventually moved to ABC as its Latin American correspondent in 1977. While in this role, he covered the Jonestown tragedy and interviewed Cuban President Fidel Castro. Shaw returned to Washington, D.C., in 1979 and finished the decade covering Capitol Hill and the hostage crisis in Iran.

On June 1, 1980, Shaw helped launch CNN as its chief anchor. He also broke new ground by moderating a presidential debate in 1988, covering the protests by Chinese students at Tiananmen Square in 1989, and scooping the world with on-the-scene coverage of the first U.S. bombing of Baghdad, Iraq, in 1991. He retired from CNN's anchor desk in 2001. Among the numerous awards Shaw earned were the George Foster Peabody Award (1990), the University of Missouri's Honor Medal for Distinguished Service

in Journalism (1992), and the Congress of Racial Equality's Dr. Martin Luther King Jr. Award for Outstanding Achievement (1993).

PAINTERS AND PHOTOGRAPHERS

Although early African Americans were heirs to the bountiful legacy in the visual arts of Western Africa, whence most slaves or their ancestors were brought, slavery allowed few opportunities and left little energy for artistic expression. Still, during the 19th century self-taught African American painters and sculptors created folk art. Arguably the most important of these folk artists was Horace Pippin. More polished in his technique and formally (though not academically) trained was Jacob Lawrence. Probably the most renowned African American photographer, Gordon Parks, Jr., documented the black experience both in still photos and as the director of motion pictures.

JACOB LAWRENCE

(b. Sept. 7, 1917, Atlantic City, N. J., U.S.—d. June 9, 2000, Seattle, Wash.)

Painter Jacob Lawrence portrayed scenes of black life and history with vivid, stylized realism.

At age 13 Lawrence moved with his family to the Harlem section of New York City. At free art classes he showed

Jacob Lawrence, 1958. Robert W. Kelley/
Time & Life Pictures/Getty Images

a talent for creating lively, decorative masks, a motif that would later figure strongly in his narrative painting. At the Harlem Art Workshop (sponsored by the Works Progress Administration) in 1932 he studied under Charles H. Alston.

Gouache and tempera were Lawrence's characteristic media. His use of sombre browns and black for shadows and outlines in an otherwise vibrant palette lent his work a distinctive overtone. His best-known works are his series on historical or social themes, including *...And the Migrants Kept Coming* (1940),

Life in Harlem (1942), and *War* (1947). In 1964 he visited Nigeria, where he painted scenes of local life. His later works include a powerful series on the struggles of desegregation. Lawrence taught at various schools and colleges and became a professor of art at the University of Washington in Seattle in 1971; he retired in 1986.

GORDON PARKS

(b. Nov. 30, 1912, Fort Scott, Ks.,
U.S.—d. March 7, 2006, New York, N.Y.)

Author, photographer, and film director Gordon Parks was prodigiously talented in a variety of art forms.

The son of a tenant farmer, Parks grew up in poverty. After dropping out of high school, he held a series of odd jobs, including pianist and waiter. In 1938 he bought a camera and initially made a name for himself as a portrait and fashion photographer. After moving to Chicago, he began chronicling life on the city's impoverished South Side. These photographs led to a Julius Rosenwald Fellowship, and in 1942 he became a photographer at the Farm Security Administration (FSA). While with the FSA, he took perhaps his best-known photograph, *American Gothic*, which featured an African American cleaning woman holding a mop and broom while standing in front of an American flag.

In 1948 Parks became a staff photographer for *Life* magazine, the first African American to hold that position. Parks,

American Gothic, *featuring cleaning woman Ella Watson, 1942.* Gordon Parks/Hulton Archive/Getty Images

who remained with the magazine until 1972, became known for his portrayals of ghetto life, black nationalists, and the civil rights movement. A photo-essay about a child from a Brazilian slum was expanded into a television documentary (1962) and a book with poetry (1978), both titled *Flavio*. Parks also was noted for his intimate portraits of such public figures as Ingrid Bergman, Barbra Streisand, Gloria Vanderbilt, and Muhammad Ali.

Parks's first work of fiction was *The Learning Tree* (1963), a coming-of-age novel about a black adolescent in Kansas in the 1920s. He also wrote forthright autobiographies—*A Choice of Weapons* (1966), *To Smile in Autumn* (1979), and *Voices in the Mirror* (1990). He combined poetry and photography in *A Poet and His Camera* (1968), *Whispers of Intimate Things* (1971), *In Love* (1971), *Moments Without Proper Names* (1975), and *Glimpses Toward Infinity* (1996). Other works included *Born Black* (1971), a collection of essays, the novel *Shannon* (1981), and *Arias in Silence* (1994).

In 1968 Parks became the first African American to direct a major motion picture with his film adaptation of *The Learning Tree*. He also produced the movie and wrote the screenplay and musical score. He next directed *Shaft* (1971), which centred on a black detective. A major success, it helped give rise to the genre of African American action films known as "blaxploitation." A sequel, *Shaft's Big Score*, appeared in 1972. Parks later directed the comedy *The Super Cops* (1974) and the drama *Leadbelly* (1976) as well as several television films.

Gordon Parks. Hulton Archive/Getty Images

HORACE PIPPIN

(b. Feb.22, 1888, West Chester, Pa., U.S.—d. July 6, 1946, West Chester)

Folk painter Horace Pippen is known for his depictions of African American life and of the horrors of war.

Pippin's childhood was spent in Goshen, N.Y., a town that sometimes appears in his paintings. There he drew horses at the local racetrack and, according to his own account, painted biblical scenes on frayed pieces of muslin. He was variously employed as an ironworker, junk dealer, and porter, until World War I, when he served in the infantry. He was wounded in 1918 and discharged with a partially paralyzed right arm. He settled in West Chester, Pa., and eventually began to paint by burning designs into wood panels with a red-hot poker and then painting in the outlined areas.

His first large canvas was an eloquent protest against war, *End of the War: Starting Home* (1931–34), which was followed by other antiwar pictures, such as *Shell Holes and Observation Balloon* (1931) and many versions of *Holy Mountain* (all from c. 1944–45). His most frequently used theme centred on the African American experience, as seen in his series entitled *Cabin in the Cotton* (mid-1930s) and his paintings of episodes in the lives of the antislavery leader John Brown and Abraham Lincoln. After the art world discovered Pippin in 1937, these pictures in particular brought him wide acclaim as the greatest black painter of his time. He enjoyed the enthusiastic support of art collectors Christian Brinton, Albert C. Barnes, and Edith Halpert, owner of the New York Gallery in New York City. His work was featured in the landmark exhibition "Masters of Popular Painting," held at the Museum of Modern Art in New York in 1938. Pippin also executed portraits and biblical subjects. His early works are characterized by their heavy impasto and restricted use of colour. His later works are more precisely painted in a bolder palette.

DANCERS AND CHOREOGRAPHERS

In the early colonial period, slaves were almost universally forbidden to dance, yet they secretly circumvented this prohibition under the full glare of their owners by moving their torsos and hips (with little arm movement) and gliding their feet, the lifting off the ground of which constituted dancing in the eyes of their masters. The resulting shuffles would become building blocks of dance forms later developed by African Americans, as would the important dance rituals brought to the New World from Africa. The Great Migration of African Americans from the rural South to cities in the North and the West allowed for the increased interaction between black people whose ancestors came from different parts of Africa and for a mixing of ancestral dance styles. Partly as a result of the centrality of juke joints, new dance steps proliferated among African Americans in the 1920s, including the Charleston and the jitterbug. Tap dancing, a staple of later plantation life, also grew in importance. Among the most pivotal later contributions to African American dance came from Katherine Dunham, Alvin Ailey, and Savion Glover.

ALVIN AILEY, JR.

(b. Jan. 5, 1931, Rogers, Texas,
U.S.—d. Dec. 1, 1989, New York, N.Y.)

Dancer, choreographer, and director Alvin Ailey formed his own dance company, the Alvin Ailey American Dance Theater.

Having moved with his family to Los Angeles in 1942, Ailey became involved with the Lester Horton Dance Theater there in 1949. Following Horton's death in 1953, Ailey was director of the company until it disbanded in 1954. He moved to New York City that year. There he performed in various stage productions and studied acting with Stella Adler and

Alvin Ailey, Jr., 1960. Courtesy of Zachary Freyman

dance with Martha Graham, Hanya Holm, Charles Weidman, and others.

In 1958 Ailey formed the Alvin Ailey American Dance Theater. Composed primarily of blacks, it toured extensively both in the United States and abroad. In addition to works by Ailey, the company performed the works of several pioneer choreographers of modern dance, including Horton, Pearl Primus, and Katherine Dunham. The company's signature piece is *Revelations* (1960), a powerful, early work by Ailey that is set to African American spirituals.

Ailey subsequently continued to choreograph works for his own and other modern-dance companies. The Alvin Ailey American Dance Theater, through its highly successful tours on every continent, made him the best-known American choreographer abroad from the 1960s through the '80s.

KATHERINE DUNHAM

(b. June 22, 1909, Glen Ellyn, Ill., U.S.—d. May 21, 2006, New York, N.Y.)

Dancer, choreographer, and anthropologist Katherine Dunham is noted for her innovative interpretations of ritualistic and ethnic dances.

Dunham early became interested in dance. While a student at the University of Chicago, she formed a dance group that performed in concert at the Chicago World's Fair in 1934 and with the Chicago Civic Opera company in 1935–36. On graduating with a bachelor's degree in anthropology she undertook field studies in the Caribbean and in Brazil. By the time she received an M.A. from the University of Chicago,

Katherine Dunham in Tropical Revue, *1943.* Courtesy of the Dance Collection, the New York Public Library at Lincoln Center, Astor, Lenox and Tilden Foundations

she had acquired a vast knowledge of the dances and rituals of the black peoples of tropical America. (She later took a Ph.D. in anthropology.) In 1938 she joined the Federal Theatre Project in Chicago and composed a ballet, *L'Ag'Ya*, based on Caribbean dance. Two years later she formed an all-black company, which began touring extensively by 1943. *Tropics* (choreographed 1937) and *Le Jazz Hot* (1938) were among the earliest of many works based on her research.

Dunham was both a popular entertainer and a serious artist intent on tracing the roots of black culture. Many of her students, trained in her studios in Chicago and New York City, became prominent in the field of modern dance. She choreographed for Broadway stage productions and opera—including *Aida* (1963) for the New York Metropolitan Opera. She also choreographed and starred in dance sequences in such films as *Carnival of Rhythm* (1942), *Stormy Weather* (1943), and *Casbah* (1947). In addition, Dunham conducted special projects for African American high school students in Chicago; was artistic and technical director (1966–67) to the president of Senegal; and served as artist-in-residence, and later professor, at Southern Illinois University, Edwardsville, and director of Southern Illinois's Performing Arts Training Centre and Dynamic Museum in East St. Louis, Ill. Dunham was active in human rights causes, and in 1992 she staged a 47-day hunger strike to highlight the plight of Haitian refugees.

Dunham's writings, sometimes published under the pseudonym Kaye Dunn, include *Katherine Dunham's Journey to Accompong* (1946), an account of her anthropological studies in Jamaica; *A Touch of Innocence* (1959), an autobiography; *Island Possessed* (1969); and several articles for popular and scholarly journals. The recipient of numerous awards, Dunham received a Kennedy Center Honor in 1983 and the National Medal of Arts in 1989.

SAVION GLOVER

(b. Nov. 19, 1973, Newark, N.J., U.S.)

Dancer and choreographer Savion Glover became known for his unique pounding style of tap dancing, called "hitting." He brought renewed interest in dance, particularly among youths and minorities.

As a young child, Glover displayed an affinity for rhythms, and at age four he began taking drumming lessons. Deemed too advanced for the class, however, he then enrolled at the Newark Community School of the Arts and soon became the youngest person in the school's history to receive a full scholarship. At age seven he began taking tap lessons and quickly developed a passion for rhythm tap, a form that uses all parts of the foot to create sound. His talent attracted the attention of a choreographer for the Broadway musical *The Tap Dance Kid*, and Glover served as an understudy before taking the lead role in 1984. He returned to Broadway in 1989, performing in the musical revue *Black and Blue*, and was nominated for a Tony Award. A role in the motion picture *Tap* (1989) followed. Glover, who had long made a point of learning as much as he could from old tap masters, soon began teaching tap classes. He also developed his own tap style, which he christened "free-form hard core," while working with dancers such as Gregory Hines, Henry Le Tang, and Sammy Davis, Jr.

In 1990 Glover created his first choreography, for a festival at New York City's Apollo Theatre. Two years later he became the youngest-ever recipient of a National Endowment for the Arts grant. He portrayed a young Jelly Roll Morton in the musical *Jelly's Last Jam*, which debuted in Los Angeles in 1991 before opening on Broadway the following year and touring in 1994. In 1995 *Bring in 'Da Noise, Bring in 'Da Funk* opened Off-Broadway. Glover choreographed and starred in the musical, which featured a series of vignettes that chronicled African American history. A huge success, the show soon moved to Broadway, and in 1996 it won four Tony Awards, including a best choreographer award for Glover. His numerous other appearances included a regular role (1990–95) on the children's television show *Sesame Street*. In 2000 Glover appeared in director Spike Lee's film *Bamboozled*.

In addition to the artistry of journalism, the focus of this chapter has been on practitioners of fine art. Art, of course, comes in many forms, including those of sight and sound that are at the centre of popular culture. The next two chapters will examine African American contributions to the popular performing arts.

CHAPTER 5

STAGE AND SCREEN

The first black faces to appear onstage did not belong to African Americans; instead, they were created by burnt cork makeup worn by white minstrels whose song, dance, and shtick were intended to represent black life and language but were in fact demeaning stereotypes of African Americans that had little basis in the original African American art forms they purported to present. Even after African Americans began to appear onstage and later in films and on television, it would be decades before realistic portrayals of rounded black characters would be anything but exceptions.

The initial stage and screen depictions of African Americans were most often stereotypes, presenting characters who were subservient and simpleminded or confined to a narrow range of mostly disreputable roles (criminals, gang members, prostitutes, and pimps, or domestics) or, later, roles as noble vessels, whose symbolic function outweighed any attempts at the portrayal of multidimensional human beings. The actors, directors, playwrights, and comedians studied in this chapter were among those artists whose work brought to theatre, film, and television fully realized portrayals of African Americans and whose masterful performances and creations reflected not just African American experience but human experience in all of its complexity.

ACTORS

One need look no farther than the world of difference between the role of Mammy in *Gone with the Wind* (1939), for which Hattie McDaniel won an Academy Award as Best Supporting Actress, and that of Leticia Musgrove in *Monster's Ball* (2001), for which Halle Berry became the first African American to win an Oscar as Best Actress, to see the enormous changes in the African American presence on the screen. Certainly one of the most important contributors to that evolution was Sidney Poitier, an actor of tremendous versatility and artistry who destroyed stereotype after stereotype with a long string of extraordinary performances in the 1950s, '60s, and '70s. Today many of Hollywood's biggest stars and most reliable box-office attractions are African Americans.

HALLE BERRY

(b. Aug. 14, 1966, Cleveland, Ohio, U.S.)

Actress Halle Berry has given many memorable performances in a wide variety of roles, none more nuanced than her Oscar-winning portrayal of the down-on-her-luck Leticia Musgrove in *Monster's Ball* (2001).

Berry was a teenage finalist in national beauty pageants, worked in modeling, and began acting on television in 1989. Film roles in *Jungle Fever* (1991), directed by Spike Lee, and in *Boomerang* (1992), starring Eddie Murphy, first brought her notice. She costarred with Jessica Lange in *Losing Isaiah* (1995), a drama about adoption, before earning acclaim for her portrayal of film star Dorothy Dandridge, the first African American to be nominated for a best actress Oscar, in the television film *Introducing Dorothy Dandridge* (1999). That performance earned her Emmy and Golden Globe awards. Berry was also cast in action roles in *X-Men* (2000) and its sequels, *Swordfish* (2001), and *Die Another Day* (2002), an installment in the James Bond spy series. *Gothika* (2003) and *Catwoman* (2004) were the first films in which she received top billing.

OSSIE DAVIS

(b. Dec. 18, 1917, Cogdell, Ga., U.S.—d. Feb. 4, 2005, Miami Beach, Fla.)

Writer, actor, director, and social activist Ossie Davis (born Raiford Chatman Davis) was known for his contributions to African American theatre and film and for his passionate support of civil rights and humanitarian causes. He was also noted for his artistic partnership with his wife, Ruby Dee, which was considered one of the theatre and film world's most distinguished.

After attending Howard University in Washington, D.C., Davis moved to New York City to pursue a career as a writer. He served in the army during World War

Ruby Dee and Ossie Davis in the television play Seven Times Monday, c. *1962*. Hulton Archive/Getty Images

II but returned to New York City after the war with an interest in acting. In 1946 he made his Broadway debut in *Jeb*, during the run of which he met Dee, whom he married in 1948.

Davis and Dee frequently appeared together onstage, screen, and television—most notably in *Purlie Victorious* (1961), a play written by Davis and later adapted for the screen as *Gone Are the Days* (1963). Davis directed and wrote the films *Cotton Comes to Harlem* (1970) and *Countdown at Kusini* (1976). He continued to work into the 21st century, combining his acting pursuits with writing and civil rights campaigning. Davis made several films with Spike Lee, including *Do the Right Thing* (1989) and *Malcolm X* (1992), in which he reenacted the real-life eulogy he had given for the fallen civil rights leader. Davis also spoke at the funeral of Martin Luther King, Jr., in 1968. The recipients of numerous honours, Davis and Dee were jointly awarded the National Medal of Arts in 1995 and a Kennedy Center Honor in 2004.

RUBY DEE

(b. Oct. 27, 1924, Cleveland, Ohio, U.S.)

Beyond her creative partnership with husband Ossie Davis, actress Ruby Dee (born Ruby Ann Wallace) is remembered for her pioneering work in African American theatre and film and for her outspoken civil rights activism.

After completing her studies at Hunter College in Manhattan, Dee served an apprenticeship with the American Negro Theatre and began appearing on Broadway. In addition to *Purlie Victorious*, Davis and Dee's most notable joint stage appearance was *A Raisin in the Sun* (1959; Dee also starred in the film version in 1961). Dee joined Davis in acting in *Do the Right Thing* (1989) and appeared in another film directed by Spike Lee, *Jungle Fever* (1991). Among Dee and Davis's television credits are *Roots: The Next Generation* (1978), *Martin Luther King: The Dream and the Drum* (1986), and *The Stand* (1994). The couple's partnership extended into their activism as well; they served as master and mistress of ceremonies for the 1963 March on Washington, which they had helped organize.

Dee continued to act into the early 21st century, and her later films include *The Way Back Home* (2006) and *American Gangster* (2007). Her performance as the mother of a drug kingpin (played by Denzel Washington) in the latter film earned Dee her first Academy Award nomination. She also appeared in numerous television productions, notably *Their Eyes Were Watching God* (2005), an adaptation of Zora Neale Hurston's novel. In addition to her acting, Dee authored several books. Dee and Davis were jointly awarded the National Medal of Arts in 1995 and a Kennedy Center Honor in 2004.

Jamie Foxx

(b. Dec. 13, 1967, Terrell, Texas, U.S.)

Comedian, musician, and actor Jamie Foxx (born Eric Bishop) became known for his impersonations on the television sketch-comedy show *In Living Color* and later proved himself a versatile film actor, especially noted for his Oscar-winning portrayal of Ray Charles in *Ray* (2004).

Foxx's parents separated soon after his birth, and he was adopted by his maternal grandparents. He began playing piano about age five and became keenly interested in music, later earning a scholarship to United States International University (now Alliant International University) in San Diego to study classical piano and music theory. It was while Foxx was a student in San Diego that he began performing at local comedy clubs. At open-microphone nights he delighted audiences with his bitingly funny impersonations of former U.S. president Ronald Reagan, boxer Mike Tyson, and comedian Bill Cosby. Foxx discovered, however, that it was easier for women to get stage time at open-microphone nights, so he adopted the gender-neutral name of Jamie Foxx. In 1991 Foxx won the Bay Area Black Comedy Competition, which led to an audition for the Fox television network's hit show *In Living Color*. His impersonations and his drag character Wanda, an ugly yet sexually aggressive woman, impressed the show's creator and star, Keenen Ivory Wayans, and earned Foxx

a job as a regular. At that time Foxx also had a recurring role on the sitcom *Roc*.

Foxx's success on television led to new opportunities in music, television, and film. In 1994 he released his debut album, *Peep This*, which he also produced and composed. Two years later he landed his own television sitcom, *The Jamie Foxx Show*, which lasted five seasons. Foxx's first feature role in a movie was in the sex comedy *Booty Call* (1997), but his breakthrough performance came with *Any Given Sunday* (1999), in which Foxx played a young quarterback who is outwardly cocky but terrified of failure. That performance, along with his role as cornerman Drew ("Bundini") Brown in the biopic *Ali* (2001), showed that Foxx's acting abilities extended well beyond simple comedic impersonations.

In 2005 Foxx collected a best actor Academy Award for his riveting performance of soul singer Ray Charles in *Ray*. He not only mastered Charles's physical mannerisms but also captured the blind singer's warmth, determination, and recklessness. That year Foxx was also nominated for an Oscar for best supporting actor for his role in the thriller *Collateral* (2004), in which he appeared as a taxi driver abducted by a professional killer (played by Tom Cruise). Foxx released his second album, *Unpredictable*, in 2005, and it quickly rose to the top of the charts. He also sang with Kanye West on the hit single *Gold Digger* (2005). Foxx's later movies include *Jarhead* (2005), a film set during the Persian Gulf War, and the musical *Dreamgirls* (2006), in which he starred as a record executive opposite Eddie Murphy and Beyoncé. In 2009 Foxx portrayed a homeless man who was once a musical prodigy in *The Soloist* and a prosecutor in the thriller *Law Abiding Citizen*.

MORGAN FREEMAN

(b. June 1, 1937, Memphis, Tenn., U.S.)

Morgan Freeman's emotional depth and versatility made him one of the most respected performers of his generation. Over a career that included numerous memorable performances onstage, screen, and television, Freeman was one of the few African American actors who consistently received roles that were not specifically written for black actors.

As a young man, Freeman had aspirations of being a fighter pilot; however, a stint in the U.S. Air Force (1955–59) proved disappointing, and he turned his attention to acting. He made his Broadway debut in an all-black production of *Hello Dolly!* in 1967. In the 1970s he continued to work onstage and also appeared on the educational children's television show *The Electric Company* as the character Easy Reader. Freeman's performance in the film *Brubaker* (1980) and on the soap opera *Another World* (1982–84), along with several enthusiastic reviews for his theatrical work in the early 1980s, led to more challenging film roles. His portrayal of a dangerous hustler in *Street Smart* (1987) earned Freeman his first Academy Award nomination, for best supporting actor. He was later nominated for a best-actor Oscar for his work in *Driving Miss Daisy* (1989), in which he re-created the role of Hoke after first performing it onstage. A third Oscar nomination came for his soulful turn as a convict in *The Shawshank Redemption* (1994).

At the beginning of the 21st century, Freeman appeared in several crime dramas, including *Along Came a Spider* (2001), a sequel to his earlier role as a detective in *Kiss the Girls* (1997), both based on James Patterson novels, as well as *The Sum of All Fears* (2002). In 2005 he played Lucius Fox, a research and development guru, in *Batman Begins*. That year he also won an Academy Award for best supporting actor for his performance as a former boxer in Clint Eastwood's *Million Dollar Baby* (2004). Freeman's later films include *The Bucket List* (2007), in which he and Jack Nicholson played terminally ill cancer patients who make the most of their remaining time, and *Dark Knight* (2008), the sequel to *Batman Begins*. In 2008 Freeman returned to Broadway after nearly 20 years away from the stage, taking the role of Frank Elgin, a talented yet dispirited actor who has lost the will to perform, in *The Country Girl*. The following year he reteamed with Eastwood on *Invictus*, a drama in which he played Nelson Mandela, who sought to unite divided South Africa by supporting the national rugby team's quest to win the 1995 World Cup.

Freeman won acclaim onstage for performances that ranged from drunks to Shakespearean leads. On screen he thrived in roles written specifically for black actors, such as a disciplinarian principal in *Lean on Me* (1989) and a hard-hearted Civil War soldier in *Glory* (1989), as well as in roles that most often fall to white actors, such as an aging gunslinger in *Unforgiven* (1992) and an analytical detective in *Seven* (1995). He made his directorial debut with the anti-apartheid film *Bopha!* (1993). Freeman was the recipient of numerous awards, and in 2008 he received the Kennedy Center's Lifetime Achievement Award.

JAMES EARL JONES

(b. Jan. 17, 1931, Arkabutla, Miss., U.S.)

James Earl Jones made his name in leading stage roles in Shakespeare's *Othello* and in *The Great White Hope*, a play about the tragic career of the first black heavyweight boxing champion, loosely based on the life of Jack Johnson. Beginning in the 1970s, he appeared frequently on television and in film.

His father, the actor Robert Earl Jones, left his family before James Earl Jones was born, and the youth was raised largely by his grandparents in Michigan. He attended the University of Michigan (B.A., 1953), majoring in drama, and, after a brief stint in the U.S. Army, went to New York City, studying at the American Theatre Wing with Lee Strasberg. He acted in his first Off-Broadway production in 1957 and subsequently with the New York Shakespeare Festival in 1961–73. He

won a Tony Award for his boxer role in Howard Sackler's *The Great White Hope* (1968) and later starred in the film version (1970). He received critical acclaim for the two-character stage play *Paul Robeson* (1978) and in the title role of *Othello*, opposite Christopher Plummer's Iago (1981–82).

A part in the film *Dr. Strangelove* (1964) began a prolific career in pictures for Jones, whose roles included an evil ruler in the fantasy film *Conan the Barbarian* (1982), a coal miner fighting for the right to form a union in *Matewan* (1987), and an African king who lets his son (played by Eddie Murphy) travel to the United States in the comedy *Coming to America* (1988). He appeared as Admiral James Greer in the film adaptations of Tom Clancy's novels about CIA agent Jack Ryan: *The Hunt for Red October* (1990), *Patriot Games* (1992), and *Clear and Present Danger* (1994). In 1995 he portrayed Rev. Stephen Kumalo in the film version of Alan Paton's classic novel *Cry, the Beloved Country*. Jones next starred opposite Robert Duvall in *A Family Thing* (1996). In 2008 he appeared as Big Daddy in a Broadway production of Tennessee Williams's *Cat on a Hot Tin Roof* that featured an all-black cast.

Known for his deep, resonant voice, Jones was cast in many voice-over roles in television advertising and in films, both as a narrator and for animated characters. He is perhaps best known for giving voice to the villain Darth Vader in the *Star Wars* series of movies, which began in 1977. In 1994 he provided the voice of Mufasa in Disney's *The Lion King*.

HATTIE McDANIEL

(b. June 10, 1895, Wichita, Kan., U.S.—d. Oct. 26, 1952, Hollywood, Calif.)

Actress and singer Hattie McDaniel was the first African American to be honoured with an Academy Award.

McDaniel was raised in Denver, Colo., where she early exhibited her musical and dramatic talent. She left school in 1910 to become a performer in several traveling minstrel groups and later became one of the first black women to be broadcast over American radio. With the onset of the Great Depression, however, little work was to be found for minstrel or vaudeville players, and to support herself McDaniel went to work as a bathroom attendant at Sam Pick's club in Milwaukee, Wisconsin. Although the club as a rule hired only white performers, some of its patrons became aware of McDaniel's vocal talents and encouraged the owner to make an exception. McDaniel performed at the club for more than a year until she left for Los Angeles, where her brother found her a small role on a local radio show, *The Optimistic Do-Nuts*; known as Hi-Hat Hattie, she became the show's main attraction before long.

Two years after McDaniel's film debut in 1932, she landed her first major part in John Ford's *Judge Priest* (1934), in which she had an opportunity to sing a duet with humorist Will Rogers. Her role as a happy Southern servant in *The Little Colonel* (1935) made her a controversial figure in the liberal black community, which sought to end Hollywood's stereotyping. When criticized for taking such roles, McDaniel responded that she would rather play a maid in the movies than be one in real life; and during the 1930s she played the role of maid or cook in nearly 40 films, including *Alice Adams* (1935), in which her comic characterization of a grumbling, far-from-submissive maid made the dinner party scene one of the best remembered from the film. She is probably most often associated with the supporting role of Mammy in the 1939 film *Gone with the Wind*, a role for which she became the first African American to win an Academy Award.

At the end of World War II, during which McDaniel organized entertainment for black troops, the NAACP (National Association for the Advancement of Colored People) and other liberal black groups lobbied Hollywood for an end to the stereotyped roles in which McDaniel had become typecast, and consequently her Hollywood opportunities declined. Radio, however, was slower to respond, and in 1947 she became the first African American to star in a weekly radio program aimed at a general audience when she agreed to play the role of a maid on *The Beulah Show*. In 1951, while filming the first six segments of a television version of the popular show, she had a heart attack. She recovered sufficiently to tape a number of radio shows in 1952 but died soon thereafter of breast cancer.

EDDIE MURPHY

(b. April 3, 1961, Brooklyn, N.Y., U.S.)

Comedian and actor Eddie Murphy was one of the dominant comedic presences in the United States during the 1980s. His comedy was largely personal and observational, yet it was at times raunchy and cruel. He was also a skillful impersonator.

Murphy began doing stand-up comedy in New York City as a teenager and was only 19 years old when he joined the cast of *Saturday Night Live* in 1980. He quickly emerged as the show's top performer, creating memorable characters such as Mister Robinson (a spoof on the children's show host Mister Rogers), convict-poet Tyrone Green, and a very grumpy take on the animated clay character Gumby. Murphy scored a major

Eddie Murphy in Dreamgirls *(2006)*. © Paramount Pictures Corporation and Dreamworks LLC.

hit in his first film, *48 Hours* (1982). He followed with three more box-office successes—*Trading Places* (1983), *Beverly Hills Cop* (1984) and *The Golden Child* (1986). He left *Saturday Night Live* in 1984 to focus on his film and stand-up career. In addition to sequels to *48 Hours* and *Beverly Hills Cop*, Murphy showed his versatility in *Raw* (1987), which documented two of his live performances, and the comedy *Coming to America* (1988), in which he played four different roles. He recorded several comedy albums during the 1980s and also scored a minor pop-music hit with the single *Party All the Time* in 1985. He wrote, directed, and starred in *Harlem Nights* (1989), which was a critical and commercial disappointment. After a series of flops in the early 1990s, Murphy triumphed again with *The Nutty Professor* (1996) and *Dr. Dolittle* (1998), both updated versions of previous films. He also found success with animated family films, providing the voice of Mushu in *Mulan* (1998) and that of Donkey in *Shrek* (2001), *Shrek 2* (2004), and *Shrek the Third* (2007). In 2007 Murphy earned his first Academy Award nomination—for best supporting actor, for his performance in *Dreamgirls* (2006). His later films include *Meet Dave* (2008) and *Imagine That* (2009).

SIDNEY POITIER

(b. Feb. 20, 1927?, Miami, Fla., U.S.)

Bahamian American actor and motion-picture director and producer Sidney Poitier is recognized as the actor who broke the colour barrier in the American motion-picture industry and made the careers of other black actors possible.

Poitier was born prematurely in the United States while his parents were visiting from The Bahamas. He grew up on Cat Island, Bahamas, and returned as a teenager to the United States, where he enlisted in the U.S. Army during World War II and served a brief stint in an army medical unit. Upon his discharge, he applied to the American Negro Theatre (ANT) in New York City. Refused a place because of his accent, he practiced American enunciation while listening to the accents of radio voices and reapplied to the ANT six months later. This time he was accepted, and he began studying acting while appearing in a series of ANT productions. He made his feature-length movie debut as Dr. Luther Brooks, a black doctor who treats a bigoted white criminal, in *No Way Out* (1950). This film established a significant pattern both for Poitier himself and for the black actors who followed him; by refusing roles that played to a racial stereotype, Poitier pushed the restrictive boundaries set by Hollywood and made inroads into the American mainstream. Another of his notable early roles was Gregory Miller, an alienated high school student in the film adaptation of Evan Hunter's novel *The Blackboard Jungle* (1955). Despite his budding film career, Poitier continued to perform in live theatre and won critical acclaim on Broadway in 1959 with his starring role in Lorraine Hansberry's

(From left) *Ruby Dee, Sidney Poitier, Claudia McNeil, and Diana Sands in* A Raisin in the Sun *(1961).* © 1961 Columbia Pictures Corporation

A Raisin in the Sun. He also starred in the 1961 film adaptation of the drama.

Among Poitier's other early notable film roles were Noah Cullen in *The Defiant Ones* (1958), which earned him an Academy Award nomination as best actor, Porgy in *Porgy and Bess* (1959), Homer Smith in *Lilies of the Field* (1963)— for which he received the Academy Award for best actor—and Gordon Raife in *A Patch of Blue* (1965). He was the second black actor to win an Academy Award (Hattie McDaniel had won a best

supporting actress Oscar for *Gone with the Wind* in 1939) and the first to insist that productions upon which he worked have a certain percentage of black crew members. Poitier also starred in three popular movies in 1967—*In the Heat of the Night, To Sir with Love*, and *Guess Who's Coming to Dinner*.

In 1969 Poitier founded the First Artists Production Company, and in 1972 he made his directorial debut with *Buck and the Preacher*. Among other films he directed are *Uptown Saturday Night*

(1974), *Stir Crazy* (1980), and *Ghost Dad* (1990). After a long absence from the screen, Poitier appeared in *Shoot to Kill* (1988) and continued to act in feature films and made-for-television movies into the 21st century. In 2001, Poitier, the recipient of many prestigious acting awards, was presented with an honorary Academy Award for "his remarkable accomplishments as an artist and as a human being." A dual citizen of the United States and The Bahamas, he was appointed ambassador to Japan for The Bahamas in 1997. In 2009 Poitier was awarded the U.S. Presidential Medal of Freedom.

WILL SMITH

(b. Sept. 25, 1968, Philadelphia, Pa., U.S.)

Relying on charisma, clean-cut good looks, and his quick wit, Will Smith skillfully made the transition from rapper to successful actor.

Smith was given the nickname "Prince Charming" in high school, which he adapted to "Fresh Prince" in order to reflect a more hip-hop sound when he began his musical career. He formed an alliance with schoolmate and deejay Jeffrey Townes, whom he met in 1981. They began recording as DJ Jazzy Jeff and the Fresh Prince and released their first single, *Girls Ain't Nothing but Trouble*, in 1986, later followed by the album *Rock the House*. In 1988 the group released the groundbreaking single *Parents Just Don't Understand*, which went on to win a Grammy Award (the first Grammy ever presented in the rap performance category).

Smith's act, notable for its wide crossover appeal, was sometimes characterized as "light rap" because of the lack of hard-core lyrics and themes in his compositions. Platinum-certified recordings and accompanying videos subsequently brought him to the attention of television producers. The television sitcom *The Fresh Prince of Bel-Air*, which began in 1990 and was loosely based on Smith's real-life persona, ran on NBC for six successful seasons, ending at the star's request. During the series' run, Smith garnered two Golden Globe nominations and produced several episodes.

Buoyed by his small-screen success, Smith expanded into cinema with *Where the Day Takes You* (1992). His first dramatic role was in the film version of the successful stage play *Six Degrees of Separation* (1993). The action comedy-thriller *Bad Boys* (1995), however, proved to be the turning point in his film career. While the movie was not a critical success, it made more than $100 million worldwide, proving Smith's star power. In 1996 he starred in that year's number one movie, *Independence Day*. He again broke box-office records the next year with the science-fiction comedy *Men in Black*, for which he also recorded the Grammy-winning title song; the sequel to the film appeared in 2002. In 1998 Smith released his first solo album, *Big Willie Style*, which included the hit *Gettin' Jiggy*

Will Smith, 2009. Chris Jackson/Getty Images

Wit It, and starred in the dramatic thriller *Enemy of the State.*

After releasing the album *Willennium* in 1999, Smith demonstrated his remarkable versatility as an actor, playing an enigmatic golf caddy in *The Legend of Bagger Vance* (2000); the boxer Muhammad Ali in the biopic *Ali* (2001); and a "date doctor" helping a romantically inept man find love in *Hitch* (2005). *Lost and Found,* Smith's fourth solo album, was released in March 2005. The next year he starred in and coproduced *The Pursuit of Happyness,* and his performance as a single father who overcomes adversity earned him an Academy Award nomination for best actor. In *I Am Legend* (2007), Smith appeared as a scientist who is perhaps the last human on Earth following an epidemic. *Hancock* (2008) featured Smith as a superhero trying to revamp his unpopular image, and in *Seven Pounds* (2008) he played a man seeking redemption after accidentally killing seven people in a car accident.

WOODY STRODE

(b. July 28, 1914, Los Angeles, Calif., U.S.—d. Dec. 31, 1994, Glendora, Calif.)

Character actor Woody Strode was part of director John Ford's "family" of actors, appearing in nearly a dozen of Ford's films. Strode also had a brief career as a professional gridiron football player and was among the first African Americans to play in the National Football League.

While a student at the University of California, Los Angeles, Strode starred on the football team along with two other African American players, Jackie Robinson and Kenny Washington. In 1946 Strode and Washington signed with the Los Angeles Rams, thus (along with two others) integrating professional football in the United States. After a single season with the Rams, Strode played football in Canada and also did a stint as a professional wrestler. He made his film debut in *Sundown* in 1941, but it was not until the 1950s that he worked regularly in the movie industry. He appeared as the king of Ethiopia in *The Ten Commandments* (1956). He also gave memorable performances in *Spartacus* (1960) and *Once Upon a Time in the West* (1968), as well as the Ford-directed films *Sergeant Rutledge* (1960), *Two Rode Together* (1961), and *The Man Who Shot Liberty Valance* (1962). In *Sergeant Rutledge* Strode played the lead role of a cavalry officer wrongly accused of rape and murder. In 1968 he starred in *Black Jesus,* an Italian production of a story based on the life of African nationalist leader Patrice Lumumba.

DENZEL WASHINGTON

(b. Dec. 28, 1954, Mount Vernon, N.Y., U.S.)

Actor Denzel Washington is celebrated for his engaging and powerful performances. Throughout his career he has been regularly praised by critics, and his

Denzel Washington, 2010. Bryan Bedder/Getty Images

consistent success at the box office helped to dispel the perception that African American actors could not draw mainstream white audiences.

After graduating from Fordham University (B.A., 1977), Washington began to pursue acting as a career and joined the American Conservatory Theater in San Francisco. After several successful stage performances in California and New York, he made his screen debut in the comedy *Carbon Copy* (1981). He first began to receive national attention for his work on the television drama *St. Elsewhere* (1982–87). For the film *Cry Freedom* (1987), Washington portrayed South African activist Stephen Biko, and he received an Oscar nomination for best supporting actor. Two years later he won the Oscar for best supporting actor for his performance as a freed slave fighting in the Union army in the Civil War film *Glory* (1989).

Washington's skill as an actor and his popular appeal as a leading man were firmly established in the 1990s. He gave memorable performances in the romantic comedy *Mississippi Masala* (1991), the Shakespearean comedy *Much Ado About Nothing* (1993), the courtroom drama *Philadelphia* (1993), the hard-boiled mystery *Devil in a Blue Dress* (1995), and the military thriller *Crimson Tide* (1995). During this time he frequently worked with director Spike Lee, starring in *Mo' Better Blues* (1990), *He Got Game* (1998), and most significantly *Malcolm X* (1992). Portraying the civil rights activist Malcolm X, Washington

gave a complex and powerful performance and earned an Academy Award nomination for best actor. He received a second best-actor nomination for his portrayal of boxer Rubin Carter in the film *The Hurricane* (1999).

In *Training Day* (2001), Washington played a corrupt and violent police detective, the performance for which he became only the second African American actor (the first was Sidney Poitier) to win an Oscar for best actor. In 2002 Washington made his directorial debut with the film *Antwone Fisher*. After starring in director Jonathan Demme's 2004 update of the 1962 thriller *The Manchurian Candidate*, Washington reteamed with Lee for the crime drama *Inside Man* (2006). He later appeared as a drug kingpin opposite Russell Crowe's determined narcotics officer in *American Gangster* (2007) and as a dispatcher caught in the middle of a subway train hijacking in *The Taking of Pelham 1 2 3* (2009).

OPRAH WINFREY

(b. Jan. 29, 1954, Kosciusko, Miss., U.S.)

Television personality, actress, and entrepreneur Oprah Winfrey became one of the richest and most influential women in the United States primarily as a result of the success of her syndicated daily talk show, which was among the most popular of the genre.

Winfrey moved to Milwaukee, Wis., at age six to live with her mother. In her

Oprah Winfrey in The Color Purple.
Gordon Parks/© 1985 Warner Bros., Inc.;
photograph from a private collection

early teens she was sent to Nashville, Tenn., to live with her father, who proved to be a positive influence in her life.

At age 19, Winfrey became a news anchor for the local CBS television station. Following her graduation from Tennessee State University in 1976, she was made a reporter and coanchor for the ABC news affiliate in Baltimore, Md. She found herself constrained by the objectivity required of news reporting, and in 1977 she became cohost of the Baltimore morning show *People Are Talking*. Winfrey excelled in the casual and

personal talk-show format, and in 1984 she moved to Chicago to host the faltering talk show *AM Chicago*. Winfrey's honest and engaging personality quickly turned the program into a success, and in 1985 it was renamed *The Oprah Winfrey Show*. Syndicated nationally in 1986, the program became the highest-rated television talk show in America and earned several Emmy Awards.

In 1985 Winfrey appeared in Steven Spielberg's adaptation of Alice Walker's 1982 novel *The Color Purple*. Her critically acclaimed performance led to other roles, including a performance in the television miniseries *The Women of Brewster Place* (1989). Winfrey formed her own television production company, Harpo Productions, Inc., in 1986, and a film production company, Harpo Films, in 1990. The companies began buying film rights to literary works, including Connie May Fowler's *Before Women Had Wings*, which appeared in 1997 with Winfrey as both star and producer, and Toni Morrison's *Beloved*, which appeared in 1998, also with Winfrey in a starring role. In 1998 Winfrey expanded her media entertainment empire when she cofounded Oxygen Media, which operates a cable television network for women. She brokered a partnership with Discovery Communications in 2008, through which the Oprah Winfrey Network (OWN) was scheduled to replace the Discovery Health Channel in 2011. In 2009 Winfrey announced that her television talk show would end in September 2011; it

Book cover of Live Your Best Life: A Treasury of Wisdom, Wit, Advice, Interviews, and Inspiration from O, the Oprah Magazine *(2005).* PRNewsFoto/Oxmoor House/AP Images

was speculated that she would focus on OWN.

Winfrey broke new ground in 1996 by starting an on-air book club. She announced selections two to four weeks in advance and then discussed the book on her show with a select group of people. Each book chosen quickly rose to the top of the best-seller charts, and Winfrey's effect on the publishing industry was significant. Winfrey further expanded her presence in the publishing industry with the highly successful launch of *O, the Oprah Magazine* in 2000 and with *O at Home*, launched in 2004. In 2006 the Oprah & Friends channel debuted on satellite radio.

Winfrey has engaged in numerous philanthropic activities, including the creation of Oprah's Angel Network, which sponsors charitable initiatives worldwide. In 2007 she opened a $40 million school for disadvantaged girls in South Africa. She is an outspoken crusader against child abuse and has received many honours and awards from civic, philanthropic, and entertainment organizations.

DIRECTORS, PRODUCERS, AND PLAYWRIGHTS

As early as the 1920s Oscar Micheaux had established himself as an auteur of authentic African American cinema, and in the 1960s and '70s a series of so-called blaxploitation films, starring and directed by African Americans (notably Melvin Van Peebles and Gordon Parks)

and targeted specifically at black audiences, made their mark. With the notable exception of director Michael Schultz, it was not until the 1980s, however, that mainstream movie-making had a significant black presence behind the camera, when a clutch of talented young African American filmmakers, headed by Spike Lee and including Charles Burnett, John Singleton, and Robert Townsend, burst onto the scene.

In the 1940s and '50s, African Americans were in the limelight in stage productions such as *Porgy and Bess* and *Carmen Jones* that featured black characters but were written and directed by whites. In the early 1960s African American playwrights came to the fore, often with plays with civil rights themes—most notably Lorraine Hansberry's powerful *Raisin in the Sun*, which African American playwright, producer, and director George Wolfe parodied as a "Momma on the Couch" play in his 1980s production *The Colored Museum*. Later, in the 1960s and '70s, black theatre became a major cultural force, especially the works by Amiri Baraka, and grew to encompass a wide range of works by talented playwrights and directors that culminated in the sweeping oeuvre of August Wilson.

AMIRI BARAKA

(b. Oct. 7, 1934, Newark, N.J., U.S.)

Writer Amiri Baraka (born LeRoi Jones) presented the experiences and anger of

African Americans with an affirmation of black life.

As LeRoi Jones, he graduated from Howard University (B.A., 1953) and served in the U.S. Air Force. After military duty, he joined the Beat movement, attended graduate school, and published his first major collection of poetry, *Preface to a Twenty Volume Suicide Note,* in 1961. In 1964 his play *Dutchman* appeared off-Broadway to critical acclaim. In its depiction of an encounter between a white woman and a black intellectual, it exposes the suppressed anger and hostility of American blacks toward the dominant white culture. After the assassination of Malcolm X, Jones took the name Amiri Baraka and began to espouse black nationalism.

In 1965 he founded the Black Arts Repertory Theatre in Harlem. He published much during this period, including *Black Art* (1966) and *Black Magic* (1969). In addition to poetry and drama, Baraka wrote several collections of essays, an autobiographical novel (*The System of Dante's Hell* [1965]), and short stories. In the mid-1970s he became a Marxist, though his goals remained similar. "I [still] see art as a weapon and a weapon of revolution," he said. "It's just now that I define revolution in Marxist terms." In addition to writing, Baraka taught at several American universities. *The Autobiography of LeRoi Jones/Amiri Baraka* was published in 1984.

CHARLES BURNETT

(b. April 13, 1944, Vicksburg, Miss., U.S.)

American filmmaker Charles Burnett gained critical acclaim for his realistic and intimate portrayals of African American families. Burnett's films were revered by critics yet rarely enjoyed any commercial success. His film *Killer of Sheep* (1977) was placed on the Library of Congress's National Film Registry in 1990.

Burnett grew up in Los Angeles and studied film at the University of California, Los Angeles. He began filming *Killer of Sheep* while a student, shooting on weekends. The film, completed in 1973 but not publicly screened until 1977, is a collection of vignettes centred on an impoverished African American family in Los Angeles. A 1980 Guggenheim Fellowship allowed Burnett to begin production on his second feature film, *My Brother's Wedding* (1983), a portrait of a family and its feelings toward the inner city neighbourhood in which it lives. In 1988 Burnett received a MacArthur Foundation Fellowship, which provided him with the financial support to make *To Sleep with Anger* (1990), another portrait of an African American family coming to grips with both its past and its present. *To Sleep with Anger* gained widespread critical acclaim and was Burnett's first film to enjoy a modicum of commercial success. *The Glass Shield* (1994), about a black cop working with a racist police unit, was Burnett's first major commercial effort, but it enjoyed only limited success. He subsequently turned to television and documentary films and in 1996 made the highly praised *Nightjohn*, a fictional film about American slaves teaching themselves to read. He followed that with the television movie *Selma, Lord, Selma* (1999), about the 1965 civil rights march from Selma to Montgomery, Ala., and the documentaries *Nat Turner: A Troublesome Property* (2003) and *Namibia: The Struggle for Liberation* (2007).

LONNE ELDER III

(b. Dec. 26, 1931, Americus, Ga., U.S.—d. June 11, 1996, Woodland Hills, Calif.)

Playwright Lonne Elder III's critically acclaimed masterwork, *Ceremonies in Dark Old Men* (1965, revised 1969), depicted the dreams, frustrations, and ultimate endurance of a black family living in 1950s Harlem.

Orphaned as a boy, Elder was raised in New Jersey by an aunt and an uncle who ran a numbers game (i.e., an illegal lottery) out of their home. As a young man, he moved to New York City, where he worked a number of odd jobs while learning the acting trade and writing poems, short stories, and, finally, plays. From 1959 to 1962 he played the role of Bobo in the classic drama *A Raisin in the Sun*, at the personal invitation of Lorraine Hansberry.

Ceremonies in Dark Old Men was presented as a dramatic reading in 1965 and then produced for the stage by the Negro Ensemble Company in 1969. The drama centres on the fractured Parker family, whose aging patriarch dreams of lost youth while his daughter toils at a dead-end office job, his two hustling sons sell bootleg liquor and engage in petty thievery, and a smooth-talking con artist runs numbers out of their decrepit barber shop. The play enjoyed instantaneous success, bringing Elder many prizes and being produced for television in 1975.

By that time Elder had moved to Los Angeles, where he wrote scripts for television shows, for the motion picture *Sounder* (1972; Academy Award nominee for best screenplay), and for *A Woman Called Moses* (1978), a television miniseries based on the life of abolitionist Harriet Tubman. Elders's only other play to be staged, *Charades on East Fourth Street* (1967), was produced for a New York social service agency.

SPIKE LEE

(b. March 20, 1957, Atlanta, Ga., U.S.)

Filmmaker Spike Lee (born Shelton Jackson Lee) is known for his uncompromising, provocative approach to controversial subject matter.

The son of the jazz composer Bill Lee, he was reared in a middle-class Brooklyn neighbourhood. He majored in communications at Atlanta's Morehouse College, where he directed his first

Super-8 films and met his future coproducer, Monty Ross. In 1978 Lee entered New York University's Graduate Film School, where he met another future collaborator, cinematographer Ernest Dickerson. Lee gained national attention with his master's thesis, the short subject *Joe's Bed-Stuy Barbershop: We Cut Heads* (as he explained at the time, the barbershop "is second only in importance to the church in the black community"), which earned him the Academy of Motion Picture Arts and Science's Student Award.

Lee's feature film debut was *She's Gotta Have It* (1986), a prismatic character study about the love life of a contemporary black woman. Establishing a career-long pattern, Lee not only wrote, produced, directed, and edited the film but also played a key supporting role. The film, which was made on a $175,000 budget, was hailed as "Godardesque" at the Cannes Film Festival. His next film, based on his experiences at Morehouse, was *School Daze* (1988), a scatological satire of colour prejudice, snobbery, and betrayal within the black academic community. The infamous Howard Beach incident, in which a black man was chased and killed by rampaging white youths, was the inspiration for Lee's third feature, *Do the Right Thing* (1989), an impassioned but evenhanded work that neither blamed any specific group for racial violence nor absolved any from it. Virtually all his subsequent films dealt head-on with issues of race and racism in the United States—interracial relationships in *Jungle Fever* (1991) and the diversity of opinions within the black community in *Get on the Bus* (1996).

With the notable exception of his monumental biographical film *Malcolm X* (1992), many of Lee's later works received mixed reviews. Some observers complained about the excessive length of his films; others criticized his perpetuation of ethnic stereotypes, notably the Jewish characters in *Mo' Better Blues* (1990) and the Italian Americans in *Summer of Sam* (1999); while still others condemned his treatment of his female characters. The outspoken Lee cited what he perceived as Hollywood's antiblack bias, noting that, while *Do the Right Thing*, *Malcolm X*, and his poignant documentary *4 Little Girls* (1997) all received Academy Award nominations, he was repeatedly denied an Oscar win.

Lee's later films include *He Got Game* (1998), a family drama that is both an exposé of college basketball recruiting practices and paean to the sport, and *25th Hour* (2002), which focuses on the last day of freedom for a convicted drug dealer. *Inside Man* (2006), starring Denzel Washington and Jodie Foster, centres on the negotiations between the police and the bank robbers engaged in a hostage situation. In 2006 Lee also released the documentary *When the Levees Broke*, a four-part HBO series outlining the U.S. government's inadequate response to Hurricane Katrina. The mystery *Miracle at St. Anna* (2008) focuses on the experiences of African American soldiers in World War II.

Spike Lee. Francois Guillot/AFP/Getty Images

Many of Lee's films can be classified as family affairs: his father, Bill, contributed music to *She's Gotta Have It* and *Mo' Better Blues*, among others; his sister, Joie, played major roles in several productions; and his brother David Charles Lee was the still photographer.

OSCAR MICHEAUX

(b. Jan. 2, 1884, Metropolis, Ill., U.S.—d. March 25, 1951, Charlotte, N.C.)

Prolific producer and director Oscar Micheaux made films independently of the Hollywood film industry from the silent era until 1948.

While working as a Pullman porter, Micheaux purchased a relinquished South Dakota homestead in 1906. Although he lost the farm because of family entanglements, his experiences became the subject of a series of self-published books, including *The Homesteader* (1917), which he sold door-to-door. In 1917 he was approached by an African American film company for movie rights to *The Homesteader*. He refused the offer but liked the idea and made his own film version, thus launching his career as an independent filmmaker.

Between 1919 and 1948 he wrote, produced, directed, and distributed more than 45 films for African American audiences, who watched these "race" (all-black) films in the 700 theatres that were part of the "ghetto circuit." Micheaux was one of the few black independents to survive the sound era, doing so largely because of his tenacity, personal charisma, and talent for promoting his work. While on promotional tours, he used his completed films, which he often distributed by hand to waiting theatres, to secure from personal investors the financing for his next project.

Micheaux's features emulated familiar Hollywood genres, and he used a modest version of the studio star system to lure audiences to his movies. His gangster films, mysteries, and jungle adventures featured Lorenzo Tucker (called the "coloured Valentino"), Ethel Moses (the "black Harlow"), and Bee Freeman (the "sepia Mae West"), among others. Despite Micheaux's understanding of certain Hollywood conventions, his films reveal a consciousness of race as a force in the lives of African Americans, and some deal directly with racial issues; these include his examination of white prejudice (*Within Our Gates*, 1920), interracial romance (*The Exile*, 1931), and skin-tone issues within the African American community (*God's Step Children*, 1937).

Micheaux's necessarily low budgets forced him to cut costs and resulted in technically inferior films with poor lighting, little editing, flubbed lines, continuity problems, and poor sound. Yet he treated issues that were important to his audience, offered an alternative to the stereotyping of blacks by Hollywood, and successfully operated outside the mainstream film industry during the powerful studio era.

NTOZAKE SHANGE

(b. Oct. 18, 1948, Trenton, N.J., U.S.)

Author Ntozake Shange (born Paulette Linda Williams) is known for plays, poetry, and fiction steeped in feminist themes and racial and sexual anger.

Shange attended Barnard College (B.A., 1970) and the University of Southern California (M.A., 1973). From 1972 to 1975 she taught humanities, women's studies, and Afro-American studies at California colleges. During this period she also made public appearances as a dancer and reciter of poetry. Her 1975 theatre piece *For Colored Girls Who Have Considered Suicide/When the Rainbow Is Enuf* quickly brought her fame. Written for seven actors, *For Colored Girls* is a group of 20 poems on the power of black women to survive in the face of despair and pain. It ran for seven months Off-Broadway in New York City, then moved to Broadway and was subsequently produced throughout the United States and broadcast on television.

Shange created a number of other theatre works that employed poetry, dance, and music (known as "choreopo-ems") while abandoning conventions of plot and character development. One of the most popular of these was her 1980 adaptation of Bertolt Brecht's *Mother Courage,* featuring a black family in the time of the American Civil War. Some of Shange's other works for the stage are *Where the Mississippi Meets the Amazon* (1977), *Three Views of Mt. Fuji* (1987), and *The Love Space Demands: A Continuing Saga* (1992).

Shange's poetry collections include *Nappy Edges* (1978) and *Ridin' the Moon in Texas* (1987). She also published the novels *Sassafrass, Cypress & Indigo* (1982), about the diverging lives of three sisters and their mother; the semiauto-biographical *Betsey Brown* (1985); and *Liliane: Resurrection of the Daughter* (1994), a coming-of-age story about a wealthy black woman in the American South. In addition, Shange wrote a number of children's books, including *Whitewash* (1997), *Daddy Says* (2003), and *Ellington Was Not a Street* (2004).

MELVIN VAN PEEBLES

(b. Aug. 21, 1932, Chicago, Ill., U.S.)

Filmmaker Melvin Van Peebles wrote, directed, and starred in *Sweet Sweetback's Baadasssss Song* (1971), a groundbreak-ing film that spearheaded the rush of blaxploitation films in the 1970s. He also served as the film's composer and editor.

After graduating from Ohio Wesleyan University (B.A., 1953), Van Peebles traveled extensively in Europe, Mexico, and the United States, working a vari-ety of jobs that included painter, postal worker, and street performer, along with a stint in the U.S. Air Force. While living in Paris, he wrote several English-language novels including *La Permission,* which he later turned into his first film *The Story of the Three Day Pass* (1967). He made his Hollywood directorial debut with *Watermelon Man* (1970), a comedy about racial bigotry. He then turned to his pet project, *Sweet Sweetback's Baadasssss Song.* Using mostly his own money and relying largely on nonprofessional actors and technicians, Van Peebles told the story of one black man's battle against white authority. Violent, sexy, and angry, the film scored a huge success with African American audiences (it was one of the top box-office earners that year), while angering many white critics.

Next Van Peebles went to Broadway, where he produced the musical comedies *Ain't Supposed to Die a Natural Death* (1971) and *Don't Play Us Cheap* (1972). Thereafter he continued to write, act, compose, and direct for films and televi-sion. Later films in which he appeared include *The Hebrew Hammer* (2003) and *Blackout* (2007). He also wrote the screenplays for *Badasssss!* (2003) and *Confessionsofa Ex-Doofus-ItchyFooted Mutha* (2008), the latter of which he also directed. In addition to his film career, Van Peebles became involved in com-modities trading in the 1980s and was the first African American to hold a seat on the American Stock Exchange.

Van Peebles's son Mario, who played the character Sweetback as a boy in the 1971 film, became a noted film actor and director in his own right.

COMEDIANS

The tradition of African American comedy stretches from the performances of genuine black performers in minstrel shows to Bert Williams and the "Tomfoolery" of Stepin Fetchit and Amos and Andy (the latter duo were portrayed by white actors on radio but African Americans on television) on to the political incisiveness of stand-up comics such as Dick Gregory. Beginning in the 1970s, some of the most gifted of these stand-up comedians also went on to become motion picture stars, including Richard Pryor, Eddie Murphy, and Chris Rock. By the 1980s and '90s, sketch comedy shows, notably *In Living Color*, and situation comedies such as the hugely popular *The Cosby Show* had become important showcases for African American comedic actors.

BILL COSBY

(b. July 12, 1937, Philadelphia, Pa., U.S.)

Actor, comedian, and producer Bill Cosby played a major role in the development of a more positive portrayal of blacks on television.

Cosby left high school without earning his diploma and joined the U.S. Navy in 1956. While enlisted he passed a high school equivalency exam, and after his discharge he received an athletic scholarship to Temple University in Philadelphia in 1961. During his sophomore year he left Temple to entertain at the Gaslight Cafe in Greenwich Village, New York City, where he began to establish a trademark comedic style characterized by a friendly and accessible stage persona and a relaxed, carefully timed delivery. During the 1960s Cosby toured major U.S. and Canadian cities, commanding ever-higher performance fees. In 1965 he made his first appearance on *The Tonight Show Starring Johnny Carson*.

Cosby's first acting assignment, in the espionage series *I Spy* (1965–68), made him the first black actor to perform in a starring dramatic role on network television. His portrayal of a black secret agent won him three Emmy Awards and helped to advance the status of African Americans on television. Cosby's subsequent projects for television included the series of *Bill Cosby Specials* (1968–71, 1975), the situation comedy *The Bill Cosby Show* (1969–71), the variety show *The New Bill Cosby Show* (1972–73), and the successful cartoon *Fat Albert and the Cosby Kids* (1972–84, 1989). He appeared in numerous commercials and on children's shows such as *Sesame Street* and *Electric Company*; he also made several feature films, which enjoyed limited success.

Cosby's most successful work, *The Cosby Show*, appeared on NBC from 1984 to 1992, becoming one of the most

Bill Cosby. Brad Barket/Getty Images

Massachusetts in 1977 and was inducted into the Television Hall of Fame in 1984. His comedy records earned him eight Grammy awards. In 1986 he wrote the best-selling book *Fatherhood.* In 1997 Cosby's son, Ennis, was shot and killed while changing a tire on a Los Angeles freeway; that same year he and his wife, Camille, founded the Hello Friend/Ennis William Cosby Foundation in their son's memory to fund teachers of students with learning disabilities. Cosby was outspoken about the need for African Americans to pursue higher education and to support their families. In 2008 he released the hip-hop album *Cosby Narratives Vol. 1: State of Emergency,* which blended jazz, pop, and funk but shied away from the profanity he said was typical of most hip-hop music.

WHOOPI GOLDBERG

(b. Nov. 13, 1955, New York, N.Y., U.S.)

popular situation comedies in television history. *The Cosby Show* depicted a stable, prosperous black family—Cosby's character was a doctor and his wife a lawyer—and avoided racial stereotypes. The show had broad cross-cultural appeal and won several major awards. After the show ended he starred in the series *Cosby* (1996–2000), in which his *Cosby Show* costar Phylicia Rashād again played his wife.

Cosby was awarded a doctorate in education from the University of

Comedian, actress, and producer Whoopi Goldberg (born Caryn Elaine Johnson) is known for her work in theatre, film, television, and recordings. An accomplished performer with a wide repertoire, her work ranges from dramatic leading roles to controversial comedic performances.

Goldberg spent her early years in a Manhattan housing project. She began performing at age eight with a children's theatre group and later, as a young adult, went on to perform in the choruses of Broadway shows. She moved to

California in 1974 and soon became active in the theatre community there, as well as establishing a presence as a stand-up comedian. Eventually she developed *The Spook Show*, a one-woman stage show noted for its humour, satire, and drama, which she performed throughout the United States and Europe. That performance became the basis for the critically acclaimed Broadway show *Whoopi Goldberg*, which debuted in 1984, and in 1985 Goldberg won a Grammy Award for the show's recording. Soon afterward she made her Hollywood debut in *The Color Purple* (1985), for which she garnered an Oscar nomination and a Golden Globe Award. Goldberg went on to perform in less-successful films before appearing in *Ghost* (1990), for which she won both the Academy Award and the Golden Globe Award for best supporting actress. Goldberg followed up with numerous performances in film and television, including hosting her own talk show for a brief stint, serving as host of the Academy Awards show on several occasions, and starring in the television show *Whoopi* (2003–04). In addition, Goldberg began producing works for television and stage in the late 1990s, and in 2002 she won a Tony Award for producing the Broadway show *Thoroughly Modern Millie*. In 2007 she became a cohost on the daytime talk television show *The View*. Goldberg is also known as an activist on behalf of several causes, including human rights, AIDS research, and children's issues.

DICK GREGORY

(b. Oct. 12, 1932, St. Louis, Mo., U.S.)

American comedian, civil rights activist, and spokesman for health issues Dick Gregory became nationally recognized in the 1960s for a biting brand of comedy that attacked racial prejudice. By addressing his hard-hitting satire to white audiences, he gave a comedic voice to the rising civil rights movement. In the 1980s his nutrition business venture targeted unhealthy diets of black Americans.

Reared in poverty in St. Louis, Gregory began working at an early age to help support his family. He was involved in sports and social causes in high school, and he entered Southern Illinois University on an athletic scholarship in 1951, excelling as a middle-distance runner. He was named the university's outstanding student athlete in 1953, the same year he left college to join the U.S. Army, where he hosted and performed comedy routines in military shows.

After a brief return to his alma mater in 1955-56, Gregory sought entrance to the national comedy circuit in Chicago. His breakthrough came in 1961, when a one-nighter at the Chicago Playboy Club turned into a six-week stint that earned him a profile in *Time* magazine and a television appearance on "The Jack Paar Show." In his numerous subsequent television, nightclub, and concert routines, he targeted poverty, segregation, and racial discrimination. Active in the civil rights

Dick Gregory, 1962. Three Lions/Hulton Archive/Getty Images

movement, he participated in numerous demonstrations and was arrested for civil disobedience several times; in 1963 he was jailed in Birmingham, Ala. His activism spurred him to run for mayor of Chicago in 1966 and for president of the United States in 1968.

In the early 1970s Gregory abandoned comedy to focus on his political interests, which widened from race relations to include such issues as violence, world hunger, capital punishment, drug abuse, and poor health care. He generated particular attention for his many hunger fasts. At this time he became a vegetarian, a marathon runner, and an expert on nutrition. He soon began a successful business venture with his nutritional product, the "Bahamian Diet," around which he built Dick Gregory Health Enterprises, Inc. Through his company, he targeted the lower life expectancy of black Americans, which he attributed to poor nutrition and drug and alcohol abuse.

Gregory wrote many books, including *Nigger: An Autobiography* (1964) and *No More Lies: The Myth and the Reality of American History* (1971). He made a brief return to the comedy circuit in the mid-1990s.

RICHARD PRYOR

(b. Dec. 1, 1940, Peoria, Ill., U.S.—d. Dec. 10, 2005, Los Angeles, Calif.)

Comedian and actor Richard Pryor was one of the leading comics of the 1970s and '80s. His comedy routines drew on a variety of downtrodden urban characters, rendered with brutal emotional honesty.

Pryor began working in clubs in the early 1960s, developing his brand of controversial, race-based humour. His success influenced many later comics. He appeared in motion pictures such as *Lady Sings the Blues* (1972) and *Silver Streak* (1976), becoming a major box-office attraction. He also had success with his own concert films, including *Richard Pryor: Live on the Sunset Strip* (1982). In 1986 he starred in the autobiographical *Jo Jo Dancer, Your Life Is Calling*. His stand-up performances also were documented in comedy albums, for which he won five Grammy Awards. As a comedy writer, Pryor received an Emmy for the Lily Tomlin television special *Lily* (1973) and a Writers Guild Award as cowriter of the screenplay for *Blazing Saddles* (1974).

Pryor struggled with drug problems, and in 1980 he was seriously burned in what was reported as a cocaine-related incident. Diagnosed with multiple sclerosis in 1986, he made few appearances after the early 1990s. Pryor was presented with the Kennedy Center's Mark Twain Prize in 1998. His autobiography, *Pryor Convictions and Other Life Sentences* (cowritten with Todd Gold), was published in 1995.

CHRIS ROCK

(b. Feb. 7, 1966, Georgetown, S.C., U.S.)

Comedian Chris Rock's popular stand-up routines often address racial matters.

Rock grew up in the impoverished Bedford-Stuyvesant section of Brooklyn, N.Y. After dropping out of high school at 17 (he later received a high-school-equivalency diploma), Rock played small clubs in the New York area, where he was discovered by comedian-actor Eddie Murphy. After landing parts in Murphy's film *Beverly Hills Cop II* (1987) and director Keenan Ivory Wayans's *I'm Gonna Git You Sucka* (1988), Rock got his big break by earning a spot in 1990 as a cast member of *Saturday Night Live*. He left the show in 1993 to join Fox Network's *In Living Color*, which was taken off the air shortly thereafter. After starring in and writing the script for the film *CB4* (1993), he covered the 1996 presidential campaign for ABC's *Politically Incorrect*. Rock then appeared in the first of his Home Box Office (HBO) comedy specials, *Big Ass Jokes* (1994), which won the 1994 Cable Ace Award. Soon after, however, Rock found his popularity as an actor and comedian beginning to fade.

In an effort to reignite his career, Rock went on the road in 1996, playing small clubs. There he honed his comedic repertoire, touching on subjects that were often considered taboo, such as race relations, drug addiction, and black poverty, all the while revealing the humorous aspects of some of the more serious, painful truths of the black experience. Bolstered by the positive reaction he received while touring, Rock once again appeared in an HBO special, *Bring the Pain* (1997), which won two Emmy

Awards and brought Rock widespread fame and critical acclaim. Riding the crest of his newfound popularity, Rock went on to star in the television series *The Chris Rock Show* (1997–2000), write the best-selling book *Rock This!* (1997), costar in the film *Lethal Weapon 4* (1998), and provide the voice for Rodney the guinea pig in another Murphy movie, *Dr. Dolittle* (1998).

In 1999 Rock starred in his third HBO comedy special, *Bigger and Blacker*, and then appeared in a series of films, including *Nurse Betty* (2000) and *Down to Earth* (2001). In 2001 he provided the voice of the title character in the animated movie *Osmosis Jones*. He later starred opposite Anthony Hopkins in the thriller *Bad Company* (2002). In 2003 Rock made his directorial debut with *Head of State*, which centred on a presidential election. After the popular HBO comedy special *Never Scared* (2004), he cocreated a television series based on his childhood, *Everybody Hates Chris*. The show premiered in 2005 and was a critical and commercial success. Rock also hosted the Academy Awards ceremony that year. His later films include *The Longest Yard* (2005), in which he costarred with Adam Sandler, and the animated movies *Madagascar* (2005) and *Madagascar: Escape 2 Africa* (2008). In 2007 he directed and starred in *I Think I Love My Wife*. Two years later Rock investigated the hairstyles of African American women in the documentary *Good Hair*.

Chris Rock. Astrid Stawiarz/Getty Images

BERT WILLIAMS

(b. *c.* 1876, New Providence, Bah.—d. March 4, 1922, New York City)

Comedian Bert Williams portrayed the slow-witted, shuffling black man that was then a standard role in vaudeville.

As a child Williams went to California with his family and worked in the mining and lumber camps of the West. In 1895 his partnership with George W. Walker began. They became one of the most successful comedy teams of their era; within a year they were appearing in New York City, where their song "Good Morning Carrie" became famous. In 1903 the partnership had graduated to full-scale musical comedy. The all-black show *In Dahomey* was a Broadway success and in London the following year played a command performance at Buckingham Palace. Other successes followed, notably *Abyssinia* (1906), *Bandanna Land* (1908), and *Mr. Lode of Koal* (1909). After Walker's death in 1909, Williams became a regular comic in the shows of Florenz Ziegfeld, starring in the *Follies* from 1910 through 1919 and writing much of his own material. Of his many musical compositions, "Nobody" (1905), with its wry, fatalistic lyric, is probably the best example of his work.

The fusion of the personal and the political is at the heart of many of the most influential performances by African Americans onstage and on screen. That is also the case in much of the most powerful music created by African Americans. Sometimes a love song is just love song, but often music is a reflection of social and political developments, as the next chapter will demonstrate.

CHAPTER 6

MUSIC

As cultural critic Adam Gopnik has observed, every epoch since the Renaissance has had an art form that seems to become a kind of universal language, one dominant artistic form and language that sweeps the world and becomes the common property of an entire civilization, from one country to another. Italian painting in the 15th century, German music in the 18th century, and French painting in the 19th and early 20th centuries transcended their local sources and became the one essential soundscape or visual representation of their time. Gopnik is then quick to add that at the beginning of the 21st century, and seen from a worldwide perspective, it is the American popular music that had its origins among African Americans at the end of the 19th century that (in all its many forms— ragtime, jazz, swing, jazz-influenced popular song, blues, rock and roll and the last's more self-consciously "serious" legacy as rock and later hip-hop) has become America's greatest contribution to the world's culture—the one indispensable and unavoidable art form of the 20th century.

The recognition of this fact was a long time coming and has had to battle prejudice and misunderstanding that continues today. Indeed, jazz-inspired American popular music has not always been well served by its own defenders, who have tended to romanticize rather than explain and describe. In broad outlines, the history of American popular music involves the adulteration of a "pure" form of folk music, largely inspired by the work and the music of African Americans. But it involves less the adulteration of those pure forms by commercial motives and commercial sounds than the constant, fruitful hybridization of folk forms by other sounds, other musics—art and avant-garde and commercial, Bach and Broadway meeting at Birdland. Most of the watershed years turn out to be permeable; as the man who is by now recognized by many as the greatest of all American musicians, Louis Armstrong, once said, "There ain't but two kinds of music in this world. Good music and bad music, and good music you tap your toe to." This chapter examines a raft of very good musicians, considered by genre.

JAZZ

For historian Gerald Early, jazz is the pinnacle of African American music. In Ken Burns's monumental documentary film *Jazz*, Early commented, "When they study our civilization two thousand years from now, there will only be three things that Americans will be known for: the Constitution, baseball, and jazz music. They're the three most beautiful things that Americans have created." Burns's film puts Louis Armstrong and Duke Ellington in a class of their own at the top of the pantheon of jazz artists, yet, as the multitude of talented jazz performers profiled here shows, jazz is an art form that is the province of much genius but is enabled by endless improvisational collaboration.

LOUIS ARMSTRONG

(b. Aug. 4, 1901, New Orleans, La., U.S.—d. July 6, 1971, New York, N.Y.)

Louis Armstrong, known as Satchmo (for "Satchel Mouth"), was the most-renowned trumpeter in jazz history and one of the most influential artists in the cultural history of the United States.

Armstrong grew up in dire poverty in New Orleans when jazz was very young. As a child he worked at odd jobs and sang in a boys' quartet. In 1913 he was sent to the Colored Waif's Home as a juvenile delinquent. There he learned to play cornet in the home's band, and playing music

Louis Armstrong. AFP/Getty Images

quickly became a passion; in his teens he learned music by listening to the pioneer jazz artists of the day, including the leading New Orleans cornetist, King Oliver. Armstrong developed rapidly: he played in marching and jazz bands, becoming skillful enough to replace Oliver in the important Kid Ory band about 1918, and in the early 1920s he played in Mississippi riverboat dance bands.

Fame beckoned in 1922 when Oliver, then leading a band in Chicago, sent for Armstrong to play second cornet. Oliver's Creole Jazz Band was the apex of the early, contrapuntal New Orleans ensemble style, and it included outstanding musicians such as the brothers Johnny and Baby Dodds and pianist Lil Hardin, who married Armstrong in 1924. The young Armstrong became popular through his ingenious ensemble lead and second cornet lines, his cornet duet passages (called "breaks") with Oliver, and his solos. He recorded his first solos as a member of the Oliver band in such pieces as "Chimes Blues" and "Tears," which Lil and Louis Armstrong composed.

Encouraged by his wife, Armstrong quit Oliver's band to seek further fame. He played for a year in New York City in Fletcher Henderson's band and on many recordings with others before returning to Chicago and playing in large orchestras. There he created his most important early works, the Armstrong Hot Five and Hot Seven recordings of 1925–28, on which he emerged as the first great jazz soloist. By then the New Orleans ensemble style, which allowed few solo opportunities, could no longer contain his explosive creativity. He retained vestiges of the style in such masterpieces as "Hotter than That," "Struttin' with Some Barbecue," "Wild Man Blues," and "Potato Head Blues" but largely abandoned it while accompanied by pianist Earl Hines ("West End Blues" and "Weather Bird"). By that time Armstrong was playing trumpet, and his technique was superior to that of all competitors. Altogether, his immensely compelling swing; his brilliant technique; his sophisticated, daring sense of harmony; his ever-mobile, expressive attack, timbre, and inflections; his gift for creating vital melodies; his dramatic, often complex sense of solo design; and his outsized musical energy and genius made these recordings major innovations in jazz.

Armstrong was a famous musician by 1929, when he moved from Chicago to New York City and performed in the theatre review *Hot Chocolates*. He toured America and Europe as a trumpet soloist accompanied by big bands; for several years beginning in 1935, Luis Russell's big band served as the Louis Armstrong band. During this time he abandoned the often blues-based original material of his earlier years for a remarkably fine choice of popular songs by such noted composers as Hoagy Carmichael, Irving Berlin, and Duke Ellington. With his new repertoire came a new, simplified style: he created melodic paraphrases and variations as well as chord-change-based improvisations on these songs. His trumpet range continued to expand, as demonstrated in the high-note show-pieces in his repertoire. His beautiful tone and gift for structuring bravura solos with brilliant high-note climaxes led to such masterworks as "That's My Home," "Body and Soul," and "Star Dust." One of the inventors of scat singing, he began to sing lyrics on most of his recordings, varying melodies or decorating with scat phrases in a gravel voice that was immediately identifiable. Although he sang such humorous songs as "Hobo, You Can't Ride This Train," he also sang many standard songs, often with an intensity and creativity that equaled those of his trumpet playing.

Louis and Lil Armstrong separated in 1931. From 1935 to the end of his life, Armstrong's career was managed by Joe Glaser, who hired Armstrong's bands and guided his film career (beginning with *Pennies from Heaven*, 1936) and radio appearances. Though his own bands usually played in a more conservative style, Armstrong was the dominant influence on the swing era, when most trumpeters attempted to emulate his inclination to dramatic structure, melody, or technical virtuosity. Trombonists, too, appropriated Armstrong's phrasing, and saxophonists as different as Coleman Hawkins and Bud Freeman modeled their styles on different aspects of Armstrong's. Above all else, his swing-style trumpet playing influenced virtually all jazz horn players who followed him, and the swing and rhythmic suppleness of his vocal style were important influences on singers from Billie Holiday to Bing Crosby.

In most of Armstrong's movie, radio, and television appearances, he was featured as a good-humoured entertainer. He played a rare dramatic role in the film *New Orleans* (1947), in which he also performed in a Dixieland band. This prompted the formation of Louis Armstrong's All-Stars, a Dixieland band that at first included such other jazz greats as Hines and trombonist Jack Teagarden. For most of the rest of Armstrong's life, he toured the world with changing All-Stars sextets; indeed, "Ambassador Satch" in his later years was noted for his almost nonstop touring schedule. It was the period of his greatest popularity; he produced hit recordings such as "Mack the Knife" and "Hello, Dolly!" and outstanding albums such as his tributes to W.C. Handy and Fats Waller. In his last years ill health curtailed his trumpet playing, but he continued as a singer. His last film appearance was in *Hello, Dolly!* (1969).

More than a great trumpeter, Armstrong was a bandleader, singer, soloist, film star, and comedian. One of his most remarkable feats was his frequent conquest of the popular market with recordings that thinly disguised authentic jazz with Armstrong's contagious humour. He nonetheless made his greatest impact on the evolution of jazz itself, which at the start of his career was popularly considered to be little more than a novelty. With his great sensitivity, technique, and capacity to express emotion, Armstrong not only ensured the survival of jazz but led in its development into a fine art.

Armstrong's autobiographies include *Swing That Music* (1936, reprinted with a new foreword, 1993) and *Satchmo: My Life in New Orleans* (1954).

COUNT BASIE

(b. Aug. 21, 1904, Red Bank, N.J., U.S.—d. April 26, 1984, Hollywood, Fla.)

Jazz musician Count Basie was noted for his spare, economical piano style and for his leadership of influential and widely heralded big bands.

William Basie studied music with his mother and was later influenced by the Harlem pianists James P. Johnson and Fats Waller, receiving informal tutelage on the organ from the latter. He began his professional career as an accompanist on the vaudeville circuit. Stranded in Kansas City, Mo., in 1927, Basie remained there and eventually (in 1935) assumed the leadership of a nine-piece band composed of former members of the Walter Page and Bennie Moten orchestras. One night, while the band was broadcasting on a shortwave radio station in Kansas City, he was dubbed "Count" Basie by a radio announcer who wanted to indicate his standing in a class with aristocrats of jazz such as Duke Ellington. Jazz critic and record producer John Hammond heard the broadcasts and promptly launched the band on its career. Though rooted in the riff style of the 1930s swing-era big bands, the Basie orchestra played with the forceful drive and carefree swing of a small combo. They were considered a

model for ensemble rhythmic conception and tonal balance—this despite the fact that most of Basie's sidemen in the 1930s were poor sight readers; mostly, the band relied on "head" arrangements (so called because the band had collectively composed and memorized them, rather than using sheet music).

The early Basie band was also noted for its legendary soloists and outstanding rhythm section. It featured such jazzmen as tenor saxophonists Lester Young (regarded by many as the premier tenor player in jazz history) and Herschel Evans, trumpeters Buck Clayton and Harry "Sweets" Edison, and trombonists Benny Morton and Dicky Wells. The legendary Billie Holiday was a vocalist with Basie for a short stint (1937–38), although she was unable to record with the band because of her contract with another record label; mostly, vocals were handled by Jimmy Rushing, one of the most renowned "blues bawlers." The rhythm unit for the band—pianist Basie, guitarist Freddie Green (who joined the Basie band in 1937 and stayed for 50 years), bassist Walter Page, and drummer Jo Jones—was unique in its lightness, precision, and relaxation, becoming the precursor for modern jazz accompanying styles. Basie began his career as a stride pianist, reflecting the influence of Johnson and Waller, but the style most associated with him was characterized by spareness and precision. Whereas other pianists were noted for technical flash and dazzling dexterity, Basie was known for his use of silence and for reducing his solo passages to the minimum amount of notes required for maximum emotional and rhythmic effect. As one Basie band member put it, "Count don't do nothin'. But it sure sounds good."

The Basie orchestra had several hit recordings during the late 1930s and early '40s, among them "Jumpin' at the Woodside," "Every Tub," "Lester Leaps In," "Super Chief," "Taxi War Dance," "Miss Thing," "Shorty George," and "One O'Clock Jump," the band's biggest hit and theme song. It had continued success throughout the war years, but, like all big bands, it had declined in popularity by the end of the 1940s. During 1950 and '51, economy forced Basie to front an octet, the only period in his career in which he did not lead a big band. In 1952 increased demand for personal appearances allowed Basie to form a new orchestra that in many ways was as highly praised as his bands of the 1930s and '40s. (Fans distinguish the two major eras in Basie bands as the "Old Testament" and "New Testament.") The Basie orchestra of the 1950s was a slick, professional unit that was expert at sight reading and demanding arrangements. Outstanding soloists such as tenor saxophonists Lucky Thompson, Paul Quinichette, and Eddie "Lockjaw" Davis and trumpeters Clark Terry and Charlie Shavers, figured prominently. Singer Joe Williams, whose authoritative, blues-influenced vocals can be heard on hit recordings such as "Every Day I Have the Blues" and "Alright, Okay, You Win," was also a major component

in the band's success. Arrangers Neal Hefti, Buster Harding, and Ernie Wilkins defined the new band's sound on recordings such as "Li'l Darlin'," "The Kid from Red Bank," "Cute," and "April in Paris" and on celebrated albums such as *The Atomic Mr. Basie* (1957).

The 1950s band showcased the sound and style Basie was to employ for the remainder of his career, although there were to be occasional—and successful—experiments such as *Afrique* (1970), an album of African rhythms and avant-garde compositions that still managed to remain faithful to the overall Basie sound. Throughout the 1960s, Basie's recordings were often uninspired and marred by poor choice of material, but he remained an exceptional concert performer and made fine records with singers Ella Fitzgerald, Sarah Vaughan, and Frank Sinatra. When jazz record producer Norman Granz formed his Pablo label in the 1970s, several established jazz artists, including Basie, signed on in order to record unfettered by commercial demands. Basie benefited greatly from his association with Granz and made several recordings during the '70s that rank among his best work. He recorded less often with his big band during this era (although when he did, the results were outstanding), concentrating instead on small-group and piano-duet recordings. Especially noteworthy were the albums featuring the duo of Basie and Oscar Peterson, with Basie's economy and Peterson's dexterous virtuosity proving an effective study in contrasts. Many of Basie's albums of the '70s were Grammy Award winners or nominees.

Suffering from diabetes and chronic arthritis during his later years, Basie continued to front his big band until a month before his death in 1984. The band itself carried on into the next century, with Thad Jones, Frank Foster, and Grover Mitchell each assuming leadership for various intervals. Basie's autobiography, *Good Morning Blues*, written with Albert Murray, was published posthumously in 1985. Along with Duke Ellington, Count Basie is regarded as one of the two most important and influential bandleaders in the history of jazz.

BUDDY BOLDEN

(b. Sept. 6, 1877, New Orleans, La., U.S.—d. Nov. 4, 1931, Jackson, La.)

Cornetist Buddy Bolden is widely considered the founding father of jazz. Many jazz musicians, including Jelly Roll Morton and Louis Armstrong, acclaimed Bolden (born Charles Joseph Bolden) as one of the most powerful musicians ever to play jazz.

Little is known about the details of Bolden's career, but it is documented that by about 1895 he was leading a band. The acknowledged king of New Orleans lower musical life, Bolden often worked with six or seven different bands simultaneously. In 1906 his emotional stability began to crumble, and the following year

he was committed to the East Louisiana State Hospital, from which he never emerged.

CAB CALLOWAY

(b. Dec. 25, 1907, Rochester, N.Y., U.S.—d. Nov. 18, 1994, Hockessin, Del.)

Bandleader, singer, and all-around entertainer Cab Calloway was known for his exuberant performing style and for leading one of the most highly regarded big bands of the swing era.

After graduating from high school, Cabell "Cab" Calloway III briefly attended a law school in Chicago but quickly turned to performing in nightclubs as a singer. He began directing his own bands in 1928 and in the following year went to New York City. There he appeared in an all-black musical, Fats Waller's *Connie's Hot Chocolates*, in which he sang the Waller classic "Ain't Misbehavin'." In 1931 he was engaged as a bandleader at the Cotton Club; his orchestra, along with that of Duke Ellington's, became one of the two house bands most associated with the legendary Harlem nightspot. In the same year, Calloway first recorded his most famous composition, "Minnie the Moocher," a song that showcased his ability at scat singing. Other Calloway hits from the 1930s include "Kickin' the Gong Around," "Reefer Man," "The Lady with the Fan," "Long About Midnight," "The Man from Harlem," and "Minnie the Moocher's Wedding Day."

Cab Calloway. Schomburg Center for Research in Black Culture; The New York Public Library; Astor, Lenox and Tilden Foundations

Calloway was an energetic and humorous entertainer whose performance trademarks included eccentric dancing and wildly flinging his mop of hair; his standard accoutrements included a white tuxedo and an oversized baton. He was a talented vocalist with an enormous range and was regarded as "the most unusually and broadly gifted male singer of the '30s" by jazz scholar Gunther Schuller. Although his band rose to fame largely on the strength of his personal appeal, some critics felt that Calloway's antics drew focus away from one of the best assemblages of musicians in jazz. Calloway led a tight, professional unit during the early 1930s, but many regard his band of 1937–42 to be his best. Featured sidemen during those years included legendary jazz players such as pianist Bennie Payne, saxophonists Chu Berry and Ike Quebec, trombonist-vibraphonist Tyree Glenn, drummer Cozy Cole, and trumpeters Dizzy Gillespie, Doc Cheatham, Jonah Jones, and Shad Collins. The decline in popularity of big bands forced Calloway to disband his orchestra in 1948, and he continued for several years with a sextet.

Calloway also had a successful side career as an actor. He appeared in several motion pictures, including *The Big Broadcast* (1932), *Stormy Weather* (1943), *Sensations of 1945* (1944), and *The Cincinnati Kid* (1965). George Gershwin had conceived the role of "Sportin' Life" in his 1935 jazz opera *Porgy and Bess* for Calloway; the entertainer finally got his chance at the part during a heralded world tour of the show in 1952–54. In the 1960s, Calloway appeared on Broadway and on tour in *Hello, Dolly!*, portraying the role of Horace Vandergelder opposite Pearl Bailey as Dolly Levi, and he again starred on Broadway in the 1970s in the hit musical *Bubbling Brown Sugar*. His best-known acting performance was also his last, as a jive-talking music promoter in director John Landis's comedy *The Blues Brothers* (1980). The film featured

Calloway singing "Minnie the Moocher" every bit as energetically and eccentrically as he had performed it in 1931.

ORNETTE COLEMAN

(b. March 9, 1930, Fort Worth, Texas, U.S.)

Saxophonist, composer, and bandleader Ornette Coleman was the principal initiator and leading exponent of "free jazz" in the late 1950s.

Coleman began playing alto, then tenor saxophone as a teenager and soon became a working musician in dance bands and rhythm-and-blues groups. Early in his career, his approach to harmony was already unorthodox and led to his rejection by established musicians in Los Angeles, where he lived for most of the 1950s. While working as an elevator operator, he studied harmony and played an inexpensive plastic alto saxophone at obscure nightclubs. Until then, all jazz improvisation had been based on fixed harmonic patterns. In the "harmolodic theory" that Coleman developed in the 1950s, however, improvisers abandoned harmonic patterns ("chord changes") in order to improvise more extensively and directly upon melodic and expressive elements. Because the tonal centres of such music changed at the improvisers' will, it became known as "free jazz."

In the late 1950s Coleman formed a group with trumpeter Don Cherry, drummer Billy Higgins, and bassist Charlie Haden, with whom he recorded his first album, *Something Else* (1958). His classic recordings *The Shape of Jazz to Come* and *Change of the Century* in 1959 preceded his move that year to New York City, where his radical conception of structure and the urgent emotionality of his improvisations aroused widespread controversy. His recordings *Free Jazz* (1960), which used two simultaneously improvising jazz quartets, and "Beauty Is a Rare Thing," in which he successfully experimented with free metres and tempos, also proved influential.

In the 1960s Coleman taught himself to play the violin and trumpet, using unorthodox techniques. By the 1970s he was performing only irregularly, preferring instead to compose. His most notable extended composition is the suite *Skies of America,* which was recorded in 1972 by the London Symphony Orchestra joined by Coleman on alto saxophone. Influenced by his experience of improvising with native musicians in the Rif Mountains of Morocco in 1973, Coleman formed an electric band called Prime Time, whose music was a fusion of rock rhythms with harmonically free collective improvisations; this band remained his primary performance vehicle until the 1990s. In 2005, with a quartet made up of two acoustic double bass players (one bowing his instrument, the other plucking), a drummer, and Coleman himself (playing alto saxophone, trumpet, and violin), he recorded *Sound Grammar* during a live performance in Italy; the work, which was said to hearken back to his music of the 1960s, was awarded the Pulitzer Prize for music in 2007. Coleman's early style influenced not only fellow saxophonists but also players of all other instruments in jazz.

JOHN COLTRANE

(b. Sept. 23, 1926, Hamlet, N.C., U.S.—d. July 17, 1967, Huntington, N.Y.)

Saxophonist, bandleader, and composer John Coltrane was one of the most iconic figures of 20th-century jazz.

Coltrane's first musical influence was his father, a tailor and part-time musician. John studied clarinet and alto saxophone as a youth and then moved to Philadelphia in 1943 and continued his studies at the Ornstein School of Music and the Granoff Studios. He was drafted into the navy in 1945 and played alto sax with a navy band until 1946; he switched to tenor saxophone in 1947. During the late 1940s and early '50s, he played in nightclubs and on recordings with such musicians as Eddie ("Cleanhead") Vinson, Dizzy Gillespie, Earl Bostic, and Johnny Hodges. Coltrane's first recorded solo can be heard on Gillespie's "We Love to Boogie" (1951).

Coltrane (who was nicknamed Trane) came to prominence when he joined Miles Davis's quintet in 1955. His abuse of drugs and alcohol during this period led to unreliability, and Davis fired him in early 1957. He embarked on a six-month stint with Thelonious Monk and began to make recordings under his own name;

each undertaking demonstrated a new-found level of technical discipline, as well as increased harmonic and rhythmic sophistication.

During this period Coltrane developed what came to be known as his "sheets of sound" approach to improvisation, as described by poet LeRoi Jones (before he assumed the name Amiri Baraka): "The notes that Trane was playing in the solo became more than just one note following another. Notes came so fast, and with so many overtones and undertones, that they had the effect of a

John Coltrane, 1966. Reprinted with permission of *Down Beat* magazine

piano player striking chords rapidly but somehow articulating separately each note in the chord, and its vibrating subtones." Or, as Coltrane himself said, "I start in the middle of a sentence and move both directions at once." The cascade of notes during his powerful solos showed his infatuation with chord progressions, culminating in the virtuoso performance of "Giant Steps" (1959).

Coltrane's tone on the tenor sax was huge and dark, with clear definition and full body, even in the highest and lowest registers. His vigorous, intense style was original, but traces of his idols Johnny Hodges and Lester Young can be discerned in his legato phrasing and portamento (or, in jazz vernacular, "smearing," in which the instrument glides from note to note with no discernible breaks). From Monk he learned the technique of multiphonics, by which a reed player can produce multiple tones simultaneously by using a relaxed embouchure (i.e., position of the lips, tongue, and teeth), varied pressure, and special fingerings. In the late 1950s, Coltrane used multiphonics for simple harmony effects (as on his 1959 recording of "Harmonique"); in the 1960s, he employed the technique more frequently, in passionate, screeching musical passages.

Coltrane returned to Davis's group in 1958, contributing to the "modal phase" albums *Milestones* (1958) and *Kind of Blue* (1959), both considered essential examples of 1950s modern jazz. (Davis at this point was experimenting with modes—i.e., scale patterns other than major and minor.) His work on these recordings was always proficient and often brilliant, though relatively subdued and cautious.

After ending his association with Davis in 1960, Coltrane formed his own acclaimed quartet, featuring pianist McCoy Tyner, bassist Jimmy Garrison, and drummer Elvin Jones. At this time Coltrane began playing soprano saxophone in addition to tenor. Throughout the early 1960s Coltrane focused on mode-based improvisation in which solos were played atop one- or two-note accompanying figures that were repeated for extended periods of time (typified in his recordings of Richard Rodgers and Oscar Hammerstein's "My Favorite Things"). At the same time, his study of the musics of India and Africa affected his approach to the soprano sax. These influences, combined with a unique interplay with the drums and the steady vamping of the piano and bass, made the Coltrane quartet one of the most noteworthy jazz groups of the 1960s. Coltrane's wife, Alice (also a jazz musician and composer), played the piano in his band during the last years of his life.

During the short period between 1965 and his death in 1967, Coltrane's work expanded into a free, collective (simultaneous) improvisation based on prearranged scales. It was the most radical period of his career, and his avant-garde experiments divided critics and audiences.

Coltrane's best-known work spanned a period of only 12 years (1955–67), but, because he recorded prolifically, his musical development is well-documented. His somewhat tentative, relatively melodic early style can be heard on the Davis-led albums recorded for the Prestige and Columbia labels during 1955 and '56. *Thelonious Monk and John Coltrane* (1957) reveals Coltrane's growth in terms of technique and harmonic sense, an evolution further chronicled on Davis's albums *Milestones* and *Kind of Blue*. Most of Coltrane's early solo albums are of a high quality, particularly *Blue Train* (1957), perhaps the best recorded example of his early hard bop style. Recordings from the end of the decade, such as *Giant Steps* (1959) and *My Favorite Things* (1960), offer dramatic evidence of his developing virtuosity. Nearly all of the many albums Coltrane recorded during the early 1960s rank as classics; *A Love Supreme* (1964), a deeply personal album reflecting his religious commitment, is regarded as especially fine work. His final forays into avant-garde and free jazz are represented by *Ascension* and *Meditations* (both 1965), as well as several albums released posthumously.

Miles Davis

(b. May 26, 1926, Alton, Ill., U.S.—d. Sept. 28, 1991, Santa Monica, Calif.)

Although he was a great trumpeter, it was as a bandleader and composer that Miles Davis became one of the major influences on jazz in the late 1940s.

Starting Out

Davis grew up in East St. Louis, Ill., where his father was a prosperous dental surgeon. (In later years he often spoke of his comfortable upbringing, sometimes to rebuke critics who assumed that a background of poverty and suffering was common to all great jazz artists.) He began studying trumpet in his early teens; fortuitously, in light of his later stylistic development, his first teacher advised him to play without vibrato. Davis played with jazz bands in the St. Louis area before moving to New York City in 1944 to study at the Institute of Musical Art (now the Juilliard School)—although he skipped many classes and instead was schooled through jam sessions with masters such as Dizzy Gillespie and Charlie Parker. Davis and Parker recorded together often during the years 1945–48.

Davis's early playing was sometimes tentative and not always fully in tune, but his unique, intimate tone and his fertile musical imagination outweighed his technical shortcomings. By the early 1950s Davis had turned his limitations into considerable assets. Rather than emulate the busy, wailing style of such bebop pioneers as Gillespie, Davis explored the trumpet's middle register, experimenting with harmonies and rhythms and varying the phrasing of his improvisations.

With the occasional exception of multi-note flurries, his melodic style was direct and unornamented, based on quarter notes and rich with inflections. The deliberation, pacing, and lyricism in his improvisations are striking.

COOL JAZZ AND MODAL JAZZ

In the summer of 1948, Davis formed a nonet that included the renowned jazz artists Gerry Mulligan, J.J. Johnson, Kenny Clarke, and Lee Konitz, as well as players on French horn and tuba, instruments rarely heard in a jazz context. Mulligan, Gil Evans, and pianist John Lewis did most of the band's arrangements, which juxtaposed the flexible, improvisatory nature of bebop with a thickly textured orchestral sound. The group was short-lived but during its brief history recorded a dozen tracks that were originally released as singles (1949–50). These recordings changed the course of modern jazz and paved the way for the West Coast styles of the 1950s. The tracks were later collected in the album *Birth of the Cool* (1957).

During the early 1950s Davis struggled with a drug addiction that affected his playing, yet he still managed to record albums that rank among his best, including several with such jazz notables as Sonny Rollins, Milt Jackson, and Thelonious Monk. In 1954, having overcome the addiction, Davis embarked on a two-decade period during which he was considered the most innovative musician in jazz. He formed classic small groups in the 1950s that featured saxophone legends John Coltrane and Cannonball Adderley, pianists Red Garland and Bill Evans, bassist Paul Chambers, and drummers "Philly" Joe Jones and Jimmy Cobb. Davis's albums recorded during this era, including *'Round About Midnight* (1956), *Workin'* (1956), *Steamin'* (1956), *Relaxin'* (1956), and *Milestones* (1958), affected the work of numerous other artists. He capped this period of his career with *Kind of Blue* (1959), perhaps the most celebrated album in the history of jazz. A mellow, relaxed collection, the album includes the finest recorded examples of modal jazz, a style in which improvisations are based upon sparse chords and nonstandard scales rather than on complex, frequently changing chords. The modal style lends itself to solos that are focused on melody; this accessible quality ensured *Kind of Blue*'s popularity with jazz fans.

Released concurrently with the small-group recordings, Davis's albums with pieces arranged and conducted by Gil Evans—*Miles Ahead* (1957), *Porgy and Bess* (1958), and *Sketches of Spain* (1960)—were also monuments of the genre. The Davis-Evans collaborations were marked by complex arrangements, a near-equal emphasis on orchestra and soloist, and some of Davis's most soulful and emotionally powerful playing. Davis and Evans occasionally collaborated in later years, but never again so memorably as on these three masterful albums.

Miles Davis. Express Newspapers/Hulton Archive/Getty Images

FREE JAZZ AND FUSION

The early 1960s were transitional, less-innovative years for Davis, although his music and his playing remained top-calibre. He began forming another soon-to-be-classic small group in late 1962 with bassist Ron Carter, pianist Herbie Hancock, and teenage drummer Tony Williams; tenor saxophonist Wayne Shorter joined the lineup in 1964. Davis's new quintet was characterized by a light, free sound and a repertoire that extended from the blues to avant-garde and free jazz. Compared with the innovations of other modern jazz groups of the 1960s, the Davis quintet's experimentations in polyrhythm and polytonality were more subtle but equally daring. *Live at the Plugged Nickel* (1965), *E.S.P.* (1965), *Miles Smiles* (1966), and *Nefertiti* (1967) were among the quintet's timeless, influential recordings. About the time of *Miles in the Sky* and *Filles de Kilimanjaro* (both 1968), Davis began experimenting with electronic instruments. With other musicians, including keyboardists Chick Corea and Joe Zawinul and guitarist John McLaughlin, Davis cut *In a Silent Way* (1969), regarded as the seminal album of the jazz fusion movement. It was considered by purists to be Davis's last true jazz album.

Davis won new fans and alienated old ones with the release of *Bitches Brew* (1969), an album on which he fully embraced the rhythms, electronic instrumentation, and studio effects of rock music. A cacophonous kaleidoscope of layered sounds, rhythms, and textures, the album's influence was heard in such 1970s fusion groups as Weather Report and Chick Corea's Return to Forever. Davis continued in this style for a few years, with the album *Live-Evil* (1970) and the film sound track *A Tribute to Jack Johnson* (1970) being particular highlights.

LEGACY

Davis was injured in an auto accident in 1972, curtailing his activities, then retired from 1975 through 1980. When he returned to public notice with *The Man with the Horn* (1981), critics felt that Davis's erratic playing showed the effects of his five-year layoff, but he steadily regained his powers during the next few years. He dabbled in a variety of musical styles throughout the 1980s, concentrating mostly on jazz-rock dance music, but there were also notable experiments in other styles, such as a return to his blues roots (*Star People*, 1982) and a set of Gil Evans-influenced orchestral numbers (*Music from Siesta*, 1987). Davis won several Grammy Awards during this period for such albums as *We Want Miles* (1982), *Tutu* (1986), and *Aura* (1989). One of the most-memorable events of Davis's later years occurred at the Montreux Jazz Festival in 1991, when he joined with an orchestra conducted by Quincy Jones to perform some of the classic Gil Evans arrangements of the late 1950s. Davis died less than three months later. His final album, *Doo-Bop* (1992), was released posthumously.

Although critics dismissed much of the music Davis released after *Bitches Brew*, his excursions helped keep jazz popular with mainstream audiences. In later years he ignored the critics, and he defied convention by wandering around the stage, often playing with his back to the audience. In his much-praised and revealing autobiography, *Miles* (1989; with Quincy Troupe), he wrote frankly of his hedonistic past and of the racism he saw in the music industry. Along with Louis Armstrong, Duke Ellington, and Charlie Parker, Davis is regarded as one of the four most important and influential musicians in jazz history, as well as the music's most eclectic practitioner.

DUKE ELLINGTON

(b. April 29, 1899, Washington, D.C., U.S.—d. May 24, 1974, New York, N.Y.)

Pianist Duke Ellington was the greatest composer and bandleader in the history of jazz. One of the originators of big-band jazz, Ellington led his band for more than half a century, composed thousands of scores, and created one of the most distinctive ensemble sounds in all of Western music.

Born Edward Kennedy Ellington, he grew up in a secure middle-class family in Washington, D.C. His family encouraged his interests in the fine arts, and he began studying piano at age seven. He became engrossed in studying art during his high-school years, and he was awarded, but did not accept, a scholarship to the Pratt Institute, Brooklyn, N.Y. Inspired by ragtime performers, he began to perform professionally at age 17.

Ellington first played in New York City in 1923. Later that year he moved there and, in Broadway nightclubs, led a sextet that grew in time into a 10-piece ensemble. The singular blues-based melodies; the harsh, vocalized sounds of his trumpeter, Bubber Miley (who used a plunger ["wa-wa"] mute); and the sonorities of the distinctive trombonist Joe ("Tricky Sam") Nanton (who played muted "growl" sounds) all influenced Ellington's early "jungle style," as seen in such masterpieces as "East St. Louis Toodle-oo" (1926) and "Black and Tan Fantasy" (1927).

Extended residencies at the Cotton Club in Harlem (1927–32, 1937–38) stimulated Ellington to enlarge his band to 14 musicians and to expand his compositional scope. He selected his musicians for their expressive individuality, and several members of his ensemble—

including trumpeter Cootie Williams (who replaced Miley), cornetist Rex Stewart, trombonist Lawrence Brown, baritone saxophonist Harry Carney, alto saxophonist Johnny Hodges, and clarinetist Barney Bigard—were themselves important jazz artists. (The most popular of these was Hodges, who rendered ballads with a full, creamy tone and long portamentos.) With these exceptional musicians, who remained with him throughout the 1930s, Ellington made hundreds of recordings, appeared in films and on radio, and toured Europe in 1933 and 1939.

The expertise of this ensemble allowed Ellington to break away from the conventions of band-section scoring. Instead, he used new harmonies to blend his musicians' individual sounds and emphasized congruent sections and a supple ensemble that featured Carney's full bass-clef sound. He illuminated subtle moods with ingenious combinations of instruments; among the most famous examples is "Mood Indigo" in his 1930 setting for muted trumpet, unmuted trombone, and low-register clarinet. In 1931 Ellington began to create extended works, including such pieces as *Creole Rhapsody, Reminiscing in Tempo,* and *Diminuendo in Blue/Crescendo in Blue.* He composed a series of works to highlight the special talents of his soloists. Williams, for example, demonstrated his versatility in Ellington's noted miniature concertos "Echoes of Harlem" and "Concerto for Cootie." Some of Ellington's numbers—notably "Caravan" and "Perdido" by trombonist Juan Tizol—were cowritten or entirely composed by sidemen. Few of Ellington's soloists, despite their importance to jazz history, played as effectively in other contexts; no one else, it seemed, could match the inspiration that Ellington provided with his sensitive, masterful settings.

A high point in Ellington's career came in the early 1940s, when he composed several masterworks—including the above-mentioned "Concerto for Cootie," his fast-tempo showpieces "Cotton Tail" and "Ko-Ko," and the uniquely structured, compressed panoramas "Main Stem" and "Harlem Air Shaft"—in which successions of soloists are accompanied by diverse ensemble colours. The variety and ingenuity of these works, all conceived for three-minute, 78-rpm records, are extraordinary, as are their unique forms, which range from logically flowing expositions to juxtapositions of line and mood. Tenor saxophonist Ben Webster and bassist Jimmy Blanton, both major jazz artists, were with this classic Ellington band. By then, too, Billy Strayhorn, composer of what would become the band's theme song, "Take the 'A' Train," had become Ellington's composing-arranging partner.

Not limiting himself to jazz innovation, Ellington also wrote such great popular songs as "Sophisticated Lady," "Rocks in My Bed," and "Satin Doll"; in other songs, such as "Don't Get Around Much Any More," "Prelude to a Kiss," "Solitude," and "I Let a Song Go out of My Heart," he made wide interval leaps an Ellington trademark. A number of these hits were introduced by Ivie Anderson, who was the band's female vocalist in the 1930s.

During these years Ellington became intrigued with the possibilities of composing jazz within classical forms. His musical suite *Black, Brown and Beige* (1943), a portrayal of African American history, was the first in a series of suites he composed, usually consisting of pieces linked by subject matter. It was followed by, among others, *Liberian Suite* (1947); *A Drum Is a Woman* (1956), created for a television production; *Such Sweet Thunder* (1957), impressions of William Shakespeare's scenes and characters; a recomposed, reorchestrated version of *Nutcracker Suite* (1960; after Peter Tchaikovsky); *Far East Suite* (1964); and *Togo Brava Suite* (1971). Ellington's symphonic *A Rhapsody of Negro Life* was the basis for the film short *Symphony in Black* (1935), which also features the voice of Billie Holiday (uncredited). Ellington wrote motion-picture scores for *The Asphalt Jungle* (1950) and *Anatomy of a Murder* (1959) and composed for the ballet and theatre—including, at the height of the civil rights movement, the show *My People* (1964), a celebration of African American life. In his last decade he composed three pieces of sacred music: *In the Beginning God* (1965), *Second Sacred Concert* (1968), and *Third Sacred Concert* (1973).

Although Ellington's compositional interests and ambitions changed over the decades, his melodic, harmonic, and rhythmic characteristics were for the most part fixed by the late 1930s, when he was a star of the swing era. The broken, eighth-note melodies and arrhythms of bebop had little impact on him, though on occasion he recorded with musicians who were not band members—not only with other swing-era luminaries such as Louis Armstrong, Ella Fitzgerald, and Coleman Hawkins but also with later bop musicians John Coltrane and Charles Mingus. Ellington's stylistic qualities were shared by Strayhorn, who increasingly participated in composing and orchestrating music for the Ellington band. During 1939–67 Strayhorn collaborated so closely with Ellington that jazz scholars may never determine how much the gifted deputy influenced or even composed works attributed to Ellington.

The Ellington band toured Europe often after World War II; it also played in Asia (1963–64, 1970), West Africa (1966), South America (1968), and Australia (1970) and frequently toured North America. Despite this grueling schedule, some of Ellington's musicians stayed with him for decades; Carney, for example, was a band member for 47 years. For the most part, later replacements fit into roles that had been created by their distinguished predecessors; after 1950, for instance, the Webster-influenced Paul Gonsalves filled the band's solo tenor saxophone role originated by Webster. There were some exceptions to this generalization, such as trumpeter-violinist Ray Nance and high-note trumpet specialist Cat Anderson.

Not least of the band's musicians was Ellington himself, a pianist whose style originated in ragtime and the stride piano idiom of James P. Johnson and Willie "The Lion" Smith. He adapted his style for orchestral purposes, accompanying with vivid harmonic colours and, especially in later years, offering swinging solos with angular melodies. An elegant man, Ellington maintained a regal manner

Duke Ellington, c. 1974. Central Press/ Hulton Archive/ Getty Images

as he led the band and charmed audiences with his suave humour. His career spanned more than half a century—most of the documented history of jazz. He continued to lead the band until shortly before his death in 1974.

Ellington's sense of musical drama and of his players' special talents and his wide range of moods were rare indeed. His gift of melody and his mastery of sonic textures, rhythms, and compositional forms translated his often subtle, often complex perceptions into a body of music unequaled in jazz history. Charles Ives is perhaps his only rival for the title of the greatest American composer. Ellington's autobiography, *Music Is My Mistress,* was published in 1973.

ELLA FITZGERALD

(b. April 25, 1917, Newport News, Va., U.S.—d. June 15, 1996, Beverly Hills, Calif.)

Ella Fitzgerald, 1962. Keystone/Hulton Archive/Getty Images

Singer Ella Fitzgerald was world famous for the wide range and rare sweetness of her voice. She became an international legend during a career that spanned some six decades.

Singing in a style influenced by the jazz vocalist Connee Boswell, Fitzgerald won amateur talent contests in New York City before she joined the Chick Webb orchestra in 1935; Webb became the teenaged Fitzgerald's guardian when her mother died. She made her first recording, "Love and Kisses," in 1935, and her

first hit, "A-Tisket, A-Tasket," followed in 1938. After Webb's death in 1939, she led his band until it broke up in 1942. She then soloed in cabarets and theatres, toured internationally with such pop and jazz stars as Benny Goodman, Louis Armstrong, Duke Ellington, the Mills Brothers, the Ink Spots, and Dizzy Gillespie, and recorded prolifically.

During much of her early career she had been noted for singing and recording novelty songs. Her status rose dramatically in the 1950s when jazz impresario

Norman Granz became her manager. From 1956 to 1964 she recorded a 19-volume series of "songbooks," in which she interpreted nearly 250 outstanding songs by Richard Rodgers, Cole Porter, George Gershwin, Duke Ellington, Jerome Kern, Irving Berlin, and Johnny Mercer. This material, combined with the best jazz instrumental support, clearly demonstrated Fitzgerald's remarkable interpretative skills. Although her diction was excellent, her rendition of lyrics was intuitive rather than studied. For many years the star attraction of Granz's Jazz at the Philharmonic concert tours, she was also one of the best-selling jazz vocal recording artists in history. She appeared in films (notably *Pete Kelly's Blues* in 1955), on television, and in concert halls throughout the world. She also recorded a number of live concert albums and produced a notable duet version of *Porgy and Bess* (1957) with Armstrong. During the 1970s she began to experience serious health problems, but she continued to perform periodically, even after heart surgery in 1986, until about 1993.

Fitzgerald's clear tone and wide vocal range were complemented by her mastery of rhythm, harmony, intonation, and diction. She was an excellent ballad singer, conveying a winsome, ingenuous quality. Her infectious scat singing brought excitement to such concert recordings as *Mack the Knife: Ella in Berlin* and was widely imitated by others. She won 12 Grammy Awards and several other honours.

Dizzy Gillespie

(b. Oct. 21, 1917, Cheraw, S.C., U.S.—d. Jan. 6, 1993, Englewood, N.J.)

Trumpeter, composer, and bandleader Dizzy Gillespie was one of the seminal figures of the bebop movement.

Gillespie's father was a bricklayer and amateur bandleader who introduced his son to the basics of several instruments. After his father died in 1927, Gillespie (born John Birks Gillespie) taught himself the trumpet and trombone; for two years he attended the Laurinburg Institute in North Carolina, where he played in the band and took music classes. His first professional job was in Frankie Fairfax's band in Philadelphia; his early style showed the strong influences of his idol, trumpeter Roy Eldridge. Gillespie's penchant for clowning and capriciousness earned him the nickname Dizzy. In 1937 he was hired for Eldridge's former position in the Teddy Hill Orchestra and made his recording debut on Hill's version of "King Porter Stomp."

In the late 1930s and early '40s, Gillespie played in a number of bands, including those led by Cab Calloway, Ella Fitzgerald, Earl Hines, Duke Ellington, and Billy Eckstine. He also took part in many late-night jam sessions at Minton's Playhouse, a New York City nightclub, and was among the club's regulars who pioneered the bebop sound and style (others included Charlie Parker, Charlie Christian, Thelonious Monk, and Max Roach). In 1944 the first bebop recording session included Gillespie's "Woody 'n' You" and featured Gillespie and Coleman Hawkins. Ultimately, Charlie Parker and Gillespie were regarded as cofounders of the bebop movement; the two worked together in several small groups in the 1940s and early '50s. Although Parker was easily irritated by Gillespie's onstage antics, their musical relationship seemed to benefit from their personal friction and their competitive solos were inventive, even inspired.

Gillespie formed his own orchestra in the late 1940s, and it was considered to be one of the finest large jazz ensembles. Noted for complex arrangements and instrumental virtuosity, its repertoire was divided between the bop approach—from such arrangers as Tadd Dameron, John Lewis, George Russell, and Gillespie himself—and Afro-Cuban jazz (or, as Gillespie called it, "Cubop")—in such numbers as "Manteca," "Cubano Be," and "Cubano Bop," featuring conga drummer Chano Pozo. Gillespie formed other bands sporadically throughout the remainder of his career, but he played mostly in small groups from the 1950s onward.

To many, Gillespie ranks as the greatest jazz trumpeter of all time, with the possible exception of Louis Armstrong. He took the saxophone-influenced lines of Roy Eldridge and executed them faster, with greater ease and harmonic daring, playing his jagged melodies with abandon, reaching into the highest registers of the trumpet range, and improvising into precarious situations from which he seemed always to extricate himself. Gillespie helped popularize the interval of the augmented eleventh (flat fifth) as a characteristic sound in modern jazz, and he used certain stock phrases in his improvisations that became clichés when two generations of jazz musicians incorporated them into their own solos. His late 1940s look—beret, hornrim glasses, and goatee—became the unofficial "bebop uniform" and a precursor to the beatnik styles of the 1950s. Other personal trademarks included his bent-bell trumpet and his enormous puffy cheeks that ballooned when playing. Gillespie was also a noted composer whose songbook is a list of bebop's greatest hits; "Salt Peanuts," "Woody 'n' You," "Con Alma," "Groovin' High," "Blue 'n' Boogie," and "A Night in Tunisia" all became jazz standards.

Dizzy Gillespie, c. 1974. Hulton Archive/ Getty Images

Although his most innovative period was over by the end of the 1950s, Gillespie continued to perform at the highest level. During the 1970s he made several big band, small-group, and duet recordings (with such players as Oscar Peterson and Count Basie) that rank among his best work. As an active musical ambassador, Gillespie led several overseas tours sponsored by the U.S. State Department and traveled the world extensively, sharing his knowledge with younger players. During his last few years, he was the leader of the United Nations Orchestra, which featured such Gillespie protégés as Paquito D'Rivera and Arturo Sandoval. Gillespie's memoirs, *To Be, or Not . . . to Bop*, were published in 1979.

LIONEL HAMPTON

(b. April 20, 1908, Louisville, Ky., U.S.—d. Aug. 31, 2002, New York, N.Y.)

Jazz musician and bandleader Lionel Hampton was known for the rhythmic vitality of his playing and his showmanship as a performer. Best known for his work on the vibraphone, "Hamp" was also a skilled drummer, pianist, and singer.

As a boy, Hampton lived with his mother in Kentucky and Wisconsin before finally settling in Chicago, where he received tuition on the xylophone from percussionist Jimmy Bertrand. Hampton got his start playing drums in the Chicago Defender Newsboys' Band before moving to California in the late 1920s. There he played drums in a succession of bands, the most notable being Paul Howard's Quality Serenaders, with which Hampton made his recording debut in 1929. He next joined Les Hite's band and accompanied Louis Armstrong on several recordings. At one session in 1930, Armstrong asked Hampton to play a vibraphone that had been fortuitously left in the studio. The results were "Memories of You" and "Shine," the first jazz recordings to feature improvised vibraphone solos. From this point on, the vibes became Hampton's main instrument.

During the early 1930s, Hampton studied music for a brief period at the University of Southern California and appeared in a few films featuring Armstrong and Hite. After leaving Hite, Hampton led his own band in Los Angeles's Paradise Cafe, where he was discovered by Benny Goodman in 1936. Soon thereafter, the Benny Goodman Trio (Goodman, pianist Teddy Wilson, and drummer Gene Krupa) became a quartet with the addition of Hampton. As a member of the Goodman group for the next four years, Hampton made some of his most heralded recordings, taking memorable solos on such songs as "Dizzy Spells," "Avalon," and "Moonglow." Hampton was an energetic performer who provided the Goodman quartet with drive and dynamism. He was also, for a brief period, drummer with the Goodman orchestra after Gene Krupa left in 1938.

While still with Goodman, Hampton led recording sessions under his own name during the years 1937–39. The majority of these represent some of the best jazz of the era and feature such legendary musicians as Coleman Hawkins, Benny Carter, Nat Cole, Cootie Williams, Harry James, Red Allen, Ben Webster, and Charlie Christian. On these recordings, Hampton occasionally plays piano (on which he performed vibraphone-style with two fingers) or drums, but most feature him on the vibes and reveal him to be as sensitive with ballads as he is extroverted on up-tempo numbers.

Hampton left Goodman and formed his own band in 1940. He had his first major hit in 1942 with "Flying Home," the number that became his perennial theme song. One of the most long-lived and popular assemblages in jazz, Hampton's band included such noted musicians as Wes Montgomery, Clifford Brown, Art Farmer, Dexter Gordon, Quincy Jones, Jimmy Cleveland, and Cat Anderson; and the band's vocalists included Joe Williams, Dinah Washington, Betty Carter, and Aretha Franklin. The band's hit recordings of the 1940s included "Hamp's Boogie Woogie," "Midnight Sun," "Million Dollar Smile," and "Central Avenue Breakdown." As the 1940s progressed, Hampton's band incorporated bebop stylings into the arrangements, but it returned to old styles and played rhythm and blues with greater frequency (especially evident in the saxophone work of Illinois Jacquet) in the '50s. It was also during this decade that Hampton released two of his most celebrated recordings, "September in the Rain" (1953) and "Stardust" (1955), both featuring some of his most beautiful and creative vibes solos.

Hampton continued to lead big bands and small groups for the remainder of his career, which extended into the 21st century. He participated in an outstanding series of combo recordings during the mid 1950s on which he proved himself one of the few musicians not to be intimidated by the genius of pianist Art Tatum. In the 1960s Hampton started his own record label and undertook extensive tours of Europe, Africa, Japan, and the Philippines. He had a few reunions with the Benny Goodman Quartet throughout the years, none so memorable or poignant as an appearance at the 1973 Newport Jazz Festival, a few months before Gene Krupa's death. In the 1980s and '90s, Hampton was still drawing sellout crowds throughout the world. Despite bouts of ill health, he continued to perform on a limited basis into his 90s.

Although Red Norvo is credited as the first jazz musician to play the vibraphone, it was Hampton who extended the instrument's possibilities and made it a standard item in the jazz world, especially in small-group settings. A true jazz icon, Hampton received numerous awards and honours, including 15 honorary doctorates from universities throughout the world, and the music school at the University of Idaho is named in his honour.

COLEMAN HAWKINS

(b. Nov. 21, 1904, St. Joseph, Mo., U.S.—d. May 19, 1969, New York, N.Y.)

Coleman Hawkins was the first major saxophonist in the history of jazz. His improvisational mastery of the tenor saxophone, which had previously been viewed as little more than a novelty, helped establish it as one of the most popular instruments in jazz.

At age four Hawkins began to study the piano, at seven the cello, and at nine the saxophone. He became a professional musician in his teens, and, while playing with Fletcher Henderson's big band between 1923 and 1934, he reached his artistic maturity and became acknowledged as one of the great jazz artists. He left the band to tour Europe for five years and then crowned his return to the United States in 1939 by recording the hit "Body and Soul," an outpouring of irregular, double-timed melodies that became one of the most imitated of all jazz solos.

Hawkins was one of the first jazz horn players with a full understanding of intricate chord progressions, and he influenced many of the great saxophonists of the swing era (notably Ben Webster and Chu Berry) as well as such leading figures of modern jazz as Sonny Rollins and John Coltrane. Hawkins's deep, full-bodied tone and quick vibrato were the expected style on jazz tenor until the advent of Lester Young, and even after Young's appearance many players continued to absorb Hawkins's approach.

Coleman Hawkins, c. 1943. Reprinted with permission of *Down Beat* magazine

One of the strongest improvisers in jazz history, Hawkins delivered harmonically complex lines with an urgency and authority that demanded the listener's attention. He was also a noted ballad player who could create arpeggiated, rhapsodic lines with an intimate tenderness that contrasted with his gruff attack and aggressive energy at faster tempos.

Hawkins gave inspired performances for decades, managing to convey fire in his work long after his youth. From the 1940s on he led small groups, recording frequently and playing widely in the United States and Europe with Jazz at the Philharmonic and other tours. He willingly embraced the changes that occurred in jazz over the years, playing with Dizzy Gillespie and Max Roach in what were apparently the earliest bebop recordings (1944). In time he also became an outstanding blues improviser, with harsh low notes that revealed a new ferocity in his art. Despite alcoholism and ill health, he continued playing until shortly before his death in 1969.

FLETCHER HENDERSON

(b. Dec. 18, 1897, Cuthbert, Ga., U.S.—d. Dec. 29, 1952, New York, N.Y.)

Musical arranger, bandleader, and pianist Fletcher Henderson was a leading pioneer in the sound, style, and instrumentation of big band jazz.

Henderson was born into a middle-class family; his father was a school principal and his mother a teacher. He changed his name from James Fletcher Henderson to Fletcher Hamilton Henderson, Jr. (James was his grandfather's name, Fletcher Hamilton his father's), in 1916 when he entered Atlanta University, from which he graduated as a chemistry and math major. In 1920 he moved to New York, intending to work as a chemist while pursuing a graduate degree. Although he found a part-time laboratory job, he immediately began

getting work as a pianist. Within months he was a full-time musician, and he began working for W.C. Handy's music publishing company as a song plugger (i.e., promoting songs to performers). In 1921 he took a position as musical factotum for Black Swan records, the first black-owned recording company, for which he organized small bands to provide backing for such singers as Ethel Waters. He played piano for leading black singers on more than 150 records between 1921 and 1923 and then began a full-time career as a bandleader.

Although Henderson had shown an interest in music from childhood, when his mother taught him piano, he knew little about jazz until he was in his 20s. His orchestra, made up of well-established New York musicians, at first played standard dance-band fare, with occasional ragtime and jazz inflections. The band became more jazz-oriented in 1924 when Henderson hired the young trumpeter Louis Armstrong. At about the same time, the band's musical director and alto saxophonist, Don Redman, conceived the arrangements and instrumentation that would become the standard for big bands. The rhythm section was established as piano, bass, guitar, and drums; and the trumpet, trombone, and reed sections composed the front line. Arrangements were constructed in the call-and-response manner (e.g., the brass section "calls," the reed section "responds"), and many tunes were based upon "riffs," identifiable musical passages repeated throughout the song. After Redman left the band in

1927, Henderson used the same approach in his own arrangements.

Henderson (whose nickname was Smack) was a superb arranger but a poor businessman. Although the band had played major venues and been heard on the radio and in recordings, the band's finances were frequently in disarray, and musicians often left without notice to join other bands. He nevertheless managed to keep his band going until the mid-1930s, at which time he sold many of his arrangements to Benny Goodman, who used them to define the sound of his new band. "King Porter Stomp," "Down South Camp Meetin'," "Bugle Call Rag," "Sometimes I'm Happy," and "Wrappin' It Up" are among the Henderson arrangements that became Goodman hits.

Through the Goodman band, Henderson's arrangements became a blueprint for the sound of the swing era. (Other arrangers, including Henderson's brother Horace, also contributed to the big band sound of the 1930s.) Henderson arranged for Goodman for several years and formed a short-lived band of his own in 1936 that included Roy Eldridge, Chu Berry, John Kirby, and Sid Catlett. That year, Henderson issued "Christopher Columbus," which became the biggest hit released under his own name. Henderson had little success in his subsequent attempts to organize bands and spent most of the 1940s arranging for Goodman, Count Basie, and others. He formed a sextet in 1950 that became the house band at New York's Cafe Society, but he suffered a stroke soon thereafter and was forced to retire.

BILLIE HOLIDAY

(b. April 7, 1915, Philadelphia, Pa., U.S.—d. July 17, 1959, New York, N.Y.)

Jazz singer Billie Holiday, who thrilled audiences from the 1930s to the '50s, was one of the most renowned vocalists in the history of American popular music.

Born Elinore Harris (her preferred spelling was Eleanora), she was the daughter of Clarence Holiday, a professional musician who for a time played guitar with the Fletcher Henderson band. She and her mother used her maternal grandfather's surname, Fagan, for a time; then in 1920 her mother married a man surnamed Gough, and both she and Eleanora adopted his name. It is probable that in neither case did her mother have Eleanora's name legally changed. The singer later adopted her natural father's last name and took the name Billie from a favourite movie actress, Billie Dove. In 1928 she moved with her mother from Baltimore (where she had spent her childhood), to New York City, and after three years of subsisting by various means, she found a job singing in a Harlem nightclub. She had had no formal musical training, but, with an instinctive sense of musical structure and with a wealth of experience gathered at the root level of jazz and blues, she developed a singing style that was deeply moving and individual.

Billie Holiday, 1958. Reprinted with permission of *Down Beat* magazine

In 1933 Holiday made her first recordings, with Benny Goodman and others. Two years later a series of recordings with Teddy Wilson and members of Count Basie's band brought her wider recognition and launched her career as the leading jazz singer of her time. She toured with Basie and with Artie Shaw in 1937 and 1938 and in the latter year opened at the plush Café Society in New York City. About 1940 she began to perform exclusively in cabarets and in concert. Her recordings between 1936 and 1942 marked her peak years. During that period she was often associated with saxophonist Lester Young, who gave her the nickname "Lady Day."

In 1947 Holiday was arrested for a narcotics violation and spent a year in a rehabilitation centre. No longer able to obtain a cabaret license to work in New York City, Holiday nonetheless packed New York's Carnegie Hall 10 days after her release. She continued to perform in concert and in clubs outside of New York City, and she made several tours during her later years. Her constant struggle with heroin addiction ravaged her voice, although not her technique.

Holiday's dramatic intensity rendered the most banal lyric profound. Among the songs identified with her were "Strange Fruit" (based on a poem about lynching), "Fine and Mellow," "The Man I Love," "Billie's Blues," "God Bless the Child," and "I Wished on the Moon." The vintage years of Holiday's professional and private liaison with Young were marked by some of the best recordings of the interplay between a vocal line and an instrumental obbligato. In 1956 she wrote an autobiography, *Lady Sings the Blues* (with William Dufty), that was made into a motion picture in 1972.

JOHN LEWIS

(b. May 3, 1920, La Grange, Ill., U.S.—d. March 29, 2001, New York, N.Y.)

Pianist and composer-arranger John Lewis was an influential member of the Modern Jazz Quartet, one of the longest-lived and best-received groups in jazz history.

Reared in New Mexico by academically oriented parents, Lewis studied piano from childhood and, until 1942, anthropology and music at the University of New Mexico. He served in the U.S. Army (1942–45) and subsequently worked as a pianist with Dizzy Gillespie, arranging "Two Bass Hit," "Emanon," "Minor Walk," and his own "Toccata for Trumpet and Orchestra" for Gillespie's big band. His restrained piano style, which was influenced by classical music, made him a highly sought-after sideman, and he worked with Miles Davis (having arranged "Move," "Budo," and "Rouge" for Davis's album *Birth of the Cool*), Charlie Parker, Lester Young, and Illinois Jacquet.

In 1952 Lewis became the leader of the Modern Jazz Quartet (known as the MJQ), which featured vibraphonist Milt Jackson, bassist Percy Heath, and drummer Connie Kay. The MJQ's music was subtle and polite, quite close to Baroque chamber music, and often classed in the "cool jazz" category. Lewis also composed for nonjazz settings and wrote musical scores for cinema, ballet, and theatre. "Django" is the Lewis composition most frequently played by others. Among his solo recordings are *Midnight in Paris* (1988) and *Evolution* (1999), and he made several albums, including *The Chess Game, Vol. 1-2*, with his wife, Mirjana, a harpsichordist.

Lewis also was noted for promoting jazz among younger performers. After receiving a master's degree from the Manhattan School of Music in 1953, he taught at several institutions and helped establish the Lenox School of Jazz in Massachusetts. In addition, he served as the musical director for the Monterey Jazz Festival in California (1958–82) and for the American Jazz Orchestra (1985–92).

CHARLES MINGUS

(b. April 22, 1922, Nogales, Ariz., U.S.—d. Jan. 5, 1979, Cuernavaca, Mex.)

By integrating loosely composed passages with improvised solos, composer, bassist, bandleader, and pianist Charles Mingus both shaped and transcended jazz trends of the 1950s, '60s, and '70s.

Mingus studied music as a child in Los Angeles and at 16 began playing bass. The foundation of his technique was laid in five years of study with a symphonic musician. After stints with Louis Armstrong and Kid Ory in the early 1940s, Mingus wrote and played for the Lionel Hampton big band from 1947 to 1948 and recorded with Red Norvo. In the early 1950s he formed his own record label and the Jazz Composer's Workshop, a musicians' cooperative, in an attempt to circumvent the commercialism of the music industry.

Mingus drew inspiration from Duke Ellington, Charlie Parker, Thelonious Monk, African American gospel music, and Mexican folk music, as well as traditional jazz and 20th-century concert music. Though most of his best work represents close collaborations with improvising musicians such as trumpeter Thad Jones, drummer Dannie Richmond, alto saxophonist Jackie McLean, and woodwind-player Eric Dolphy, Mingus also wrote for larger instrumentations and composed several film scores.

As a bassist, Mingus was a powerhouse of technical command and invention; he was always more effective as a soloist than as an accompanist or sideman. The Mingus composition most frequently recorded by others is "Goodbye, Porkpie Hat," a tribute to Lester Young, and his most frequently cited extended work is "Pithecanthropus Erectus," a musical interpretation of human evolution. His volatile personality and opinions were captured in his autobiography, *Beneath the Underdog*, published in 1971.

MODERN JAZZ QUARTET (MJQ)

The Modern Jazz Quartet was noted for delicate percussion sonorities, innovations in jazz forms, and consistently high performance standards sustained over a long career. For most of its existence it was composed of Milt Jackson, vibes; John Lewis, piano; Percy Heath, bass; and Connie Kay, drums.

Jackson, Lewis, and drummer Kenny Clarke were pioneer bop musicians who had played together in the 1948 Dizzy Gillespie big band and pursued separate careers before adding Heath to form the Modern Jazz Quartet in 1952. Its early career was distinguished by introducing Lewis compositions such as "Django" and "Concorde." Clarke's departure in 1955 resulted in a loss of some of the group's rhythmic energy; his replacement was Kay, whose playing helped place the interplay of Jackson and Lewis in the foreground. Jackson, whose dynamic sensitivity and technical mastery brought a rare expressive quality to his instrument, was a virtuoso of melody, rhythmic detail, and swing. Lewis accompanied him not with the customary harmonic punctuations but rather with riffs (repeated melodic patterns) and melodic variations in a rhythmically simplified style that resulted in unique extended counterpoint; Heath, an uncommonly melodic bassist, and Kay accompanied.

Lewis's interest in baroque forms led him to compose fugues for the MJQ, and his classical-music-inspired works such as *The Comedy* (1962) and the film score *No Sun in Venice* (1957) are among the group's successes. Popular and jazz standards and Jackson songs were also part of its repertoire; in the 1980s it played, less successfully, arrangements of Duke Ellington compositions. In its album *Third Stream Music* (1957) the MJQ is joined by a string quartet and others in extended works by jazz and classical composers.

Its members also pursued separate careers during periods when the MJQ was not performing together, and in 1974 it disbanded. It began reuniting for annual tours in the 1980s. Following Kay's death in 1994, Albert "Tootie" Heath, brother of Percy, became the MJQ's drummer.

THELONIOUS MONK

(b. Oct. 10, 1917, Rocky Mount, N.C., U.S.—d. Feb. 17, 1982, Englewood, N.J.)

Pianist and composer Thelonious Monk was among the first creators of modern jazz.

As the pianist in the band at Minton's Play House, a nightclub in New York City, in the early 1940s, Monk had great influence on the other musicians who later developed the bebop movement. For much of his career Monk performed and recorded with small groups. His playing was percussive and sparse, often being described as "angular," and he used complex and dissonant harmonies and unusual intervals and rhythms. Monk's music was known for its humorous, almost playful, quality. He was also one of the most prolific composers in the history of jazz. Many of his compositions, which were generally written in the 12-bar blues or the 32-bar ballad form, became jazz standards. Among his best-known works are "Well, You Needn't," "I Mean You," "Straight, No Chaser," "Criss-Cross," "Mysterioso," "Epistrophy," "Blue Monk," and "'Round Midnight." He influenced the flavour of much modern jazz, notably the work of George Russell, Randy Weston, and Cecil Taylor.

JELLY ROLL MORTON

(b. Oct. 20, 1890, New Orleans, La., U.S.—d. July 10, 1941, Los Angeles, Calif.)

Composer and pianist Jelly Roll Morton pioneered the use of prearranged, semiorchestrated effects in jazz-band performances.

Morton (born Ferdinand Joseph La Menthe) learned the piano as a child and from 1902 was a professional pianist in the bordellos of the Storyville district of New Orleans. He was one of the pioneer ragtime piano players, but he would later invite scorn by claiming to have "invented jazz in 1902." He was, nevertheless, an important innovator in the transition from early jazz to orchestral jazz that took place in New Orleans about the turn of the century. About 1917 he moved west to California, where he played in night-clubs until 1922. He made his recording debut in 1923, and from 1926 to 1930 he made, with a group called Morton's Red Hot Peppers, a series of recordings that gained him a national reputation. Morton's music was more formal than the early Dixieland jazz, though his arrange-ments only sketched parts and allowed for improvisation. By the early 1930s, Morton's fame had been overshadowed by that of Louis Armstrong and other emerging innovators.

As a jazz composer, Morton is best remembered for such pieces as "Black Bottom Stomp," "King Porter Stomp," "Shoe Shiner's Drag," and "Dead Man Blues."

KING OLIVER

(b. May 11, 1885, Abend, La., U.S.—d. April 8, 1938, Savannah, Ga.)

Cornetist King Oliver was a vital link between the semimythical prehistory of jazz and the firmly documented history of jazz proper. He is also remembered for choosing as his protégé the man generally considered to have been the greatest of all New Orleans musicians, Louis Armstrong.

Born on a plantation, Joseph Oliver went to New Orleans as a boy and began playing the cornet in 1907. By 1915 he was an established bandleader and two years later was being billed as "King." In the following year, after the closing down of Storyville, the city's red-light district, Oliver moved to Chicago. Four years later he sent for Armstrong to join him as sec-ond cornetist, thus indirectly ensuring the spread of jazz across the continent and eventually the world. In 1928 he went to New York City, and from this point his fortunes declined. Plagued by dental trouble and outflanked by rapidly evolv-ing jazz styles, he died in obscurity while working as a poolroom marker.

CHARLIE PARKER

(b. Aug. 29, 1920, Kansas City, Kan., U.S.—d. March 12, 1955, New York, N.Y.)

Alto saxophonist, composer, and bandleader Charlie Parker is generally considered the greatest jazz saxophon-ist. A lyric artist, Parker was the principal stimulus of the modern jazz idiom known as bebop, and—together with Louis Armstrong and Ornette Coleman—he was one of the three great revolutionary geniuses in jazz.

Parker grew up in Kansas City, Mo., during the great years of Kansas City jazz and began playing alto saxophone when he was 13. At 14 he quit school and began performing with youth bands, and at 16 he was married—the first of his four marriages. The most significant of his early stylistic influences were tenor saxophone innovator Lester Young and the advanced swing-era alto saxophonist Buster Smith, in whose band Parker played in 1937. Two years later Parker experienced a personal stylistic breakthrough during a jam session in New York City. He described this moment of revelation in *Hear Me Talkin' to Ya* (1955), edited by Nat Hentoff and Nat Shapiro:

> *I'd been getting bored with the stereotyped changes (harmonies) that were being used all the time. ...I found that by using the higher intervals of a chord as a melody line and backing them with appropriately related changes I could play the thing I'd been hearing. I came alive.*

Parker recorded his first solos as a member of Jay McShann's band, with whom he toured the eastern United States in 1940–42. It was at this time that his childhood nickname "Yardbird" was shortened to "Bird." His growing friendship with trumpeter Dizzy Gillespie led Parker to develop his new music in avant-garde jam sessions in New York's Harlem. Bebop grew out of these experiments by Parker, Gillespie, and their adventurous colleagues; the music featured chromatic harmonies and, influenced especially by Parker, small note values and seemingly impulsive rhythms. Parker and Gillespie played in Earl Hines's swing-oriented

Charlie Parker, 1949. AP

band and Billy Eckstine's more modern band. In 1944 they formed their own small ensemble, the first working bebop group. The next year Parker made a series of classic recordings with Red Norvo, with Gillespie's quintet ("Salt Peanuts" and "Shaw Nuff"), and for his own first solo recording session ("Billie's Bounce," "Now's the Time," and "Koko"). The new music he was espousing aroused controversy but also attracted a devoted audience. By this time Parker had been addicted to drugs for several years. While working in Los Angeles with Gillespie's group and others, Parker collapsed in the summer of 1946, suffering from heroin and alcohol addiction, and was confined to a state mental hospital.

Following his release after six months, Parker formed his own quintet, which included trumpeter Miles Davis and drummer Max Roach. He performed regularly in New York City and on tours to major U.S. cities and abroad, played in a Gillespie concert at Carnegie Hall (1947), recorded with Machito's Afro-Cuban band (1949–50), and toured with the popular Jazz at the Philharmonic troupe (1949). A Broadway nightclub, Birdland, was named after him, and he performed there on opening night in late 1949; Birdland became the most famous of 1950s jazz clubs.

The recordings Parker made for the Savoy and Dial labels in 1945–48 (including the "Koko" session, "Relaxin' at Camarillo," "Night in Tunisia," "Embraceable You," "Donna Lee," "Ornithology," and "Parker's Mood") document his greatest period. He had become the model for a generation of young saxophonists. His alto tone was hard and ideally expressive, with a crying edge to his highest tones and little vibrato. One of his most influential innovations was the establishment of eighth notes as the basic units of his phrases. The phrases themselves he broke into irregular lengths and shapes and applied asymmetrical accenting. His brilliant, innovative technique—speed of execution, full sound in all registers, and precision during very fast tempos—was widely imitated.

Parker's most popular records, recorded in 1949–50, featured popular song themes and brief improvisations accompanied by a string orchestra. These recordings came at the end of a period of years when his narcotics and alcohol addictions had a less disruptive effect on his creative life. By the early 1950s, however, he had again begun to suffer from the cumulative effects of his excesses; while hospitalized for treatment of an ulcer, he was informed that he would die if he resumed drinking. He was banned from playing in New York City nightclubs for 15 months. He missed engagements and failed to pay his accompanying musicians, and his unreliability led his booking agency to stop scheduling performances for him. Even Birdland, where he had played regularly, eventually fired him. His two-year-old daughter died; his fourth marriage fell apart. He twice attempted suicide and again spent time in a mental hospital.

If Parker's life was chaotic in the 1950s, he nonetheless retained his creative edge. From roughly 1950 he abandoned his quintet to perform with a succession of usually small, ad hoc jazz groups; on occasion he performed with Latin American bands, big jazz bands (including Stan Kenton's and Woody Herman's), or string ensembles. Recording sessions with several quartets and quintets produced such pieces as "Confirmation," "Chi-Chi," and "Bloomdido," easily the equals of his best 1940s sessions. Outstanding performances that were recorded at concerts and in nightclubs also attest to his vigorous creativity during this difficult period. He wanted to study with classical composer Edgard Varèse, but, before the two could collaborate, Parker's battle with ulcers and cirrhosis of the liver got the better of him. While visiting his friend Baroness Nica de Koenigswarter, he was persuaded to remain at her home because of his illness; there, a week after his last engagement, he died of a heart attack.

Parker's concepts of harmony and melody were as influential as those of his tone and technique. Rejecting the diatonic scales common to earlier jazz, Parker improvised melodies and composed themes using chromatic scales. Often he played phrases that implied added harmonies or created passages that were only distantly related to his songs' harmonic foundations (chord changes). Yet for all the tumultuous feelings in his solos, he created flowing melodic lines. At slow tempos as well as fast, his were intense improvisations that communicated complex, often subtle emotions. The harmonies and inflections of the blues, which he played with passion and imagination, reverberated throughout his improvisations. Altogether, Parker's lyric art was a virtuoso music resulting from a coordination of nerve, muscle, and intellect that pressed human agility and creativity to their limits.

Parker's influence upon modern jazz was immense. His many followers included Ornette Coleman, John Coltrane, and Albert Ayler—leading figures in the development of free jazz. His difficult life was the subject of *Bird* (1988), a film directed by Clint Eastwood.

MAX ROACH

(b. Jan. 10, 1924, Newland, N.C., U.S.—d. Aug. 16, 2007, New York, N.Y.)

Jazz drummer and composer Max Roach was one of the most influential and widely recorded modern percussionists.

Roach grew up in New York City, and, as a child, he played drums in gospel bands. In the early 1940s he began performing with a group of innovative musicians—including Charlie Parker and Dizzy Gillespie—at such notable nightclubs as Monroe's Uptown House and Minton's Playhouse. Their jam sessions gave rise to bebop, a style of jazz that moved the fixed pulse from the bass drum to the ride cymbal and created a polyrhythmic, percussive texture by exploiting the flexibility of the trap-drum set. By carefully developing thematic ideas on his drums, Roach elevated the percussionist to the equal of melodic improvisers.

Roach participated in recordings by Parker's quintet in 1947–48 and in the Miles Davis sessions that were later collected in the album *Birth of the Cool* (1957). In 1954 he became coleader of a quintet with trumpeter Clifford Brown. The group produced a number of influential recordings before a car accident in 1956 killed Brown and another band member. Roach subsequently formed other ensembles, many of which did not include a pianist. In 1960 he composed, with lyricist Oscar Brown, Jr., "We Insist! Freedom Now Suite" for his future wife, vocalist Abbey Lincoln, a chorus, instrumental soloists, and ensemble. The work's theme of racial equality reflected Roach's political activism. In the early 1970s he established an all-percussion ensemble, M'Boom, and in 1972 he began teaching at the University of Massachusetts (Amherst). In 1980 he embarked on a series of duets with such avant-garde improvisers as pianist Cecil Taylor and saxophonist Anthony Braxton. Often involved in unusual projects, Roach performed with a rapper and accompanied authors' readings. His Max Roach Double Quartet was unique for its inclusion of improvising string players. Roach continued to tour into the early 21st century. Among his numerous compositions were works for plays, films, and dance pieces. Roach received many honours, including a MacArthur Foundation grant (1988).

SONNY ROLLINS

(b. Sept. 7, 1930, New York, N.Y., U.S.)

Tenor saxophonist Sonny Rollins was among the finest improvisers on the instrument to appear since the mid-1950s.

Rollins (born Theodore Walter Rollins) grew up in a neighbourhood where Thelonious Monk, Coleman Hawkins (his early idol), and Bud Powell were playing. After recording with the latter in 1949, Rollins began recording with Miles Davis in 1951. During the next three years he composed three of his best-known tunes, "Oleo," "Doxy," and "Airegin," and continued to work with Davis, Charlie Parker, and others. Following his withdrawal from music in 1954 to cure a heroin addiction, Rollins reemerged with the Clifford Brown–Max Roach quintet in 1955, and the next four years proved to be his most fertile.

Beginning with a style drawn primarily from Parker, Rollins became a master of intelligent and provocative spontaneity that was combined with an excellent command of the tenor sax. The clarity of thought evident in his improvisations stands out in jazz history. Rollins, whose nickname was "Newk," displayed an interest in unaccompanied saxophone improvisation and gross manipulations of tone colour long before such techniques became common in modern jazz. He was also one of the first to successfully improvise when alternately ignoring tempo and swinging within a single solo while his accompanists adhered to a preset tempo and chord progression. In these respects he was particularly influential with avant-garde saxophonists of the 1960s and '70s.

BILLY STRAYHORN

(b. Nov. 29, 1915, Dayton, Ohio,
U.S.—d. May 31, 1967, New York, N.Y.)

Pianist and composer Billy Strayhorn spent his entire career in collaboration with and as amanuensis to the composer and bandleader Duke Ellington.

Educated privately, Strayhorn applied to Ellington in 1938 for work as a lyricist, using his own composition "Lush Life" as a credential. In 1939 Ellington made his first recording of a Strayhorn composition; it was the first of many, including the highly popular "Take the 'A' Train" and "Chelsea Bridge," an excellent example of the composer's refined, impressionistic style. Strayhorn was also an accomplished pianist who rarely did justice to his own talent. His work as a composer became so intertwined with Ellington's that it was said that eventually neither man was able to distinguish his own contributions to their joint work. Strayhorn worked on most of Ellington's major concert works and unquestionably exerted a great influence upon him.

SUN RA

(b. May 22, 1914, Birmingham, Ala.,
U.S.—d. May 30, 1993, Birmingham)

Composer and keyboard player Sun Ra led a free jazz big band known for its innovative instrumentation and the theatricality of its performances.

Sun Ra, who claimed to have been born on the planet Saturn, grew up in Birmingham as Herman "Sonny" Blount, studied piano under noted teacher Fess Wheatley, and attended Alabama Agricultural and Mechanical College (now University). By the mid-1940s he was living in Chicago and scoring music for nightclub floor shows. In 1946–47 he was apprenticed to swing bandleader-arranger Fletcher Henderson. From the 1950s he led his own bands, the variously constituted Arkestras, which played his own music: an expanded hard bop that included tympani, electric piano, and flute—instruments then rare in jazz. He also was a pioneer of modal jazz settings; among his early works, "Ancient Aiethopia" most successfully unites the diverse strands of his composing.

Sun Ra's music became increasingly exotic with the addition of African and Latin-American instruments. After the Arkestra moved to New York about 1960, he became wholly involved with free jazz; he dispensed with composition entirely, creating works by conducting his improvisers. Among his free jazz recordings, *The Magic City* (1965/66) is the most significant. The Arkestra, which included dancers, dressed in fantastical costumes inspired by ancient Egyptian attire and the space age, and Sun Ra (whose formal name was Le Sony'r Ra) conducted while wearing flowing robes and futuristic helmets. He was highly regarded for his atonal solos on synthesizer, an instrument that he virtually pioneered in jazz.

During the 1970s and '80s Sun Ra's Arkestra made increasing use of earlier compositions of his own and of composers such as Henderson, Duke Ellington, and Thelonious Monk. He and his music are featured in the films *The Cry of Jazz* (1959), *Space Is the Place* (1971), and *Sun Ra: A Joyful Noise* (1980).

ART TATUM

(b. Oct. 13, 1910, Toledo, Ohio, U.S.—d. Nov. 5, 1956, Los Angeles, Calif.)

Blind, self-taught pianist Art Tatum is considered one of the greatest technical virtuosos in jazz.

At 13, after starting on violin, Tatum concentrated on the piano and was soon performing on local radio programs. At 21 he moved to New York City, where he made his most impressive recordings during the 1930s and '40s using a stride-style left hand and highly varied right-hand stylings. In 1943 he organized a trio with guitarist Tiny Grimes and bassist Slam Stewart, and he played mostly in the trio format for the rest of his life.

In his improvisations Tatum was given to spontaneously inserting entirely new chord progressions (sometimes with a new chord on each beat) into the small space of one or two measures. His reharmonization of pop tunes became a standard practice among modern jazz musicians, horn players as well as pianists. In rhythmically unpredictable spurts he often generated lines with notes cascading across each other while weaving in and out of tempo.

Few jazz pianists fail to incorporate at least one favourite Tatum run or embellishment in their playing. Several jazz pianists—including Bud Powell, Lennie Tristano, and Oscar Peterson—as well as other jazz musicians clearly exhibit and credit Tatum's influence.

SARAH VAUGHAN

(b. March 27, 1924, Newark, N.J., U.S.—d. April 3, 1990, Hidden Hills, Calif.)

Vocalist and pianist Sarah Vaughan was known for her rich voice, with an unusually wide range, and for the inventiveness and virtuosity of her improvisations.

Vaughan was the daughter of amateur musicians. She began studying piano and organ at age seven and sang in the church choir. After winning an amateur contest at Harlem's famed Apollo Theatre in 1942, she was hired as a singer and second pianist by the Earl Hines Orchestra. A year later she joined the singer Billy Eckstine's band, where she met Dizzy Gillespie and Charlie Parker. Vaughan's singing style was influenced by their instruments—"I always wanted to imitate the horns." Gillespie, Parker, and Vaughan recorded "Lover Man" together in 1945.

By the mid-1940s, Vaughan began singing with John Kirby and appearing on television variety shows. During the 1950s her audience grew as she toured both the United States and Europe and she signed with Mercury Record Corporation and EmArcy, Mercury's jazz label, in 1953 to sing both pop and jazz. She also appeared in three movies in this period, *Jazz Festival* (1956), *Disc Jockey* (1951), and *Basin Street Revue* (1956).

A contralto with a range of three octaves who earned the nicknames "Sassy" and "the Divine One," she came to be regarded as one of the greatest of all jazz singers. Among her best-known songs were "It's Magic," "Make Yourself Comfortable," "Broken-Hearted Melody," "Misty," and "Send in the Clowns." Vaughan died in 1990, the same year in which she was inducted into the Jazz Hall of Fame.

FATS WALLER

(b. May 21, 1904, New York, N.Y., U.S.—d. Dec. 15, 1943, Kansas City, Mo.)

Pianist and composer Fats Waller was one of the few outstanding jazz musicians to win wide commercial fame, though this was achieved at a cost of obscuring his purely musical ability under a cloak of broad comedy.

Born Thomas Wright Waller but better known as Fats, Waller overcame opposition from his clergyman father to become a professional pianist at 15, working in cabarets and theatres. Soon he was deeply influenced by James P. Johnson, the founder of the stride school of jazz piano. By the late 1920s he was also an established songwriter whose work often appeared in Broadway revues. From 1934 on he made hundreds of recordings with his own small band, in which excellent jazz was mixed with slapstick in a unique blend.

His best-known songs include "Ain't Misbehavin'," "Honeysuckle Rose," and his first success, "Squeeze Me" (1925), written with Clarence Williams. He was the first jazz musician to master the organ, and he appeared in several films, including *Stormy Weather* (1943). Usually remembered as a genial clown, he is of lasting importance as one of the greatest of all jazz pianists and as a gifted songwriter, whose work in both fields was rhythmically contagious.

LESTER YOUNG

(b. Aug. 27, 1909, Woodville, Miss., U.S.—d. March 15, 1959, New York, N.Y.)

Tenor saxophonist Lester Young emerged in the mid-1930s Kansas City, Mo., jazz world with the Count Basie band and introduced an approach to improvisation that provided much of the basis for modern jazz solo conception.

Young's tone was a striking departure from the accepted full-bodied, dark, heavy variety, with its quick vibrato, because his was light in weight, colour, and texture, with a slow vibrato. The swinging,

DECCA RECORDS

Formed as an American division by its British parent company in 1934, Decca was the only major company to stand by its roster of African American musicians during the 1940s, although most of its artists—including vocal groups (the Mills Brothers and the Ink Spots) and big bands (led by Lionel Hampton and Buddy Johnson)—worked in prewar idioms. Decca's black roster was supervised by Milt Gabler, a jazz fan who had previously run his own Commodore label. At Decca, Gabler formed a close relationship with Louis Jordan, whose hugely popular and influential jump-blues combo topped the black music market's best-seller chart for an unrivaled total of 118 weeks during the 1940s.

When Jordan left Decca to join the independent Aladdin label in 1954, Gabler signed a white group with a comparable style: Bill Haley and His Comets. The first sessions with Haley, recorded at Manhattan's Pythian Temple, resulted in two extremely influential hits—a cover version of Joe Turner's recent rhythm-and-blues hit "Shake Rattle and Roll" and the record that was to become one of the best-selling rock-and-roll hits of all time, "Rock Around the Clock." In an attempt to take advantage of the more flexible procedures of the independent sector (notably in radio promotion), Decca set up two independently distributed subsidiary labels, Brunswick and Coral, whose rosters included Buddy Holly, the Crickets, and Jackie Wilson.

rhythmic feeling in his improvisations was far more relaxed and graceful than that usually heard in the work of others during the 1930s. His lines were streamlined, logical, and refreshingly melodic. The impact of his style was so broad that he has been cited as a favourite by such diverse modern jazz figures as Charlie Parker, Stan Getz, and John Coltrane. Much of the West Coast "cool" style was a direct product of Lester Young's approach, many saxophonists playing his lines note for note in their own performances. He was so important that singer Billie Holiday called him president of tenor saxophonists, and he was known thereafter as Pres (or Prez). His best-known performances include "Taxi War Dance," "D.B. Blues," and "Lester Leaps In."

Lester Young, c. *1955*. Reprinted with permission of *Down Beat* magazine

FOLK AND BLUES

Blues began in the South, thrived as acoustic country blues, especially in the Mississippi Delta, and moved to the North as part of the Great Migration. Blues became electrified in Chicago, largely to be heard above the din of the patrons in the bars in which it was played. Blues is the sound of survival, the poking of an exposed wound by the injured to prove that he or she is down but not out. As the 20th century blended into the 21st, blues became more peripheral to African American popular culture, more of interest to musicologists and a narrower audience of devotees, many of whom were not black; however, blues remains an essential part of African American cultural history. In addressing that ongoing significance in his book *Blues People*, LeRoi Jones (Amiri Baraka) wrote, "As I began to get into the history of the music, I found that this was impossible without, at the same time, getting deeper into the history of the people. The music was the score, the creative reflection of Afro-American life, explaining the history as the history was explaining the music."

BIG BILL BROONZY

(b. June 26, 1893, Scott, Miss., U.S.—d. Aug. 14, 1958, Chicago, Ill.)

Blues singer and guitarist Big Bill Broonzy was the epitome of the tradition of itinerant folk blues.

Broonzy (born William Lee Conley Broonzy) grew up in Arkansas. He served in the army (1918–19) and moved to Chicago in 1920, where six years later he made his recording debut as guitar accompanist to black blues singers. Later he became a singer himself and by 1940 was recognized as one of the best-selling blues recording artists. His New York City concert debut was made at Carnegie Hall in 1938. In 1951 he visited Europe and soon became popular across that continent. At the height of his popularity in 1957, his vocal effectiveness was reduced by a lung operation, and he died the following year of cancer. Many students of the blues have found his work almost as fascinating for its sociological as for its strictly musical content. His mother, who was born a slave, died in 1957 at the age of 102, having survived to see Broonzy become a world-famous figure. His autobiography, *Big Bill Blues,* appeared in 1955.

WILLIE DIXON

(b. July 1, 1915, Vicksburg, Miss., U.S.—d. Jan. 29, 1992, Burbank, Calif.)

As record producer, bassist, and prolific songwriter, Willie Dixon exerted a major influence on the post-World War II Chicago Blues style.

Dixon's mother wrote religious poetry, and he sang in a gospel quartet before moving to Chicago in 1936. The following year he won the Illinois Golden Glove amateur heavyweight boxing championship. He began playing the double bass in

1939 and worked extensively with the Big Three Trio (1946–52). When that group dissolved, he began working full-time for Chess Records, serving as a house bassist and arranger on recording sessions. Dixon's upbeat blues compositions, which he sold for as little as $30, helped usher in the Chicago blues sound of the 1950s.

Among his best-known songs are "I'm Your Hoochie Coochie Man" and "I'm Ready," written for Muddy Waters; "Little Red Rooster" and "Back Door Man," for Howlin' Wolf; "My Babe," for Little Walter; "Bring It on Home," for the second Sonny Boy Williamson (Alex "Rice" Miller); and "The Seventh Son" and "Wang Dang Doodle." In the late 1950s he worked with the short-lived Cobra label; in the 1960s he toured Europe with the American Folk Blues Festival and formed the Chicago Blues All-Stars, which traveled widely throughout the United States and Europe. Rock performers such as the Rolling Stones, Jimi Hendrix, Elvis Presley, and Led Zeppelin recorded his songs. He was the founder of the Blues Heaven Foundation, a nonprofit organization designed to benefit destitute blues performers and provide scholarships to young musicians. His autobiography is entitled *I Am the Blues* (1989).

W.C. HANDY

(b. Nov. 16, 1873, Florence, Ala., U.S.—d. March 28, 1958, New York, N.Y.)

Composer W.C. Handy changed the course of popular music by integrating the blues idiom into then-fashionable ragtime music. Among his best-known works is the classic *St. Louis Blues*.

William Christopher Handy was a son and grandson of Methodist ministers, and he was educated at Teachers Agricultural and Mechanical College in Huntsville, Ala. Going against family tradition, he began to cultivate his interest in music at a young age and learned to play several instruments, including the organ, piano, and guitar; he was a particularly skilled cornetist and trumpet player. Longing to experience the world beyond Florence, Handy left his hometown in 1892. He traveled throughout the Midwest, taking a variety of jobs with several musical groups. He also worked as a teacher in 1900–02. He conducted his own orchestra, the Knights of Pythias from Clarksdale, Miss., from 1903 to 1921. During the early years of this period of his life, Handy was steeped in the music of the Mississippi Delta and of Memphis, and he began to arrange some of those tunes for his band's performances. Unable to find a publisher for the songs he was beginning to write, Handy formed a partnership with Harry Pace and founded Pace & Handy Music Company (later Handy Brothers Music Company).

Handy worked during the period of transition from ragtime to jazz. Drawing on the vocal blues melodies of African American folklore, he added harmonizations to his orchestral arrangements. His work helped develop the conception of the blues as a harmonic framework within which to improvise. With his "Memphis

W.C. Handy. Michael Ochs Archives/ Getty Images

Blues" (published 1912) and especially his "St. Louis Blues" (1914), he introduced a melancholic element, achieved chiefly by use of the "blue" or slightly flattened seventh tone of the scale, which was characteristic of African American folk music. Later he wrote other blues pieces (*Beale Street Blues,* 1916; *Loveless Love*) and several marches and symphonic compositions. He issued anthologies of African American spirituals and blues (*Blues: An Anthology*, 1926; *W.C. Handy's Collection of Negro Spirituals*, 1938; *A Treasury of the Blues*, 1949) and studies of black American musicians (*Negro*

Authors and Composers of the United States, 1938; *Unsung Americans Sung*, 1944). His autobiography, *Father of the Blues*, was published in 1941.

ALBERTA HUNTER

(b. April 1, 1895, Memphis, Tenn., U.S.—d. Oct. 17, 1984, New York, N.Y.)

Blues singer Alberta Hunter achieved international fame in the 1930s for her vigorous and rhythmically infectious style.

Hunter's father abandoned the family soon after her birth. Her mother, who worked as a domestic in a brothel, remarried about 1906, but Alberta did not get along with her new family.

Hunter ran away to Chicago about the age of 11 (the reports of dates and age vary). There she took a job in a boardinghouse for $6 a week, plus room and board. By dressing up to look older she was able to sneak into clubs, where she asked for a chance as a singer. By 1915 she was singing—though not among the headliners—at the Panama Café, home to many leading blues singers of the day.

Sometime between 1913 and 1915, her mother moved to live with her. Hunter later relocated to New York City. Although she bought several homes in New York and was based there for most of the rest of her life, the city always represented a constant struggle for work. For one of her jobs she traveled on the Keith-Albee vaudeville circuit. Hunter's original song

"Downhearted Blues" brought her recognition in 1923 when it was recorded by Bessie Smith, and in 1926 she replaced Smith in the leading role of *How Come?* on Broadway. In 1927 Hunter began her legendary travels between New York City, Europe, and Chicago, performing in nightclubs and theatre productions, most successfully in Europe, including the 1928–29 London production of *Showboat* with Paul Robeson. She returned to the United States in 1929, but the Great Depression eroded even the dubious security of vaudeville; in 1933 she headed back to Europe, where work was more plentiful and racism less evident. In 1935 she played a role in the English film *Radio Parade* and was part of the final sequence, shot in colour. In 1937 she caught the attention of NBC executives, and she returned briefly to New York City for a job with NBC radio. She settled in the United States permanently in late 1938, when the State Department warned of imminent war in Europe.

Hunter toured extensively for the USO during World War II and again later during the Korean War. After World War II she performed in England, toured Canada, and played long residences in Chicago. She retired from active performing in 1954.

Against the advice of friends, Hunter then began a second career as a practical nurse. Lying about her age, she enrolled in a three-year YWCA training program. She was offered a job before her training ended, and she completed 20 years of service before reaching the mandatory retirement age of 70 in 1977. (She was actually 82.) When completing a form requesting welfare, she indicated that she was actively looking for work and had only left nursing because she had been forced to retire. By all accounts she was an excellent practical nurse and had particularly good rapport with her patients.

Unbeknownst to her nursing colleagues, Hunter was coaxed into making two recordings during her nursing career, with Lovie Austin in 1961 and Jimmy Archey in 1962. Five months after her retirement party, she returned to performing at the Cookery, a nightclub in Greenwich Village, New York City. Her comeback led to greater fame than she had ever experienced during her earlier singing career. Hunter continued performing until a few months before her death.

ELMORE JAMES

(b. Jan. 27, 1918, Richland, Miss., U.S.—d. May 24, 1963, Chicago, Ill.)

Blues singer-guitarist Elmore James is remembered for the urgent intensity of his singing and guitar playing. He also was a significant influence on the development of rock music.

Born into a sharecropping family, James (born Elmore Brooks) played guitar in his teens and toured the Mississippi Delta with Robert Johnson, the principal influence on his music, in the late 1930s.

He then performed in the South with the second Sonny Boy Williamson (Alex "Rice" Miller) before becoming a mainstay of Chicago blues in the 1950s. He recorded several versions of his 1952 hit "Dust My Broom" and repeated that song's opening guitar chorus on many later recordings. Characteristically, his singing was harsh, including shouted phrases, and his vivid slide guitar replies featured heavy amplifier reverberation. His most-praised work began in 1958 and included the slow blues songs "The Sky Is Crying" (1959) and "It Hurts Me Too" (1965). Numerous rock musicians, including the Rolling Stones and Eric Clapton, adopted his hard-driving style and often recorded his songs. James was inducted into the Rock and Roll Hall of Fame in 1992.

ROBERT JOHNSON

(b. c. 1911, Hazlehurst, Miss., U.S.—d. Aug. 16, 1938, near Greenwood, Miss.)

The eerie falsetto singing voice and masterful, rhythmic slide guitar playing of Robert Johnson influenced both his contemporaries and many later blues and rock musicians.

Johnson was the product of a confusing childhood, with three men serving as his father before he reached age seven. Little is known about his biological father (Noah Johnson, whom his mother never married), and the boy and his mother lived on various plantations in the Mississippi Delta region before settling briefly in Memphis, Tenn., with her first husband (Robert Dodds, who had changed his surname to Spencer). The bulk of Johnson's youth, however, was spent in Robinsonville, Miss., with his mother and her second husband (Dusty Willis). There Johnson learned to play the Jew's harp and harmonica before taking up the guitar. In 1929 he married 16-year-old Virginia Travis, whose death in childbirth (along with that of their baby) in April 1930 devastated Johnson.

In Robinsonville he came in contact with well-known Mississippi Delta bluesmen Willie Brown, Charley Patton, and Son House—all of whom influenced his playing and none of whom was particularly impressed by his talent. They were dazzled by his musical ability, however, when he returned to town after spending as much as a year away. That time away is central to Johnson's mythic status. According to legend, during that period Johnson made a deal with Satan at a crossroads, acquiring his prodigious talent as a guitarist, singer, and songwriter in exchange for the stipulation that he would have only eight more years to live. (A similar story circulated in regard to another Mississippi bluesman, Tommy Johnson.) Music historian Robert Palmer, in his highly regarded book *Deep Blues* (1981), instead ascribes Robert Johnson's remarkable musical attainments to the time he had to hone his skills as a guitarist under the instruction of Ike Zinneman as a result of the financial support he received from the older woman he married near Hazlehurst, Miss. (Johnson's birthplace), and to the wide variety of music to which he was exposed during his hiatus from Robinsonville, including the single-string picking styles of Lonnie Johnson and Scrapper Blackwell.

After returning briefly to Robinsonville, Johnson settled in Helena, Ark., where he played with Elmore James, Robert Nighthawk, and Howlin' Wolf, among others. He also became involved with Estella Coleman and informally adopted her son, Robert Lockwood, Jr., who later became a notable blues musician under the name Robert Jr. Lockwood. Johnson traveled widely throughout Mississippi, Arkansas, Texas, and Tennessee and as far north as Chicago and New York, playing at house parties, juke joints, and lumber camps and on the street. In 1936–37 he made a series of recordings in a hotel room in San Antonio, Texas, and a warehouse in Dallas. His repertoire included several blues songs by House and others, but Johnson's original numbers, such as "Me and the Devil Blues," "Hellhound on My Trail," "Sweet Home Chicago," "I Believe I'll Dust My Broom," "Ramblin' on My Mind," and "Love in Vain" are his most compelling pieces. Unlike the songs of many of his contemporaries—which tended to unspool loosely, employing combinations of traditional and improvised lyrics— Johnson's songs were tightly composed, and his song structure and lyrics were praised by Bob Dylan. Despite the limited number of his recordings, Johnson had a major impact on other musicians, including Muddy Waters, Elmore James, Eric Clapton, and the Rolling Stones. Johnson died of poisoning after drinking strychnine-laced whiskey in a juke joint.

B.B. KING

(b. Sept. 16, 1925, Itta Bena, near Indianola, Miss., U.S.)

Guitarist and singer B.B. King was a principal figure in the development of blues and from whose style leading popular musicians drew inspiration.

Riley B. King was reared in the Mississippi Delta, and gospel music in church was the earliest influence on his singing. To his own impassioned vocal calls, King played lyrical single-string guitar responses with a distinctive vibrato; his guitar style was influenced by T-Bone Walker, by delta blues players (including his cousin Bukka White), and by such jazz guitarists as Django Reinhardt and Charlie Christian. He worked for a time as a disk jockey in Memphis, Tenn. (notably at station WDIA), where he acquired the name B.B. (for Blues Boy) King. In 1951 he made a hit record of "Three O'Clock Blues," which led to virtually continuous tours of clubs and theatres throughout the country. He often played 300 or more one-night stands a year with his 13-piece band. A long succession of hits, including "Every Day I Have the Blues," "Sweet Sixteen,"

B.B. King, 1974. Mike Moore/Hulton Archive/Getty Images

and "The Thrill Is Gone," enhanced his popularity. By the late 1960s rock guitarists acknowledged his influence and priority; they introduced King and his guitar, Lucille, to a broader white public, who until then had heard blues chiefly in derivative versions.

King's relentless touring strengthened his claim to the title of undisputed king of the blues, and he was a regular fixture on the *Billboard* charts through the mid-1980s. His strongest studio albums of this era were those that most closely tried to emulate the live experience, and he found commercial success through a series of all-star collaborations. On *Deuces Wild* (1997), King enlisted such artists as Van Morrison, Bonnie Raitt, and Eric Clapton to create a fusion of blues, pop, and country that dominated the blues charts for almost two years. Clapton and King collaborated on the more straightforward blues album *Riding with the King* (2000), which featured a collection of standards from King's catalog. He recaptured the pop magic of *Deuces Wild* with *80* (2005), a celebration of his 80th birthday that featured Sheryl Crow, John Mayer, and a standout performance by Elton John. King returned to his roots with *One Kind Favor* (2008), a collection of songs from the 1940s and '50s including blues classics by the likes of John Lee Hooker and Lonnie Johnson. Joining King in the simple four-part arrangements on the T-Bone Burnett-produced album were stalwart New Orleans pianist Dr. John, ace session drummer Jim

Keltner, and stand-up bassist Nathan East. The album earned King his 15th Grammy Award.

In 2008 the B.B. King Museum and Delta Interpretive Center opened in Indianola, with exhibits dedicated to King's music, his influences, and the history of the delta region. King's autobiography, *Blues All Around Me*, written with David Ritz, was published in 1996.

LEADBELLY

(b. Jan. 21, 1885?, Jeter Plantation, near Mooringsport, La., U.S.—d. Dec. 6, 1949, New York, N.Y.)

Huddie William Ledbetter, known to the world as Leadbelly (or Lead Belly), was a folk-blues singer, songwriter, and guitarist whose ability to perform a vast repertoire of songs, in conjunction with his notoriously violent life, made him a legend.

Musical from childhood, Leadbelly played accordion, 6- and 12-string guitar, bass, and harmonica. He led a wandering life, learning songs by absorbing oral tradition. For a time he worked as an itinerant musician with Blind Lemon Jefferson. In 1918 he was imprisoned in Texas for murder. According to tradition he won his early release in 1925 by singing a song for the governor of Texas when he visited the prison.

Resuming a life of drifting, Leadbelly was imprisoned for attempted murder in 1930 in the Angola, La., prison farm.

There he was "discovered" by the folklorists John Lomax and Alan Lomax, who were collecting songs for the Library of Congress. A campaign spearheaded by the Lomaxes secured his release in 1934, and he embarked on a concert tour of eastern colleges. Subsequently he published 48 songs and commentary (1936) about Depression-era conditions of blacks and recorded extensively. His first commercial recordings were made for the American Record Corporation, which did not take advantage of his huge folk repertory but rather encouraged him to sing blues. He settled in New York City in 1937. He struggled to make enough money, and in 1939–40 he was jailed again, this time for assault. When he was released, he worked with Woody Guthrie, Sonny Terry, Brownie McGhee, and others as the Headline Singers, performed on radio, and, in 1945, appeared in a short film. In 1949, shortly before his death, he gave a concert in Paris.

Leadbelly died penniless, but within six months his song "Goodnight, Irene" had become a million-record hit for the singing group the Weavers; along with other pieces from his repertoire, among them "The Midnight Special" and "Rock Island Line," it became a standard.

Leadbelly's legacy is extraordinary. His recordings reveal his mastery of a great variety of song styles and his prodigious memory; his repertory included more than 500 songs. His rhythmic guitar playing and unique vocal accentuations make his body of work both instructive and compelling. His influence on later rock musicians—including Eric Clapton, Bob Dylan, Janis Joplin, and Kurt Cobain—was immense.

MA RAINEY

(b. April 26, 1886, Columbus, Ga., U.S.—d. Dec. 22, 1939, Rome, Ga.)

Singer Ma Rainey, the "mother of the blues," is recognized as the first great African American professional blues vocalist.

Gertrude Malissa Nix Pridgett made her first public appearance about the age of 14 in a local talent show called "Bunch of Blackberries" at the Springer Opera House in her native Columbus, Ga. Little else is known of her early years. In February 1904 she married William Rainey, a vaudeville performer known as Pa Rainey, and for several years they toured with African American minstrel groups as a song-and-dance team. In 1902, in a small Missouri town, she first heard the sort of music that was to become known as the blues.

Ma Rainey, as she was known, began singing blues songs and contributed greatly to the evolution of the form and to the growth of its popularity. In her travels she appeared with jazz and jug bands throughout the South. While with the Tolliver's Circus and Musical Extravaganza troupe, she exerted a direct influence on young Bessie Smith. Her deep contralto voice, sometimes verging on harshness, was a power-ful instrument by which to convey the pathos of her simple songs of everyday life and emotion.

In 1923 Ma Rainey made her first phonograph recordings for the Paramount company. Over a five-year span she recorded some 92 songs for Paramount—such titles as "See See Rider," "Prove It on Me," "Blues Oh Blues," "Sleep Talking," "Oh Papa Blues," "Trust No Man," "Slave to the Blues," "New Boweavil Blues," and "Slow Driving Moan"—that later became the only per-manent record of one of the most influential popular musical artists of her time. She continued to sing in public into the 1930s. In 2008 a small museum opened in a house she had built in Columbus for her mother; she lived there herself from 1935 until her death.

Bessie Smith, c. *1935.* Three Lions/Hulton Archive/Getty Images

BESSIE SMITH

(b. April 15, 1898?, Chattanooga, Tenn., U.S.—d. Sept. 26, 1937, Clarksdale, Miss.)

It would be hard to find someone to argue that Bessie Smith was not one of the greatest of blues vocalists.

Elizabeth "Bessie" Smith grew up in poverty and obscurity. She may have made a first public appearance at the age of eight or nine at the Ivory Theatre in her hometown. About 1919 she was dis-covered by Gertrude "Ma" Rainey, one of the first of the great blues singers, from whom she received some training. For

several years Smith traveled through the South singing in tent shows and bars and theatres in small towns and in such cit-ies as Birmingham, Ala.; Memphis, Tenn.; and Atlanta and Savannah, Ga. After 1920 she made her home in Philadelphia, and it was there that she was first heard by Clarence Williams, a representative of Columbia Records. In February 1923 she made her first recordings, includ-ing the classic "Down Hearted Blues," which became an enormous success, selling more than two million copies. She made 160 recordings in all, in many of which she was accompanied by some of the great jazz musicians of the time, including Fletcher Henderson, Benny Goodman, and Louis Armstrong.

Bessie Smith's subject matter was the classic material of the blues: poverty and oppression, love—betrayed or unrequited—and stoic acceptance of defeat at the hands of a cruel and indifferent world. The great tragedy of her career was that she outlived the topicality of her idiom. In the late 1920s her record sales and her fame diminished as social forces changed the face of popular music and bowdlerized the earthy realism of the sentiments she expressed in her music. Her gradually increasing alcoholism caused managements to become wary of engaging her, but there is no evidence that her actual singing ability ever declined.

Known in her lifetime as the "Empress of the Blues," Smith was a bold, supremely confident artist who often disdained the use of a microphone and whose art expressed the frustrations and hopes of a whole generation of black Americans. Her tall figure and upright stance, and above all her handsome features, are preserved in a short motion picture, *St. Louis Blues* (1929), banned for its realism and now preserved in the Museum of Modern Art, New York City. She died from injuries sustained in a road accident. It was said that, had she been white, she would have received earlier medical treatment, thus saving her life, and Edward Albee made this the subject of his play *The Death of Bessie Smith* (1960).

MUDDY WATERS

(b. April 4, 1915, Rolling Fork, Miss., U.S.—d. April 30, 1983, Westmont, Ill.)

Dynamic guitarist and singer Muddy Waters played a major role in creating the post-World War II electric blues.

McKinley Morganfield, whose nickname, Muddy Waters, came from his proclivity for playing in a creek as a boy, grew up in the cotton country of the Mississippi Delta, where he was raised principally by his grandmother on the Stovall plantation near Clarksdale, Miss. He taught himself to play harmonica as a child and took up guitar at age 17. He eagerly absorbed the classic Delta blues styles of Robert Johnson, Son House, and others while developing a style of his own. As a young man, he drove a tractor on the sharecropped plantation, and on weekends he operated the cabin in which he lived as a "juke house," where visitors could party and imbibe moonshine whiskey made by Waters. He performed both on his own and in a band, occasionally earning a little money playing at house parties. He was first recorded in 1941, for the U.S. Library of Congress by archivist Alan Lomax, who had come to Mississippi in search of Johnson (who had already died by that time).

In 1943 Waters—like millions of other African Americans in the South who moved to cities in the North and West during the Great Migration from 1916 to 1970—relocated to Chicago. There he began playing clubs and bars on the city's South and West sides while earning a living working in a paper mill and later driving a truck. In 1944 he bought his first electric guitar, which cut more easily through the noise of crowded bars. He soon broke with country blues by playing electric guitar in a shimmering slide style. In 1946 pianist Sunnyland Slim, another Delta native, helped Waters land a contract with Aristocrat Records, for which he made several unremarkable recordings. By 1948 Aristocrat had become Chess Records (taking its name from Leonard and Phil Chess, the Polish immigrant brothers who owned and operated it), and Waters was recording a string of hits for it that began with "I Feel Like Going Home" and "I Can't Be Satisfied." His early, aggressive, electrically amplified band—including pianist Otis Spann, guitarist Jimmie Rodgers, and harmonica virtuoso Little Walter—created closely integrated support for his passionate singing, which featured dramatic shouts, swoops, and falsetto moans. His repertoire, much of which he composed, included lyrics that were mournful ("Blow Wind Blow," "Trouble No More"), boastful ("Got My Mojo Working," "I'm Your Hoochie Coochie Man"), and frankly sensual (the unusual 15-bar blues "Rock Me"). In the process Waters became the foremost exponent of modern Chicago blues.

Tours of clubs in the South and Midwest in the 1940s and '50s gave way after 1958 to concert tours of the United

Muddy Waters, c. 1979. Keystone/ Hulton Archive/Getty Images

States and Europe, including frequent dates at jazz, folk, and blues festivals. Over the years, some of Chicago's premier blues musicians did stints in Waters's band, including harmonica players James Cotton and Junior Wells, as well as guitarist Buddy Guy. Toward the end of his career, Waters concentrated on singing and played guitar only occasionally. A major influence on a variety of rock musicians—most notably the Rolling Stones (who took their name from his song "Rollin' Stone" and made a pilgrimage to Chess to record)—Waters was inducted into the Rock and Roll Hall of Fame in 1987.

RHYTHM AND BLUES

"The blues had a baby and they named it rock and roll," Muddy Waters famously sang, but it is probably more accurate to identify that first offspring as rhythm and blues and to see rock and roll as more of a stepchild. Rhythm and blues (R&B) was an outgrowth of the post-World War II electric blues and the jump blues of Louis Jordan, with stepped-up tempos anchored with a forceful backbeat (the second and fourth beats of the measure). To say that rock and roll was simply rhythm and blues played by white people ignores the role that country music played in the genesis of rock and roll; at the same time, there is no question that the music that pioneering disc jockey Alan Freed named *rock and roll* was rhythm and blues played by African Americans.

Some have made a distinction between rock and roll and rhythm and blues based on the lyrics. According to this distinction, rock and roll (including recordings by African American artists such as Chuck Berry and Little Richard) focused on teenage concerns, while R&B addressed more mature topics. Before journalist-turned-producer Jerry Wexler coined the term *rhythm and blues*, the music industry called these recordings "race" music, meaning that it was made by and for African Americans. What was wrong with this pigeon-holing was that this music's audience increasingly came to include whites. Whether Elvis Presley and those who followed in his wake "appropriated" black music may be less important, however, than the "race mixing" this music engendered and the role it played in breaking down racial barriers.

CHUCK BERRY

(b. Oct. 18, 1926, St. Louis, Mo., U.S.)

Singer, songwriter, and guitarist Chuck Berry was one of the most popular and influential performers in rhythm-and-blues and rock-and-roll music in the 1950s, '60s, and '70s.

Raised in a working-class African American neighbourhood on the north side of the highly segregated city of St. Louis, Berry grew up in a family proud of its African American and Native American ancestry. He gained early exposure to music through his family's participation in the choir of the Antioch Baptist Church, through the blues and country-western music he heard on the radio, and through music classes, especially at Sumner High School. Berry was still attending high school when he was sent to serve three years for armed robbery at a Missouri prison for young offenders. After his release and return to St. Louis, he worked at an auto plant, studied hairdressing, and played music in small nightclubs. Berry traveled to Chicago in search of a recording contract; Muddy Waters directed him to the Chess brothers. Leonard and Phil Chess signed him for their Chess label, and in 1955 his first recording session produced

"Maybellene" (a country-and-western-influenced song that Berry had originally titled "Ida Red"), which stayed on the pop charts for 11 weeks, cresting at number five. Berry followed this success with extensive tours and hit after hit, including "Roll Over Beethoven" (1956), "School Day" (1957), "Rock and Roll Music" (1957), "Sweet Little Sixteen" (1958), "Johnny B. Goode" (1958), and "Reelin' and Rockin'" (1958). His vivid descriptions of consumer culture and teenage life, the distinctive sounds he coaxed from his guitar, and the rhythmic and melodic virtuosity of his piano player (Johnny Johnson) made Berry's songs staples in the repertoire of almost every rock-and-roll band.

At the peak of his popularity, federal authorities prosecuted Berry for violating the Mann Act, alleging that he transported an underage female across state lines "for immoral purposes." After two trials tainted by racist overtones, Berry was convicted and remanded to prison. Upon his release he placed new hits on the pop charts, including "No Particular Place to Go" in 1964, at the height of the British Invasion, whose prime movers, the Beatles and the Rolling Stones, were hugely influenced by Berry (as were the Beach Boys). In 1972 Berry achieved his first number one hit, "My Ding-A-Ling." Although he recorded more sporadically in the 1970s and '80s, he continued to appear in concert, most often performing with backing bands comprising local musicians. Berry's public visibility increased in 1987 with the publication of his book *Chuck Berry: The Autobiography*

Chuck Berry performing at the Birmingham Odeon in England, May 6, 1977. Keystone/Hulton Archive/Getty Images

and the release of the documentary film *Hail! Hail! Rock 'n' Roll*, featuring footage from his 60th birthday concert and guest appearances by Keith Richards and Bruce Springsteen.

Berry is undeniably one of the most influential figures in the history of rock music. In helping to create rock and roll from the crucible of rhythm and blues, he combined clever lyrics, distinctive guitar sounds, boogie-woogie rhythms, precise diction, an astounding stage show, and musical devices characteristic of country-western music and the blues in his many best-selling single records and albums. A distinctive if not technically dazzling guitarist, Berry used electronic effects to replicate the ringing sounds of bottleneck blues guitarists in his recordings. He drew upon a broad range of musical genres in his compositions, displaying an especially strong interest in Caribbean music on "Havana Moon" (1957) and "Man and the Donkey" (1963), among others. Influenced by a wide variety of artists—including guitar players Carl Hogan, Charlie Christian, and T-Bone Walker and vocalists Nat King Cole, Louis Jordan, and Charles Brown—Berry played a major role in broadening the appeal of rhythm-and-blues music during the 1950s. He fashioned his lyrics to appeal to the growing teenage market by presenting vivid and humorous descriptions of high-school life, teen dances, and consumer culture. His recordings serve as a rich repository of the core lyrical and musical building blocks of rock and roll. In addition to the Beatles and the Rolling Stones, Elvis Presley, Buddy Holly, Linda Ronstadt, and a multitude of significant popular-music performers have recorded Berry's songs.

An appropriate tribute to Berry's centrality to rock and roll came when his song "Johnny B. Goode" was among the pieces of music placed on a copper phonograph record attached to the side of the Voyager 1 satellite, hurtling through outer space, in order to give distant or future civilizations a chance to acquaint themselves with the culture of the planet Earth in the 20th century. In 1984 he was presented with a Grammy Award for lifetime achievement. He was inducted into the Rock and Roll Hall of Fame in 1986.

RUTH BROWN

(b. Jan. 12, 1928, Portsmouth, Va., U.S.—d. Nov. 17, 2006, Las Vegas, Nev.)

Singer and actress Ruth Brown earned the sobriquet "Miss Rhythm" while dominating the rhythm-and-blues charts throughout the 1950s. Her success helped establish Atlantic Records ("The House That Ruth Built") as the era's premier rhythm-and-blues label.

The oldest of seven children, Brown (born Ruth Alston Weston) was steered away from "the devil's music" by her father, a church choir director, but by her late teens she was singing in clubs in Virginia's Tidewater region and had begun to perform with touring bands. In 1949, after spending nine months in a hospital recovering from an automobile accident, Brown released her first recording, "So Long." Abetted by Atlantic's cofounder Herb Abramson and songwriter Rudy Toombs, she became the most popular female rhythm-and-blues singer of the 1950s with a string of number one hits that included "Teardrops from My Eyes" (1950), "5-10-15 Hours" (1952), and her signature tune, "(Mama) He Treats Your Daughter Mean" (1953). After years of having her records covered by white performers, she experienced crossover pop success with "Lucky Lips" (1957) and "This Little Girl's Gone Rockin'" (1958).

Her career began a long decline in the early 1960s. Having survived four failed marriages, she spent the next decade driving a bus and cleaning houses while raising two sons. She began acting in the mid-1970s, first in television situation comedies and then in films and on the stage. In 1989 she won a Tony Award for best performance by a leading actress for the musical *Black and Blue,* and in 1990 she won a Grammy Award for best jazz vocal by a female. A champion of musicians' rights, she spoke out against exploitative contracts, and in the 1980s she eventually received some back royalties from Atlantic. Brown, whose principal influences were Ella Fitzgerald and Billie Holiday, was inducted into the Rock and Roll Hall of Fame in 1993. Her memoir, *Miss Rhythm* (cowritten with Andrew Yule), was published in 1996.

RAY CHARLES

(b. Sept. 23, 1930, Albany, Ga., U.S.—d. June 10, 2004, Beverly Hills, Calif.)

Pianist, singer, composer, and bandleader Ray Charles is credited with the early development of soul music through his melding of gospel, rhythm and blues, and jazz music. In the process he was dubbed "the Genius."

When Charles (born Ray Charles Robinson) was an infant his family moved to Greenville, Fla., and he began his musical career at age five on a piano in a neighbourhood café. He began to go blind at six, possibly from glaucoma, completely losing his sight by age seven. He attended the St. Augustine School for the Deaf and Blind, where he concentrated on musical studies, but left school at age 15 to play the piano professionally after his mother died from cancer (his father had died when the boy was 10).

Charles built a remarkable career based on the immediacy of emotion in his performances. After emerging as a blues and jazz pianist indebted to Nat King Cole's style in the late 1940s, Charles recorded the boogie-woogie classic "Mess Around" and the novelty song "It Should've Been Me" in 1952–53. His arrangement for Guitar Slim's "The Things That I Used to Do" became a blues million-seller in 1953. By 1954 Charles had created a successful combination of blues and gospel influences and signed on with Atlantic Records. Propelled by Charles's distinctive raspy voice, "I've Got a Woman" and "Hallelujah I Love You So" became hit records. "What'd I Say" led the rhythm and blues sales charts in 1959 and was Charles's own first million-seller.

Charles's rhythmic piano playing and band arranging revived the "funky" quality of jazz, but he also recorded in many other musical genres. He entered the pop market with the best-sellers "Georgia on My Mind" (1960) and "Hit the Road, Jack" (1961). His album *Modern Sounds in Country and Western Music* (1962) sold more than one million copies, as did its single, "I Can't Stop Loving You." Thereafter his music emphasized jazz standards and renditions of pop and show tunes.

From 1955 Charles toured extensively in the United States and elsewhere with his own big band and a gospel-style female backup quartet called The

Ray Charles, 1963. Express Newspapers/Hulton Archive/Getty Images

Raeletts. He also appeared on television and worked in films such as *Ballad in Blue* (1964) and *The Blues Brothers* (1980) as a featured act and sound track composer. He formed his own custom recording labels, Tangerine in 1962 and Crossover Records in 1973. The recipient of many national and international awards, he received 13 Grammy Awards, including a lifetime achievement award in 1987. In 1986 Charles was inducted into the Rock and Roll Hall of Fame and received a Kennedy Center Honor. He published an autobiography, *Brother Ray, Ray Charles' Own Story* (1978), written with David Ritz.

SAM COOKE

(b. Jan. 22, 1931, Clarksdale, Miss., U.S.—d. Dec. 11, 1964, Los Angeles, Calif.)

Singer, songwriter, producer, and entrepreneur Sam Cooke is a major figure in the history of popular music and, along with Ray Charles, one of the most influential black vocalists of the post-World War II period. If Charles represents raw soul, Cooke symbolizes sweet soul. To his many celebrated disciples—Smokey Robinson, James Taylor, and Michael Jackson among them—he is viewed as an icon of unrivaled stature.

Cooke's career came in two phases. As a member of the groundbreaking Soul Stirrers, a premier gospel group of the 1950s, he electrified the African American church community nationwide with a light, lilting vocal style that soared rather than thundered. "Nearer to Thee" (1955), "Touch the Hem of His Garment" (1956), and "Jesus, Wash Away My Troubles" (1956) were major gospel hits and, in the words of Aretha Franklin, "perfectly chiseled jewels."

Cooke's decision to turn his attention to pop music in 1957 had tremendous implications in the black musical community. There long had been a taboo against such a move, but Cooke broke the mold. He reinvented himself as a romantic crooner in the manner of Nat King Cole. His strength was in his smoothness. He wrote many of his best songs himself, including his first hit, the ethereal "You Send Me," which shot to number one on all charts in 1957 and established Cooke as a superstar.

While other rhythm-and-blues artists stressed visceral sexuality, Cooke was essentially a spiritualist, even in the domain of romantic love. When he did sing dance songs—"Twistin' the Night Away" (1962), "Shake" (1965)—he did so with a delicacy theretofore unknown in rock music. Cooke also distinguished himself as an independent businessman, heading his own publishing, recording, and management firms. He broke new ground by playing nightclubs, such as the Copacabana in New York City, previously off-limits to rhythm-and-blues acts.

The tragedy of his demise in 1964—he was shot to death at age 33 by a motel manager—is shrouded in mystery. But the mystery has done nothing to damage the strength of his legacy. "A Change Is Gonna Come" (1965) remains his signature song, an anthem of hope and boundless optimism that expresses the genius of his poetry and sweetness of his soul. Cooke was inducted into the Rock and Roll Hall of Fame in 1986.

BO DIDDLEY

(b. Dec. 30, 1928, McComb, Miss., U.S.—d. June 2, 2008, Archer, Fla.)

Singer, songwriter, and guitarist Bo Diddley was one of the most influential performers of rock music's early period.

Raised mostly in Chicago by his adoptive family, from whom he took the surname McDaniel (his original name was Ellas Bates), he recorded for the legendary blues record company Chess as Bo Diddley (a name most likely derived from the diddley bow, a one-stringed African guitar popular in the Mississippi Delta region). Diddley scored few hit records but was one of rock's most influential artists nonetheless, because he had something nobody else could claim, his own beat: chink-a-chink-chink, ca-chink-chink. That syncopated beat (also known as "hambone" or "shave-and-a-haircut—two-bits") had surfaced in a few big-band rhythm-and-blues charts of the 1940s, but Diddley stripped it down and beefed it up. He made it, with its obvious African roots, one of the irresistible dance sounds in rock and roll. It was appropriated by fellow 1950s rockers (Johnny Otis's "Willie and the Hand Jive" [1958]), 1960s garage bands (the Strangeloves' "I Want Candy" [1965]), and budding superstars (the Rolling Stones' version of Buddy Holly's Diddley-influenced "Not Fade Away" [1964]). For all that, Diddley hit the pop charts just five times and the Top 20 only once (even though his 1955 debut single, "Bo Diddley," backed with "I'm a Man," was number one on the rhythm-and-blues charts).

After playing for several years on Chicago's legendary Maxwell Street, signed with Chess subsidiary Checker in 1955. The lyrics to his songs were rife with African American street talk, bluesy imagery, and raunchy humour (e.g., "Who Do You Love" [1957]). He used tremolo, fuzz, and feedback effects to create a guitar sound on which only Jimi Hendrix has expanded (consider sonic outbursts like "Bo Diddley"). His stage shows—featuring his half sister the Duchess on vocals and rhythm guitar and Jerome Green on bass and maracas—made an art out of bad taste. Commonly dressed in a huge black Stetson and loud shirts, Diddley no doubt influenced the dress of British Invasion groups such as the Rolling Stones. The odd-shaped guitars that he played reinforced his arresting look.

In the 1960s he recorded everything from surf music to straight-ahead blues with equal aplomb. But his last conquest was the sublime "You Can't Judge a Book by the Cover" (1962), until the British Invasion put him back on the map long enough for a minor 1967 hit, "Ooh Baby." Always outspoken about how black musicians have been underpaid, he toured only sporadically after the 1970s, appeared in a few movies, and made occasional albums. He was inducted into the Rock and Roll Hall of Fame in 1987.

FATS DOMINO

(b. Feb. 26, 1928, New Orleans, La., U.S.)

Singer and pianist Fats Domino, a rhythm-and-blues star who became one of the first rock-and-roll stars, helped define the New Orleans sound. Altogether his relaxed, stylized recordings of the 1950s and '60s sold some 65 million copies, making him one of the most popular performers of the early rock era.

From a musical family, Antoine "Fats" Domino, Jr., received early training from his brother-in-law, guitarist Harrison Verrett. He began performing in clubs in his teens and in 1949 was discovered by Dave Bartholomew—the bandleader, songwriter, and record producer who helped bring New Orleans's J&M Studio to prominence and who became Domino's exclusive arranger. Domino's first recording, "The Fat Man" (1950), became the first of a series of rhythm-and-blues hits that sold 500,000 to one million copies. His piano playing consisted of simple rhythmic figures, often only triad chords over a boogie pattern, forcefully played and joined by simple saxophone riffs and drum afterbeats (accents in a measure of music that follow the downbeat). These accompanied the smooth, gently swinging vocals he delivered in a small, middle baritone range, with even dynamics and a slight New Orleans accent, all of which made Domino one of the most distinctive rock-and-roll stylists.

With "Ain't That a Shame" (1955) Domino became a favourite of white as well as black audiences. "Blueberry Hill" (1956), his most popular recording, was one of several rock-and-roll adaptations of standard songs. The piano-oriented Domino-Bartholomew style was modified somewhat in hits such as "I'm Walkin'" (1957) and "Walking to New Orleans" (1960). He appeared in the 1956 film *The Girl Can't Help It*. One of his last hits was a version of the Beatles' "Lady Madonna" (1968). Domino was inducted into the Rock and Roll Hall of Fame in 1986.

JIMI HENDRIX

(b. Nov. 27, 1942, Seattle, Wash., U.S.—d. Sept. 18, 1970, London, Eng.)

Guitarist, singer, and composer Jimi Hendrix fused the American traditions of blues, jazz, rock, and soul with techniques of British avant-garde rock to redefine the electric guitar in his own image.

Though his active career as a featured artist lasted a mere four years, Hendrix altered the course of popular music and became one of the most successful and influential musicians of his era. An instrumentalist who radically redefined the expressive potential and sonic palette of the electric guitar, he was the composer of a classic repertoire of songs ranging from ferocious rockers to delicate, complex ballads. He also was the most charismatic in-concert performer of his generation. Moreover, he was a visionary who collapsed the genre boundaries of rock, soul, blues, and jazz and an iconic figure whose appeal linked the concerns of white hippies and black revolutionaries by clothing black anger in the colourful costumes of London's Carnaby Street.

A former paratrooper whose honourable medical discharge exempted him from service in the Vietnam War, Hendrix (who changed his formal name from John Allen Hendrix to James Marshall Hendrix), spent the early 1960s working as a freelance accompanist for a variety of musicians, both famous and obscure. His unorthodox style and penchant for playing at high volume, however, limited him to subsistence-level work until he was discovered in a small New York City club and brought to England in August 1966. Performing alongside two British musicians, bassist Noel Redding and drummer Mitch Mitchell, he stunned London's clubland with his instrumental virtuosity and extroverted showmanship, numbering members of the Beatles, the Rolling Stones, and the Who among his admirers. It proved a lot easier for him to learn their tricks than it was for them to learn his.

Hendrix had an encyclopaedic knowledge of the musical roots on which the cutting-edge rock of his time was based, but, thanks to his years on the road with the likes of Little Richard and the Isley Brothers, he also had hands-on experience of the cultural and social worlds in which those roots had developed and a great admiration for the work of Bob Dylan, the Beatles, and the Yardbirds. Speedily adapting the current musical and sartorial fashions of late 1966 London to his own needs, he was soon able not only to match the likes of the Who at their own high-volume, guitar-smashing game but also to top them with what rapidly became the hottest-ticket show in town.

By November his band, the Jimi Hendrix Experience, had their first Top

Jimi Hendrix, 1970. Evening Standard/Hulton Archive/Getty Images

Ten single, "Hey Joe." Two more hits, "Purple Haze" and "The Wind Cries Mary," followed before their first album, *Are You Experienced?*, was released in the summer of 1967, when it was second in impact only to the Beatles' *Sgt. Pepper's Lonely Hearts Club Band.* Its immediate successor, *Axis: Bold as Love,* followed that December. On Paul McCartney's recommendation, Hendrix was flown to California for a scene-stealing appearance at the Monterey Pop Festival, which rendered him a sensation in his homeland less than a year after his departure.

Relocating back to the United States in 1968, Hendrix enjoyed further acclaim with the sprawling, panoramic double album *Electric Ladyland,* but the second half of his career proved frustrating. Legal complications from an old contract predating his British sojourn froze his recording royalties, necessitating constant touring to pay his bills; and his audiences were reluctant to allow him to progress beyond the musical blueprint of his earliest successes. He was on the verge of solving both these problems when he died of an overdose of barbiturates, leaving behind a massive stockpile of works-in-progress that were eventually edited and completed by others.

For Hendrix, the thunderous drama of his hard rock band was but a fraction of what he aspired to: he wanted to compose more complex music for larger ensembles, rather than simply to improvise endlessly in front of a rhythm section for audiences waiting for him to smash or burn his guitar. Nevertheless, in his all-too-brief career,

he managed to combine and extend the soaring improvisational transcendence of John Coltrane, the rhythmic virtuosity of James Brown, the bluesy intimacy of John Lee Hooker, the lyrical aesthetic of Bob Dylan, the bare-knuckle onstage aggression of the Who, and the hallucinatory studio fantasias of the Beatles. Hendrix's work provides a continuing source of inspiration to successive generations of musicians to whom he remains a touchstone for emotional honesty, technological innovation, and an all-inclusive vision of cultural and social brotherhood.

HOWLIN' WOLF

(b. June 20, 1910, West Point, Miss., U.S.—d. Jan. 10, 1976, Hines, Ill.)

Singer and composer Howlin' Wolf was one of the principal exponents of the urban blues style of Chicago.

Chester Arthur Burnett was brought up on a cotton plantation; the music he heard was the traditional tunes of the region. As Howlin' Wolf, he started singing professionally when quite young and in the 1920s and '30s performed throughout Mississippi, playing in small clubs. He was influenced by the music of Blind Lemon Jefferson, Sonny Boy Williamson, and Charley Patton. In the 1940s he went to Arkansas, where there was a flourishing blues tradition, and formed his own group, which included James Cotton and Little Jr. Parker, both of whom became noted blues performers in their own right.

Wolf accompanied himself on guitar and harmonica, but his main instrument was his guttural and emotionally suggestive voice, which gave his songs power and authenticity. After his first record, "Moanin' at Midnight" (1951), became a hit, Wolf moved to Chicago, where he, along with Muddy Waters, made the city a centre for the transformation of the (acoustic) Mississippi Delta blues style into an electrically amplified style for urban audiences. His work was known only to blues audiences until the Rolling Stones and other British and American rock stars of the 1960s and '70s acknowledged his influence. Wolf was noted for his brooding lyrics and his earthy, aggressive stage presence.

Etta James, c. 2006. PRNewsFoto/RCA Records/AP Images

ETTA JAMES

(b. Jan. 25, 1938, Los Angeles, Calif., U.S.)

Over time, popular rhythm-and-blues entertainer Etta James became a successful ballad singer.

With bandleader Johnny Otis, James as a teenager composed a reply song to Hank Ballard and the Midnighters' suggestive hits "Work with Me, Annie" and "Annie Had a Baby"; originally titled "Roll with Me, Henry," "The Wallflower" became a rhythm-and-blues hit for James and then a million-seller in a sanitized cover version ("Dance with Me, Henry") by Georgia Gibbs. A veteran of grueling tours on the rhythm-and-blues theatre circuit, James (born Jamesetta Hawkins)

battled drug addiction for much of her career. Her highly dramatic qualities became evident on her 1960s ballads such as "All I Could Do Was Cry," "I'd Rather Go Blind," and the sensuous "At Last." Over the years James's voice changed—growing rougher and deeper and losing its little-girl quality—and she became one of the first women to sing in the style that became soul. She continued to perform and record into the early 21st century.

QUINCY JONES

(b. March 14, 1933, Chicago, Ill., U.S.)

Performer, producer, arranger, and composer Quincy Jones's work encompasses virtually all forms of popular music.

Jones was born in Chicago and reared in Bremerton, Wash., where he studied the trumpet and worked locally with the then-unknown pianist-singer Ray Charles. In the early 1950s Jones studied briefly at the prestigious Schillinger House (now Berklee College of Music) in Boston before touring with Lionel Hampton as a trumpeter and arranger. He soon became a prolific freelance arranger, working with Clifford Brown, Gigi Gryce, Oscar Pettiford, Cannonball Adderley, Count Basie, Dinah Washington, and many others. He toured with Dizzy Gillespie's big band in 1956, recorded his first album as a leader in the same year, worked in Paris for the Barclay label as an arranger and producer in the late 1950s, and continued to compose. Some of his more successful compositions from this period include "Stockholm Sweetnin'," "For Lena and Lennie," and "Jessica's Day."

Back in the United States in 1961, Jones became an artists-and-repertoire (or "A&R" in trade jargon) director for Mercury Records. In 1964 he was named a vice president at Mercury, thereby becoming one of the first African Americans to hold a top executive position at a major American record label. In the 1960s Jones recorded occasional jazz dates, arranged albums for many singers (including Frank Sinatra, Peggy Lee, and Billy Eckstine), and composed music for several films, including *The Pawnbroker* (1964), *In the Heat of the Night* (1967), and *In Cold Blood* (1967). Jones next worked for the A&M label from 1969 to 1981 (with a brief hiatus as he recovered from a brain aneurysm in 1974) and moved increasingly away from jazz toward pop music. During this time, "Q," as he is sometimes called, became one of the most famous producers in the world, his success enabling him to start his own record label, Qwest, in 1980.

Jones's best-known work includes producing an all-time best-selling album, Michael Jackson's *Thriller* (1982), organizing the all-star charity recording "We Are the World" (1985), and producing the film *The Color Purple* (1985) and the television series *The Fresh Prince of Bel-Air* (1990–96). In 1993 he founded the magazine *Vibe*, which he sold in 2006. Throughout the years, Jones has worked with a "who's who" of figures from all fields of popular music. He was nominated for more than 75 Grammy Awards (winning more than 25) and seven Academy Awards and received an Emmy Award for the theme music he wrote for the television miniseries *Roots* (1977). *Q: The Autobiography of Quincy Jones* was published in 2001.

LITTLE RICHARD

(b. Dec. 5, 1932, Macon, Ga., U.S.)

Flamboyant singer and pianist Little Richard's hit songs of the mid-1950s were defining moments in the development of rock and roll.

Born into a family of 12 children, Richard Wayne Penniman learned gospel music in Pentecostal churches of the Deep South. As a teenager he left home to perform rhythm and blues in medicine shows and nightclubs, where he took the name "Little Richard," achieving notoriety for high-energy onstage antics. His first recordings in the early 1950s, produced in the soothing jump-blues style of Roy Brown, showed none of the soaring vocal reach that would mark his later singing. His breakthrough came in September 1955 at a recording session at J & M Studio in New Orleans, where Little Richard, backed by a solid rhythm-and-blues band, howled "Tutti Frutti," with its unforgettable exhortation, "A wop bop a loo bop, a lop bam boom!" In the year and a half that followed, he released a string of songs on Specialty Records that sold well among both black and white audiences: "Rip It Up," "Long Tall Sally," "Ready Teddy," "Good Golly, Miss Molly," and "Send Me Some Lovin'," among others. With a phenomenal voice able to generate croons, wails, and screams unprecedented in popular music, Little Richard scored hits that combined childishly amusing lyrics with sexually suggestive undertones. Along with Elvis Presley's records for the Sun label in the mid-1950s, Little Richard's sessions from the same period offer models of singing and musicianship that have inspired rock musicians ever since.

As his success grew, Little Richard appeared in some of the earliest rock-and-roll movies: *Don't Knock the Rock* and *The Girl Can't Help It* (both 1956) and *Mr. Rock and Roll* (1957). In the latter he stands at the piano belting out songs with a dark intensity that, in the bland Eisenhower years, seemed excessive, an impression amplified by his bizarre six-inch pompadour, eyeliner, and pancake makeup. At the very peak of his fame, however, he concluded that rock and roll was the Devil's work; he abandoned the music business, enrolled in Bible college, and became a traveling Evangelical preacher. When the Beatles skyrocketed onto the music scene in 1964, they sang several of his classic songs and openly acknowledged their debt to their great forebear. This renewed attention inspired Little Richard to return to the stage and the recording studio for another shot at stardom. Although a new song, "Bama Lama Bama Loo" (1964), invoked the fun and vitality of his heyday, record-buying youngsters were not impressed. A major recording contract in the early 1970s produced three albums for Reprise Records—*The Rill Thing, King of Rock'n' Roll,* and *Second Coming*—collections that showed Little Richard in fine voice but somewhat out of his element in the hard rock styles of the period.

In the late 1990s Little Richard continued to appear at concerts and festivals, performing songs that had become cherished international standards. He remained a frequent guest on television talk shows and children's programs, but his madcap mannerisms, so threatening to parents in the 1950s, had come to seem amusingly safe. Having weathered a career marked by extraordinary changes in direction, Little Richard survived not only as the self-proclaimed "architect of rock and roll" but also as a living treasure of 20th-century American culture.

TINA TURNER

(b. Nov. 26, 1939, Brownsville, Tenn., U.S.)

Singer Tina Turner found success in the rhythm-and-blues, soul, and rock genres in a career that spanned five decades.

Anna Mae Bullock was born into a sharecropping family in rural Tennessee. She began singing as a teenager and, after moving to St. Louis, Mo., immersed herself in the local rhythm-and-blues scene. She met Ike Turner at a performance by his band, the Kings of Rhythm, in 1956, and soon became part of the act. She began performing as Tina Turner, and her electric stage presence quickly made her the centrepiece of the show. The ensemble, which toured as the Ike and Tina Turner Revue, was renowned for its live performances but struggled to find recording success. That changed in 1960, when "A Fool in Love" hit the pop charts, and a string of hit singles followed. Ike and Tina were married in 1962, although the date is subject to some speculation (during the couple's divorce proceedings in 1977, Ike claimed that the two were never legally married). The Phil Spector-produced album *River Deep—Mountain High* (1966) was a hit in Europe, and its title track is arguably the high point of Spector's "wall of sound" production style, but it sold poorly in the United States. Ike and Tina's final hits as a couple were the cover version of Creedence Clearwater Revival's "Proud Mary" (1971) and "Nutbush City Limits" (1973).

Tina divorced Ike in 1978, alleging years of physical abuse and infidelity. After a series of guest appearances on the albums of other artists, she released her debut solo album, *Private Dancer*, in 1984. It was a triumph, both critically and commercially, garnering three Grammy Awards and selling more than 20 million copies worldwide. She followed her musical success with a role in the film *Mad Max Beyond Thunderdome* (1985), and she wrote her autobiography, *I, Tina*

Tina Turner on stage at London's Wembley Arena, March 19, 1985. Dave Hogan/Hulton Archive/Getty Images

(1986; adapted as the film *What's Love Got to Do with It*, 1993). Later albums include *Break Every Rule* (1986), *Foreign Affair* (1989), and *Wildest Dreams* (1996). Her greatest-hits compilation *All the Best* was released in 2004, and Turner continued touring into the 21st century. Ike and Tina were inducted into the Rock and Roll Hall of Fame in 1991.

JACKIE WILSON

(b. June 9, 1934, Detroit, Mich., U.S.—d. Jan. 21, 1984, Mount Holly, N.J.)

Singer Jackie Wilson was a pioneering exponent of the fusion of 1950s doo-wop, rock, and blues styles into the soul music of the 1960s.

Wilson was one of the most distinctively dynamic soul performers of the 1960s. Few singers could match his vocal range or his pure physicality onstage. He was a genuine original, and his stylistic innovations in the 1950s were as important in the evolution of American pop, rock, and soul as those of James Brown, Nat King Cole, or Sam Cooke, despite the fact that his recordings seldom enjoyed the commercial impact that theirs did.

Wilson—who possessed a dynamic multioctave tenor—started singing professionally while still a teenager, and in 1953 he replaced Clyde McPhatter as the lead singer of the vocal group the Dominoes, led by Billy Ward, with whom he sang until he became a solo performer in 1957. Wilson had to deal with the routine forms of racial segregation that made it difficult for African American male artists to secure mainstream success. The commercial and stylistic barriers between so-called "race music" and the predominantly white pop Top 40 forced singers like Wilson to agonize over their choice of material as they sought to display their talents to the fullest without provoking racially motivated marginalization. This was the challenge songwriter and fellow Detroiter Berry Gordy, Jr., took on when he and Roquel ("Billy") Davis (also known as Tyran Carlo) wrote Wilson's first solo single, "Reet Petite," in 1957. Two years later Gordy formed Motown Records, where his goal was crossover success—that is, to take black performers from the rhythm-and-blues chart onto the pop chart. Both Gordy and Wilson had earlier pursued careers as boxers, possibly the source of Wilson's phenomenal stamina and breath control onstage. Gordy's affinity for Wilson's masculine, highly physical persona led him to cowrite (with his sister Gwendolyn and Davis) several of the singer's most successful singles, including "Lonely Teardrops" (1958), "To Be Loved" (1958), and "That's Why (I Love You So)" (1959), the first of which topped the rhythm-and-blues chart and reached number seven on the pop chart.

Once Wilson's solo career was launched, he toured constantly, creating a reputation as a consummate showman. In 1963 he scored a Top Five pop record with the deep-soul rave-up "Baby Workout,"

APOLLO THEATER

Established in 1913 at 253 West 125th Street in the Harlem district of New York City, the Apollo was the central theatre on Harlem's main commercial street, and its position reflects its central role in Harlem's culture. Designed by New York architect George Keister, the building was leased by Jules Hurtig and Harry Seamon and opened as Hurtig and Seamon's New (Burlesque) Theater. After a few years it was purchased by a competitor and renamed the 125th Street Apollo Theater. The district surrounding the building was opened up during the 1910s to African Americans making the Great Migration out of the South, and in the 1920s Harlem was transformed into a black residential and commercial area.

The Apollo was again under new ownership in 1932; burlesque shows began to give way to musical revues, and the theatre's new owners began to tailor shows to the area's most recent residents. The building opened its doors to African Americans for the first time on Jan. 26, 1934. That year the long-standing weekly talent show called Amateur Night at the Apollo was born, and one of its early winners was the young Ella Fitzgerald. These Wednesday night shows became legendary, not only for the individuals and groups discovered there (including Lena Horne, Sam Cooke, the Orioles, Marvin Gaye, James Brown, and many others) but also for the highly sophisticated and critical audience that attended. Many performers—including Brown, Moms Mabley, B.B. King, and Clyde McPhatter—recorded live albums at the theatre; these recordings document the Apollo's trademark performer-audience dialogue.

In addition to introducing a vast number of rising stars, the Apollo quickly became a vital stop for any black entertainer, and virtually every major African American musical act performed there at least once—as did several white acts (notably Buddy Holly), who often were booked because they were assumed to be black. The management maintained a policy of alternating live stage shows with B movies (allegedly to clear the house). The Apollo was the pinnacle of the "chitlin circuit" of venues—including the Regal Theater in Chicago and the Howard Theater in Washington, D.C.—that catered to African American audiences. As a show of respect for its legacy, the building was left untouched during the riots of the 1960s. In 1977 the shows were discontinued, and the theatre was operated (unsuccessfully) as a movie theatre. A year later the building was closed. Purchased by investors in 1981, the Apollo received landmark status in 1983, was renovated, and was reopened to the public in 1985.

but he did not have another big hit until 1967, when—at the peak of Beatlemania—Wilson's soaring rendition of "(Your Love Keeps Lifting Me) Higher and Higher" reached number six on the pop chart. Unlike other stars at Stax and Motown, Wilson was not always backed by first-rate session musicians or provided with quality arrangements; however, Chicago-based producer Carl Davis hired the Motown rhythm section for "Higher and Higher," investing the record with a trendy, contemporary beat. Yet, despite Davis's imaginative contributions, Wilson's later records had limited commercial success, largely because Brunswick Records did not give them the necessary promotional push to secure radio play. Wilson resorted to touring to reignite public interest in his career. In September 1975, as he was about to mount a major comeback with the just-completed album *Nobody but You,* Wilson suffered a heart attack during a live performance that left him semicomatose for almost eight years until his death in 1984. He was inducted into the Rock and Roll Hall of Fame in 1987.

SOUL

If rhythm and blues was lost to white audiences and performers as rock and roll, the development of soul marked black popular music's return to its roots—gospel and blues. Through the work of Ray Charles and others, pure gospel songs were secularized into soul music but remained suffused in the expression of profound emotion and in the yearning for transcendence. Usually a distinction is made between Southern soul and the soul produced in Northern cities. The former was generally more raw, while the latter, especially the meticulously crafted recordings produced by Motown, was more polished and primed for crossover appeal.

JAMES BROWN

(b. May 3, 1933, Barnwell, S.C., U.S.—d. Dec. 25, 2006, Atlanta, Ga.)

Singer, songwriter, arranger, and dancer James Brown was one of the most important and influential entertainers in 20th-century popular music and whose remarkable achievements earned him the sobriquet "the Hardest-Working Man in Show Business."

Brown was raised mainly in Augusta, Ga., by his great-aunt, who took him in at about the age of five when his parents divorced. Growing up in the segregated South during the Great Depression of the 1930s, Brown was so impoverished that he was sent home from grade school for "insufficient clothes," an experience that he never forgot and that perhaps explains his penchant as an adult for wearing ermine coats, velour jumpsuits, elaborate capes, and conspicuous gold jewelry. Neighbours taught him how to play drums, piano, and guitar, and he learned about gospel music in churches and at tent revivals, where preachers would scream, yell, stomp their feet, and fall to their knees during sermons to provoke responses from the congregation. Brown sang for his classmates and competed in local talent shows but initially thought more about a career in baseball or boxing than in music.

At age 15 Brown and some companions were arrested while breaking into cars. He was sentenced to 8 to 16 years of incarceration but was released after 3 years for good behaviour. While at the Alto Reform School, he formed a gospel group. Subsequently secularized and renamed the Flames (later the Famous Flames), it soon attracted the attention of rhythm-and-blues and rock-and-roll shouter Little Richard, whose manager helped promote the group. Intrigued by their demo record, Ralph Bass, the artists-and-repertoire man for the King label, brought the group to Cincinnati, Ohio, to record for King Records's subsidiary Federal. The label's owner, Syd Nathan, hated Brown's first recording, "Please, Please, Please" (1956), but the record eventually sold three million copies and launched Brown's extraordinary career. Along with placing nearly 100 singles and almost 50 albums on the best-seller charts, Brown broke new ground with two of the first successful "live and in concert" albums—his landmark *Live at the Apollo* (1963), which stayed on the charts for 66 weeks, and his 1964 follow-up, *Pure Dynamite! Live at the Royal*, which charted for 22 weeks.

During the 1960s Brown was known as "Soul Brother Number One." His hit recordings of that decade have often been associated with the emergence of the black aesthetic and black nationalist movements, especially the songs "Say It Loud—I'm Black and I'm Proud" (1968), "Don't Be a Drop-Out" (1966), and "I Don't Want Nobody to Give Me Nothin' (Open Up the Door, I'll Get It Myself)" (1969). Politicians recruited him to help calm cities struck by civil insurrection and avidly courted his endorsement. In the 1970s Brown became "the Godfather of Soul," and his hit songs stimulated several dance crazes and were featured on the sound tracks of a number of "blaxploitation" films (sensational, low-budget, action-oriented motion pictures with African American protagonists). When hip-hop emerged as a viable commercial music in the 1980s, Brown's songs again assumed centre stage as hip-hop disc jockeys frequently incorporated samples (audio snippets) from his records. He also appeared in several motion pictures, including *The Blues Brothers* (1980) and *Rocky IV* (1985), and attained global status as a celebrity, especially in Africa, where his tours attracted enormous crowds and generated a broad range of new musical fusions. Yet Brown's life continued to be marked by difficulties, including the tragic death of his third wife, charges of drug use, and a period of imprisonment for a 1988 high-speed highway chase in which he tried to escape pursuing police officers.

Brown's uncanny ability to "scream" on key, to sing soulful slow ballads as well as electrifying up-tempo tunes, to plumb the rhythmic possibilities of the human voice and instrumental accompaniment, and to blend blues, gospel, jazz, and country vocal styles together made him one of the most influential vocalists of the 20th century. His extraordinary dance routines featuring deft deployment of microphones and articles of clothing as props, acrobatic leaps, full-impact knee landings, complex rhythmic patterns, dazzling footwork, dramatic entrances, and melodramatic exits redefined public performance within popular music and inspired generations of imitators (not least Michael Jackson). His careful attention to every aspect of his shows, from arranging songs to supervising sidemen, from negotiating performance fees to selecting costumes, guaranteed his audiences a uniformly high level of professionalism every night and established a precedent in artistic autonomy. In the course of an extremely successful commercial career, Brown's name was associated with an extraordinary number and range of memorable songs, distinctive dance steps, formative fashion trends, and even significant social issues. A skilled dancer and singer with an extraordinary sense of timing, Brown played a major role in bringing rhythm to the foreground of popular music. In addition to providing melody and embellishment, the horn players in his bands functioned as a rhythm section (they had to think like drummers), and musicians associated with him (Jimmy Nolan, Bootsy Collins, Fred Wesley, and Maceo Parker) have played an important role in creating the core vocabulary and grammar of funk music. Brown was inducted into the Rock and Roll Hall of Fame in 1986.

James Brown. Hulton Archive/Getty Images

THE FOUR TOPS

The vocal group the Four Tops was one of Motown's most popular acts in the 1960s. The members were Renaldo ("Obie") Benson (b. June 14, 1936, Detroit, Mich.,

U.S.—d. July 1, 2005, Detroit), Abdul ("Duke") Fakir (b. Dec. 26, 1935, Detroit), Lawrence Payton (b. 1938, Detroit—d. June 20, 1997, Southfield, Mich.), and Levi Stubbs (byname of Levi Stubbles; b. June 6, 1936, Detroit—d. Oct. 17, 2008, Detroit).

The Four Tops formed after singing together at a party in 1953, calling themselves until 1956 the Four Aims. They spent a decade performing primarily jazz-oriented material in clubs and releasing poorly received singles before signing with Motown Records. Under the stewardship of Motown's premier songwriting and producing team, Holland-Dozier-Holland (Brian Holland, Lamont Dozier, and Eddie Holland), the Four Tops became consistent hit makers, registering their first hit, "Baby I Need Your Loving," in 1964. "I Can't Help Myself" (number one on the pop and rhythm-and-blues charts in the United States) and "It's the Same Old Song" followed in 1965, establishing the group's signature sound: Stubbs's gruff, passionate lead vocals set against gentler background harmonies. The group reached a pinnacle of fame in 1966 with its second million-seller, "Reach Out I'll Be There." Splitting with Motown in 1972 when the label relocated to California but returning for another five-year stint with the company in the mid-1980s, the group's original lineup continued to tour and record together throughout the 1970s, '80s, and '90s. The Four Tops were inducted into the Rock and Roll Hall of Fame in 1990.

ARETHA FRANKLIN

(b. March 25, 1942, Memphis, Tenn., U.S.)

Singer Aretha Franklin defined the golden age of soul music of the 1960s. Franklin's mother, Barbara, was a gospel singer and pianist. Her father, C.L. Franklin, presided over the New Bethel Baptist Church of Detroit and was a minister of national influence. A singer himself, he was noted for his brilliant sermons, many of which were recorded by Chess Records.

Her parents separated when she was six, and Franklin remained with her father in Detroit. Her mother died when Aretha was 10. As a young teen, Franklin performed with her father on his gospel programs in major cities throughout the country and was recognized as a vocal prodigy. Her central influence, Clara Ward of the renowned Ward Singers, was a family friend. Other gospel greats of the day—Albertina Walker and Jackie Verdell—helped shape young Franklin's style. Her album *The Gospel Sound of Aretha Franklin* (1956) captures the electricity of her performances as a 14-year-old.

At age 18, with her father's blessing, Franklin switched from sacred to secular music. She moved to New York City, where Columbia Records executive John Hammond, who had signed Count Basie and Billie Holiday, arranged her recording contract and supervised sessions highlighting her in a blues-jazz vein. From that first session, "Today I Sing the Blues" (1960) remains a classic. But, as her Detroit friends on the Motown label enjoyed hit after hit, Franklin struggled to achieve crossover success. Columbia placed her with a variety of producers who marketed her to both adults ("If Ever You Should Leave Me," 1963) and teens ("Soulville," 1964). Without targeting any particular genre, she sang everything from Broadway ballads to youth-oriented rhythm and blues. Critics recognized her talent, but the public remained lukewarm until 1966, when she switched to Atlantic Records, where producer Jerry Wexler allowed her to sculpt her own musical identity.

At Atlantic, Franklin returned to her gospel-blues roots, and the results were sensational. "I Never Loved a Man (the Way I Love You)" (1967), recorded at Fame Studios in Florence, Ala., was her first million-seller. Surrounded by sympathetic musicians playing spontaneous arrangements and devising the background vocals herself, Franklin refined a style associated with Ray Charles—a rousing mixture of gospel and rhythm and blues—and raised it to new heights. As a civil-rights-minded nation lent greater support to black urban music, Franklin was crowned the "Queen of Soul." "Respect," her 1967 cover of Otis Redding's spirited composition, became an anthem operating on personal, sexual, and racial levels. "Think" (1968), which Franklin wrote herself, also had more than one meaning. For the next half-dozen years, she became a hit maker of

unprecedented proportions; she was "Lady Soul."

In the early 1970s she triumphed at the Fillmore West in San Francisco before an audience of flower children and on whirlwind tours of Europe and Latin America. Her return to church, *Amazing Grace* (1972), is considered one of the great gospel albums of any era. By the late 1970s disco cramped Franklin's style and eroded her popularity. But in 1982, with help from singer-songwriter-producer Luther Vandross, she was back on top with a new label, Arista, and a new dance hit, "Jump to It," followed by "Freeway of Love" (1985). A reluctant interviewee, Franklin kept her private life private, claiming that the popular perception associating her with the unhappiness of singers Bessie Smith and Billie Holiday was misinformed.

In 1987 Franklin became the first woman inducted into the Rock and Roll Hall of Fame. While her album sales in the 1990s and 2000s failed to approach the numbers of previous decades, Franklin remained the Queen of Soul, and in 2009 she electrified a crowd of more than one million with her performance of "My Country 'Tis of Thee" at the presidential inauguration of Barack Obama.

Marvin Gaye

(b. April 2, 1939, Washington, D.C., U.S.—d. April 1, 1984, Los Angeles, Calif.)

Soul singer-songwriter-producer Marvin Gaye, to a large extent, ushered in the era

Aretha Franklin sings at the inauguration of U.S. Pres. Barack Obama, Jan. 20, 2009. Robyn Beck/AFP/Getty Images

of artist-controlled popular music of the 1970s. Gaye's father was a storefront preacher; his mother was a domestic worker. Gaye (born Marvin Pentz Gay, Jr.) sang in his father's Evangelical church in Washington, D.C., and became a member of a nationally known doo-wop group, the Moonglows, under the direction of Harvey Fuqua, one of the genre's foremost maestros, who relocated the group to Chicago.

When doo-wop dissipated in the late 1950s, Gaye had already absorbed Fuqua's lessons in close harmony. After disbanding the Moonglows, Fuqua took the 20-year-old Gaye to Detroit, where Berry Gordy, Jr., was forming Motown Records.

Gaye, who also played drums and piano, bucked the Motown system and its emphasis on teen hits. He was set on being a crooner in the Nat King Cole-Frank Sinatra vein, but his first efforts in that style failed. His break came with "Stubborn Kinda Fellow" (1962), the first of a long string of hits in the Motown mold—mainly songs written and produced by others, including "I'll Be Doggone" (1965), by Smokey Robinson, and "I Heard It Through the Grapevine" (1968), by Norman Whitfield. Gaye also enjoyed a series of successful duets, most notably with Tammi Terrell ("Ain't Nothing Like the Real Thing" [1968]).

Blessed with an exceptionally wide range that encompassed three distinct vocal styles—a piercing falsetto, a smooth mid-range tenor, and a deep gospel growl—Gaye combined great technical prowess with rare musical individuality. Rebellious by nature, he turned the tables on Motown's producer-driven hierarchy by becoming his own producer for *What's Going On* (1971), the most significant work of his career. A suite of jazz-influenced songs on the nature of America's political and social woes, this concept album—still a novel format at the time—painted a poignant landscape of America's black urban neighbourhoods. Gaye also displayed dazzling virtuosity by overdubbing (building sound track by track onto a single tape) his own voice three or four times to provide his own rich harmony, a technique he would employ for the rest of his career. *What's Going On* was a critical and commercial sensation in spite of the fact that Gordy, fearing its political content (and its stand against the Vietnam War), had argued against its release.

Other major artists—most importantly Stevie Wonder—followed Gaye's lead and acted as producer of their own efforts. In 1972 Gaye wrote the soundtrack for the film *Trouble Man*, with lyrics that mirrored his own sense of insecurity. *Let's Get It On*, released in 1973, displayed Gaye's sensuous side. *I Want You* (1976) was another meditation on libidinous liberation. *Here, My Dear* (1979) brilliantly dealt with Gaye's divorce from Gordy's sister Anna (the first of the singer's two tumultuous divorces).

Gaye's growing addiction to cocaine exacerbated his psychological struggles. Deeply indebted to the Internal Revenue Service, he fled the country, living in exile in England and Belgium, where he wrote "Sexual Healing" (1982), the song that signaled his comeback and led to his only Grammy Award.

Back in Los Angeles, his home from the 1970s, his essential conflict—between the sacred and secular—grew more intense. His 1983 "Sexual Healing" tour, his last, was marked by chaos and confusion. On April 1, 1984, during a family dispute, Gaye initiated a violent fight with his father, who shot him to death. Those close to the singer theorized that it was a death wish come true. For months

before, he had toyed with suicide. Gaye, who cited his chief influences as Ray Charles, Clyde McPhatter, Rudy West (lead singer for the doo-wop group the Five Keys), and Little Willie John, was inducted into the Rock and Roll Hall of Fame in 1987.

As an artist who employed urban soul music to express social and personal concerns, as well as a singer of exquisite sensitivity and romantic grace, Gaye left a legacy that has widened since his demise, and his music has become a permanent fixture in American pop.

BERRY GORDY, JR.

(b. Nov. 28, 1929, Detroit, Mich., U.S.)

Marvin Gaye, 1977. Pictorial Parade/ Hulton Archive/Getty Images

Businessman Berry Gordy, Jr., founded Motown Record Corporation (1959), the most successful black-owned music company in the United States. Through Motown, he developed the majority of the great rhythm-and-blues performers of the 1960s and '70s, including Diana Ross and the Supremes, Smokey Robinson and the Miracles, the Marvelettes, Stevie Wonder, Marvin Gaye, the Temptations, and Michael Jackson and the Jackson Five. Gordy was said to have masterminded the popular "Motown sound," a ballad-based blend of traditional black harmony and gospel music with the lively beat of rhythm and blues. By 1982, the company boasted revenues of $104 million, and Motown acts had recorded

110 number one hits on the American pop charts.

Gordy dropped out of Northeastern High School in Detroit and pursued a featherweight boxing career before joining the U.S. Army (c. 1951–53). Shortly thereafter he returned to Detroit to open a record store and begin producing recordings of his own compositions.

By the time Gordy founded Motown, he was at the apex of Detroit's black music scene and had already discovered Smokey Robinson. During the early 1960s Motown produced a string of hits that included Martha Reeves and the Vandellas' "Dancing in the Street" and the Temptations' "My Girl." Also about this time Gordy developed the Supremes, Motown's first superstar act. Powered by Diana Ross's sweet voice and quiet grace, the group went on to become one of the most successful female singing trios of all time. By the early 1970s Gordy had relocated the company to Hollywood and begun producing films, including *Lady Sings the Blues* (1972), featuring Ross in her film debut as Billie Holiday.

Gordy was honoured for lifetime achievement at the American Music Awards in 1975 and was inducted into the Rock and Roll Hall of Fame in 1988.

AL GREEN

(b. April 13, 1946, Forrest City, Ark., U.S.)

Singer-songwriter Al Green was the most popular performer of soul music in the 1970s. By further transforming the essential relationship in soul music between the sacred and the secular, Green followed the musical and spiritual path of his greatest inspiration, Sam Cooke. At the height of his commercial success, however, Green sacrificed his fame in order to fully dedicate himself to his religious faith.

In 1964, after his family moved from Arkansas to Michigan, Green (born Albert Greene) and some friends formed the Creations and toured the chitlin circuit in the South before renaming themselves Al Green and the Soul Mates three years later. They formed their own record label, releasing the single "Back Up Train," which enjoyed moderate success on the rhythm-and-blues charts in 1968. The watershed moment for Green came in Texas in 1968 when he met Willie Mitchell, a former bandleader who served as chief producer and vice president of Hi Records in Memphis. Obscurity was threatening to end Green's fledgling career, but with Mitchell's help he became a star in short order. After releasing a cover version of the Beatles' "I Want to Hold Your Hand" in 1969, which exhibited his awe-inspiring vocal agility, Green recorded a fine remake of the Temptations' "I Can't Get Next to You," which reached number one on the soul charts in 1971. But it was "Tired of Being Alone" (1971), written by Green, which suggested his extraordinary potential. It sold more than a million copies, preparing the way for "Let's Stay Together," the title track from Green's first gold album.

Al Green performing at RFK Stadium, Washington, D.C., Oct. 21, 2001. Paul J. Richards/AFP/ Getty Images

That single was his biggest hit, reaching number one on both the rhythm-and-blues and pop charts in 1972. Written by Green, Mitchell, and Al Jackson, the drummer for Booker T. and the MG's, the song reflected Mitchell's musical vision. In comparison with the grittier sound of Memphis neighbour Stax/Volt Records, Green's recordings with Mitchell offered a sophisticated and softened melody cradled by a distinctive bass sound. Green delivered gospel intensity, effortlessly soaring to the highest falsetto or plunging into a husky groan cloaked in hushed sensuality. From the tender "I'm Still in Love with You" (1972) and "Call Me (Come Back Home)" (1973) to the earthy "Love and Happiness" (1973) and "Here I Am (Come and Take Me)" (1973), Green and Mitchell experienced a string of hits through the early 1970s.

In the mid-1970s, facing a profound identity crisis, Green became a minister, establishing his own church. By 1980 he had devoted himself completely to his ministry and to gospel music. Later in that decade he cautiously reemerged from his spiritual seclusion and resumed performances of his most celebrated works alongside his popular gospel recordings. After a commercially disappointing comeback effort in 1995, Green came close to recapturing his trademark 1970s sound on *I Can't Stop* (2003). He followed with *Everything's OK* (2005) and won a new generation of fans with *Lay It Down* (2008). The latter album featured guest vocals by neo-soul artists John Legend, Anthony Hamilton, and Corinne Bailey Rae, and it earned Green a pair of Grammy Awards. Green was inducted into the Rock and Roll Hall of Fame in 1995.

JANET JACKSON

(b. May 16, 1966, Gary, Ind., U.S.)

Singer and actress Janet Jackson's increasingly mature version of dance-pop music made her one of the most popular recording artists of the 1980s and '90s.

The youngest of nine siblings in Motown's famed Jackson family, Janet Damita Jo Jackson parlayed her family's success into an independent career that spanned recordings, television, and film. She appeared as a regular on the 1970s television comedy series *Good Times* and later as a teenager in the dance-oriented series *Fame*. Following an unremarkable recording debut in 1982 and a 1984 follow-up album, Jackson took control of her career, moved out on her own, and developed her own sound and influential style.

She reemerged in 1986 with her breakthrough record *Control*, which featured five singles that topped the rhythm-and-blues charts, including two Top Ten pop hits, "What Have You Done for Me Lately" and "Nasty." Her fierce independence struck a chord with the youth of the day, and Jackson rose to a level of stardom that rivaled that of Michael Jackson, the most famous of her brothers. Her collaborations with the production team of Jimmy Jam and Terry Lewis (based in Minneapolis, Minn.) produced bold, beat-heavy, catchy songs that defined the punch and power of 1980s dance and pop music. Jackson returned in 1989 with her most diverse work, *Janet Jackson's Rhythm Nation 1814*. The album delivered seven pop Top Ten hit singles, including "Miss You Much," "Escapade," and "Love Will Never Do (Without You)."

Jackson continued to enjoy worldwide popularity and critical acclaim in the 1990s with the albums *janet.* (1993), *Design of a Decade* (1995), and *The Velvet Rope* (1997). Between the release of *All for You* (2001), which continued in the sensual vein of *janet.*, and *Damita Jo* (2004), Jackson was at the centre of a debate on decency standards on television, when a "wardrobe malfunction" (that some argued was accidental and others premeditated) caused a scandal during her live performance at halftime of the 2004 Super Bowl.

MICHAEL JACKSON

(b. Aug. 29, 1958, Gary, Ind., U.S.—d. June 25, 2009, Los Angeles, Calif.)

Singer, songwriter, and dancer Michael Jackson was the most popular entertainer in the world in the early and mid-1980s. Reared in Gary, Ind., in one of the most acclaimed musical families of the rock era, Michael Joseph Jackson was the youngest and most talented of five brothers whom his father, Joseph, shaped into a dazzling group of child stars known as the Jackson 5. In addition to Michael, the members of the Jackson 5 were Jackie Jackson (byname of Sigmund Jackson; b. May 4, 1951, Gary), Tito Jackson (byname of Toriano Jackson; b. Oct. 15, 1953, Gary), Jermaine Jackson (b. Dec. 11, 1954, Gary), and Marlon Jackson (b. March 12, 1957, Gary).

Motown Records president Berry Gordy, Jr., was impressed with the group and signed them in 1969. Sporting the loudest fashions, the largest Afros, the snappiest choreography, and a youthful, soulful exuberance, the Jackson 5 became an immediate success. They scored four consecutive number one pop hits with "I Want You Back," "ABC," "The Love You Save," and "I'll Be There" in 1970. With Michael topping the pop charts as a solo performer with Ben and reaching number two with "Rockin' Robin," and with the Jackson 5 producing trendsetting dance tracks such as "Dancing Machine," the family's string of hits for Motown lasted through 1975. As Michael matured, his voice changed, family tensions arose, and a contract standoff ensued. The group finally broke with Motown, moving to Epic Records as the Jacksons. Jermaine remained at Motown as a solo performer and was replaced by his youngest brother, Randy Jackson (in full Steven Randall Jackson; b. Oct. 29, 1961). As a recording act, the Jacksons enjoyed consistent success through 1984, and their sister Janet Jackson embarked on her own singing career in the early 1980s; however, Michael's solo albums took on an entirely different status.

Jackson's first solo effort for Epic, *Off the Wall* (1979), exceeded all expectations and was the best-selling album of the year (and has since sold more 20 million copies). Produced by industry veteran Quincy Jones, *Off the Wall* yielded the massive international hit singles "Don't Stop 'til You Get Enough" and "Rock with You," both of which showcased Michael's energetic style and capitalized on the contemporary disco dance fad. Three years later he returned with another collaboration with Jones, *Thriller*, a tour de force that featured an array of guest stars and elevated him to a worldwide superstar. *Thriller* captured a slew of awards, including a record-setting eight Grammys; remained on the charts for more than two years; and sold more than 40 million copies, long holding the distinction of being the best-selling album in history. The first single on the album, "The Girl Is Mine," an easygoing duet with

Michael Jackson, 1996. AFP/Getty Images

Paul McCartney, went to number one on the rhythm-and-blues charts and number two on the pop charts in the fall of 1982. The follow-up single, "Billie Jean," an electrifying dance track and the vehicle for Jackson's trademark "moonwalk" dance, topped the pop charts, as did "Beat It," which featured a raucous solo from famed guitarist Eddie Van Halen. Moreover, "Beat It" helped break down the artificial barriers between black and white artists on the radio and in the emerging format of music videos on television.

By 1984 Jackson was renowned worldwide as the "King of Pop." His much anticipated Victory reunion tour with his brothers was one of the most popular concert events of 1984. In 1985 Jackson and Lionel Richie cowrote "We Are the World," the signature single for USA for Africa, an all-star project aimed at famine relief. Further solo albums—*Bad* (1987), which produced five chart-topping hits, and *Dangerous* (1991), much of which was produced by New Jack Swing sensation Teddy Riley—solidified Jackson's dominance of pop music. In 2001 he was inducted into the Rock and Roll Hall of Fame; the Jackson 5 were inducted in 1997.

Jackson's eccentric, secluded lifestyle grew increasingly controversial in the early 1990s. His reputation was seriously damaged in 1993 when he was accused of child molestation by a 13-year-old boy he had befriended; a civil suit was settled out of court. In 1994 Jackson secretly married Lisa Marie Presley, daughter of Elvis Presley, but their marriage lasted less than two years. Shortly thereafter Jackson married again, this marriage producing children, though it too ended in divorce. While he remained an international celebrity, his image in the United States was slow to recover, and it suffered even more in November 2003 when he was arrested and charged with child molestation. After a 14-week trial that became something of a media circus, Jackson was acquitted in 2005.

In the wake of these events, Jackson suffered a financial collapse that resulted in the sale of many of his considerable assets, including, ultimately, his lavish Neverland ranch. He was preparing for a series of high-profile concerts he hoped would spark a comeback when he died suddenly of cardiac arrest on June 25, 2009—prompting a widespread outpouring of grief from his fans that culminated in a memorial celebration of his life and legacy on July 7 at the Staples Center in Los Angeles, featuring tributes by friends and luminaries such as Stevie Wonder, Berry Gordy, Jr., Brooke Shields, and Al

Sharpton. In August 2009 it was revealed that the coroner had ruled Jackson's death a homicide; the cause was a lethal combination of sedatives and propofol, an anesthetic. The documentary film *This Is It*, which drew from more than 100 hours of footage compiled during rehearsals for Jackson's scheduled 50-concert comeback engagement in London, premiered in October 2009.

CURTIS MAYFIELD

(b. June 3, 1942, Chicago, Ill, U.S.—d. Dec. 26, 1999, Roswell, Ga.)

Singer, songwriter, guitarist, producer, and entrepreneur Curtis Mayfield was one of the principal architects of Chicago-based soul music during the 1960s and '70s. Beginning with his earliest songs—such as "Gypsy Woman" (1961), "It's All Right" (1963), "Keep On Pushing" (1964), and "People Get Ready" (1965)—when he was lead vocalist of the Impressions, Mayfield wrote highly inspirational, humanistic pieces concerned with African American uplift. His compositions became standards in the repertoires of artists as varied as Rod Stewart, Bob Marley, and Brian Hyland.

Mayfield entered the music business in 1957, when he became a vocalist and guitarist with the Impressions, whose other members were Jerry Butler, Sam Gooden, and brothers Richard and Arthur Brooks. Butler left in 1958 and was replaced by Fred Cash; the Brooks brothers left in 1962. With the group reduced to a trio, Mayfield, along with Gooden and Cash, devised a much-imitated vocal style, a pronounced three-part alternating lead, which allowed Mayfield's delicate high tenor to be balanced by Gooden's bass and Cash's low tenor. Derived from gospel music, this switch-off technique called for each vocalist to take a turn with the lead part while the others provided backing harmony. It was later adopted by groups such as Sly and the Family Stone and Earth, Wind and Fire.

A remarkably innovative guitarist, the self-taught Mayfield tuned his instrument to a natural chord to achieve a subtle, lyrical sound. Many other guitarists in Chicago imitated his playing, and the Mayfield style showed up on innumerable soul records made in his hometown. Mayfield also was a major contributor of songs to other soul performers—most of them from Chicago. Among those who recorded his compositions were Jan Bradley, Jerry Butler, Gene Chandler, Aretha Franklin, Walter Jackson, Gladys Knight and the Pips, Major Lance, and the Staple Singers. In the late 1960s, with such songs as "We're a Winner" (1967) and "Choice of Colors" (1969), recorded with the Impressions, Mayfield played a crucial role in transforming black popular music into a voice for social concern during the struggle for civil rights.

In 1961 he became one of the first African Americans to found his own music publishing company. Six years later he established the highly successful Curtom Records, which became a leading producer of soundtrack albums for black-oriented films and for which Mayfield and such artists as Gene Chandler, Major Lance, and the Five Stairsteps recorded. Mayfield left the Impressions in 1970 to work as a soloist and subsequently became a major force in the development of funk, with such songs as "(Don't Worry) If There's a Hell Below We're All Going to Go," "Beautiful Brother of Mine," and "We People Who Are Darker Than Blue." Although he achieved considerable recognition for such albums as *Curtis* (1970) and *Curtis/Live!* (1971), it was through the recording of soundtracks for motion pictures that Mayfield achieved his biggest success, particularly with *Superfly* (1972). Mayfield's last Top Ten rhythm-and-blues hit was *Only You Babe* in 1976. He struggled during the subsequent disco era and by the mid-1980s was no longer a factor on the rhythm-and-blues or pop charts.

Mayfield was paralyzed from the neck down by a freak accident during a concert in 1990. He was inducted into the Rock and Roll Hall of Fame as a member of the Impressions in 1991 and as a solo artist in 1999. He is the author of *Poetic License: In Poem & Song* (1996), a book of poetry and song lyrics.

OTIS REDDING

(b. Sept. 9, 1941, Dawson, Ga., U.S.—d. Dec. 10, 1967, near Madison, Wis.)

Singer-songwriter Otis Redding was one of the great soul stylists of the 1960s. Redding was raised in Macon,

Ga., where he was deeply influenced by the subtle grace of Sam Cooke and the raw energy of Little Richard. In the late 1950s Redding joined Richard's band, the Upsetters, after Richard had gone solo. It was as a Little Richard imitator that Redding experienced his first minor hit, "Shout Bamalama," for the Confederate label of Athens, Ga.

The story of Redding's breakthrough is part of soul music mythology. Redding joined Johnny Jenkins's Pinetoppers, a local Georgia band, and also served as the group's driver. When the group traveled to Memphis, Tenn., to record at the famed Stax studios, Redding sang two songs of his own at the end of the session. One of the two, "These Arms of Mine" (1962), launched his career, attracting both a record label executive (Jim Stewart) and a manager (Phil Walden) who passionately believed in his talent.

Redding's open-throated singing became the measure of the decade's great soul artists. Unabashedly emotional, he sang with overwhelming power and irresistible sincerity. "Otis wore his heart on his sleeve," said Jerry Wexler, whose Atlantic label handled Stax's distribution, thus bringing Redding to a national market.

The hits came fast and furiously— "I've Been Loving You Too Long (to Stop Now)" (1965), "Respect" (1965), "Satisfaction" (1966), "Fa-Fa-Fa-Fa-Fa (Sad Song)" (1966). Redding's influence extended beyond his gritty vocals. As a composer, especially with his frequent partner Steve Cropper, he introduced a new sort of rhythm-and-blues line—lean, clean, and steely strong. He arranged his songs as he wrote them, singing horn and rhythm parts to the musicians and, in general, sculpting his total sound. That sound, the Stax signature, would resonate for decades to come. Redding became a de facto leader presiding over a band that would prove as influential as the great rhythm-and-blues aggregations that preceded it, units associated with Ray Charles and James Brown.

The rapport between Redding and his rhythm section—Cropper on guitar, Donald ("Duck") Dunn on bass, Al Jackson on drums, and Booker T. Jones on keyboards (known collectively as Booker T. and the MG's)—was extraordinary. Redding proved to be an adept duet partner as well; his hits with labelmate Carla Thomas ("Tramp" and "Knock on Wood," 1967) added to his romantic aura.

When the Stax/Volt Revue stormed Europe, Redding led the brigade. He converted hippiedom to soul music at the 1967 Monterey (Calif.) Pop Festival and was just entering a new phase of popularity when tragedy struck. On Dec. 10, 1967, a chartered plane crashed into a Wisconsin lake. Victims included Redding and his backing band. Redding was 26 years old.

Ironically, the across-the-board success Redding had sought was realized only after his death. His most haunting composition, cowritten with Cropper, shot to the top of the charts and became his only number one hit: "(Sittin' on) The Dock of the Bay" (1968), a bittersweet lament of indolence and love. The public mourned his passing by playing his records. During 1968 three other Redding songs—"The Happy Song (Dum Dum)," "Amen," and "Papa's Got a Brand New Bag"—hit the charts. He remains a giant of the genre, a much-revered master of straight-ahead soul singing. Redding was inducted into the Rock and Roll Hall of Fame in 1989.

SMOKEY ROBINSON AND THE MIRACLES

Led by one of the most gifted, influential singer-songwriters in 20th-century popular music, Smokey Robinson and the Miracles helped define the Motown sound of the 1960s. In addition to Smokey Robinson (byname of William Robinson; b. Feb. 19, 1940, Detroit, Mich., U.S.), the principal members of the group were Warren Moore (b. Nov. 19, 1939, Detroit), Bobby Rogers (b. Feb. 19, 1940, Detroit), Ronnie White (b. April 5, 1939, Detroit), and Claudette Rogers (b. 1942). Whether writing for fellow artists Mary Wells, the Temptations, or Marvin Gaye or performing with the Miracles, singer-lyricist-arranger-producer Robinson created songs that were supremely balanced between the joy and pain of love. At once playful and passionate, Robinson's graceful lyrics led Bob Dylan to call him "America's greatest living poet."

Coming of age in the doo-wop era and deeply influenced by jazz vocalist Sarah Vaughan, Robinson formed the Five Chimes with school friends in the mid-1950s. After some personnel changes, the group, as the Matadors, auditioned unsuccessfully for Jackie Wilson's manager; however, they greatly impressed Wilson's songwriter Berry Gordy, who soon became their manager and producer. Most importantly, Gordy became Robinson's mentor, harnessing his prodigious but unformed composing talents, and Robinson, assisted by the Miracles, became Gordy's inspiration for the creation of Motown Records.

With the arrival of Claudette Rogers, the group changed its name to the Miracles and released "Got a Job" on End Records in 1958. The Miracles struggled onstage in their first performance at the Apollo Theater that year, but good fortune came their way in the form of Marv Tarplin, guitarist for the Primettes, who were led by Robinson's friend Diana Ross. Tarplin became an honorary (but essential) Miracle, while Robinson introduced Gordy to the Primettes, who soon became the Supremes. In 1959 Robinson and Claudette Rogers were married, and "Bad Girl," licensed to Chess Records, peaked nationally at number 93. The fiery "Way Over There" and the shimmering "(You Can) Depend on Me" were followed in 1960 by "Shop Around," the second version of which became an enormous hit, reaching number one on the rhythm-and-blues charts and number two on the pop charts.

While Robinson was writing such vital songs as "My Guy" for Mary Wells, "I'll Be Doggone" for Marvin Gaye, and

"My Girl" for the Temptations, he and the Miracles proceeded to record stunning compositions, including "You've Really Got a Hold on Me" (1962), "I'll Try Something New" (1962), "Ooo Baby Baby" (1965), "Choosey Beggar" (1965), "The Tracks of My Tears" (1965), and "More Love" (1967, written following the premature birth and death of Robinson's twin daughters). The Miracles complemented their songs of aching romance and mature love with buoyant numbers such as "Mickey's Monkey" (1963), "Going to a Go-Go" (1965), "I Second That Emotion" (1967), and "The Tears of a Clown" (1970).

In 1972 Robinson left the Miracles to pursue a solo career. Without him, the Miracles enjoyed moderate success in subsequent years (the disco-era "Love Machine [Part 1]" hit number one on the pop charts in 1975), while Robinson produced such solo hits as "Cruisin'" (1979) and "Being with You" (1981). He also unintentionally inspired the new soul radio format that took its name from the title track of his 1975 conceptual album *A Quiet Storm*. Robinson was inducted into the Rock and Roll Hall of Fame in 1987.

THE SUPREMES

The pop-soul vocal group the Supremes was among the most successful musical groups of the 1960s and the flagship act of Motown Records. The principal members of the group were Diana Ross (byname of Diane Earle; b. March 26, 1944, Detroit, Mich., U.S.), Florence Ballard (b. June 30, 1943, Detroit—d. Feb. 22, 1976, Detroit), Mary Wilson (b. March 6, 1944, Greenville, Miss.), and Cindy Birdsong (b. Dec. 15, 1939, Camden, N.J.).

Not only were the Supremes the Motown label's primary crossover act, they also helped change the public image of African Americans during the civil rights era. With their sequined evening gowns and the sophisticated pop-soul swing given them by the songwriting-production team of Brian Holland, Lamont Dozier, and Eddie Holland from 1964 to 1967, the Supremes were the idealized look and sound of the "integrated Negro." Indeed, the youth of America learned many of its first lessons about racial equality from teen magazines that documented every hyperglamourized move the Supremes made as they went from topping the pop chart to appearances on *The Ed Sullivan Show* to sold-out Las Vegas bookings.

Their story began humbly enough when a group of working-class girls from Detroit's Brewster public housing project formed a singing group called the Primettes, their name derived from their sister-act association with the Primes, a forerunner of the Temptations. The details of the group's formation (namely, who came first) have been disputed, but, from a series of permutations of five principals (including, initially, Betty McGlown), a quartet emerged that comprised Ballard, Barbara Martin, Ross, and Wilson. After recording briefly with Lupine Records, the quartet signed with Berry Gordy's Motown Records in 1960. They changed

The Supremes performing, mid-1960s. From left to right, Cindy Birdsong, Diana Ross, and Mary Wilson. Archive Photos/Getty Images

their name to the Supremes before releasing their first Motown single in 1961, and upon the subsequent departure of Martin the remaining trio went on to score five U.S. number one hits in a row between 1964 and 1965.

But the Supremes didn't catch on right away. It took a while to create the distinctive look and sound that ultimately made them famous. Gordy unsuccessfully paired the group with different musicians and songs for three years until he finally stumbled upon the right formula. In 1964 Holland-Dozier-Holland gave the Supremes their first number one single with "Where Did Our Love Go." Embellishing Ross's precise, breathy phrasing with chiming bells and a subdued rhythm section gave the Supremes an intentional lack of identifiable ethnicity. Not really sounding "white" or stereotypically "black," hit singles like "Baby Love" and "Come See About Me" (both 1964) sounded modern, upwardly mobile, and stylishly sensual in a way that appealed equally to adults and teens of all persuasions.

The group continued to rack up chart-topping hits but was ultimately pulled apart by conflicting individual and corporate ambitions. By the end of 1967, the Supremes had lost both Ballard (who was replaced by Birdsong) and producers Holland-Dozier-Holland. The group continued recording for two more years as Diana Ross and the Supremes, largely to prepare the public for Ross's solo career. Jean Terrell became the first of many new group members who helped Wilson keep the Supremes alive and recording for seven years after Ross departed in 1970.

Ross's solo career was greatly aided by starring roles in films financed by her longtime mentor, Gordy. *Lady Sings the Blues* (1972), *Mahogany* (1975), and *The Wiz* (1978) and their soundtrack albums kept Ross in the public eye and ear for most of the 1970s. *The Boss* (1979), produced by Nickolas Ashford and Valerie Simpson, and *Diana* (1980), produced by Chic's Nile Rodgers and Bernard Edwards, were both hits, but aside from a controversial concert in Central Park, New York City, in 1983 and some American television appearances, Ross spent the rest of the 1980s and '90s cultivating a foreign fan base that outstripped her popularity in the United States.

The Supremes were inducted into the Rock and Roll Hall of Fame in 1988.

THE TEMPTATIONS

Recording primarily for Motown, the Temptations, noted for their smooth harmonies and intricate choreography, were among the most popular performers of soul music in the 1960s and '70s. The principal members of the group were Otis Williams (original name Otis Miles; b. Oct. 30, 1949, Texarkana, Texas, U.S.), Paul Williams (b. July 2, 1939, Birmingham, Ala.—d. Aug. 17, 1973, Detroit, Mich.), Melvin Franklin (original name David English; b. Oct. 12, 1942, Montgomery, Ala.—d. Feb. 23, 1995, Los Angeles, Calif.), Eddie Kendricks (b. Dec. 17, 1939, Union Springs, Ala.—d.

Oct. 5, 1992, Birmingham), David Ruffin (byname of Davis Eli Ruffin; b. Jan. 18, 1941, Meridian, Miss.—d. June 1, 1991, Philadelphia, Pa.), and Dennis Edwards (b. Feb. 3, 1943, Birmingham).

Originally called the Elgins, the Temptations were formed in 1961 from the coupling of two vocal groups based in Detroit—the Primes, originally from Alabama, and the Distants. That same year they signed with Motown. After a slow start—with the addition of Ruffin and largely under the direction of song-writer-producer Smokey Robinson—the Temptations turned out a string of roman-tic hits, beginning with "The Way You Do the Things You Do" (1964) and including "My Girl" (1964), "Get Ready" (1966), and "Beauty Is Only Skin Deep" (1966). Bass Franklin, baritone Otis Williams, and occasional lead Paul Williams provided complex harmonies, and the two regular lead singers, Ruffin and Kendricks, strik-ingly complemented each other. Ruffin had a remarkable sandpaper baritone and Kendricks a soaring tenor. Paragons of sleek fashion and practitioners of ath-letic choreography (provided by Paul Williams and Motown's house chore-ographer, Cholly Atkins), the "Tempts" epitomized sophisticated cool.

In the late 1960s they shifted to a more funk-oriented sound and to more socially conscious material when Norman Whitfield became the group's producer and principal songwriter (along with partner Barrett Strong). Influenced by psychedelic rock and with Edwards replacing Ruffin (who had embarked on a solo career), the Temptations produced hits such as "Cloud Nine" (1968), "Runaway Child, Running Wild" (1969), "Psychedelic Shack" (1970), "Ball of Confusion (That's What the World Is Today)" (1970), and the Grammy Award-winning "Papa Was a Rollin' Stone" (1972). In 1968–69 they were paired with Diana Ross and the Supremes for two television specials and recordings that included "I'm Gonna Make You Love Me" (1968) and "I'll Try Something New" (1969). In 1971 Kendricks left to pursue a solo career, notable for "Keep On Truckin'" (1973). From the mid-1970s the Temptations changed personnel fre-quently and produced occasional hits, but they never regained the form that earned them induction into the Rock and Roll Hall of Fame in 1989.

STEVIE WONDER

(b. May 13, 1950, Saginaw, Mich., U.S.)

A child prodigy, singer, songwriter, and multi-instrumentalist, Stevie Wonder developed into one of the most creative musical figures of the late 20th century.

Blind from birth and raised in inner-city Detroit, Steveland Judkins was a skilled musician by age eight. Renamed Little Stevie Wonder by Motown Records president Berry Gordy, Jr.,—to whom he was introduced by Ronnie White, a member of the Miracles—Wonder made his recording debut at age 12. The soul-ful quality of his high-pitched singing and the frantic harmonica playing that characterized his early recordings were evident in his first hit single, "Fingertips (Part 2)," recorded during a show at Chicago's Regal Theatre in 1963. But Wonder was much more than a prepubescent imitation of Ray Charles, as audiences discovered when he demonstrated his prowess with piano, organ, harmonica, and drums. By 1964 he was no longer described as "Little," and two years later his fervent delivery of the pounding soul of "Uptight (Everything's Alright)," which he also had written, suggested the emergence of both an unusually compelling performer and a composer to rival Motown's stable of skilled songwriters. (He had already cowritten, with Smokey Robinson, "The Tears of a Clown.")

Over the next five years Wonder had hits with "I Was Made to Love Her," "My Cherie Amour" (both cowritten with producer Henry Cosby), and "For Once in My Life," songs that suited dancers as well as lovers. *Where I'm Coming From,* an album released in 1971, hinted not merely at an expanded musical range but, in its lyrics and its mood, at a new introspection. *Music of My Mind* (1972) made his concerns even more plain. In the interim he had been strongly influenced by Marvin Gaye's *What's Going On,* the album in which his Motown stablemate moved away from the label's "hit factory" approach to confront the divisive social issues of the day. Any anxieties Gordy may have felt about his protégé's declaration of independence were amply calmed by the run of recordings with which Wonder obliterated the competition in

the mid-1970s. Those albums produced a steady stream of classic hit songs, among them "Superstition," "You Are the Sunshine of My Life," "Higher Ground," "Living for the City," "Don't You Worry 'Bout a Thing," "Boogie On Reggae Woman," "I Wish," and "Sir Duke."

Although still only in his mid-20s, Wonder appeared to have mastered virtually every idiom of African American popular music and to have synthesized them all into a language of his own. His command of the new generation of electronic keyboard instruments made him

Stevie Wonder. PRNewsFoto/BET Black Entertainment Television/AP Images

a pioneer and an inspiration to rock musicians, the inventiveness of his vocal phrasing was reminiscent of the greatest jazz singers, and the depth and honesty of his emotional projection came straight from the black church music of his childhood. Such a fertile period was unlikely to last forever, and it came to an end in 1979 with an overambitious extended work called *Stevie Wonder's Journey Through the Secret Life of Plants*. Thereafter his recordings became sporadic and often lacked focus, although his concerts were never less than rousing. The best of his work formed a vital link between the classic rhythm-and-blues and soul performers of the 1950s and '60s and their less commercially constrained successors. Yet, however sophisticated his music became, he was never too proud to write something as apparently slight as the romantic gem "I Just Called to Say I Love You" (1984). He was inducted into the Rock and Roll Hall of Fame in 1989 and received a Grammy Award for lifetime achievement in 2005. In 2008 the Library of Congress announced that Wonder was the recipient of its Gershwin Prize for Popular Song.

FUNK

Driven by thumping bass lines and syncopated drumbeats, with an emphasis on "the one" (the first beat of measure), funk revels in rhythmic counterplay and demands that listeners submit to the power of "the groove" and the pull of the dance floor. Although James Brown and his band were important innovators of the funk sound and George Clinton (leader of Parliament-Funkadelic) was its avatar, funk has been ably "brought" by a range of African American performers, including Sly and the Family Stone, the Ohio Players, and Prince.

PARLIAMENT-FUNKADELIC

Parliament-Funkadelic, a massive group of performers that greatly influenced black music in the 1970s, scored 13 Top Ten rhythm-and-blues and pop hits from 1967 to 1983 (including six number one rhythm-and-blues hits) under a variety of names, including the Parliaments, Funkadelic, Bootsy's Rubber Band, and the Brides of Funkenstein, as well as under the name of its founding father, George Clinton.

The original members were Clinton (b. July 22, 1941, Kannapolis, N.C., U.S.), Raymond Davis (b. March 29, 1940, Sumter, S.C.), Calvin Simon (b. May 22, 1942, Beckley, W.Va.), Fuzzy Haskins (byname of Clarence Haskins; b. June 8, 1941, Elkhorn, W.Va.), and Grady Thomas (b. Jan. 5, 1941, Newark, N.J.). Later members included Michael Hampton (b. Nov. 15, 1956, Cleveland, Ohio), Bernie Worrell (b. April 19, 1944, Long Beach, N.J.), Billy Bass Nelson (byname of William Nelson, Jr.; b. Jan. 28, 1951, Plainfield, N.J.), Eddie Hazel (b. April 10, 1950, Brooklyn, N.Y.— d. Dec. 23, 1992), Tiki Fulwood (byname of Ramon Fulwood; b. May 23, 1944, Philadelphia, Pa.—d. Oct. 29, 1979), Bootsy Collins (byname of William Collins; b.

Oct. 26, 1951, Cincinnati, Ohio), Fred Wesley (b. July 4, 1943, Columbus, Ga.), Maceo Parker (b. Feb. 14, 1943, Kinston, N.C.), Jerome Brailey (b. Aug. 20, 1950, Richmond, Va.), Garry Shider (b. July 24, 1953, Plainfield), Glen Goins (b. Jan. 2, 1954, Plainfield—d. July 29, 1978, Plainfield), and Gary ("Mudbone") Cooper (b. Nov. 24, 1953, Washington, D.C.).

The band, often referred to simply as P-Funk, combined the hard rock of Jimi Hendrix, the funky rhythms of James Brown, and the showstopping style of Sly and the Family Stone to fashion an outrageous tribal funk experience. P-Funk emphasized the aesthetics of funk as a means of self-fulfillment; to "give up the funk" meant to achieve transcendence.

Organized and produced by Clinton, the original Parliaments began as a doo-wop quintet based in Plainfield. The group's first charting single, "(I Wanna) Testify," in 1967 led to their first tour, but legal problems that arose with the demise of their record company resulted in the loss of the group's name. Performing throughout the northeastern United States and recording in Detroit, the group began to emphasize its backing band, Funkadelic. Led by bassist Nelson, guitarist Hazel, drummer Fulwood, and classically trained keyboardist Worrell, Funkadelic incorporated the influence of amplified, psychedelic rock into its distinctive sound.

By 1970 Clinton was producing albums for both the renamed Parliament and Funkadelic—essentially the same entity recording for different labels. In the process he recruited key new performers: Collins on bass, Wesley on trombone, and Parker on saxophone (all from James Brown's band the JBs), along with drummer Brailey, vocalist Cooper, lead guitarist Hampton, and vocalist-guitarists Shider and Goins. Success came in 1976 with the release of Parliament's album *Mothership Connection* and the single "Give Up the Funk (Tear the Roof Off the Sucker)," which earned a gold record. Other hit singles followed, including "Flash Light" (1977) by Parliament, "One Nation Under a Groove" (1978) by Funkadelic, and "Atomic Dog" (1982) by Clinton.

P-Funk reached its peak in the late 1970s, sporting a massive stage act (with more than 40 performers) that showcased Clinton's visionary album concepts, Collins's spectacular bass effects, and Worrell's synthesizer innovations. However, by the early 1980s the large overhead and multifaceted legal identity of the group led to a collapse of the enterprise.

P-Funk defined the dance music of its time and influenced a range of styles from hard rock to house music. The P-Funk catalog is among the most sampled by rap music producers. Parliament-Funkadelic was inducted into the Rock and Roll Hall of Fame in 1997.

PRINCE

(b. June 7, 1958, Minneapolis, Minn., U.S.)

Prince, a singer, guitarist, songwriter, producer, dancer, and performer on keyboards, drums, and bass, was among the most talented American musicians of his generation. Like Stevie Wonder, he was a rare composer who could perform at a professional level on virtually all the instruments he required, and a considerable number of his recordings feature him in all the performing roles. Prince's recording career began with funk and soul marketed to a black audience; his early music also reflected the contemporary musical impact of disco. Later records incorporated a vast array of influences, including jazz, punk, heavy metal, the Beatles, and hip-hop, usually within an overall approach most informed by funky up-tempo styles and soulful ballads; the latter often featured his expressive falsetto singing.

Taking an early interest in music, Prince (born Prince Rogers Nelson) began playing the piano at age 7 and mastered the guitar and drums by the time he joined his first band at age 14. With very few African American residents, his hometown, Minneapolis, Minn., was an unlikely site for the development of a major black star, but Prince even managed to lead other local musicians, most notably Jimmy Jam and Terry Lewis, to major success.

Mirrored by correspondingly intense music, Prince's lyrics often address sexuality and desire with frankness and imagination. Much of his work, in its lyrics and imagery, struggles with the constriction of social conventions and categories. As one of his biographers put it, "The whole thrust of Prince's art can be understood in terms of a desire to escape the social identities thrust upon him by simple virtue of his being small, black, and male."

Prince explored typographical oddities in his song titles and lyrics as another way of evading convention. In 1993 he announced that he had changed his name to a combination of the male and female gender signs— ⚤. (At other junctures he went by the name, the Artist Formerly Known as Prince and the Artist.) There is also a strong religious impulse in some of his music, sometimes fused into a kind of sacred erotic experience that has roots in African American churches.

"Little Red Corvette" (1983) was Prince's first big crossover hit, gaining airplay on MTV at a time when virtually no black artists appeared on the influential new medium. *Purple Rain* (1984) made him one of the major stars of the 1980s and remains his biggest-selling album. Three of its singles were hits: the frenetic "Let's Go Crazy," the androgynous but vulnerable "When Doves Cry," and the anthemic title cut. Thereafter he continued to produce inventive music of broad appeal; outside the United States he was particularly popular in Britain and the rest of Europe.

Throughout most of his career, Prince's prolific inventiveness as a songwriter clashed with his record company's policy of releasing only a single album each year. As a backlog of his completed but unreleased recordings piled up, he

Prince performs at the Grand Palais, Paris, Oct. 11, 2009. Bertrand Guay/AFP/Getty Images

gave songs to other performers—some of whom recorded at and for Paisley Park, the studio and label he established in suburban Minneapolis—and even organized ostensibly independent groups, such as the Time, to record his material. His 1996 album *Emancipation* celebrated the forthcoming end of his Warner Brothers contract, which enabled him to release as much music as he liked on his NPG label. Later he explored marketing his work on the Internet and through private arrangements with retail chains as a means of circumventing the control of large record companies. In 1999, however, he released *Rave Un2 the Joy Fantastic* under the Arista label; a collaboration with Sheryl Crow, Chuck D, Ani DiFranco, and others, the album received mixed reviews and failed to find a large audience. Prince (who, following the formal termination of his contract with Warner Brothers in 1999, stopped using the symbol as his name) was inducted into the Rock and Roll Hall of Fame in 2004. That year he also released *Musicology*, an album that both sold well and was much praised by critics.

SLY AND THE FAMILY STONE

Sly and the Family Stone became widely popular in the late 1960s with a string of anthemlike pop singles, stirring socially relevant albums, and memorable live performances. The members were Sly Stone (original name Sylvester Stewart; b. March 15, 1943, Denton, Texas, U.S.),

Freddie Stone (original name Freddie Stewart; b. June 5, 1946, Vallejo, Calif.), Rosie Stone (original name Rose Stewart; b. March 21, 1945, Vallejo), Cynthia Robinson (b. Jan. 12, 1946, Sacramento, Calif.), Jerry Martini (b. Oct. 1, 1943, Boulder, Colo.), Larry Graham (b. Aug. 14, 1946, Beaumont, Texas), and Greg Errico (b. Sept. 1, 1946, San Francisco, Calif.). As a performer, songwriter, and social satirist, bandleader Sly Stone stood among the giants of rock.

The band's style combined a range of influences (including rock, funk, jazz, psychedelic rock, standards, and nursery rhymes) with the spirit of a Pentecostal church revival and produced some of the era's most energizing and compelling songs. "Everyday People" and "Thank You (Falletinme Be Mice Elf Agin)"—both of which reached number one on the pop and rhythm-and-blues charts—as well as "Hot Fun in the Summertime" and "I Want to Take You Higher" all became classics of popular music.

Based in the San Francisco Bay area, the unpredictable and innovative Family Stone was one of the first acts to feature blacks and whites and men and women all performing and singing simultaneously. The loud colours and individualistic dress of the players reflected and influenced the counterculture of the 1960s; musically, Sly and the Family Stone laid the foundation for much of the street funk, soul, and disco music of the 1970s.

Raised in a churchgoing family in Vallejo, the charismatic Sylvester Stewart learned to perform at an early age. He established himself in the Bay Area music industry by working at Autumn Records producing national pop hits for Bobby Freeman ("C'mon and Swim") in 1964 and the Beau Brummels ("Laugh Laugh") in 1965. He was among the area's top soul music deejays when, adopting his radio name, Sly Stone, he founded the Family Stone in 1967. The group comprised his brother Freddie (guitar) and younger sister Rose (piano), trumpeter Robinson, saxophonist Martini, drummer Errico, and bassist Graham.

Signed to Epic in 1967, the band scored its first charting single with the raucous "Dance to the Music" in 1968. That smash hit led to a national tour and television appearances. In 1969 Sly captured the moods of the nation with the *Stand!* album, which showcased an unprecedented combination of joy, optimism, and rage and established Sly Stone as a lightning rod for social commentary. The band's engaging performance at the Woodstock festival in August 1969 was a high point of the legendary concert and the zenith of Sly's career.

The 1970 release of *Greatest Hits* provided the band's second gold album, but Sly was faltering—delving into drugs and missing concerts. He returned with the single "Family Affair" (number one on the pop and rhythm-and-blues charts) and album *There's a Riot Goin' On* in 1971, which surprised critics with its brooding, introspective tone.

Graham, who had pioneered the funk bass style of "thumping" and "plucking," left the band in 1972 to form his own successful group, Graham Central Station, and later to pursue a solo singing career. With a new bassist, Rusty Allen, Sly produced his final gold album, *Fresh,* in 1973, but thereafter recordings and sales dropped sharply.

Interest in Sly Stone resurfaced with the "sampling" of many of his songs (and Graham's bass lines) by hip-hop producers in the 1990s. Sly and the Family Stone were inducted into the Rock and Roll Hall of Fame in 1993.

HIP-HOP

Hip-hop emerged from the South Bronx neighbourhood of New York City as a multi-faceted cultural movement, gaining wide popularity in the 1980s and '90s. Its hugely popular musical component is frequently referred to simply as rap, though rapping (also known as ryhming and MCing), the performance-poetry vocal component of hip-hop, is just one element of a mix that is equally reliant on the contributions of the producer, who creates the musical backdrop. In appropriating "samples" from older recordings that serve as vital hooks, hip-hop developed a distinctly high-tech, postmodern approach to music making. Along the way hip-hop developed from a spontaneous locally produced art into a multi-million dollar business that includes fashion, music videos, and advertising.

DIDDY

(b. Nov. 4, 1970, New York, N.Y., U.S.)

American rapper, record producer, and clothing designer Diddy founded an entertainment empire in the 1990s.

Sean John Combs was born and raised in Harlem, where his father was murdered when Combs was three. Nine years later the family moved to suburban Mount Vernon, N.Y., where Combs attended prep school and supposedly received the nickname "Puffy" for his habit of puffing up his chest during football practice. He attended Howard University in Washington, D.C., but he left college after two years to become an intern at Uptown Records in New York City; within a year he had moved up to vice president. In December 1991 9 people were crushed to death and 29 were injured as crowds pushed their way into a charity basketball game Combs had promoted at the City College of New York.

In 1993 Combs was fired from Uptown, and he turned his energies to his own label, Bad Boy Entertainment. He soon discovered and befriended a street hustler named Christopher Wallace, who rapped as Biggie Smalls and recorded as the Notorious B.I.G. By 1994 Wallace was a rising rap star, and Combs had negotiated a $15 million deal to move Bad Boy to Arista Records, which gained him a growing industry-wide reputation as a rap impresario and entrepreneur. In spring 1997 the Notorious B.I.G. was murdered, and Combs's first album, *No Way Out*—released that summer under the moniker Puff Daddy—included the single "I'll Be Missing You," a musical eulogy featuring the voice of Wallace's widow and the melody from the Police's "Every Breath You Take." Several more singles from *No Way Out* dominated the pop charts in 1997.

In 1998 Combs toured in support of *No Way Out* and maintained his presence on the airwaves; for the movie *Godzilla* he enlisted guitarist Jimmy Page to concoct the single "Come with Me," a thunderous reworking of Page's Led Zeppelin song "Kashmir." That year Combs took home two Grammy Awards, for rap album (*No Way Out*) and rap performance ("I'll Be Missing You"), and he also launched the Sean John clothing line.

Legal troubles, however, soon overshadowed Combs's music and fashion achievements. In 1999 he was found partially liable for the City College stampede and was made to pay settlements on several resulting claims. Later that year, he pleaded guilty to second-degree harassment after an altercation with a record company executive, and in December 1999 he was present during a shooting at a Manhattan nightclub. Charged with several crimes, including illegal gun possession, he was acquitted in 2001 on all counts. He subsequently made a symbolic break with his past by changing his name to P. Diddy and releasing his second album, *The Saga Continues* (2001). He claimed another Grammy in 2004 for his collaboration with the rapper Nelly (Cornell Haynes, Jr.) on "Shake Ya Tailfeather," and later that year he was honoured by the Council of Fashion Designers of America as their menswear designer of the year. He publicly dropped the "P." from his name in 2005 and released his third album, *Press Play*, the following year as Diddy.

JAY-Z

(b. Dec. 4, 1970, Brooklyn, N.Y., U.S.)

American rapper and entrepreneur Jay-Z was one of the most influential figures in hip-hop in the 1990s and 2000s.

Shawn Carter grew up in Brooklyn's often dangerous Marcy Projects, where he was raised mainly by his mother. His firsthand experience with illicit drug dealing would inform his lyrics when he began rapping under the stage name Jazzy, soon shortened to Jay-Z (a name that may also have been derived from the proximity of the J and Z subway lines to the Marcy Projects). Jay-Z and two friends founded their own company, Roc-a-Fella Records, to release his debut album, *Reasonable Doubt* (1996), which climbed the *Billboard* charts, reaching number 23 on the pop chart and number 3 on the rhythm-and-blues chart.

A string of successful albums followed at a rate of at least one per year through 2003. *Vol. 2: Hard Knock Life* (1998) not only was the first of Jay-Z's releases to top the *Billboard* 200 album sales chart but also won a Grammy Award for best rap album. In 2001 he pleaded guilty to assault relating to a 1999 nightclub stabbing and received three years' probation. In 2003, with the release of *The Black Album*, Jay-Z announced his retirement as a performer. In 2004 he assumed the presidency of Def Jam Recordings, making him one of the most highly placed African American executives in the recording industry at the time.

Postretirement, Jay-Z stayed remarkably active, collaborating with the rock group Linkin Park in 2004 and appearing as a guest vocalist on the recordings of numerous other artists, including Kanye West and Beyoncé; Jay-Z and Beyoncé were married in 2008. He developed a large portfolio of business ventures and investments, including Roc-a-Fella Films, a clothing line, and a stake in the New Jersey Nets of the National Basketball Association. He formally returned to recording in 2006 with *Kingdom Come*. In December 2007 he stepped down as Def Jam president shortly after releasing the album *American Gangster*. Jay-Z proved that he remained one of rap's most bankable acts when he embarked on a highly successful tour with Mary J. Blige in 2008. The following year he won a Grammy Award for best rap performance for "Swagga Like Us," a collaboration

Jay-Z performing in Jersey City, N.J., July 31, 2009. Jason Kempin/Getty Images

with T.I., Kanye West, and Lil Wayne, and that September, he released *The Blueprint 3*, which featured guest vocals from Alicia Keys and production by West and Timbaland.

PUBLIC ENEMY

Public Enemy's dense, layered sound and radical political message made them among the most popular, controversial, and influential hip-hop artists of the late 1980s and early 1990s. The group's original members were Chuck D (original name Carlton Ridenhour; b. Aug. 1, 1960, New York, N.Y., U.S.), Flavor Flav (original name William Drayton; b. March 16, 1959, New York), Terminator X (original name Norman Lee Rogers; b. Aug. 25, 1966, New York), and Professor Griff (original name Richard Griffin).

Public Enemy was formed in 1982 at Adelphi University on Long Island, N.Y., by a group of African Americans who came primarily from the suburbs. Chuck D, Hank Shocklee, Bill Stephney, and Flavor Flav collaborated on a program on college radio. Reputedly, Def Jam producer Rick Rubin was so taken with Chuck D's booming voice that he begged him to record. Public Enemy resulted and brought radical black political ideology to pop music in an unprecedented fashion on albums with titles that read like party invitations for leftists and warning stickers for the right wing: *Yo! Bum Rush the Show* (1987), *It Takes a Nation of Millions to Hold Us Back* (1988), *Fear of a Black Planet* (1990), and *Apocalypse 91: The Enemy Strikes Black* (1991).

Acclaimed as Public Enemy's masterpiece, *Nation of Millions* revived the messages of the Black Panther Party and Malcolm X. On tracks such as "Night of the Living Baseheads," "Black Steel in the Hour of Chaos," and "Don't Believe the Hype," the strident, eloquent lyrics of Chuck D combined with bombastic, dissonant, and poignantly detailed backing tracks created by Public Enemy's production team, the Bomb Squad (Shocklee, his brother Keith, Chuck D, and Eric "Vietnam" Adler), to produce songs challenging the status quo in both hip-hop and racial politics. The Bomb Squad sampled (composed with other recordings) a wide variety of genres and sounds, including classic funk tracks by James Brown, jazz, the thrash-metal of Anthrax, sirens, and agitprop speeches. Flavor Flav provided a comic foil for Chuck D.

Comments by Professor Griff to the *Washington Times* in 1989 brought charges of anti-Semitism, which ultimately resulted in his leaving the group. Public Enemy's open admiration for the Nation of Islam leader Louis Farrakhan also brought it into conflict with Jewish organizations. While Public Enemy's activism inspired other artists to take up topical themes, the group's influence waned in the early 1990s as younger, more "ghettocentric" performers such as N.W.A. and Snoop Doggy Dogg came to the fore. The group seemed to have folded after *Muse Sick N Hour Mess Age* (1994), but in 1998 they produced a new album of songs for Spike Lee's film *He Got Game* and went on tour.

RUN-D.M.C.

Rap group Run-D.M.C. brought hip-hop into the musical and cultural mainstream, introducing what became known as "new-school" rap. The members were Run (original name Joseph Simmons; b. Nov. 14, 1964, New York, N.Y., U.S.), D.M.C.

(original name Darryl McDaniels; b. May 31, 1964, New York, N.Y.), and Jam Master Jay (original name Jason Mizell; b. Jan. 21, 1965, New York, N.Y.—d. Oct. 30, 2002, New York).

Formed in 1982 in Hollis—a middle-class, predominantly African American section of the New York City borough Queens—Run-D.M.C. was managed by Russell Simmons, who was the brother of group member Run and was cofounder of Def Jam, one of the most successful black-owned record companies. Run,

Run-D.M.C. at the Montreux Pop Festival in Switzerland, May 1988. From left to right, Jam Master Jay (Jason Mizell), D.M.C. (Darryl McDaniels), and Run (Joseph Simmons). Dave Hogan/Hulton Archive/Getty Images

whose nickname came from his quick turntable manipulation, began his musical career as a deejay for old-school rapper Kurtis Blow. Later Run, D.M.C., and Jam Master Jay began performing in New York City clubs. In 1983 Profile Records released the group's groundbreaking single "It's Like That/Sucker MCs," which featured a spare, forceful rhythm track and overlapping vocals (group members interweaving lines and words). Not only was their sound different, so, too, was their dress. Whereas earlier rap stars fashioned their looks after the spangled superhero costumes of 1970s funk acts like Parliament-Funkadelic and Rick James, Run-D.M.C. appeared in their signature bowler hats, black leather jackets, unlaced Adidas athletic shoes, and black denim pants, establishing the more casual look of hip urban youth as de rigueur stage wear for rappers.

They were the first rappers to have a gold album—*Run-D.M.C.* (1984)—and the first rap act to appear on MTV, becoming popular with the cable channel's largely white audience via their fusion of hardcore hip-hop and screaming guitar solos on hits such as "Rock Box" (1984) and a 1986 remake of Aerosmith's "Walk This Way" (featuring the song's hard-rocking originators). Other hits by Run-D.M.C. include "King of Rock" (1985), "My Adidas" (1986), which led to the first endorsement deal between hip-hop artists and a major corporation, and "It's Tricky" (1987). Although the group never officially disbanded, their recording and performing activities decreased significantly in the 1990s. In 2002 Jam Master Jay was fatally shot at a recording studio in Jamaica, Queens. Run-D.M.C was inducted into the Rock and Roll Hall of Fame in 2009.

TUPAC SHAKUR

(b. June 16, 1971, Brooklyn, N.Y., U.S.—d. Sept. 13, 1996, Las Vegas, Nev.)

Rapper and actor Tupac Shakur was one of the leading names in 1990s gangsta rap.

Lesane Parish Crooks was born to Alice Faye Williams, a member of the Black Panther Party, and she renamed him Tupac Amaru Shakur—after Peruvian revolutionary Tupac Amaru II—when he was a year old. He spent much of his childhood on the move with his family, which in 1986 settled in Baltimore, Md., where Shakur attended the elite Baltimore School of the Arts. He distinguished himself as a student, both creatively and academically, but his family relocated to Marin City, Calif., before he could graduate. There Shakur took to the streets, selling drugs and becoming involved in the gang culture that would one day provide material for his rap lyrics. In 1990 he joined Digital Underground, an Oakland-based rap group that had scored a *Billboard* Top 40 hit with the novelty single "The Humpty Dance." Shakur performed on two Digital Underground albums in 1991, *This Is an EP Release* and *Sons of the P*, before his solo debut, *2Pacalypse Now*, later that year.

2Pacalypse Now was a radical break from the dance party sound of Digital

Tupac Shakur, 1993. Al Pereira/Michael Ochs Archives/Getty Images

Underground, and its tone and content were much closer to the works of Public Enemy and West Coast gangsta rappers N.W.A. The lack of a clear single on the album limited its radio appeal, but it sold well, especially after Vice Pres. Dan Quayle criticized the song "Soulja's Story" during the 1992 presidential campaign. That same year Shakur (who was also known as 2Pac and Makaveli) joined the ranks of other rappers-turned-actors, such as Ice Cube and Ice-T, when he was cast in the motion picture *Juice*, an urban crime drama. The following year

he appeared in *Poetic Justice*, opposite Janet Jackson, and he released his second album, *Strictly 4 My N.I.G.G.A.Z.* The album did not stray far from the activist lyricism of his debut, but singles such as "Holler If Ya Hear Me" and "Keep Ya Head Up" made it much more radio-friendly.

With increased fame and success came greater scrutiny of Shakur's gangsta lifestyle. A string of arrests culminated with a conviction for sexual assault in 1994; he was incarcerated when his third album, *Me Against the World*, was released in 1995. Shakur was paroled after serving eight months in prison, and he signed with Suge Knight's Death Row Records for his next release. That album, *All Eyez on Me* (1996), was a two-disc paean to the "thug life" that Shakur embodied. It debuted at number one on the *Billboard* charts and sold more than five million copies within its first year of release. Quick to capitalize on his most recent success, Shakur returned to Hollywood, where he starred in *Bullet* (1996) and *Gridlock'd* (1997).

On the evening of Sept. 7, 1996, Shakur was leaving a Las Vegas casino, where he had just attended a prizefight featuring heavyweight champion Mike Tyson, when he was shot by an unknown assailant. The incident, believed by many to be the result of an ongoing rivalry between the East Coast and West Coast rap communities, shocked the entertainment world. Shakur died six days later. In spite of his relatively short recording career, Shakur left an enduring legacy within the hip-hop community. His popularity was undiminished after his death, and a long succession of posthumous releases (many of them were simply repackaged or remixed existing material, and most were of middling quality), ensured that "new" 2Pac albums continued to appear well into the 21st century.

KANYE WEST

(b. June 8, 1977, Atlanta, Ga., U.S.)

Producer and rapper Kanye West parlayed his production success in the late 1990s and early 2000s into a career as a popular, critically acclaimed solo artist.

West, the child of a photographer and former Black Panther father and a college professor mother, grew up in Chicago and attended Chicago State University for one year before dropping out to pursue a career in music. Early on he demonstrated his considerable abilities as a producer, contributing to Jermaine Dupri's album *Life in 1472* (1998) before relocating to the New York City area, where he made his name with his production work for Roc-a-Fella Records, especially on rapper Jay-Z's album *Blueprint* (2001). West's skillful use of accelerated sample-based beats soon made him much in demand as a producer, but he struggled to be allowed to make his own recordings (partly because of the perception that his middle-class background denied him credibility as a rapper). When he finally released his debut solo album, *The College Dropout* (2004), it was massively successful: sales soared, and critics gushed over its sonic sophistication and clever wordplay, which blended humour, faith, insight, and political awareness on songs such as "Through the Wire" and the gospel-choir-backed "Jesus Walks," which won a Grammy Award for best rap song—to go along with the awards for best rap album and best rhythm-and-blues song for "You Don't Know My Name."

Abetted by his flamboyant personality, West quickly rose to stardom. His second album, *Late Registration* (2005), repeated the commercial success of his first, with a number of hit singles (including "Diamonds in Sierra Leone" and "Gold Digger"), and earned West three more Grammy Awards. He also gained notoriety for his widely quoted assertion that the federal government's slow response to the Hurricane Katrina disaster in New Orleans in 2005 demonstrated that U.S. Pres. George Bush "doesn't care about black people."

Throughout his career, West continued to produce for high-profile artists such as Ludacris, Alicia Keys, and Janet Jackson. He also founded GOOD Music, a record label under the auspices of Sony BMG. His third release, *Graduation* (2007), produced the hit singles "Good Life" and "Stronger" and garnered him four more Grammy Awards. In 2008 West released *808s and Heartbreak*, an album that dwelled on feelings of personal loss and regret. Its sound differed radically from his previous releases, as West chose to sing (with the assistance of a vocal production tool called an Auto-Tuner) rather than rap his lyrics.

CABARET, GOSPEL, OPERA, AND SHOW MUSIC

Gospel music, though pioneered by African Americans such as Thomas Andrew Dorsey, is not the sole province of African Americans. Neither, of course, are opera, cabaret, show music, and any number of other genres that make up the tapestry of American popular music to which African Americans have made important contributions. Some

performers excel in many genres; others are such originals that their music cannot be shoehorned into a genre. The following is an amalgam of performers who are known for their work in one genre—Dorsey and Mahalia Jackson (gospel), Leontyne Price and Jessye Norman (opera)—and those who have earned distinction in several—Sammy Davis, Jr., Nat King Cole, and Lena Horne.

NAT KING COLE

(b. March 17, 1917, Montgomery, Ala., U.S.—d. Feb. 15, 1965, Santa Monica, Calif.)

Nat King Cole has been hailed as one of the best and most influential pianists and small-group leaders of the swing era. Cole attained his greatest commercial success, however, as a vocalist specializing in warm ballads and light swing.

Nathaniel Adams Cole (whose family name was originally Coles) grew up in Chicago where, by age 12, he sang and played organ in the church where his father was pastor. He formed his first jazz group, the Royal Dukes, five years later. In 1937, after touring with a black musical revue, he began playing in jazz clubs in Los Angeles. There he formed the King Cole Trio (originally King Cole and His Swingsters), with guitarist Oscar Moore and bassist Wesley Prince (later replaced by Johnny Miller). The trio specialized in swing music with a delicate touch in that they did not employ a drummer; also unique were the voicings of piano and guitar, often juxtaposed to sound like a single instrument. An influence on jazz pianists such as Oscar Peterson, Cole was known for a compact, syncopated piano style with clean, spare, melodic phrases.

During the late 1930s and early '40s the trio made several instrumental recordings, as well as others that featured their harmonizing vocals. They found their greatest success, however, when Cole began doubling as a solo singer. Their first chart success, "Straighten Up and Fly Right" (1943), was followed by hits such as "Sweet Lorraine," "It's Only a Paper Moon," "(I Love You) For Sentimental Reasons," and "Route 66." Eventually, Cole's piano playing took a backseat to his singing career. Noted for his warm tone and flawless phrasing, Cole was regarded among the top male vocalists, although jazz critics tended to regret his near-abandonment of the piano. He first recorded with a full orchestra (the trio serving as rhythm section) in 1946 for "The Christmas Song," a holiday standard and one of Cole's biggest-selling recordings. By the 1950s, he worked almost exclusively as a singer, with such notable arrangers as Nelson Riddle and Billy May providing lush orchestral accompaniment. "Nature Boy, Mona Lisa," "Too Young," "A Blossom Fell," and "Unforgettable" were among his major hits of the period. He occasionally revisited his jazz roots, as on the outstanding album *After Midnight* (1956), which proved that Cole's piano skills had not diminished.

Cole's popularity allowed him to become the first African American to host a network variety program, *The Nat King Cole Show*, which debuted on NBC television in 1956. The show fell victim to the bigotry of the times, however, and was canceled after one season; few sponsors were willing to be associated with a black entertainer. Cole had greater success with concert performances during the late 1950s and early '60s and twice toured with his own vaudeville-style reviews, *The Merry World of Nat King Cole* (1961) and *Sights and Sounds* (1963). His hits of the early '60s—"Ramblin' Rose," "Those Lazy, Hazy, Crazy Days of Summer," and "L-O-V-E"—indicate that he was moving even farther away from his jazz roots and concentrating almost exclusively on mainstream pop. Adapting his style, however, was one factor that kept Cole popular up to his early death from lung cancer in 1965.

The prejudices of the era in which Cole lived hindered his potential for even greater stardom. His talents extended beyond singing and piano playing: he excelled as a relaxed and humorous stage personality, and he was also a capable actor, evidenced by his performances in the films *Istanbul* (1957), *China Gate* (1957), *Night of the Quarter Moon* (1959), and *Cat Ballou* (1965); he also played himself in *The Nat "King" Cole Musical Story* (1955) and portrayed blues legend W.C. Handy in *St. Louis Blues* (1958). His daughter Natalie is also a popular singer who achieved her greatest chart success in 1991 with "Unforgettable," an electronically created duet with her father.

Sammy Davis, Jr.

(b. Dec., 1925, New York, N.Y., U.S.—d. May 16, 1990, Los Angeles, Calif.)

Singer, dancer, and entertainer Sammy Davis, Jr., was one of Hollywood's most recognizable personalties in the 1960s and '70s.

At age three Davis began performing in vaudeville with his father and uncle, Will Mastin, in the Will Mastin Trio. Davis studied tap dancing under Bill "Bojangles" Robinson but never received a formal education. After serving in the U.S. Army he became the central figure of the Mastin Trio, not only singing and dancing but also playing trumpet, drums, piano, and vibraphone; moreover, he was an accomplished mime and comedian. He encountered virulent racial prejudice early in his career, but he endured to become one of the first African American stars to achieve wide popularity.

Along with his extremely successful nightclub career, Davis was a popular recording artist, and he was successful on Broadway in *Mr. Wonderful* (1956) and in a 1964 revival of Clifford Odets' *Golden Boy*, and in films, including *Porgy and Bess* (1959) and *Sweet Charity* (1969). He also appeared in a series of motion pictures with friends such as Frank Sinatra and Dean Martin, including *Ocean's Eleven* (1960), *Sergeants 3* (1962), and *Robin and the 7 Hoods* (1964). Davis wrote two autobiographical books, *Yes I Can* (1965) and *Why Me?* (1989).

Thomas Andrew Dorsey

(b. July 1, 1899, Villa Rica, Ga., U.S.—d. Jan. 23, 1993, Chicago, Ill.)

Songwriter, singer, and pianist Thomas Andrew Dorsey's many up-tempo blues arrangements of gospel music hymns earned him the title of "Father of Gospel Music."

Dorsey was the son of a revivalist preacher. He was influenced in childhood by blues pianists in the Atlanta, Ga., area and worked in secular "hokum" music as a composer, arranger, pianist, and vocalist from 1910 through 1928. In 1916 he moved to Chicago, where he attended the College of Composition and Arranging. In the 1920s he toured with Ma Rainey and his own bands, often featuring the slide guitarist Tampa Red.

From 1929 on Dorsey worked exclusively within a religious setting, consciously applying blues melodies and rhythms to spiritual concerns. Dozens of his optimistic and sentimental songs became gospel standards, notably "Precious Lord, Take My Hand" (1932). He recorded extensively in the early 1930s, publishing his own sheet music and lyrics. From 1932 Dorsey was choral director of the Pilgrim Baptist Church in Chicago. He founded the National Convention of Gospel Choirs and Choruses in Chicago in 1933, serving as its president for 40 years. He stopped recording in 1934 but toured widely into the 1940s. Thereafter, though he continued writing, he concentrated on lecturing and administrative duties.

LENA HORNE

(b. June 30, 1917, Brooklyn, N.Y., U.S.—d. May 9, 2010, New York City)

Singer and actress Lena Horne first came to fame in the 1940s.

Horne left school at age 16 to help support her ailing mother and became a dancer at the Cotton Club in Harlem, New York City. In two years at the Cotton Club she appeared with such entertainers as Cab Calloway and eventually starred in her own shows. In 1935 she joined the Noble Sissle orchestra under the name Helena Horne. Horne was married from 1937 to 1944 to Louis J. Jones. In the early 1940s she was hired to sing for Charlie Barnet's orchestra. She was discovered by producer John Hammond, and soon after she performed in a solo show at Carnegie Hall in New York City.

In 1942 Horne moved to Los Angeles, after which she appeared in such movies as *Cabin in the Sky* (1943), *Meet Me in Las Vegas* (1956), and *The Wiz* (1978). Her role in the film *Stormy Weather* (1943) included her rendition of the title song, which became her trademark. A remarkably charismatic entertainer, Horne was one of the most popular singers of her

Lena Horne on stage at Café Moulin Rouge, Paris, France, 1954. Hulton Archive/Getty Images

time. One of her albums, *Lena Horne at the Waldorf-Astoria* (1957), was a longtime best-seller, and her first featured performance on Broadway—in the musical *Jamaica* (1957)—won her a New York Drama Critics' Poll Award in 1958.

Though primarily known as an entertainer, Horne also was noted for her work with civil rights and political organizations; as an actress, she refused to play roles that stereotyped African American women. She was married to Lennie Hayton from 1947 until his death in 1971. Her one-woman show, *Lena Horne: The*

Lady and Her Music (1981), garnered many awards, including a Drama Critics' Circle Award and a special achievement Tony Award. In 1984 Horne received a Kennedy Center honour for lifetime contribution to the arts, and in 1989 a Grammy Award for lifetime achievement.

Mahalia Jackson

(b. Oct. 26, 1911, New Orleans, La., U.S.—d. Jan. 27, 1972, Evergreen Park, near Chicago, Ill.)

Singer Mahalia Jackson is known as the "Queen of Gospel Song."

Jackson was brought up in a strict religious atmosphere. Her father's family included several entertainers, but she was forced to confine her own musical activities to singing in the church choir and listening—surreptitiously—to recordings of Bessie Smith and Ida Cox as well as of Enrico Caruso. When she was 16 she went to Chicago and joined the Greater Salem Baptist Church choir, where her remarkable contralto voice soon led to her selection as a soloist.

Jackson first came to wide public attention in the 1930s, when she participated in a cross-country gospel tour singing such songs as "He's Got the Whole World in His Hands" and "I Can Put My Trust in Jesus." In 1934 her first recording, "God Gonna Separate the Wheat from the Tares," was a success, leading to a series of other recordings. Jackson's first great hit, "Move on Up a

Little Higher," appeared in 1945; it was especially important for its use of the "vamp," an indefinitely repeated phrase (or chord pattern) that provides a foundation for solo improvisation. All the songs with which she was identified—including "I Believe," "Just over the Hill," "When I Wake Up in Glory," and "Just a Little While to Stay Here"—were gospel songs, with texts drawn from biblical themes and strongly influenced by the harmonies, rhythms, and emotional force of blues. Jackson refused to sing any but religious songs or indeed to sing at all in surroundings that she considered inappropriate. But she sang on the radio and on television and, starting in 1950, performed to overflow audiences in annual concerts at Carnegie Hall in New York City. Eight of Jackson's records sold more than a million copies each.

Jackson was enormously popular abroad; her version of "Silent Night," for example, was one of the all-time best-selling records in Denmark. She made a notable appearance at the Newport (R.I.) Jazz Festival in 1957—in a program devoted entirely, at her request, to gospel songs—and she sang at the inauguration of Pres. John F. Kennedy in January 1961. In the 1950s and '60s she was active in the civil rights movement; in 1963 she sang the old African American spiritual "I Been 'Buked and I Been Scorned" for a crowd of more than 200,000 in Washington, D.C., just before civil rights leader Martin Luther King, Jr., delivered his famous "I Have a Dream" speech.

JESSYE NORMAN

(b. Sept. 15, 1945, Augusta, Ga., U.S.)

Jessye Norman was one of the finest operatic sopranos of her day. She also enjoyed a successful concert career.

Norman was reared in a musical family. Both her mother and grandmother were pianists and her father sang in church, as did the young Jessye. She won a scholarship to Howard University in Washington, D.C., where she studied voice. She graduated in 1967 and received further training at the Peabody Conservatory in Baltimore, Md., and at the University of Michigan.

After winning the Bavarian Radio Corp. International Music Competition in 1968, Norman made her operatic debut as Elisabeth in Richard Wagner's *Tannhäuser* in 1969 in Berlin. The beauty, range, and flexibility of Norman's vibrant soprano voice assured her further operatic engagements, the most notable being the title role in *Aïda* in productions in Berlin and at La Scala in Milan and the role of Cassandra in Hector Berlioz's *Les Troyens*

Jessye Norman. Sean Gallup/Getty Images

(*The Trojans;* Covent Garden, 1972). In 1989 she appeared at the Metropolitan Opera for a historic performance of that company's first single-character production, *Erwartung* by Arnold Schoenberg.

Norman also enjoyed success as a recitalist with her thorough scholarship and her ability to project drama through her voice. She toured throughout the 1970s, giving recitals of works by Franz Schubert, Gustav Mahler, Wagner, Johannes Brahms, Erik Satie, Olivier Messiaen, and several contemporary American composers. By the mid-1980s she was one of the most popular and highly regarded dramatic soprano singers in the world. She produced numerous award-winning recordings, and many of her performances were televised.

LEONTYNE PRICE

(b. Feb. 10, 1927, Laurel, Miss., U.S.)

Lyric soprano Leontyne Price was the first African American singer to achieve an international reputation in opera.

Both of Price's grandfathers had been Methodist ministers in black churches in Mississippi, and she sang in her church choir as a girl. Only when she graduated from the College of Education and Industrial Arts (now Central State College) in Wilberforce, Ohio, in 1948 did she decide to seek a career as a singer. She studied for four years at the Juilliard School of Music in New York City, where she worked under the former concert singer Florence Page Kimball, who remained her coach in later years. Her debut took place in April 1952 in a Broadway revival of *Four Saints in Three Acts* by Virgil Thomson and Gertrude Stein. Her performance in that production, which subsequently traveled to Paris, prompted Ira Gershwin to choose her to sing the role of Bess in his revival of *Porgy and Bess*, which played in New York City from 1952 to 1954 and then toured the United States and Europe. The year 1955 saw her triumphant performance of the title role in the National Broadcasting Company's television production of *Tosca*, and she sang leading roles in other operas on television in the next few years.

Price's operatic stage debut did not take place until September 1957, when she appeared in the American premiere of Francis Poulenc's *Les Dialogues des Carmélites* at the San Francisco Opera. She continued in San Francisco until 1960, appearing in such works as *Aïda*, *Thaïs*, and *The Wise Maidens*. By that time she was one of the most popular lyric sopranos in the country and had also made successful appearances in Vienna in 1959 and at Milan's La Scala in May 1960.

Despite this great success, her debut at the Metropolitan Opera in New York City was deferred until January 1961, when she appeared there in the role of Leonora in *Il Trovatore*. After a brilliant performance she became one of the Met's leading regular sopranos. Her later roles there included Cio-Cio-San in *Madama Butterfly*, Donna Anna in *Don Giovanni*, and Liu in *Turandot*.

In the 1970s Price began to devote more time to recitals, but she scored another great success in her first performance of *Ariadne auf Naxos* in San Francisco in October 1977. She was one of the most frequently recorded opera singers, and she was the recipient of more than 20 Grammy Awards from the American Society of Recording Arts and Sciences. She was awarded the Presidential Medal of Freedom in 1964, the National Medal of the Arts in 1985, and a lifetime achievement award from the National Academy of Recorded Arts and Sciences in 1989. She gave her farewell performance of *Aïda* at the Metropolitan Opera in New York in 1985 but continued to give recitals, which she described as her first love. She published a book, *Aida*, based on Giuseppe Verdi's opera, in 1990.

The realm of music has a huge constellation of African American stars and superstars that is larger than that found on the stage and screen. Perhaps only in sports are there more African Americans who are household names.

CHAPTER 7

SPORTS

L ike the field of entertainment, sports have historically offered disadvantaged groups of Americans opportunities to transcend humble beginnings. The notion of ethnic succession—that is, of successive waves of immigrant groups finding success in fields that earlier-arriving ethnic groups had dominated but largely left behind as broader avenues to success opened—is often tied to the genesis of organized crime in the United States, but it is equally applicable to entertainment and sports. Boxing, dominated at one time or another by Jewish, Irish, Italian, African American, and Latino fighters, is the classic example.

Sports have not only provided economic advancement opportunities for African Americans, they have also been pivotal to the development of black self-esteem. It is telling that the "level playing field" of sports (on which, once colour barriers to participation were broken, black achievement could not be denied or discounted) has proved to be one of the most powerful metaphors for access and equity in all endeavours. Yet, as sociologist Harry Edwards pointed out as early as the 1960s, the prevalence of African Americans in a number of sports can also be seen as a marker of the lack of opportunity available to blacks in other fields of endeavour. He and others were quick to encourage young African Americans to look for role models in places other than on the basketball court, on other playing fields, or in the ring, pointing out that only an elite few would earn livings in professional sports and that education remained the key to social mobility. Still, there is no denying the symbolic importance of the breaking of the colour barrier in sports and of the extraordinary performances by black athletes, many of the most renowned of whom are profiled in this chapter.

BASEBALL

Baseball may no longer be the most popular sport in the United States, but because it was for so long and because it remains (at least in name) the national pastime, laden with symbolism, the story of its desegregation is central not just to the history of sports and of African Americans but to that of the country. That story is grounded in the history of the Negro Leagues, some of whose best remembered players are represented here; in the dramatic smashing of major league baseball's colour barrier by Jackie Robinson; and in the accomplishments of the thousands of African American players who followed Robinson onto the diamond, including record breakers and fan favourites such as Hank Aaron, who began his career in the Negro Leagues and went on to hit more lifetime home runs that any other player in the history of the game, until his record was surpassed by another African American slugger, Barry Bonds.

HANK AARON

(b. Feb. 5, 1934, Mobile, Ala., U.S.)

During 23 seasons in the major leagues (1954–76), baseball player Hank Aaron surpassed batting records set by some of the greatest hitters in the game, including Babe Ruth, Ty Cobb, and Stan Musial.

Aaron, a right-hander (born Henry Louis Aaron), began his professional career in 1952, playing shortstop for a few months with the Indianapolis Clowns of the Negro American League. His contract was bought by the Boston Braves of

Hank Aaron. Pictorial Parade

the National League, who assigned him to minor league teams. In 1954 he moved up to the majors, playing mostly as an outfielder for the Braves (who had moved to Milwaukee, Wis., in 1953). In 1956 he won the league batting championship with an average of .328, and in 1957, having led his team to victory in the World Series, he was named the league's Most Valuable Player. By the time the Braves moved to Atlanta at the end of 1965, Aaron had hit 398 home runs. In Atlanta on April 8, 1974, he hit his 715th, breaking Babe Ruth's record, which had stood since 1935. After the 1974 season, Aaron was traded to the Milwaukee Brewers, who were at that time in the American League. Aaron retired after the 1976 season and rejoined the Atlanta Braves as an executive. He was elected to the Baseball Hall of Fame on Jan. 13, 1982.

Aaron's batting records include totals of 1,477 extra-base hits and 2,297 runs batted in. His home run record of 755 was broken by Barry Bonds in 2007. Aaron's other career statistics include 2,174 runs scored (second to Ty Cobb) and 12,364 times at bat in 3,298 games (second to Pete Rose). His hits (3,771) were exceeded only by those of Ty Cobb and Pete Rose. Aaron's lifetime batting average was .305.

COOL PAPA BELL

(b. May 17, 1903, Starkville, Miss., U.S.—d. March 7, 1991, St. Louis, Mo.)

Cool Papa Bell was reputedly the fastest baserunner of all time.

James Thomas Bell began as a pitcher for the St. Louis Stars in the Negro National League at the age of 19 and earned the nickname Cool when he struck out legendary Oscar Charleston; Bell's manager added "Papa." He played centre field for the Stars (1922–28), for the Pittsburgh Crawfords (1933–37), in the Mexican League (1938–42), for the Homestead Grays in the Negro National League (1943–45), and as player-manager of the Kansas City Monarchs in that same league (1948–50). He also played in the California Winter League and in Cuba and the Dominican Republic, as well as on occasion with other Negro teams. A right-handed batter who later became a switch hitter, his average ranged from .308 to .480. He reputedly stole 175 bases in a 200-game season. (Statistics in Negro baseball were not carefully kept.) Playing against all the greats of Negro baseball and against white All-Star teams, Bell batted .391 over a five-year period. He was elected to the Baseball Hall of Fame in 1974.

BARRY BONDS

(b. July 24, 1964, Riverside, Calif., U.S.)

A great all-around player, Barry Bonds broke the major league home run records for both a career (with his 756th home run, in 2007) and a single season (with 73 home runs in 2001).

Barry Lamar Bonds was born into a baseball family. His father, Bobby Bonds, was an outfielder for the San Francisco

Giants. His cousin was baseball great Reggie Jackson. His godfather was the legendary Willie Mays, who was a teammate of Bobby Bonds. Barry Bonds excelled at baseball from early childhood. The San Francisco Giants drafted him out of high school, but he turned down the contract the team offered him and instead chose to play college baseball for Arizona State University. Bonds was drafted by the Pittsburgh Pirates in 1985 and joined the Pirates' major league roster in 1986.

Bonds garnered numerous Gold Glove awards for his play in left field but was best known as an extremely productive hitter. In 2004 he became only the third major leaguer to hit more than 700 home runs in his career, and he became the major league all-time walks leader, surpassing Rickey Henderson. He compiled a career batting average of .300 and was such a dangerous hitter that opposing managers routinely walked him intentionally when men were on base. Bonds was also an excellent base runner, reaching the plateau of 500 career stolen bases in 2003. He was voted the National League's Most Valuable Player (MVP) seven times (1990, 1992, 1993, 2001, 2002, 2003, and 2004), the first player in either league to win the award more than three times.

Bonds became a free agent in 1992 and signed with the San Francisco Giants, with whom he continued to have record-breaking seasons. He completed the 2001 season with 73 home runs, breaking Mark McGwire's 1998 record of 70 home runs on October 5. In 2005 Bond's personal trainer pleaded guilty to distribution of banned steroids, leading to speculation that Bonds may have used the performance-enhancing drugs; however, Bonds testified before a grand jury in 2003 that he had never knowingly used steroids or received injections from his personal trainer. On Aug. 7, 2007, Bonds hit his 756th home run—off Washington Nationals pitcher Mike Bacsik in San Francisco—to surpass Hank Aaron's career record. At the end of the season, however, Bonds became a free agent after the Giants elected not to offer him a new contract. In November 2007 he was indicted on charges of perjury and obstruction of justice for his 2003 grand jury testimony.

LOU BROCK

(b. June 18, 1939, El Dorado, Ark., U.S.)

Lou Brock's career 938 stolen bases (1961–79) set a record that held until 1991, when it was broken by Rickey Henderson.

Louis Clark Brock followed his childhood interest in baseball by playing at Southern University in Baton Rouge, La., where he both pitched and played in the outfield. He threw and hit left-handed. He was signed to a contract by the Chicago Cubs in 1961 and played on their farm teams before moving to the major leagues in 1962. With the Cubs his outfield playing was erratic, and his speed on the bases was unproductive; when he went into a hitting slump in 1964 (.251 in 52 games), he was traded to the St. Louis Cardinals, where he hit .348 for the rest of the season (.315 in all). Thereafter he led the league in stolen bases (1966–69 and 1971–74), stealing 50 or more bases each year (1965–76). His batting average was .300 or higher for eight seasons and .293 in his career. In 1974 he stole 118 bases, a new season record until 1982, when Rickey Henderson stole 130. Brock hit .414 in the 1967 World Series and .464 in the 1968 series. He retired after the 1979 season and was elected to the Baseball Hall of Fame in 1985.

LARRY DOBY

(b. Dec. 13, 1923, Camden, S.C., U.S.—d. June 18, 2003, Montclair, N.J.)

Larry Doby was the second African American player in the major leagues and the first in the American League when he joined the Cleveland Indians in 1947.

The son of a semipro baseball player, Lawrence Eugene Doby excelled at baseball, basketball, and football, earning an athletic scholarship to Long Island University in New York. Doby played for the Newark Eagles of the Negro National League in 1942 and 1943 before enlisting in the U.S. Navy. He returned to the Newark Eagles for the 1946 and 1947 seasons until Bill Veeck signed him to play with the Cleveland Indians at the end of the 1947 season. Doby, whose own father had died when he was 8 years old, spoke of Veeck as a second father. When some of his new teammates refused to shake his hand, Veeck got rid of them before the

next season began. Like Jackie Robinson, Doby was excluded from many segregated hotels and restaurants frequented by teammates, received numerous death threats, and had to overcome the animosity of other players and fans; however, since the papers were already reporting Robinson's troubles, Doby's struggles were mostly ignored at the time.

In 1948 Doby starred as the Indians' centre fielder, batting .301, and his home run won a World Series game. A power hitter, he batted .326 in 1950, when he led the league in on-base percentage; twice he slugged 32 homers to lead the league; and his 126 runs batted in (RBIs) led the Indians to another pennant in 1954. Doby was an all-star for 7 of his 13 years (1947–59), which included time with the Chicago White Sox and the Detroit Tigers. He came out of retirement in 1962 to play with the Chunichi Dragons in Japan for one season. He then went on to coach for the Montreal Expos, Indians, and White Sox, before Veeck made him the White Sox manager in 1978, the second African American major league manager. Doby was elected to the Baseball Hall of Fame by the Veterans Committee in 1998.

BOB GIBSON

(b. Nov. 9, 1935, Omaha, Neb., U.S.)

Right-handed pitcher Bob Gibson was at his best in crucial games. In nine World Series games, he won seven and lost two.

At Omaha Technical High School Gibson (born Pack Robert Gibson) was a star in basketball and track, as well as a baseball catcher. He played basketball and baseball at Creighton University (Omaha) as a shortstop and outfielder. After playing professional basketball with the Harlem Globetrotters for one season, Gibson signed with baseball's St. Louis Cardinals in 1957 and played with their minor-league teams until 1959. A regular with the Cardinals from 1961, Gibson won 20 games in 1965 and 22 (including 13 shutouts) in 1968. He started 34 games in 1968, completing 28, and had an earned run average (ERA) of 1.12, the lowest single-season ERA since 1914. Gibson won both the NL Cy Young and NL Most Valuable Player awards for 1968. Two years later he added a second Cy Young Award after posting a league-high 23 wins with a 3.12 ERA. He pitched quickly, and his best pitches were a fastball and a slider. In his career Gibson had 3,117 strikeouts, the first pitcher to accumulate more than 3,000 since Walter Johnson in the 1920s. The eight-time NL All Star retired as a player in 1975. He later worked as a pitching coach for the New York Mets and Atlanta Braves, and in 1996 he became a special instructor for the Cardinals. Gibson (who was nicknamed "Hoot") was elected to the Baseball Hall of Fame in 1981.

JOSH GIBSON

(b. Dec. 21, 1911, Buena Vista, Ga., U.S.—d. Jan. 20, 1947, Pittsburgh, Pa.)

Called the black Babe Ruth, Josh Gibson was one of the greatest players kept from the major leagues by the unwritten rule (enforced until the year of his death) against hiring black ballplayers.

Gibson played as a catcher for the Pittsburgh Crawfords (1927–29 and 1932–36) and the Homestead Grays of Pennsylvania (1930–31 and 1937–46). Although precise records do not exist, he is believed to have led the Negro National League in home runs for 10 consecutive seasons and to have had a career batting average of .347. He hit 75 home runs for Homestead in 1931. His catching ability was praised by Walter Johnson and other major league stars against whom he played in exhibition games. Gibson was elected to the Baseball Hall of Fame in 1972.

RICKEY HENDERSON

(b. Dec. 25, 1958, Chicago, Ill., U.S.)

In 1991 Rickey Henderson set a record for the most stolen bases in major league baseball and in 2001 set a record for the most career runs scored.

Henderson was an All-American running back in football as a high school athlete in Oakland, Calif. He chose to play baseball over football, however, and competed in the minor leagues for four seasons. Henderson's career in the major leagues began with the Oakland Athletics in June 1979. In 1980, his first full season, he became one of only three players ever to have stolen 100 bases, breaking Ty Cobb's American League record of 96 bases. It was the first of seven consecutive seasons in which Henderson led the American League in stolen bases. In 1982 he broke Lou Brock's single-season record of 118 stolen bases, set in 1974, with 130 stolen bases. Henderson added 108 stolen bases the following year.

Henderson was traded to the New York Yankees after the 1984 season but was traded back to Oakland midway through the 1989 season and helped the Athletics win the World Series. In 1990 Henderson—having hit 28 home runs, scored 119 runs, stolen 65 bases, and batted .325—was selected American League Most Valuable Player. He set the American League career stolen-base record that year with his 893rd steal, again breaking a mark set by Cobb. Henderson stole the 939th base of his career in 1991, breaking Brock's major league record.

Henderson played for numerous teams in the 1990s. His frequent trades to different teams were fueled in part by contract disputes and the perception that he was not a team player.

The 2001 season was a landmark for Henderson. On April 25, while a member of the San Diego Padres, he broke Babe Ruth's lifetime record for bases on balls (walks). When Ruth retired from baseball in 1935, he had 2,062 bases on balls, a testament to his ability to judge pitches and intimidate pitchers, and it was thought that the record would never be broken. Ted Williams (with 2,019) had been the only other player to even top 2,000 walks until Henderson, who ended the 2001 season with 2,141 walks. (The career walk record was broken again by Barry Bonds

in 2004.) Henderson continued his record-breaking season on October 4, setting the all-time record for runs scored. His 2,246th run broke the career record for runs held by Ty Cobb, which had stood since Cobb's retirement in 1928. On October 7, the last day of the 2001 regular season, Henderson became only the 25th player in major league history to have recorded 3,000 hits.

He last appeared in a major league game in September 2003, but he continued to play for independent minor league teams over the following two years. Henderson officially retired from baseball in 2007. Two years later he was elected to the Baseball Hall of Fame in Cooperstown, N.Y. His autobiography, *Off Base: Confessions of a Thief*, was published in 1992.

REGGIE JACKSON

(b. May 18, 1946, Wyncote, Pa., U.S.)

One of baseball's great sluggers, Reggie Jackson was at his best during the major league's pressure-filled playoffs.

Reginald Martinez Jackson was encouraged in sports by his father and became a star athlete at Cheltenham High School in Pennsylvania, excelling in track and football as well as baseball. He was a good pitcher as well as a hitter, batting and throwing left-handed. He continued his athletic career at Arizona State University (Tempe), but after two years he became a professional baseball player. He played with American League

Reggie Jackson of the New York Yankees hitting his third home run in his third consecutive at-bat in game six of the 1977 World Series. Louis Requena

Kansas City Athletics farm teams (1967–68) and joined the Athletics in 1968 when the team moved to Oakland, Calif., remaining with the team through the 1975 season. He made his mark as a home-run hitter and an exceptional base runner. He led the league in home runs (1973 and 1975). Playing on the World Series-winning Athletics (1972–74), Jackson in the 1973 World Series batted .310, drove in all three runs as Oakland won the sixth game, and hit a two-run homer in the decisive seventh game.

In 1976 he was traded to the Baltimore Orioles, and in 1977 as a free agent he signed a five-year contract with the New York Yankees for nearly $3 million. He finished his career with the California Angels (1982–86). He led the league in home runs in 1980. In the final game of the 1977 World Series, he hit three consecutive home runs and drove in five runs as the Yankees won 8–4. In the 1978 World Series he hit .391 and two home runs. He earned his nickname "Mr. October" because of his outstanding performance in World Series games. From 1973 he played mainly as a designated hitter (or DH, wherein one bats for the pitcher but holds no fielding position). Jackson was elected to the Baseball Hall of Fame in 1993.

BUCK LEONARD

(b. Sept. 8, 1907, Rocky Mount, N.C., U.S.—d. Nov. 27, 1997, Rocky Mount)

Buck Leonard was considered one of the best first basemen in the Negro leagues. He was among the first Negro leaguers to receive election into the Baseball Hall of Fame.

Leonard, a left-handed hitter (born Walter Fenner Leonard), was a semi-professional player for several years in North Carolina before losing his job with a railroad and deciding to pursue full-time professional baseball in 1933. That year he played with the Portsmouth Firefighters, the Baltimore Stars, and the Brooklyn Royal Giants. He signed with the Homestead Grays in 1934 and played 17 years with them, through the 1950 season.

Leonard and catcher Josh Gibson led the Grays to nine consecutive Negro National League championships from 1937 through 1945. The Grays won a 10th pennant and their third Negro World Series title in 1948. Leonard was selected to start in the East-West All-Star game a record 11 times. He finished his Negro league career with a batting average of about .341 and a .382 mark against major leaguers in exhibition games.

In 1943 Leonard was part of Satchel Paige's All-Stars, playing against major league All-Stars and hitting .500 in eight games. But it was home runs that made Leonard and Gibson the most-feared tandem in the Negro leagues, much like Lou Gehrig and Babe Ruth of the major league New York Yankees. Clark Griffith, the owner of the Washington Senators of the major leagues, considered signing the pair but never did. After Homestead disbanded, Leonard played five more years, in Mexico and also with Portsmouth, until 1955, when he was 48 years old.

Leonard was inducted into the Baseball Hall of Fame in 1972, along with Gibson, his longtime teammate. Leonard served as vice president of the Rocky Mount Leafs in the Class-A Carolina League.

WILLIE MAYS

(b. May 6, 1931, Westfield, Ala., U.S.)

Considered by many to have been the best all-around player in the history of baseball, Willie Mays was exceptional at both batting and fielding. Mays played in major league baseball very soon after the colour bar ended, and he probably never received the respect due him based upon his skills.

Both Mays's father and his grandfather had been baseball players. Willie Mays, who batted and fielded right-handed, played semiprofessional baseball when he was 16 years old and joined the Birmingham Black Barons of the Negro

A spectacular catch made by Willie Mays of the New York Giants during the All-Star Game, July 12, 1955. UPI

National League in 1948, playing only on Sunday during the school year. The National League New York Giants paid the Barons for his contract when he graduated from Fairfield Industrial High School in 1950. After two seasons in the minor leagues, Mays went to the Giants in 1951 and was named Rookie of the Year at the end of that season—one legendary in baseball. The Giants were far behind the Brooklyn Dodgers in the pennant race. With the great play of Mays and others, the Giants tied the Dodgers in the standings on the last day of the season, and a three-game playoff for the National League championship was won with a home run, known as "the shot heard 'round the world," hit by the Giants' Bobby Thomson.

Mays (nicknamed the "Say Hey Kid") became known first for his spectacular leaping and diving catches before he established himself as a hitter. He served in the army (1952–54), and upon his return to baseball in the 1954 season, when the Giants won the National League pennant and the World Series, Mays led the league in hitting (.345) and had 41 home runs. In 1966 his two-year contract with the Giants (who had moved to San Francisco in 1958) gave him the highest salary of any baseball player of that time. He was traded to the New York Mets midseason in 1972 and retired after the 1973 season. Late in his career he played in the infield, mainly at first base. His career home run total was 660 and his batting average .302. Mays had 3,283 hits during his career, which made him one of the small group of players with more than 3,000 career hits. He led the league in home runs in 1955, 1962, and 1964–65, won 12 consecutive Gold Gloves (1957–68), and appeared in 24 All-Star Games.

After retiring as a player, Mays was a part-time coach and did public relations work for the Mets. In 1979 Mays took a public relations job with a company that was involved in gambling concerns, with the result that he was banned from baseball-related activities just three months after being elected to the Baseball Hall of Fame in Cooperstown, New York. In 1985 the ban was lifted, and in 1986 Mays became a full-time special assistant to the Giants. His autobiography, *Say Hey* (1988), was written with Lou Sahadi.

BUCK O'NEIL

(b. Nov. 13, 1911, Carrabelle, Fla., U.S.—d. Oct. 6, 2006, Kansas City, Mo.)

Buck O'Neil is remembered for his skills as both a player and manager in the Negro leagues.

John Jordan O'Neil, Jr., was raised in Sarasota, Fla., and began playing baseball on a semiprofessional level at age 12. He attended Edward Waters College in Jacksonville, Fla., after being turned away from a segregated high school. There he earned a high school diploma and completed two years of college.

In 1937 O'Neil was signed to the Memphis Red Sox in the Negro American League. He debuted as a first baseman for the Kansas City Monarchs in 1938.

During his tenure with the Monarchs, O'Neil twice led the Negro American League in batting average, batting .345 in 1940 and .350 in 1946. In 1942 the Red Sox took the Negro American League title and advanced to win the Negro World Series against the Homestead Grays. O'Neil left the team to serve in the navy from 1944 to 1945. He was the team's manager from 1948 to 1955, during which time the team won four league titles.

In 1956 he was hired as a scout for the Chicago Cubs and helped the team sign future Baseball Hall of Fame players Ernie Banks and Lou Brock. In 1962 the Cubs made O'Neil the first African American coach in major league baseball. His leading role in Ken Burns's 1994 television documentary *Baseball* brought him to the attention of new generations of baseball fans. O'Neil served as chairman of the Negro Leagues Baseball Museum in Kansas City from its creation in 1990 until his death. He was posthumously awarded the Presidential Medal of Freedom.

Satchel Paige, 1942. UPI

SATCHEL PAIGE

(b. July 7, 1906?, Mobile, Ala., U.S.—d. June 8, 1982, Kansas City, Mo.)

Pitcher Satchel Paige's prowess became legendary during his many years in the Negro leagues; he finally was allowed to enter the major leagues in 1948. A right-handed, flexible "beanpole" standing more than 6 feet 3 inches tall, Paige had considerable pitching speed, but he also developed a comprehensive mastery of slow-breaking pitches and varied deliveries. He is rated as one of the greatest players in the history of baseball.

Paige (born Leroy Robert Paige) honed his baseball skills while in reform school. He entered the Negro leagues playing for the Chattanooga Black Lookouts in 1926. He was a pitcher for various teams in the Negro Southern Association and the Negro National League. Wearing a false red beard, he also played for the House of David team (a team fielded by a communal Christian religious sect that forbade its male members to shave or cut their hair). A true "iron man," he pitched in the Dominican Republic and Mexican leagues during the northern winter. As a barnstormer, he would travel as many as 30,000 miles a year while pitching for any team willing to meet his price. He is reputed to have pitched a total of 2,500 games during his nearly 30-year career, winning 2,000 of them.

Paige was a colourful and larger-than-life figure in the Negro leagues, prone to stunts such as sending the infield players into the dugout while he pitched or deliberately loading the bases before pitching to Josh Gibson, a hitter of great renown. His showmanship and popularity caused white baseball fans to take greater notice of the players in the Negro leagues, which perhaps hastened the integration of baseball. Despite the colour bar, Paige faced the best major league players in exhibition games before 1948. He once struck out Rogers Hornsby, probably the greatest right-handed hitter in baseball history, five times in one game. In Hollywood in 1934 Paige scored a spectacular 1–0 victory in 13 innings over Dizzy Dean, who won 30 games for the St. Louis Cardinals that year.

In his later years Paige derived much amusement from the controversy about his age; his birth date is sometimes placed as early as Dec. 18, 1899. He was surely well past his prime in 1948 when team owner Bill Veeck signed him for the Cleveland Indians; whatever his exact age, he was the oldest rookie ever to play in the major leagues. He helped to spark that team to American League pennant and World Series victories that year. When Veeck purchased the St. Louis Browns, Paige joined that team, and he was its most effective relief pitcher from 1951 through 1953. He also pitched three scoreless innings for the Kansas City Athletics in 1965, which made him the oldest to pitch in the major leagues.

Paige was famous for his pithy remarks. One well-known quotation on on "How to Stay Young" reads:

1. Avoid fried meats, which angry up the blood. 2. If your stomach disputes you, lie down and pacify it with cool thoughts. 3. Keep the juices flowing by jangling around gently as you move. 4. Go very light on the vices, such as carrying on in society. The social ramble ain't restful. 5. Avoid running at all times. 6. Don't look back. Something might be gaining on you.

Paige was elected to the Baseball Hall of Fame in Cooperstown, New York, in 1971. His autobiography, *Maybe I'll Pitch Forever* (1962), written with David Lipman, was revised in 1993.

FRANK ROBINSON

(b. Aug. 31, 1935, Beaumont, Texas, U.S.)

The only player to win the Most Valuable Player (MVP) award in both the National and American leagues, Frank Robinson was also the first African American to manage a Major League Baseball team.

As a youth, Robinson played sandlot and American Legion Junior League baseball in Oakland, Calif., and at McClymonds High School, where he also played football and basketball. The right-hander played third base and pitched occasionally. After graduation he was signed by the National League (NL) Cincinnati Reds and played with their minor league teams (third base and out-field) until he joined the parent club in 1956, the year he was awarded Rookie of the Year honours. Robinson won an NL MVP award in 1961, and he batted more than .300 in 5 of the 10 years before he was traded to the American League (AL) Baltimore Orioles in 1966. In his first season with Baltimore he won the Triple Crown—leading the league in home runs (49), runs batted in (122), and batting aver-age (.316)—and he was named the 1966 AL MVP, becoming the first to win the award in both leagues. He remained with Baltimore through 1971 and then played with the NL Los Angeles Dodgers (1972) and the AL California Angels (1973–74) and Cleveland Indians (1974–76). With 586 career home runs, Robinson ranked fourth in home runs hit, after Hank Aaron (755), Babe Ruth (714), and Willie Mays (660) when he retired in 1976.

Robinson began managing the Indians in 1975, the first African American to manage a major league team. He had begun his managing career in winter baseball for the Santurce team

in the Puerto Rican League in 1968 and had also coached at Baltimore and in the minor leagues for the International League. In 1981 he became manager of the NL San Francisco Giants. In 1984 Robinson returned to the Orioles, work-ing as a coach, as a manager (he was named AL Manager of the Year in 1989), and in the front office for the team's upper management. He stayed with the Orioles until the end of the 1995 season. In 2000 Robinson was put in charge of discipline as a vice president of Major League Baseball, meting out fines and suspensions in controversial imbro-glios. In 2002 he became manager of the Montreal Expos (from 2005 known as the Washington Nationals); he was fired by the franchise in 2006. Robinson was elected to the Baseball Hall of Fame in Cooperstown, N.Y., in 1982.

JACKIE ROBINSON

(b. Jan. 31, 1919, Cairo, Ga., U.S.—d. Oct. 24, 1972, Stamford, Conn.)

Jackie Robinson was the first African American to play in the major leagues during the 20th century. On April 15, 1947, Robinson broke the decades-old colour bar of Major League Baseball when he appeared on the field for the National League Brooklyn Dodgers. He played as an infielder and outfielder for the Dodgers from 1947 through 1956.

Reared in Pasadena, Calif., Robinson became an outstanding all-around ath-lete at Pasadena Junior College and the

University of California, Los Angeles (UCLA). He excelled in football, basketball, and track as well as baseball. Robinson withdrew from UCLA in his third year to help his mother care for the family. In 1942 he entered the U.S. Army and attended officer candidate school; he was commissioned a second lieutenant in 1943. Robinson faced court-martial in 1944 for refusing to follow an order that he sit at the back of a military bus. The charges against Robinson were dismissed, and he received an honourable discharge from the military. The incident, however, presaged Robinson's future activism and commitment to civil rights. Upon leaving the army, he played professional football in Hawaii and baseball with the Kansas City Monarchs of the Negro American League, where he drew the attention of the president and general manager of the Brooklyn Dodgers, Branch Rickey.

Rickey had been planning an attempt to integrate baseball and was looking for the right candidate. Robinson's skills on the field, his integrity, and his conservative family-oriented lifestyle all appealed greatly to Rickey. Rickey's main fear concerning Robinson was that he would be unable to withstand the racist abuse without responding in a way that would hurt integration's chances for success. During a legendary meeting Rickey shouted insults at Robinson, trying to be certain that Robinson could accept taunts without incident. On Oct. 23, 1945, Rickey signed Robinson to play on a Dodger farm team, the Montreal Royals of the International League.

Robinson led that league in batting average in 1946 and was brought up to play for Brooklyn in 1947. He was an immediate success on the field. Leading the National League in stolen bases, he was chosen Rookie of the Year. In 1949 he won the batting championship with a .342 average and was voted the league's Most Valuable Player (MVP).

His personal experiences were quite different. Fans hurled bottles and invectives at him. Some Dodger teammates openly protested against having to play with an African American, while players on opposing teams deliberately pitched balls at Robinson's head and spiked him with their shoes in deliberately rough slides into bases. Not everyone in baseball was unsupportive of Robinson. When players on the St. Louis Cardinals team threatened to strike if Robinson took the field, commissioner Ford Frick quashed the strike, countering that any player who did so would be suspended from baseball. Dodger captain Pee Wee Reese left his position on the field and put an arm around Robinson in a show of solidarity when fan heckling became intolerable, and the two men became lifelong friends. However, with the ugly remarks, death threats, and Jim Crow laws that forbade a black player to stay in hotels or eat in restaurants with the rest of his team, Robinson's groundbreaking experience in the major leagues was bleak. Of this period Robinson later stated,

Plenty of times I wanted to haul off when somebody insulted me

Jackie Robinson, 1946. UPI

for the color of my skin, but I had to hold to myself. I knew I was kind of an experiment. The whole thing was bigger than me.

His career in baseball was stellar. His lifetime batting average was .311, and he led the Dodgers to six league championships and one World Series victory. As a base runner, Robinson unnerved opposing pitchers and terrorized infielders who had to try to prevent him from stealing bases.

After retiring from baseball early in 1957, Robinson engaged in business and in civil rights activism. He was a spokesperson for the NAACP and made appearances with Martin Luther King, Jr. With his induction in 1962, Robinson became the first black person in the Baseball Hall of Fame, in Cooperstown, N.Y. His autobiography, *I Never Had It Made*, was published in 1972. In 1984 Robinson was posthumously awarded the Presidential Medal of Freedom, the highest honour for an American civilian.

In April 1997, on the 50th anniversary of the breaking of the colour bar in baseball, baseball commissioner Bud Selig retired Robinson's jersey number, 42, from Major League Baseball. It was common for a team to retire the number of a player from that team, but for a number to be retired for all the professional teams within a sport was unprecedented. In 2004 Major League Baseball announced that it would annually honour Robinson each April 15, which would thenceforth be recognized as Jackie Robinson Day.

Three years later, star slugger Ken Griffey, Jr., received permission from the commissioner of baseball to wear the number 42 on Jackie Robinson Day, and the yearly "unretiring" of Robinson's number gained more adherents until, in 2009, Major League Baseball decided that all players, coaches, and umpires would wear number 42 on April 15.

BASKETBALL

African American achievement in sports is perhaps most evident in basketball, which by the second half of the 20th century had become the definitive "city game," dominated on the professional level by black players, many of whom had honed their skills on courts on inner-city playgrounds, from which college scholarships offered a way out. That the culture of the game had also been transformed by African American culture was evident not just in the emergence of an improvisational aesthetic of play akin to that of jazz but also in the psychological gamesmanship of "trash-talking."

Yet, long before the "dipper dunk" of Wilt Chamberlain, the "sky hook" of Kareem Abdul-Jabbar, and the "Air"-borne acrobatics of Michael Jordan "elevated the game" (to borrow cultural critic Nelson George's phrase), the all-black New York Renaissance (better known as the Rens) had proved themselves in the 1920s against the "original" Celtics. Later, in 1939, they did the same in the championship game of the first World Professional Basketball Tournament against the Oshkosh All-Stars of the National Basketball League, which black teams were barred from joining. In the interim, the Harlem Globetrotters (actually based in Chicago), served as the international ambassadors of black basketball, combining dazzling ball-handling magicianship with comic flair.

More than the desegregation of the National Basketball Association by Earl Lloyd in 1950, the landmark achievement in the desegregation of basketball arguably came in 1966 when Texas Western University, which started five African American players, defeated perennial powerhouse the University of Kentucky to win the National Collegiate Athletic Association championship, an event depicted in the motion picture *Glory Road* (2006).

KAREEM ABDUL-JABBAR

(b. April 16, 1947, New York, N.Y., U.S.)

One of basketball's greatest big men, Kareem Abdul-Jabbar, a 7-foot-1.75-inch centre, dominated the collegiate and then professional game throughout the 1970s and early '80s.

Born Ferdinand Lewis Alcindor, Jr., he played as Lew Alcindor for Power Memorial Academy on the varsity for four years, and his total of 2,067 points set a New York City high school record. His offensive skill was so developed coming out of high school that the collegiate basketball rules committee, fearing he would be able to score at will, made

dunking illegal prior to his enrollment at the University of California at Los Angeles (UCLA) in 1965. Despite the new rule, he set a UCLA scoring record with 56 points in his first game. Playing for coach John Wooden, Alcindor helped lead UCLA to three National Collegiate Athletic Association championships (1966–68), and during his stay at UCLA the team lost only two games. The no-dunking rule was rescinded after Alcindor graduated.

Alcindor joined the National Basketball Association (NBA) Milwaukee Bucks in 1969 and was Rookie of the Year in 1970. In 1971 the Bucks won the NBA championship, and Alcindor led in scoring (2,596 points) and game-point average (31.7); he also led in these statistics in 1972 (2,822 points; 34.8). In 1971 Alcindor, who had converted to Islam while at UCLA, took the Arabic name Kareem Abdul-Jabbar. In 1975 he was traded to the Los Angeles Lakers, who won the NBA championship in 1980, 1982, 1985, 1987, and 1988. In 1984 he surpassed Wilt Chamberlain's career scoring total of 31,419 points.

Although Abdul-Jabbar lacked the physical strength of NBA centres Wilt Chamberlain and Willis Reed, he brought an excellent shooting touch to the position and a wide range of graceful post moves, including his sweeping, nearly indefensible sky hook. He also was an outstanding passer.

Abdul-Jabbar retired at the end of the 1988–89 season, having been voted Most Valuable Player a record six times. By the end of his extraordinarily long career, he had set NBA records for most points (38,387), most field goals made (15,837), and most minutes played (57,446). He was elected to the Naismith Memorial Basketball Hall of Fame in 1995.

Away from the basketball court Abdul-Jabbar pursued interests in acting and writing. He appeared on television and in a handful of films, including a memorable turn as a copilot in the comedy *Airplane!* (1980). His autobiography, *Giant Steps*, was published in 1983. In addition to his own experiences, he has written on the African American experience, including *Black Profiles in Courage: A Legacy of African American Achievement* (1996; with Alan Steinberg) and *On the Shoulders of Giants: My Journey Through the Harlem Renaissance* (2007). He also did some basketball coaching and consulting.

KOBE BRYANT

(b. Aug. 23, 1978, Philadelphia, Pa., U.S.)

Kobe Bryant helped lead the Los Angeles Lakers to four NBA championships (2000–02; 2009).

Bryant's father, Joe ("Jelly Bean") Bryant, was a professional basketball player who spent eight seasons in the NBA and eight more playing in Italy, where Bryant went to school. When his family returned to the United States, Bryant played basketball at Lower Merion High School in Ardmore, Pa., where he

received several national Player of the Year awards and broke the southeastern Pennsylvania scoring record set by Wilt Chamberlain with 2,883 points. Bryant opted to forgo college and declared himself eligible for the NBA draft when he graduated from high school. The Charlotte Hornets chose him with the 13th pick of the 1996 draft. He was traded to the Lakers shortly thereafter and became the second youngest NBA player in history when the 1996–97 season opened. He quickly proved his merit with the Lakers and was selected for the NBA All-Star Game in just his second season, becoming the youngest all-star.

Bryant was forced to share the role of the Lakers' star player with his popular and talented teammate Shaquille O'Neal. The two had an uneasy relationship, but they found success under the leadership of Phil Jackson, who became coach of the Lakers in 1999. Bryant, a shooting guard, and O'Neal, a centre, meshed into a remarkably effective combination, and, by the time Bryant was 23, the Lakers had won three consecutive NBA championships.

After winning their third title in 2002, Bryant and the Lakers encountered difficulties. In the 2003 play-offs the Lakers were defeated in the second round. Several months later Bryant was accused of raping a young woman in Colorado. He maintained his innocence, and all charges were eventually dropped. The incident, however, greatly tarnished his image. Led by Bryant, the Lakers returned to the finals in 2004, but they were upset

Kobe Bryant autographing jerseys, 2007. TM and © Upper Deck Company, all rights reserved/
PRNewsFoto/AP Images

by the Detroit Pistons. O'Neal subsequently was traded, and Bryant emerged as the team's sole leader. He led the league in scoring during the 2005–06 and 2006–07 seasons, and in 2007 he won his second All-Star Game's Most Valuable Player (MVP) award. In 2008 he was named the league's MVP for the first time in his career. Bryant won his fourth NBA title in 2009, and he was named the finals MVP after averaging a stellar 32.4 points per game in the series. In addition to his professional accomplishments, he was also a member of the gold-medal-winning U.S. men's basketball team at the 2008 Beijing Olympic Games.

WILT CHAMBERLAIN

(b. Aug. 21, 1936, Philadelphia, Pa., U.S.—d. Oct. 12, 1999, Los Angeles, Calif.)

At more than 7 feet tall, centre Wilt Chamberlain, another of basketball's greatest big men, is considered to be one of the most dominant offensive players in the history of the game. During his 1961–62 season he became the first player to score more than 4,000 points in an NBA season, with 4,029, averaging 50.4 points per game.

As a teenager, Wilton Norman Chamberlain was sought after by more than 100 colleges and universities after his play at Overbrook High School in Philadelphia. He played two years (1956–58) at the University of Kansas, after which he joined the Harlem Globetrotters

for a year (1958–59). He went to the NBA in 1959, playing with the Philadelphia Warriors (1959–65; the team moved and became the San Francisco Warriors in 1962), going back to Philadelphia to play for the 76ers (1965–68), and finishing his career with the Los Angeles Lakers (1968–73). Chamberlain had a long-standing (but good-natured) rivalry with Boston Celtic Bill Russell, and many credit the increase in the popularity of professional basketball to the excitement generated around games featuring these two players.

With 31,419 points scored over the span of his professional career,

Wilt Chamberlain (centre), *1970*. Wen Roberts/AFP/Getty Images

Chamberlain (who was nicknamed "Wilt the Stilt" and "the Big Dipper") held the NBA record for points scored until 1984, when his record was surpassed by Kareem Abdul-Jabbar. Other highlights of Chamberlain's NBA career include a career average of 30.1 points per game, an NBA record until it was broken by Michael Jordan, and a career average of 22.9 rebounds per game. His 100 points against the New York Knicks in Hershey, Pa., on March 2, 1962, still stands as professional basketball's top single-game feat. He also scored 56 or more points 61 times in regular-season games, tallied 36 field goals in a game (March 2, 1962), and captured 55 rebounds in a game (Nov. 24, 1960). Chamberlain's proudest feat was never having fouled out of an NBA game. He was elected to the Basketball Hall of Fame in 1978.

His autobiography, written with David Shaw, *Wilt: Just Like Any Other 7-Foot Black Millionaire Who Lives Next Door*, was published in 1973. Chamberlain also published a more revealing book about his personal life entitled *A View from Above* in 1991.

CYNTHIA COOPER

(b. April 14, 1963, Chicago, Ill., U.S.)

Cynthia Cooper was the first Most Valuable Player (MVP) of the Women's National Basketball Association (WNBA). In the WNBA's inaugural season (1997), Cooper led the league in scoring while leading her team, the Houston Comets, to the championship. She was named MVP of both the regular season and the play-offs that year.

Cooper was raised in the Watts section of Los Angeles. She began playing organized basketball at age 16 and quickly took to the sport. She earned a scholarship to the University of Southern California, where she played in the shadow of Cheryl Miller while helping the team to national championships in 1983 and 1984. After college Cooper played professionally in Europe, primarily for a team in Parma, Italy, where she blossomed into a potent scorer and a tenacious defender. She was a member of the 1988 U.S. national team that won the gold medal at the Olympic Games in Seoul, S. Kor.

By the end of the WNBA's inaugural season, Cooper had established herself as the league's first great player. Along with star teammates Sheryl Swoopes and Tina Thompson, Cooper led the Comets to titles in 1998, 1999, and 2000, each time being recognized as the MVP of the play-offs. She was named the league MVP for the second time in 1998. She retired in 2004 with WNBA career per-game averages of 21 points, 4.9 assists, 3.3 rebounds, and 1.56 steals.

JULIUS ERVING

(b. Feb. 22, 1950, Roosevelt, N.Y., U.S.)

Julius Erving, known to millions as "Doctor J," was one of the most colourful and exciting figures in basketball during the 1970s and '80s. At 6 feet 6 inches tall, Erving played forward and was noted for his fast breaks, balletic leaps toward the basket, and climactic slam dunks.

While playing in high school Erving (born Julius Winfield Erving II) won an athletic scholarship to the University of Massachusetts. In two seasons there he became one of only five players ever to average more than 20 points and 20 rebounds per game in a collegiate career. He was still generally unknown, however, when he left Massachusetts after his junior year and joined the Virginia Squires of the American Basketball Association (ABA) in 1971. He was traded to the New York Nets two years later. In his five seasons in the ABA, Erving led the league in scoring three times, was the league's Most Valuable Player in its last three years, and led the Nets to championships in 1974 and 1976.

When the ABA merged with the NBA, the Nets traded Erving to the Philadelphia 76ers. Erving led the 76ers to the NBA finals four times in seven years, including their 1983 championship win. He was voted the NBA's Most Valuable Player in 1981. He retired in 1987 after having become the third professional player to have scored a career total of 30,000 points. After his playing career ended Erving spent time as a television basketball analyst (1993–97) and served in the front office of the Orlando Magic (1997–2003). In 1996 Erving was named one of the 50 greatest players in NBA history, and he was elected to the Naismith Memorial Basketball Hall of Fame in 1993.

MAGIC JOHNSON

(b. Aug. 14, 1959, Lansing, Mich., U.S.)

One of the most popular and exciting players in the history of professional basketball, charismatic Magic Johnson led the Los Angeles Lakers to five NBA championships.

The son of an auto worker, Earvin Johnson, Jr., earned the nickname "Magic" for his creative and entertaining ball handling. He was an intense competitor. He led his high school team to a state championship in 1977, Michigan State University to the National Collegiate Athletic Association championship in 1979—handing Larry Bird and Indiana State its only defeat of that season—and the U.S. team to a basketball gold medal at the 1992 Olympics in Barcelona, Spain.

Johnson achieved his greatest success in the professional ranks, where he guided the Lakers to NBA championships in 1980, 1982, 1985, 1987, and 1988. He was named the NBA's Most Valuable Player in 1987, 1989, and 1990. He played point guard and brought new versatility to that position. At 6 feet 9 inches, he was a dangerous scorer from anywhere on the court and a capable rebounder, averaging 19.5 points and 7.2 rebounds per game over his 13-year career. However, he was best-known for innovative no-look and bounce passes and a knack of making big plays in the clutch.

The battles for league supremacy between Johnson's Lakers and Bird's Boston Celtics spurred a new era of fan interest and NBA prosperity. At the time of his initial retirement due to HIV infection in 1991, Johnson was the NBA's all-time leader in assists (9,921; broken in 1995 by John Stockton). Later he served briefly as head coach of the Lakers (1994), and he returned as a player for a portion of the 1995–96 season. After his retirement from basketball, Johnson became an extremely successful entrepreneur—with estimated holdings of approximately $800 million as of 2008—and an HIV/AIDS activist. In 1996 the NBA named him one of the 50 greatest players of all time. He was elected to the Naismith Memorial Basketball Hall of Fame in 2002.

MICHAEL JORDAN

(b. Feb. 17, 1963, Brooklyn, N.Y., U.S.)

Widely considered to be the greatest all-around player in the history of basketball, Michael "Air" Jordan led the Chicago Bulls to six NBA championships (1991–93, 1996–98).

Michael Jeffrey Jordan grew up in Wilmington, N.C., and entered the University of North Carolina at Chapel Hill in 1981. As a freshman, he made the winning basket against Georgetown in the 1982 national championship game. Jordan was named College Player of the Year in both his sophomore and junior years, leaving North Carolina after his junior year. He led the U.S. basketball team to Olympic gold medals in 1984 in Los Angeles and in 1992 in Barcelona, Spain.

In 1984 Jordan was drafted by the Chicago Bulls. In his first season (1984–85) as a professional, he led the league in scoring and was named Rookie of the Year; after missing most of the following season with a broken foot, he returned to lead the NBA in scoring for seven consecutive seasons, averaging about 32 points per game. He was only the second player (after Wilt Chamberlain) to score 3,000 points in a single season (1986–87). Jordan was named the NBA's MVP five times (1988, 1991, 1992, 1996, 1998) and was also named Defensive Player of the Year in 1988. In October 1993, after leading the Bulls to their third consecutive championship, Jordan retired briefly to pursue a career in professional baseball. He returned to basketball in March 1995. In the 1995–96 season Jordan led the Bulls to a 72–10 regular season record, the best in the history of the NBA. From 1996 to 1998 the Jordan-led Bulls again won three championships in a row, and each time Jordan was named MVP of the NBA finals. After the 1997–98 season Jordan retired again. His career totals at that time included 29,277 points (31.5 points per game average), 2,306 steals, and 10 scoring titles.

Jordan remained close to the sport, buying a share of the Washington Wizards in January 2000. He was also appointed president of basketball operations for the club. However, managing rosters and salary caps was not enough for Jordan, and in September 2001 he renounced his ownership and management positions with the Wizards in order

Michael Jordan, mid-flight and pre-slam dunk, on the way to leading the Chicago Bulls to a win over the Charlotte Hornets, Nov. 3, 1995. Jonathan Daniel/Getty Images

to be a player on the team. His second return to the NBA was greeted with enthusiasm by the league, which had suffered declining attendance and television ratings since his 1998 retirement. After the 2002–03 season, Jordan announced his final retirement. He ended his career with 32,292 total points and a 30.12-points-per-game average, which was the best in league history. In 2006 Jordan became minority owner and general manager of the NBA's Charlotte Bobcats.

At 6 feet 6 inches, Jordan, a guard, was an exceptionally talented shooter and passer and a tenacious defender. He earned the nickname "Air Jordan" because of his extraordinary leaping ability and acrobatic maneuvers.

During his playing career Jordan's popularity reached heights few athletes (or celebrities of any sort) have known. He accumulated millions of dollars from endorsements (most notably for his Air Jordan basketball shoes). He also made a successful film, *Space Jam* (1996), in which he starred with animated characters Bugs Bunny and Daffy Duck. In 1996 the NBA named him one of the 50 greatest players of all time, and in 2009 he was elected to the Naismith Memorial Basketball Hall of Fame.

OSCAR ROBERTSON

(b. Nov. 24, 1938, Charlotte, Tenn., U.S.)

Oscar Robertson starred in both the collegiate and professional ranks of basketball and is considered one of the top players in the history of the game. As a player with the NBA's Cincinnati (Ohio) Royals in 1961–62, he averaged double figures in points (30.8), rebounds (12.5), and assists (11.4) per game, a feat unmatched by any other player.

Oscar Palmer Robertson grew up in Indianapolis, Ind., where he led Crispus Attucks High School to two state championships. In 1956 he received an athletic scholarship to the University of Cincinnati and became the first African American to play basketball there. In three seasons of collegiate basketball, he averaged 33.8 points per game and helped the Cincinnati Bearcats twice reach the final four of the National Collegiate Athletic Association (NCAA) basketball tournament. He set 14 NCAA records during his college days. In 1960 he won a gold medal in Rome as a member of the U.S. Olympic team.

Robertson, known as the "Big O," was the first selection of the 1960 NBA draft and earned Rookie of the Year honours that season with the Cincinnati Royals. Measuring 6 feet 5 inches and weighing more than 200 lb, Robertson was larger than most guards. He was able to use his size to gain position for scoring and rebounding. He was also a superior ball handler, leading the league in assists six times. He was named the NBA Most Valuable Player for the 1963–64 season, in which he averaged 31.4 points, 9.9 rebounds, and 11 assists per game.

Robertson was traded in 1970 to the Milwaukee Bucks, where he teamed with Lew Alcindor (Kareem Abdul-Jabbar) and won the NBA title that season. Robertson retired from the NBA in 1974 with 26,710 career points (25.7 per game), 7,804 rebounds (7.5 average), and 9,887 assists (an NBA record at the time). He was elected to the Naismith Memorial Basketball Hall of Fame in 1979.

After his playing days ended, Robertson pursued a career in business and from 1981 was chief executive officer of a Cincinnati-based chemical company.

BILL RUSSELL

(b. Feb. 12, 1934, Monroe, La., U.S.)

In his day, Bill Russell was regarded as the greatest defensive centre in the history of the NBA. He set standards by which other exceptionally tall players were judged (his height was 6 feet 10 inches). On April 18, 1966, he became the first black coach of a major professional sports team (the Boston Celtics) in the United States.

Reared in Oakland, Calif., Russell led the University of San Francisco to National Collegiate Athletic Association (NCAA) championships in two consecutive seasons (1954–55 and 1955–56). He played on the U.S. team that won the 1956 Olympic basketball gold medal in Melbourne, Austl.

The history of professional basketball changed when Celtics coach Red Auerbach traded established star "Easy" Ed Macauley to the St. Louis Hawks for the rights to draft Russell. With Russell

turning shot-blocking into an art form, Boston dominated the NBA for more than a decade. With Russell at centre, the Celtics won 9 championships (1957, 1959–66) in 10 seasons and two more (1968–69) with Russell as player and coach. He retired in 1969.

On five occasions Russell was voted the Most Valuable Player in the NBA. In 1967 the Associated Press (AP) named him one of the five members of its All-America collegiate team for the preceding 20 years; later the AP selected him the outstanding professional

Bill Russell, mid-1960s. Dick Raphael

basketball player of the 1960s. He was coach and general manager of the Seattle SuperSonics (1973–77). His autobiography, *Second Wind: The Memoirs of an Opinionated Man,* was published in 1979. After retirement from basketball, Russell was a network sports announcer, wrote a syndicated column, and did television news commentary.

BOXING

One of the earliest and most dramatic challenges to the notion of white supremacy came in the early 1900s in the sport of boxing and in the person of Jack Johnson, the gifted, proud, and flamboyant black heavyweight champion of the world, who inspired pride in African Americans and reactionary animosity in many whites. Their desire for a "Great White Hope" to defeat Johnson prompted former champion James Jeffries out of retirement in 1910, only to be knocked out by Johnson. Boxing's next great African American heavyweight champion, Joe Louis, was careful not to antagonize white Americans even as he remained a heroic symbol for black Americans. And when he twice fought German Max Schmeling—testing German dictator Adolf Hitler's theories of Aryan supremacy—a large percentage of white Americans were in Louis's corner. More in the mode of Johnson was the fighter simply known as "the Greatest," Muhmmad Ali, a brash, handsome, witty, lightning-fast former Olympic champion who converted to

Islam and whose conscientious objection to serving in the Army during the Vietnam War led to his championship title's being revoked, though he would win it back later—twice. At the height of the Vietnam War and black rebellion in U.S. cities, Ali's boxer vs. brawler classic championship fights with Joe Frazier (and later his title match with George Foreman in Africa, the "Rumble in the Jungle") were seen by some as symbolic confrontations between black militancy (represented by the outspoken Ali) and a more cautious path to equality (Frazier and Foreman).

MUHAMMAD ALI

(b. Jan. 17, 1942, Louisville, Ky., U.S.)

Muhammad Ali was the first professional boxer to win the world heavyweight championship on three separate occasions; he successfully defended this title 19 times.

Cassius Marcellus Clay, Jr., grew up in the American South in a time of segregated public facilities. His father, Cassius Marcellus Clay, Sr., supported a wife and two sons by painting billboards and signs. His mother, Odessa Grady Clay, worked as a household domestic.

When Clay was 12 years old, he took up boxing under the tutelage of Louisville policeman Joe Martin. After advancing through the amateur ranks, he won a gold medal in the 175-pound division at the 1960 Olympic Games in Rome and began a professional career under the guidance of the Louisville Sponsoring Group, a syndicate composed of 11 wealthy white men.

In his early bouts as a professional, Clay was more highly regarded for his charm and personality than for his ring skills. He sought to raise public interest in his fights by reading childlike poetry and spouting self-descriptive phrases such as "float like a butterfly, sting like a bee." He told the world that he was "the Greatest," but the hard realities of boxing seemed to indicate otherwise. Clay infuriated devotees of the sport as much as he impressed them. He held his hands unconventionally low, backed away from punches rather than bobbing and weaving out of danger, and appeared to lack true knockout power. The opponents he was besting were a mixture of veterans who were long past their prime and fighters who had never been more than mediocre. Thus, purists cringed when Clay predicted the round in which he intended to knock out an opponent, and they grimaced when he did so and bragged about each new conquest.

On Feb. 25, 1964, Clay challenged Sonny Liston for the heavyweight championship of the world. Liston was widely regarded as the most intimidating, powerful fighter of his era. Clay was a decided underdog. But in one of the most stunning upsets in sports history, Liston retired to his corner after six rounds, and Clay became the new champion. Two days later, Clay shocked the boxing establishment again by announcing that he had accepted the teachings of the Nation of Islam. On March 6, 1964, he took the name Muhammad Ali, which was given to him by his spiritual mentor, Elijah Muhammad.

For the next three years, Ali dominated boxing as thoroughly and magnificently as any fighter ever had. In a May 25, 1965, rematch against Liston, he emerged with a first-round knockout victory. Triumphs over Floyd Patterson, George Chuvalo, Henry Cooper, Brian London, and Karl Mildenberger followed. On Nov. 14, 1966, Ali fought Cleveland Williams. Over the course of three rounds, Ali landed more than 100 punches, scored four knockdowns, and was hit a total of three times. Ali's triumph over Williams was succeeded by victories over Ernie Terrell and Zora Folley.

Then, on April 28, 1967, citing his religious beliefs, Ali refused induction into the U.S. Army at the height of the war in Vietnam. This refusal followed a blunt statement voiced by Ali 14 months earlier: "I ain't got no quarrel with them Vietcong." Many Americans vehemently condemned Ali's stand. It came at a time when most people in the United States still supported the war in Southeast Asia. Moreover, although exemptions from military service on religious grounds were available to qualifying conscientious objectors who were opposed to war in any form, Ali was not eligible for such an exemption because he acknowledged that he would be willing to participate in an Islamic holy war.

Ali was stripped of his championship and precluded from fighting by every state athletic commission in the United States for three and a half years. In addition, he was criminally indicted and, on June 20, 1967, convicted of refusing induction into the U.S. armed forces and sentenced to five years in prison. Although he remained free on bail, four years passed before his conviction was unanimously overturned by the U.S. Supreme Court on a narrow procedural ground.

Meanwhile, as the 1960s grew more tumultuous, Ali's impact upon American society was growing, and he became a lightning rod for dissent. Ali's message of black pride and black resistance to white domination was on the cutting edge of the civil rights movement. Having refused induction into the U.S. Army, he also stood for the proposition that "unless you have a very good reason to kill, war is wrong." As black activist Julian Bond later observed, "When a figure as heroic and beloved as Muhammad Ali stood up and said, 'No, I won't go,' it reverberated through the whole society."

In October 1970, Ali was allowed to return to boxing, but his skills had eroded. The legs that had allowed him to "dance" for 15 rounds without stopping no longer carried him as surely around the ring. His reflexes, while still superb, were no longer as fast as they had once been. Ali prevailed in his first two comeback fights, against Jerry Quarry and Oscar Bonavena. Then, on March 8, 1971, he challenged Joe Frazier, who had become heavyweight champion during Ali's absence from the ring. It was a fight of historic proportions, billed as the "Fight of the Century." Frazier won a unanimous 15-round decision.

Following his loss to Frazier, Ali won 10 fights in a row, 8 of them against world-class opponents. Then, on March 31, 1973, a little-known fighter named Ken Norton broke Ali's jaw in the second round en route to a 12-round upset decision. Ali defeated Norton in a rematch. After that, he fought Joe Frazier a second time and won a unanimous 12-round decision. From a technical point of view, the second Ali-Frazier bout was probably Ali's best performance in the ring after his exile from boxing.

On Oct. 30, 1974, Ali challenged George Foreman, who had dethroned Frazier in 1973 to become heavyweight champion of the world. The bout (which Ali referred to as the "Rumble in the Jungle") took place in the unlikely location of Zaire (now the Democratic Republic of the Congo). Ali was received by the people of Zaire as a conquering hero, and he did his part by knocking out Foreman in the eighth round to regain the heavyweight title. It was in this fight that Ali employed a strategy once used by former boxing great Archie Moore. Moore called the maneuver "the turtle" but Ali called it "rope-a-dope." The strategy was that, instead of moving around the ring, Ali chose to fight for extended periods of time leaning back into the ropes in order to avoid many of Foreman's heaviest blows.

Muhammad Ali, right, fights then-world heavyweight boxing champion George Foreman in Kinshasa, Congo, Oct. 30, 1974. Ali won, regaining the heavyweight title. AFP/Getty Images

Over the next 30 months, at the peak of his popularity as champion, Ali fought nine times in bouts that showed him to be a courageous fighter but a fighter on the decline. The most notable of these bouts occurred on Oct. 1, 1975, when Ali and Joe Frazier met in the Philippines, 6 miles (9.5 km) outside Manila, to do battle for the third time. In what is regarded by many as the greatest prizefight of all time (the "Thrilla in Manila"), Ali was declared the victor when Frazier's corner called a halt to the bout after 14 brutal rounds.

The final performances of Ali's ring career were sad to behold. In 1978 he lost his title to Leon Spinks, a novice boxer with an Olympic gold medal but only seven professional fights to his credit. Seven months later, Ali regained the championship with a 15-round victory over Spinks. Then he retired from boxing, but two years later he made an ill-advised comeback and suffered a horrible beating at the hands of Larry Holmes in a bout that was stopped after 11 rounds. The final ring contest of Ali's career was a loss by decision to Trevor Berbick in 1981.

Ali's place in boxing history as one of the greatest fighters ever is secure. His final record of 56 wins and 5 losses with 37 knockouts has been matched by others, but the quality of his opponents and the manner in which he dominated during his prime place him on a plateau with boxing's immortals. Ali's most tangible ring assets were speed, superb footwork, and the ability to take a punch. But perhaps more important, he had courage and all the other intangibles that go into making a great fighter.

Ali's later years have been marked by physical decline. Damage to his brain caused by blows to the head have resulted in slurred speech, slowed movement, and other symptoms of Parkinson syndrome. However, his condition differs from chronic encephalopathy, or dementia pugilistica (which is commonly referred to as "punch drunk" in fighters), in that he does not suffer from injury-induced intellectual deficits.

Ali's religious views have also evolved over time. In the mid-1970s, he began to study the Qur'an seriously and turned to Orthodox Islam. His earlier adherence to the teachings of Elijah Muhammad (e.g., that white people are "devils" and there is no heaven or hell) were replaced by a spiritual embrace of all people and preparation for his own afterlife. In 1984 Ali spoke out publicly against the separatist doctrine of Louis Farrakhan, declaring, "What he teaches is not at all what we believe in. He represents the time of our struggle in the dark and a time of confusion in us, and we don't want to be associated with that at all."

Ali married his fourth wife, Lonnie (née Yolanda Williams) in 1986. He has nine children, most of whom have chosen to avoid the spotlight of which Ali was so fond. One of his daughters, however, Laila Ali, is pursuing a career as a professional boxer. While her skills are limited, she has benefited from the fact that the Ali name is still financially viable.

In 1996 Ali was chosen to light the Olympic flame at the start of the 24th Olympiad in Atlanta, Ga. The outpouring of goodwill that accompanied his appearance confirmed his status as one of the most beloved athletes in the world.

George Foreman

(b. Jan. 10, 1949, Marshall, Texas, U.S.)

George Foreman was the world heavyweight champion (1973–74, 1994–95). When Foreman regained the heavyweight title at age 45, he was the oldest world heavyweight champion.

Foreman grew up in Houston, Texas, and learned to box in a U.S. Job Corps camp in Oregon. At the 1968 Olympic Games in Mexico City, he won the gold medal in the heavyweight boxing competition. The 6-foot 3-inch, 218-pound Foreman first captured the professional heavyweight belt by knocking out Joe Frazier in two rounds at Kingston, Jam., on Jan. 22, 1973. He had won all 40 of his professional bouts, including a sequence of 24 consecutive knockouts, when he fell to Muhammad Ali in eight rounds in the "Rumble in the Jungle" in Kinshasa, Zaire (now Congo), on Oct. 30, 1974. He retired from the ring in 1977 and became an evangelist.

Foreman resumed professional boxing in 1987 at age 39 and found immediate success. Evidence later surfaced that Foreman's promoter, Bob Arum, had paid bribes to the International Boxing Federation (IBF) in order to manipulate the rankings and permit Foreman a chance at a title fight. Nevertheless, Foreman did very well when his chance at a title bout came. Despite his age and more than 30 additional pounds, Foreman remained a devastating puncher and captured the IBF and World Boxing Association (WBA) versions of the world heavyweight title by knocking out Michael Moorer in 10 rounds at Las Vegas, Nev., on Nov. 5, 1994. In March 1995 Foreman was stripped of his WBA title for refusing to fight their contender, and he resigned his IBF title in June 1995 rather than fight a rematch with IBF contender Axel Schultz. In 1997 Foreman retired from boxing again. He was inducted into the International Boxing Hall of Fame in 2003.

A colourful personality in the world of boxing, Foreman had great success as a television spokesperson for a number of products, including an eponymous home grill that was introduced in 1995; it earned him more money (and arguably more fame) than his boxing career.

Joe Frazier

(b. Jan. 12, 1944, Beaufort, S.C., U.S.)

Joe Frazier was the world heavyweight boxing champion from Feb 16, 1970, when he knocked out Jimmy Ellis in five rounds in New York City, until Jan. 22, 1973, when he was beaten by George Foreman at Kingston, Jam.

During Frazier's amateur career he was one of the best heavyweights in the United States, but he lost in the Olympic trials to Buster Mathis in 1964 and made it to the Tokyo Olympic Games as a replacement boxer only when Mathis injured his hand. He won the gold medal in his weight division and then began his professional career in August 1965. A chunky man (5 feet 11 inches tall and weighing 205 pounds) with an aggressive style and a powerful left hook, "Smokin' Joe" was likened to an earlier heavyweight champion, Rocky Marciano.

After Muhammad Ali was stripped of his heavyweight title in 1967, the heavyweight championship became muddled. On March 4, 1968, in a title bout sanctioned by the New York State Athletic Commission and similar bodies in other states, Frazier knocked out his old rival Mathis in 11 rounds. The following month, Jimmy Ellis won a championship tournament (in which Frazier declined to participate) approved by the World Boxing Association (WBA). Frazier successfully defended his New York title four times before defeating Ellis in a fifth-round knockout to claim the WBA heavyweight title.

In 1970 Ali was reinstated to the sport, and a bout between the undefeated former champion and Frazier was inevitable. On March 8, 1971, the two heavyweights met in Madison Square Garden in the fight billed as "The Fight of the Century." During the build-up for the fight the media-savvy Ali characterized Frazier as a champion of the white establishment, even calling him an "Uncle Tom," which sparked some genuine hostility between the boxers. The two fought at a furious pace for 15 rounds, but Ali had lost some of his speed during his absence from boxing, and Frazier scored a decision over him.

After his loss to Foreman in 1973, Frazier faced Ali again in 1974, losing a 12-round decision. On Oct. 1, 1975, the two faced off in the Philippines for a third time. The fight, known as the "Thrilla in Manila," was for the heavyweight championship, and this time Ali was the winner by technical knockout after 14 grueling rounds.

After a few more fights, Frazier retired in 1976. He staged an unsuccessful comeback attempt in 1981. He then retired again and began operating a gym in Philadelphia. Frazier was inducted into the International Boxing Hall of Fame in 1990. His daughter Jacqui began a professional boxing career in 2000.

MARVIN HAGLER

(b. May 23, 1954, Newark, N.J., U.S.)

Durable middleweight champion Marvin Hagler was one of the greatest fighters of the 1970s and '80s.

Marvin Nathaniel Hagler began his boxing career in Brockton, Mass., winning 57 amateur fights and the 1973 Amateur Athletic Union middleweight title before turning professional. He won his first 26 professional bouts, which included 19 knockouts, but his streak was broken in late 1974 when he fought Sugar Ray Seales to a draw. After losing two matches in 1976 to middleweights Bobby Watts and Willie Monroe, Hagler remained unbeaten for another decade.

A powerful left-hander, Hagler stood 5 feet 9 inches tall and weighed 160 pounds. In his first title fight, in 1979, he boxed world middleweight champion Vito Antuofermo to a 15-round draw. On Sept., 1980, in his 54th professional fight, Hagler took the world title from Alan Minter with a third-round knockout. Hagler went on to defend the title 12 times from 1981 through 1986. On April 15, 1985, in one of his finest bouts, he pummeled Thomas Hearns, dispatching him in three rounds.

Hagler, who had legally changed his first name to Marvelous in 1982, was now ranked among the world's preeminent boxers. On April 6, 1987, in one of the most renowned middleweight title fights, Hagler lost his long-held crown to Sugar Ray Leonard in a controversial 12-round split decision. Unable to accept the defeat, Hagler retired from boxing. Although Leonard long commanded enormous earnings for his matches, the $11 million he received for this bout was $1 million shy of Hagler's $12 million purse. After his retirement, Hagler moved to Italy, where he began an acting career. He also served as a commentator for boxing telecasts on the British Broadcasting Corporation.

Fifty-two of Hagler's 62 career wins were by knockout; he had three losses and two draws. He was inducted into the International Boxing Hall of Fame in 1993.

JACK JOHNSON

(b. March 31, 1878, Galveston, Texas, U.S.—d. June 10, 1946, Raleigh, N.C.)

Jack Johnson was the first African American to hold the heavyweight boxing championship of the world.

Johnson (born John Arthur Johnson) fought professionally from 1897 to 1928 and engaged in exhibition matches as late as 1945. He won the title by knocking out champion Tommy Burns in Sydney, Dec. 26, 1908, and lost it on a knockout by Jess Willard in 26 rounds in Havana, April 5, 1915.

Until his fight with Burns, discrimination limited Johnson's opportunities and purses. When he became champion, a hue and cry for a "Great White Hope" produced numerous opponents.

At the height of his career Johnson was excoriated by the press for having twice married white women, and he further offended white supremacists by knocking out former champion James J. Jeffries, who was induced to come out of retirement as a "Great White Hope." In connection with one of his marriages, Johnson was convicted in 1912 of violating the Mann Act in transporting his wife across state lines before their marriage. He was sentenced to a year in prison and

Jack Johnson. UPI

was released on bond, pending appeal. Disguised as a member of a black baseball team, he fled to Canada, made his way to Europe, and was a fugitive for seven years.

He defended the championship three times in Paris before agreeing to fight Willard in Cuba. Some observers thought that Johnson, mistakenly believing that the charge against him would be dropped if he yielded the championship to a white man, deliberately lost to Willard. From 1897 to 1928, Johnson had 114 bouts, winning 80, 45 by knockouts.

In 1920 Johnson surrendered to U.S. marshals and served his sentence, fighting in several bouts within the federal prison at Leavenworth, Kan. After his release he fought occasionally and appeared in vaudeville and carnival acts, appearing finally with a trained flea act. He wrote two books of memoirs, *Mes

Combats (in French, 1914) and *Jack Johnson in the Ring and Out* (1927; reprinted 1975). He died in an automobile accident.

DON KING

(b. Aug. 20, 1931, Cleveland, Ohio, U.S.)

Known for his flamboyant manner and outrageous hair style, boxing promoter Don King first came to prominence with his promotion of the 1974 "Rumble in the Jungle" bout between Muhammad Ali and George Foreman in Kinshasa, Zaire (now the Democratic Republic of the Congo).

While growing up in Cleveland, King considered becoming a lawyer. To finance his college education, he became a numbers runner (i.e., a courier of illegal betting slips), and in a short time he was one of the leading racketeers in Cleveland. King attended Western Reserve University (now Case Western Reserve University) in Cleveland for a year but quit to concentrate on his numbers business.

After being cleared of a 1954 murder charge, which a judge found to be justifiable homicide, King was sentenced to prison in 1967 on a manslaughter charge for beating a man to death. Paroled in 1971, King entered the business of boxing. The next year he persuaded Muhammad Ali to compete in a benefit exhibition to raise money for a Cleveland hospital. Buoyed by this success, and with Ali's

encouragement, King became a full-time promoter with the 1974 Ali-Foreman fight. King promised the boxers $5 million each for the fight. When financial backers proved difficult to enlist, King sought out Zaire's dictator, Mobutu Sese Seko, who agreed to put up the money from his country's treasury. Mobutu saw the match as a way of generating positive publicity about Zaire. The televised bout was a huge ratings success, and King's career was launched.

King staged seven of Ali's title bouts, including the legendary "Thrilla in Manila"—the 1975 fight between Ali and Joe Frazier that was viewed by more than a million people worldwide and earned Ali $6 million. He also promoted the fights of such pugilists as Sugar Ray Leonard, Leon Spinks, Roberto Durán, Julio César Chávez, Mike Tyson, Evander Holyfield, and Felix Trinidad. Trinidad, however, sued King and was released from his contract. A number of boxers, including Tyson, felt defrauded by King and also filed suits against him.

King's financial success continued into the 1980s and '90s. In 1983 he promoted 12 world championship bouts; in 1994 he promoted 47 such bouts. King was heavily criticized, however, for a business strategy that resulted in his control over many of the top boxers, especially in the lucrative heavyweight division. King used a contractual clause that required a boxer who wished to challenge a fighter belonging to King to agree to be promoted by King in the future should he win. Thus, no matter which boxer won, King represented the winner. Those who were unwilling to sign contracts with this obligatory clause found it very difficult to obtain fights, especially title fights, with boxers who were promoted by King.

King has been the focus of a myriad of criminal investigations and has been indicted numerous times. In 1999 the U.S. Federal Bureau of Investigation seized thousands of records from King's offices that concerned alleged payoffs by King to the president of the International Boxing Federation for the purpose of procuring more favourable rankings for King's boxers.

King has been a mixed blessing to the sport. On one hand, he has organized some of the largest purses in the history of the sport and has creatively promoted boxing and his bouts. On the other hand, King's legal problems and controversial tactics have reinforced the public perception of boxing as a corrupt sport.

SUGAR RAY LEONARD

(b. May 17, 1956, Rocky Mount, N.C., U.S.)

Known for his agility and finesse, boxer Sugar Ray Leonard won 36 of 40 professional matches and several national titles. As an amateur, he took an Olympic gold medal in the light-welterweight class at the 1976 Games in Montreal.

By his mid-teens Ray Charles Leonard proved adept at boxing, and, as an amateur, he won 145 of 150 bouts and garnered two National Golden Glove championships (1973, 1974), two Amateur Athletic Union championships (1974, 1975), and a gold medal at the 1975 Pan American Games. Following his Olympic victory in 1976, he announced his retirement from the sport but reentered the ring as a professional on Feb. 5, 1977.

In November 1979 Leonard defeated the reigning World Boxing Council (WBC) welterweight champion, Wilfred Benítez, only to lose the title in June 1980 in a famous match against Roberto Durán. Five months later Leonard regained the title by defeating Durán, and he successfully defended it thereafter, winning the World Boxing Association (WBA) version of the title with a victory over Thomas Hearns in 1981. Earlier that same year he had won the WBA junior-middleweight title with a ninth-round knockout of Ayub Kalule.

Leonard retired from prizefighting in 1982 and again in 1984 but was enticed to return in April 1987 to face the up-and-coming Marvelous Marvin Hagler, whom he defeated to capture the WBC middleweight title in what was considered one of the greatest professional boxing matches of all time.

Leonard retired again in 1991 after losing a WBC super welterweight title bout, but he returned to the ring once more in 1997, at age 40, and lost by a fifth-round technical knockout. He retired after the fight and was inducted into the International Boxing Hall of Fame later that year. After his final retirement, Leonard served as a boxing commentator and television host.

JOE LOUIS

(b. May 13, 1914, Lafayette, Ala., U.S.—d. April 12, 1981, Las Vegas, Nev.)

Joe Louis was world heavyweight champion from June 22, 1937, when he knocked out James J. Braddock in eight rounds in Chicago, until March 1, 1949, when he briefly retired. During his reign, the longest in the history of any weight division, he successfully defended his title 25 times, more than any other champion in any division, scoring 21 knockouts (his service in the U.S. Army from 1942 to 1945 no doubt prevented him from defending his title many more times). He was known as an extremely accurate and economical knockout puncher.

Louis's father, a sharecropper, was committed to a state mental hospital when Louis (born Joseph Louis Barrow) was about two years old. After his mother remarried, the family, which included eight children, moved to Detroit, where Louis took up amateur boxing. He won the U.S. Amateur Athletic Union 175-pound championship in 1934 and also was a Golden Gloves titleholder; of 54 amateur fights, Louis won 50 and lost 4. His first professional fight took place on July 4, 1934, and within 12 months he had knocked out Primo Carnera, the first of six previous or subsequent heavyweight champions who would become his victims; the others were Max Baer, Jack Sharkey, Braddock, the German champion Max Schmeling, and Jersey Joe Walcott. Louis sustained his first professional loss in 1936 at the hands of Schmeling. In 1938, after having beaten Braddock and taken the title, Louis met Schmeling in a rematch that the American media portrayed as a battle between Nazism and democracy (though Schmeling himself was not a Nazi). Louis's dramatic knockout victory in the first round made him a national hero. He was perhaps the first African American to be widely admired by whites, a fact attributable not only to his extraordinary pugilistic skills but also to his sportsmanlike behaviour in the ring (he did not gloat over his white opponents), his perceived humility and soft-spoken demeanour, and his discretion in his private life.

Louis was at his peak in the period 1939–42. From December 1940 through June 1941 he defended the championship seven times. After enlisting in the U.S. Army in 1942, he served in a segregated unit with Jackie Robinson. Louis did not see combat but fought in 96 exhibition matches before some two million troops; he also donated more than $100,000 to Army and Navy relief funds. After the war he was less active, and in 1949 he retired as the undefeated champion long enough to allow Ezzard Charles to earn recognition as his successor.

Joe Louis, 1946. Encyclopædia Britannica, Inc.

Although Louis earned nearly $5 million as a fighter, he spent or gave away nearly all of it. When the Internal Revenue Service demanded more than $1 million in back taxes and penalties, he was forced to return to the ring to pay off his debts. He fought Charles for the championship on Sept. 27, 1950, but lost a 15-round decision. In his last fight of consequence, against future champion Rocky Marciano on Oct. 26, 1951, he was knocked out in eight rounds. From 1934 to 1951, Louis had 71 bouts, winning 68, 54 by knockouts. A Hollywood movie about his life, *The Joe Louis Story*, was made in 1953.

After his second retirement Louis continued to be plagued by money problems, and he was briefly forced to work as a professional wrestler. Later he became a greeter for Caesar's Palace, a resort and casino in Las Vegas. Upon his death in 1981 he was buried in Arlington National Cemetery; one of the pallbearers at his funeral was Schmeling. Louis was inducted to the Ring Magazine Boxing Hall of Fame in 1954 and the International Boxing Hall of Fame in 1990. He was posthumously awarded the Congressional Gold Medal in 1982.

FLOYD PATTERSON

(b. Jan. 4, 1935, Waco, N.C., U.S.—d. May 11, 2006, New Paltz, N.Y.)

Floyd Patterson was the first boxer to hold the world heavyweight championship twice.

Floyd Patterson (upright) *fighting Tom McNeeley, 1961.* AP

Born into poverty in North Carolina, Patterson grew up in Brooklyn, N.Y. He learned to box while in a school for emotionally disturbed children and soon began training with Constantine ("Cus") D'Amato, who later worked with Mike Tyson. Patterson won New York Golden Gloves titles in 1951 and 1952 and earned the gold medal as a middleweight at the 1952 Olympic Games in Helsinki, Fin. His first professional fight took place on Sept. 12, 1952. Over the next four years, he lost only one bout (1954), a disputed decision in favour of the clever and far more experienced Joey Maxim, a former light-heavyweight champion.

Patterson was undersize for a heavyweight, typically weighing about 185 pounds, and had a short reach (71 inches). In the ring, he relied on his speed and a peekaboo boxing style, in which he held his gloves close to his face. On Nov. 30, 1956, he knocked out Archie Moore in five rounds in Chicago to capture the heavyweight title vacated by the retired Rocky Marciano. At the time, Patterson was the youngest person to hold the championship. He defended his title in four subsequent fights before facing Ingemar Johansson of Sweden on June 26, 1959. Although heavily favoured to win, Patterson was knocked out in the third round. On June 20, 1960, he regained the title with a fifth-round knockout of Johansson. Patterson remained heavyweight champion until Sept. 25, 1962, when he was knocked out in the first round by Sonny Liston in Chicago. He later was defeated by Liston and Muhammad Ali in his attempts to recapture the world championship. In 1968 Patterson lost to Jimmy Ellis, World Boxing Association heavyweight champion, in a match for that version of the disputed world title. He retired from the ring in 1972, having won 55 of 64 fights. Forty of his wins were by knockout.

Patterson, who was noted for his shyness and gentle manner, later ran an amateur boxing club and was athletic commissioner for the state of New York. In 1991 he was inducted into the International Boxing Hall of Fame.

SUGAR RAY ROBINSON

(b. May 3, 1921, Detroit, Mich., U.S.—d. April 12, 1989, Culver City, Calif.)

Considered by many authorities to have been the best boxer in history, Sugar Ray Robinson was six times a world champion: once as a welterweight (147 pounds), from 1946 to 1951, and five times as a middleweight (160 pounds), between 1951 and 1960.

He won 89 amateur fights without defeat, fighting first under his own name and then as Ray Robinson, using the amateur certificate of another boxer of that name in order to qualify for a bout. He won Golden Gloves titles as a featherweight in 1939 and as a lightweight in 1940.

Robinson won 40 consecutive professional fights before losing to Jake LaMotta in one of their six battles. On Dec. 20, 1946, he won the welterweight championship by defeating Tommy Bell on a 15-round decision. Robinson resigned this title on winning the middleweight championship by a 13-round knockout of LaMotta on Feb. 14, 1951. He lost the 160-pound title to Randy Turpin of England in 1951 and regained it from Turpin later that year. In 1952 he narrowly missed defeating Joey Maxim for the light-heavyweight (175-pound) crown and a few months later retired.

Robinson returned to the ring in 1954, recaptured the middleweight title from Carl (Bobo) Olson in 1955, lost it to and

Sugar Ray Robinson (right) *fighting Randy Turpin, 1951.* AP

regained it from Gene Fullmer in 1957, yielded it to Carmen Basilio later that year, and for the last time won the 160-pound championship by defeating Basilio in a savage fight in 1958. Paul Pender defeated Robinson to win the title on Jan. 22, 1960, and also won their return fight.

Robinson continued to fight until late 1965, when he was 45 years old. In 201 professional bouts, he had 109 knockouts. He suffered only 19 defeats, most of them when he was past 40. His outstanding ability and flamboyant personality made him a hero of boxing fans throughout the world. In retirement he appeared on television and in motion pictures and formed a youth foundation in 1969.

MIKE TYSON

(b. June 30, 1966, Brooklyn, N.Y., U.S.)

At age 20, Mike Tyson became the youngest heavyweight champion in boxing history.

A member of various street gangs at an early age, Michael Gerald Tyson was sent to reform school in upstate New York in 1978. At the reform school, social worker and boxing aficionado Bobby Stewart recognized his boxing potential and directed him to renowned trainer Cus D'Amato, who became his legal guardian. Tyson compiled a 24–3 record as an amateur and turned professional in 1985.

D'Amato taught Tyson a peekaboo boxing style, with hands held close to his cheeks and a continuous bobbing motion in the boxing ring that made his defense almost impenetrable. At 5 feet 11 inches tall and weighing about 218 pounds, Tyson was short and squat and lacked the classic heavyweight boxer's appearance, but his surprising quickness and aggressiveness in the ring overwhelmed most of his opponents. On Nov. 22, 1986, "Iron Mike" became the youngest heavyweight champion in history, with a second-round knockout of Trevor Berbick, to claim the crown of the World Boxing Council (WBC). On March 7, 1987, he acquired the World Boxing Association (WBA) belt when he defeated James Smith. After he defeated Tony Tucker on Aug. 1, 1987, Tyson was unanimously recognized as champion by all three sanctioning organizations (WBC, WBA, and International Boxing Federation [IBF]).

After the deaths of D'Amato and manager Jimmy Jacobs, Tyson aligned with controversial promoter Don King. He made 10 successful defenses of his world heavyweight title, including victories over former champions Larry Holmes and Michael Spinks. In 1988 Tyson married actress Robin Givens, but the couple divorced in 1989 amid allegations that Tyson had physically abused her. A myriad of assault and harassment charges were subsequently filed against Tyson.

On Feb. 11, 1990, in one of the biggest upsets in boxing history, Tyson lost the championship to lightly regarded James ("Buster") Douglas, who scored a technical knockout in the 10th round. Tyson rebounded from the loss with four straight victories. In 1991, however, he was accused of having raped a beauty pageant contestant, and he was convicted of the charge in 1992.

Following his release from prison in 1995, Tyson resumed boxing and in 1996 regained two of his championship belts with easy victories over Frank Bruno and Bruce Seldon. On Nov. 9, 1996, in a long-anticipated bout with two-time heavyweight champion Evander Holyfield, Tyson lost for the second time in his professional career, by a technical knockout in the 11th round. In a rematch against Holyfield on June 28, 1997, he was disqualified after he twice bit his opponent's ears, and, as a result of the infraction, he lost his boxing license.

Tyson eventually was relicensed, and he returned to the ring on Jan. 16, 1999, when he knocked out Franz Botha in the fifth round. On February 6, however, Tyson was sentenced to one year in jail, two years of probation, and 200 hours of community service and was fined $2,500 after he pleaded no contest to the charges that he had assaulted two elderly men following a 1998 automobile accident. Tyson was released after serving just a few months of the one-year sentence.

Nevertheless, Tyson's self-control problems continued. After the referee stopped a fight in June 2000 with American Lou Savarese, Tyson continued punching and inadvertently injured the referee. In comments made to the press after this fight, Tyson outraged boxing fans with bizarre and vicious remarks about British heavyweight champion Lennox Lewis. In his October 2000 bout with Andrew Golota, Tyson won in the third round, but the fight was later declared a no contest because Tyson tested positive for marijuana. Tyson had only one more fight between October 2000 and his June 2002 fight with Lewis.

It had been difficult to schedule this fight. Both men were contractually bound to different promoters and cable television companies. Tyson had attacked and bitten Lewis during a press conference, which also had a dampening effect. Finally, Tyson's legal problems caused him to be denied a boxing license by the sanctioning bodies of the U.S. states that usually hold major boxing matches (such as Nevada). It had been so long since Tyson had fought a boxer of his own calibre that no one knew the level of his skills. The question was settled when Lewis twice knocked Tyson to the canvas during the course of the fight before knocking him out in the eighth round.

Tyson had his final professional win in 2003, a 49-second first-round knockout. Later that year, he filed for bankruptcy, claiming to be $34 million in debt after earning an estimated $400 million over the course of his career. Tyson lost bouts in 2004 and 2005, and he retired in the aftermath of the latter fight. In 2007 he served 24 hours in prison after pleading guilty to drug possession and driving under the influence, charges that stemmed from a 2006 arrest. A documentary about his life, *Tyson*, premiered at the Cannes Film Festival in 2008.

FOOTBALL

There were exclusively African American collegiate football organizations in the early days of the game, but both college and professional football were integrated to a limited extent almost from the beginning. Until the 1950s, however, it was unusual for college teams to have more than one or two black players and a "gentleman's agreement" by owners prevented African Americans from playing in the National Football League from 1934 to 1945. Among the black collegiate stars in the 1930s and '40s were Paul Robeson, better remembered as an actor and singer, and Jackie Robinson, whose most important contributions to African American history came as a baseball player. As late as the 1950s Northern college teams honoured the "sensibilities" of Southern host teams by benching African American players.

JIM BROWN

(b. Feb. 17, 1936, St. Simons, Ga., U.S.)

Jim Brown led the National Football League (NFL) in rushing for eight of his nine seasons. He was the dominant player of his era and one of the small number of running backs rated as the best of all time.

In high school and at Syracuse University in New York, Brown displayed exceptional all-around athletic ability, excelling in basketball, baseball, track, and lacrosse as well as football. In his final year at Syracuse, Brown earned All-America honours in both football and lacrosse. Many considered Brown's best sport to be lacrosse, and he was inducted into both the Pro Football Hall of Fame and the U.S. Lacrosse National Hall of Fame.

From 1957 through 1965, Brown played for the Cleveland Browns of the NFL, and he led the league in rushing yardage every year except 1962. Standing 6 feet 2 inches and weighing 232 pounds, Brown was a bruising runner who possessed the speed to outrun opponents as well as the strength to run over them. He rushed for more than 1,000 yards in seven seasons and established NFL single-season records by rushing for 1,527 yards in 1958 (12-game schedule) and 1,863 yards in 1963 (14-game schedule), a record broken by O.J. Simpson in 1973. On Nov. 24, 1957, he set an NFL record by rushing for 237 yards in a single game, and he equaled that total on Nov. 19, 1961. At the close of his career, he had scored 126 touchdowns, 106 by rushing, had gained a record 12,312 yards in 2,359 rushing attempts for an average of 5.22 yards, and had a record combined yardage (rushing along with pass receptions) of 15,459 yards. Brown's rushing and combined yardage records stood until 1984, when both were surpassed by Walter Payton of the Chicago Bears.

At 30 years of age and seemingly at the height of his athletic abilities, Brown retired from football to pursue a career in motion pictures. He appeared in many action and adventure films, among them *The Dirty Dozen* (1967) and *100 Rifles*

(1969). Brown was also active in issues facing African Americans, forming groups to assist black-owned businesses and to rehabilitate gang members.

MARION MOTLEY

(b. June 5, 1920, Leesburg, Ga., U.S.—d. June 27, 1999, Cleveland, Ohio)

Running back Marion Motley helped desegregate professional football in the 1940s during a career that earned him induction into the Pro Football Hall of Fame in 1968. Motley's bruising running style and exceptional blocking ability marked him as one of the sport's greatest players.

Motley was a fullback and linebacker for both South Carolina State University (Orangeburg) and the University of Nevada (Reno) before playing for the Great Lakes Naval Training Station during World War II. His coach there was Paul Brown, who later was named the first coach of the Cleveland Browns in the All-America Football Conference (AAFC). Motley signed with Cleveland as a fullback in 1946, breaking professional football's 13-year colour barrier along with three other players.

Motley, 6 feet 1 inch tall and weighing 238 pounds, was the leading rusher in the four-year history of the AAFC, with 3,024 yards. The Cleveland Browns won every AAFC title and compiled a 47–4–3 regular-season record. Motley, who also contributed defensively, was an AAFC linebacker in each of his first three seasons.

When the Browns joined the National Football League (NFL) in 1950, Motley led the league with 810 yards, an average of 5.8 yards per carry, and was named to the All-Pro team. The Browns won the NFL title in 1950 and advanced to the title game in each of the next three seasons. Motley missed the 1954 season because of a knee injury. He finished his career with the Pittsburgh Steelers in 1955. In all, Motley totaled 4,720 rushing yards (a 5.7-yard average) and scored 31 touchdowns.

Motley's career has been overshadowed by later Browns fullback Jim Brown, who played in an era when the NFL attracted a broad national audience through television. However, Motley, using a similar combination of speed and power, was just as dominant during his career and was considered by many, including Coach Paul Brown, to have been the more complete player.

WALTER PAYTON

(b. July 25, 1954, Columbia, Miss., U.S.—d. Nov. 1, 1999, Barrington, Ill.)

Walter Payton's productivity and durability made him one of the game's greatest running backs. He retired in 1987 as the leading rusher in the history of the National Football League (NFL), a title he held until 2002 when he was surpassed by Emmitt Smith.

Chicago Bears running back Walter Payton tries eluding a tackle by Los Angeles Rams linebacker Jim Collins, Nov. 6, 1983. George Rose/Getty Images

21,803 yards), most seasons with 1,000 or more yards rushing (10), most yards gained in a single game (275 yards), most games with 100 or more yards gained in a career (77), and most career touchdowns earned by rushing (110).

Besides being an outstanding rusher, Payton was a capable blocker, pass receiver, and even passer. He was best known, however, for his pinball running style, in which he often bounced off would-be tacklers. His rigorous off-season training regimen contributed to his durability; he started in more than 180 consecutive games in his career.

Payton was inducted into the Pro Football Hall of Fame in 1993. Established in 1987, the Walter Payton Award is presented annually to the top player in Division I-AA college football. During his final year of life, while suffering from a rare liver disease, Payton was credited with awakening national interest in organ donation.

Payton played football in high school and at Jackson State University in Mississippi. It was during his college years that he gained the sobriquet "Sweetness" for his affable personality and graceful athleticism. In 1975 he was drafted by the NFL Chicago Bears. Payton played his entire career (12 seasons) with the Bears, filling the position of halfback for most of that time. He set NFL records for total career rushing yardage (16,726 yards), most combined career yards gained (rushing and pass receiving,

JERRY RICE

(b. Oct. 13, 1962, Starkville, Miss., U.S.)

Jerry Rice is considered by many to be the greatest wide receiver in the history of the National Football League (NFL). Playing primarily for the San Francisco 49ers, he set a host of NFL records, including those for career touchdowns (208), receptions (1,549), and reception yardage (22,895).

The son of a brick mason, Rice was celebrated for having developed strong, reliable hands by catching bricks that his brothers threw to him while working for their father. He attended Mississippi Valley State University in Itta Bena on a football scholarship. There he earned All-America honours and set 18 records in Division I-AA of the National Collegiate Athletic Association, including most catches in a single game (24).

Rice was drafted by the San Francisco 49ers in the first round of the 1985 NFL draft. He initially struggled to hold on to the ball as he concentrated on the intricate pass patterns of the San Francisco offense, but in his second season he caught 86 passes and led the league in reception yardage (1,570) and touchdown receptions (15). Rice thrived in San Francisco head coach Bill Walsh's "West Coast" offense, which relied on a large number of short, quick passes by the quarterback and precise route running by the receivers. He set a single-season record for touchdown receptions (22) in 1987, even though a players' strike limited the season to 12 games, and was named NFL Player of the Year. Standing 6 feet 2 inches tall, Rice was larger than the typical NFL wide receiver, and he used his size and strength to overmatch defenders. He was also an exceptional runner after making a catch.

Rice played on three Super Bowl championship teams with the 49ers (1988, 1989, and 1994 seasons), and he, along with quarterback Joe Montana and defensive back Ronnie Lott, became virtually synonymous with the team. He was named the Most Valuable Player of Super Bowl XXIII (1988 season), and he set numerous Super Bowl records. Rice was named to the annual Pro Bowl from 1986 through 1998. In a controversial move to develop younger players, the 49ers traded Rice to the Oakland Raiders before the 2001 season. The following season he became the first player to register more than 200 career touchdowns as he helped the Raiders reach Super Bowl XXXVII, where they were defeated by the Tampa Bay Buccaneers. In 2003 he made his 13th Pro Bowl appearance. Midway through the 2004 season, Rice was traded to the Seattle Seahawks, but he was released by the team at the end of the season. After an unsuccessful attempt to become a starting receiver for the Denver Broncos the following year, he signed a ceremonial one-day contract with San Francisco and retired as a 49er.

EDDIE ROBINSON

(b. Feb. 13, 1919, Jackson, La.,
U.S.—d. April 3, 2007, Ruston, La.)

Eddie Robinson spent his entire head-coaching career at Grambling State University in Louisiana. On Oct. 7, 1995, having guided Grambling to a 42–6 win over Mississippi Valley State, he became the first coach to claim 400 victories. He finished his career with 408 wins.

Edward Gay Robinson attended Leland College in Baker, La., where he played quarterback and led the team to a combined 18–1 record over the 1939 and 1940 seasons. During his final two years at Leland, he also served as an assistant coach. He earned his bachelor's degree in 1941 and received a master's degree from the University of Iowa in 1954.

In 1941 Grambling (then known as Louisiana Negro Normal and Industrial Institute) hired Robinson to coach football and basketball and teach physical education. In his first season he had no assistants and no budget for replacing equipment. He handled virtually everything himself, from mowing the field to taping players' ankles to writing accounts of the games for the local newspaper. That season his team posted a record of 3–5. The next season, however, he guided the team to a perfect 8–0 record.

Robinson's Grambling Tigers went on to have two more perfect seasons, capture 17 conference titles, and win several National Negro championships. In the 1960s, after several decades when football at historically black colleges went largely unnoticed by most football fans, Robinson's Grambling teams gained fame for sending more players into professional football than any school except Notre Dame. Among the more than 200 of his players who went on to compete in the National Football League were Hall of Fame members Willie Davis, Willie Brown, and Buck Buchanan. The racial integration of college football in the South in the 1970s ended this brief period of football glory for Grambling and other black colleges.

Surpassing Bear Bryant's record for wins, Robinson earned his 324th career victory on Oct. 5, 1985, with a 27–7 defeat of Prairie View A&M in Dallas. At the end of the 1997 season, he retired with a lifetime record of 408–165–15. Robinson's record of 408 career victories stood until 2003, when it was broken by John Gagliardi, coach of St. John's of Minnesota. The recipient of numerous awards, Robinson was inducted into the College Football Hall of Fame in 1997.

O.J. Simpson

(b. July 9, 1947, San Francisco, Calif., U.S.)

Known for his speed and elusiveness, O.J. Simpson was one of football's premier running backs in the 1960s and '70s. His trial on murder charges in 1995 was one of the most celebrated criminal trials in American history.

Simpson (born Orenthal James Simpson) played football at Galileo High School in San Francisco, first as a tackle and then as a fullback. He attended San Francisco City College (1965–66) to achieve a scholastic record that allowed him to play at the University of Southern California (USC), where he set team records for yards gained by rushing: 1967, 1,415 yards; 1968, 1,709 yards. He was named All-American (1967–68), played in two Rose Bowl games, and won the Heisman Trophy as the best collegiate player of the season (1968). At USC he was also a member of a world-record-setting 440-yard relay team.

Buffalo Bills running back O.J. Simpson.
Robert L. Smith/NFL/Getty Images

Simpson, who was often called "Juice" because of his energetic runs and because his initials could stand for "orange juice," was the number one draft choice of the American Football League (AFL) Buffalo Bills in 1969. The following year the AFL merged with the National Football League (NFL). The Bills were members of the American Football Conference (AFC) of the NFL when Simpson set a single-season record for yards gained rushing (2,003) in 1973. The Bills were never a contending team

during his stay, but he was a great box-office draw. Injuries to his knees prompted the Bills to trade him in 1978 to the San Francisco 49ers, but he retired after the 1979 season. His 1975 record of most touchdowns scored in a season (23) stood until 1983, and his 1973 season rushing record for most yards gained lasted until 1984, when it was broken by Eric Dickerson. Simpson led the AFC in rushing yardage four times (1972–73, 1975–76). His career total yards gained (11,236) was second in the all-time rankings at the time of his retirement. He was inducted into the Pro Football Hall of Fame in 1985.

After retiring from football, Simpson became a film and television actor and sports commentator. On June 12, 1994, his ex-wife Nicole Brown Simpson and her friend Ronald Goldman were stabbed to death outside her home in Los Angeles. Simpson was arrested and charged with the two murders on June 17; he pleaded not guilty and hired a team of prominent lawyers to handle his defense. His lengthy nationally televised trial became the focus of unprecedented media scrutiny. A jury acquitted Simpson of the murder charges on Oct. 3, 1995. In a separate civil trial decision in 1997, he was found liable for the deaths of his ex-wife and Goldman and was ordered to pay $33.5 million in damages to the families. Simpson later collaborated (with Pablo F. Fenjves) on *If I Did It*, in which he hypothesized about how he would have committed the murders. Public outrage prevented its initial publication in 2006, but a bankruptcy court subsequently awarded the book's rights to the Goldman family, who released the work in 2007.

Later that year, Simpson was arrested after he and several other men entered a Las Vegas hotel room and took memorabilia items that Simpson claimed had been stolen from him. The incident resulted in Simpson being charged with a number of crimes, including armed robbery and kidnapping. On Oct. 3, 2008, a jury found him guilty of all charges. He was later sentenced to a minimum of nine years in prison, with a possible maximum sentence of 33 years.

TRACK AND FIELD

Many African Americans have excelled in track and field, especially in the sprints, hurdles, middle-distance races, and the broad, triple, and high jumps. Decades before Carl Lewis won a total of nine gold medals in four different events at the Olympic Games of 1984, 1988, 1992, and 1996, another multitalented African American track athlete, Jesse Owens, emphatically put the lie to Hitler's theory of racial superiority during the 1936 Olympic Games at Berlin. Intended to be a world showcase for Nazi ideology, they are instead remembered for the Superman-like performance of Owens, who won four gold medals, prompting the humiliated Hitler to shun him in victory. The politics of the struggle for freedom and for civil rights were reflected at the 1968 Olympics in Mexico City when 200-metre-dash gold and bronze medalists, Tommie Smith and John Carlos, respectively, bowed their heads on the victory stand during the playing of "The Star Spangled Banner" while thrusting black-gloved fists into the air in black-power gestures.

BOB BEAMON

(b. Aug.29, 1946, Bronx, N.Y., U.S.)

Long jumper Bob Beamon set a world record of 29.2 feet at the 1968 Olympic Games in Mexico City. The new record surpassed the existing mark by an astounding 21.65 inches and stood for 23 years, until Mike Powell of the United States surpassed it in 1991.

Beamon began jumping at Jamaica High School (Long Island, N.Y.). He attended North Carolina Agricultural and Technical College (Greensboro), the University of Texas at El Paso, and Adelphi University (Long Island), where he also played basketball.

In Mexico City Beamon's athletic talent was aided by the high altitude and brisk tailwind. When he landed in the pit, he had no idea how far he had jumped or that he had just shattered the world record while also becoming the first long jumper to surpass the milestones of both 28 and 29 feet. When teammate Ralph Boston informed him that the jump was more than 29 feet, Beamon collapsed to the ground, overcome with such powerful

Bob Beamon breaking the world record in the long jump at the 1968 Olympic Games in Mexico City. UPI/Bettmann Newsphotos

emotions that he had to fight off nausea as well as tears and had to be helped to his feet by teammates.

After setting the record, Beamon competed irregularly and retired before the 1972 Olympics. Later he was a track coach, did youth work, and participated in various sports-related activities, including fund-raising for the U.S. Olympic Committee in 1984. When the U.S. Olympic Hall of Fame was established in 1983, he was among the first athletes to be inducted.

LEE EVANS

(b. Feb. 25, 1947, Madera, Calif., U.S.)

Lee Evans won two gold medals at the 1968 Olympic Games in Mexico City, and his victory in the 400-metre event there set a world record that lasted for two decades.

In 1966 Evans attracted national attention when he won the Amateur Athletic Union (AAU) 440-yard championship; the next year he won the 400-metre race at the Pan American Games, and he was the National Collegiate Athletic Association (NCAA) champion in the 400 metres in 1968. He set an unofficial world record of 44.0 seconds in the 400 metres during the 1968 Olympic trials.

When two of Evans's San Jose State University teammates were banned from the 1968 Olympics for their black militant protest during an awards ceremony, Evans threatened to drop out of the 400-metre race in a show of support. In the end, however, he elected to run, beginning with a burst of speed and winning a narrow victory. His winning time was measured by automatic timing at 43.86 seconds, setting a world record that would stand until 1988, when Butch Reynolds of the United States posted a time of 43.29 seconds; the high altitude in Mexico City was an advantage in Evans's record-setting run. At the same Olympics, Evans anchored the U.S. team that won the 4 × 400-metre relay, setting a world record of 2 min 56.1 sec. He expected to race again in the 1972 Olympics in Munich, W. Ger., after winning his last AAU championship, but a hamstring injury prevented his running in the 400 metres, and the U.S. 4 × 400 relay team, of which he was a member, did not race.

FLORENCE GRIFFITH JOYNER

(b. Dec. 21, 1959, Los Angeles, Calif., U.S.—d. Sept. 21, 1998, Mission Viejo, Calif.)

Glamorous sprinter Florence Griffith Joyner set world records in the 100 metres (10.49 seconds) and 200 metres (21.34 seconds) that have stood since 1988.

Delorez Florence Griffith started running at age seven, chasing jackrabbits to increase her speed. In 1980 she entered the University of California, Los Angeles (B.A., 1983), to train with coach Bob Kersee. At the 1984 Olympics in

Los Angeles, she won a silver medal in the 200-metre race and quickly became a media celebrity with her 6-inch decorated fingernails and eye-catching racing suits. Disappointed with her performance, however, she went into semiretirement. In 1987 she rededicated herself to the sport, adopting an intense weight-training program and altering her starting technique. That same year she married Al Joyner, winner of the 1984 gold medal in the triple jump and brother of Jackie Joyner-Kersee, a heptathlon champion. The changes produced dramatic results. At the 1988 Olympic trials, Griffith Joyner (now dubbed "FloJo") set a world record in the 100-metre sprint (10.49 seconds), beating the old mark by 0.27 second and improving her previous best by more than half a second. Later that year at the Olympics in South Korea, she captured three gold medals (100 metres, 200 metres, and 4 × 100-metre relay) and a silver (4 × 400-metre relay). In 1988 Griffith Joyner received the Sullivan Award as the nation's top amateur performer. Though her remarkable performances sparked rumours of steroid use, drug tests revealed no banned substances.

After retiring in 1989, Griffith Joyner established a foundation for underprivileged children and from 1993 to 1995 served as the cochair of the President's Council on Physical Fitness. A comeback attempt in 1996 ended following a leg injury. She was inducted into the Track and Field Hall of Fame in 1995.

CARL LEWIS

(b. July 1, 1961, Birmingham, Ala., U.S.)

Track-and-field superstar Carl Lewis won nine Olympic gold medals during the 1980s and '90s.

Lewis (born Frederick Carlton Lewis) qualified for the U.S. Olympic team in 1980 but did not compete, because of the U.S. boycott of the Moscow Games. At the 1984 Games in Los Angeles, Lewis won gold medals in the 100-metre (9.9 sec) and 200-metre (19.8 sec) races, in the long jump (28.02 feet) as a member of the U.S. 4 × 100-metre relay team, which he anchored. Lewis became the third track-and-field athlete to win four gold medals in one Olympics, joining Americans Alvin Kraenzlein (1900) and Jesse Owens, the latter of whom won the same four events at the 1936 Olympics in Berlin that Lewis won in Los Angeles.

Lewis added two more gold medals and a silver medal at the 1988 Games in Seoul, S. Kor., becoming the first Olympic athlete to win consecutive long-jump gold medals, with a leap of 28.61 feet had the four best jumps in the competition, and his Olympic title was part of a long string of consecutive long-jump victories that extended over several years during the 1980s. Lewis's other gold medal at the 1988 Games came in the 100 metres (9.92 sec), after Canadian Ben Johnson, who had won in world-record time (9.79 sec), was disqualified three days later after testing positive for anabolic steroids. Lewis settled for a silver in the 200 metres.

At the 1992 Olympics in Barcelona. won two more gold medals, including his third consecutive long-jump title, with a leap of 28.44 feet. Again anchoring the U.S. 4 × 100-metre relay team, Lewis won his eighth gold medal as the team set a world and Olympic record of 37.40 sec. At age 35 Lewis was a surprise qualifier in the long jump for the 1996 Olympics in Atlanta, where he "ran through" his first jump and notched a ho-hum 26.71 feet on his second leap. However, his last leap of 27.89 feet, though well off any records or personal bests, held up as the top jump and earned Lewis his ninth gold medal. In 1997 he retired from competition.

EDWIN MOSES

(b. Aug. 31, 1955, Dayton, Ohio, U.S.)

Hurdler Edwin Moses dominated the 400-metre hurdles event for a decade, winning gold medals in the race at the 1976 and 1984 Olympic Games.

Moses competed in cross-country, track, and football in high school and studied physics at Morehouse College (B.S., 1978) in Atlanta. There he first ran the 400-metre race and the 120-yard high hurdles but began running the 400-metre hurdles in 1976.

In the 1976 Olympic Games at Montreal, Moses won the gold medal and set his first world record of 47.64 sec.

He proceeded to set successive world records for the 400-metre hurdles of 47.45 sec (1977), 47.13 sec (1980), and 47.02 sec (1983), the last of which stood for nine years. Moses defended his Olympic title at the 1984 Games in Los Angeles. His swiftest Olympic time, 47.56 sec, earned him a bronze medal at the 1988 Games in Seoul, S. Kor. In one of the sport's best-known winning streaks, Moses was unbeaten in the 400-metre hurdles from 1977 until 1987, with victories in more than 100 consecutive finals.

Moses briefly shifted his competitive focus to bobsledding in the early 1990s, competing at a world-class level. Active in sports administration from the mid-1980s, he helped design a new drug testing program and was named president of the International Amateur Athletic Association in 1997. He received a master's degree from Pepperdine University in 1994. Also that year he was inducted into the U.S. National Track & Field Hall of Fame.

JESSE OWENS

(b. Sept. 12, 1913, Oakville, Ala., U.S.—d. March 31, 1980, Phoenix, Ariz.)

Jesse Owens set a world record in the running broad jump (also called long jump) that stood for 25 years and won four gold medals at the 1936 Olympic Games in Berlin.

As a student in a Cleveland high school, Owens (born James Cleveland

Jesse Owens, 1936. AP

Owens) won three events at the 1933 National Interscholastic Championships in Chicago. In one day, May 25, 1935, while competing for Ohio State University (Columbus) in a Western (later Big Ten) Conference track-and-field meet at the University of Michigan (Ann Arbor), Owens equaled the world record for the 100-yard dash (9.4 sec) and broke the world records for the 220-yard dash (20.3 sec), the 220-yard low hurdles (22.6 sec), and the long jump (26.67 feet).

Owens's performance at the 1936 Berlin Olympics has become legend, both for his brilliant gold-medal efforts in the 100-metre run (10.3 sec, an Olympic record), the 200-metre run (20.7 sec, a world record), the long jump (8.06 metres [26.4 feet]), and the 4 × 100-metre relay

(39.8 sec) and for events away from the track. One popular tale that arose from Owens's victories was that of the "snub," the notion that Hitler refused to shake hands with Owens because he was an African American. In truth, by the second day of competition, when Owens won the 100-metre final, Hitler had decided to no longer publicly congratulate any of the athletes. The previous day the International Olympic Committee president, angry that Hitler had publicly congratulated only a few German and Finnish winners before leaving the stadium after the German competitors were eliminated from the day's final event, insisted that the German chancellor congratulate all or none of the victors. Unaware of the situation, American papers reported the "snub," and the myth grew over the years.

Despite the politically charged atmosphere of the Berlin Games, Owens was adored by the German public, and it was German long jumper Carl Ludwig ("Luz") Long who aided Owens through a bad start in the long jump competition. Owens was flustered to learn that what he had thought was a practice jump had been counted as his first attempt. Unsettled, he foot-faulted the second attempt. Before Owens's last jump, Long suggested that the American place a towel in front of the take-off board. Leaping from that point, Owens qualified for the finals, eventually beating Long (later his close friend) for the gold.

For a time, Owens held alone or shared the world records for all sprint distances recognized by the International Amateur Athletic Federation (IAAF; later International Association of Athletics Federations).

After retiring from competitive track, Owens engaged in boys' guidance activities, made goodwill visits to India and East Asia for the U.S. Department of State, served as secretary of the Illinois State Athletic Commission, and worked in public relations.

WILMA RUDOLPH

(b. June 23, 1940, St. Bethlehem, near Clarksville, Tenn., U.S.—d. Nov. 12, 1994, Brentwood, Tenn.)

Sprinter Wilma Rudolph was the first American woman to win three track-and-field gold medals in a single Olympics.

Rudolph was sickly as a child and could not walk without an orthopedic shoe until she was 11 years old. Her determination to compete, however, made her a star basketball player and sprinter during high school in Clarksville, Tenn. She attended Tennessee State University from 1957 to 1961. At age 16 she competed in the 1956 Olympic Games at Melbourne, winning a bronze medal in the 4 × 100-metre relay race. In 1960, before the Olympic Games at Rome, she set a world record of 22.9 seconds for the 200-metre race. In the Games themselves she won gold medals in the 100-metre dash (tying the world record: 11.3 seconds), in the 200-metre dash, and as a member of the 4 × 100-metre relay team, which had set a world record of 44.4 seconds in a semifinal race. She was Amateur Athletic Union (AAU) 100-yard-dash champion (1959–62).

Her strikingly fluid style made Rudolph a particular favourite with spectators and journalists. She won the AAU's 1961 Sullivan Award as the year's outstanding amateur athlete. After retiring as a runner, Rudolph was an assistant director for a youth foundation in Chicago during the 1960s to develop girls' track-and-field teams, and thereafter she promoted running nationally. She was named to the National Track & Field Hall of Fame in 1974, the International Sports Hall of Fame in 1980, and the U.S. Olympic Hall of Fame in 1983, in the first group of inductees. Her autobiography, *Wilma*, was published in 1977.

TENNIS, GOLF, AND HORSE RACING

African American jockeys such as Isaac Burns Murphy found success in horse racing as early the late 19th century; it would be more than 50 years later before African Americans made their mark in the "country club" sports of golf and tennis, with Althea Gibson and Arthur Ashe the first black woman and man to excel on the tennis court. By the end of the century, however, women's tennis was dominated by a pair of African Americans, the Williams sisters, Serena and Venus, while Tiger Woods was unchallenged as the greatest professional golfer.

ARTHUR ASHE

(b. July 10, 1943, Richmond, Va.,
U.S.—d. Feb. 6, 1993, New York, N.Y.)

Arthur Ashe was the first African American tennis player to win a major men's singles championship.

Ashe began to play tennis at the age of seven in a neighbourhood park. He was coached by Walter Johnson of Lynchburg, Va., who had coached tennis champion Althea Gibson. Ashe moved to St. Louis, Mo., where he was coached by Richard Hudlin, before he entered the University of California at Los Angeles on a tennis scholarship. In 1963 Ashe won the U.S. hard-court singles championship; in 1965 he took the intercollegiate singles and doubles titles; and in 1967 he won the U.S. clay-court singles championship. In 1968 he captured the U.S. (amateur) singles and open singles championships. He played on the U.S. Davis Cup team (1963–70, 1975, 1977–78) and helped the U.S. team to win the Davis Cup challenge (final) round in 1968, 1969, and 1970. In the latter year he became a professional.

His criticism of South African apartheid racial policy led to denial of permission to play in that country's open tournament, and, as a consequence, on March 23, 1970, South Africa was excluded from Davis Cup competition. In 1975, when he won the Wimbledon singles and the World Championship singles, he was ranked first in world tennis. After retiring from play in 1980, he became captain of the U.S. Davis Cup team, a position he held from 1981 to 1985.

Ashe underwent coronary bypass operations in 1979 and 1983. In April 1992 he revealed that he had become infected with the virus that causes AIDS, probably through a tainted blood transfusion received during one of those operations. For the remainder of his life, Ashe devoted considerable time to efforts to educate the public about the disease.

ALTHEA GIBSON

(b. Aug. 25, 1927, Silver, S.C., U.S.—d.
Sept. 28, 2003, East Orange, N.J.)

Althea Gibson dominated women's tennis in the late 1950s. She was the first black player to win the French (1956), Wimbledon (1957–58), and U.S. Open (1957–58) singles championships.

Gibson grew up in New York City, where she began playing tennis at an early age under the auspices of the New York Police Athletic League. In 1942 she won her first tournament, which was sponsored by the American Tennis Association (ATA), an organization founded by African American players. In 1947 she captured the ATA's women's singles championship, which she would hold for 10 consecutive years. While attending Florida Agricultural and Mechanical University (B.S., 1953) in Tallahassee, she continued to play in tournaments around the country and in 1950 became the first black tennis player to enter the national grass-court championship tournament at Forest Hills in Queens, N.Y. The next year she entered the Wimbledon tournament, again as the first black player ever invited. The tall and lean Gibson soon became noted for her dominating serves and powerful play.

Until 1956 Gibson had only fair success in match tennis play, but that year she won a number of tournaments in Asia and Europe, including the French and Italian singles titles and the women's doubles title at Wimbledon. In 1957–58 she won the Wimbledon women's singles and doubles titles and took the U.S. women's

Althea Gibson plays centre court at Wimbledon, Eng., during the 1956 women's singles quarter finals. Reg Speller/ Hulton Archive/Getty Images

singles championship at Forest Hills. She also won the U.S. mixed doubles and the Australian women's doubles in 1957. That year Gibson was voted Female Athlete of the Year by the Associated Press, becoming the first African American to receive the honour; she also won the award the following year. Having worked her way to top rank in world amateur tennis, she turned professional following her 1958 Forest Hills win. She won the women's professional singles title in 1960, but, there being few tournaments and prizes for women at that time, she took up professional golf in the early 1960s. From 1973 to 1992 Gibson was active in sports administration, mainly for the state of New Jersey. Her autobiography, *I Always Wanted to Be Somebody*, appeared in 1958. In 1971 she was elected to the National Lawn Tennis Hall of Fame.

ISAAC BURNS MURPHY

(b. 1861, Fayette county, Kentucky, U.S.—d. Feb. 12, 1896, Lexington, Ky.)

Isaac Burns Murphy was the first jockey to be elected to the National Museum of Racing's Hall of Fame in Saratoga Springs, N.Y.; he is one of only two African American jockeys to have received this honour (the other is Willie Simms). Some sportswriters referred to him as the "colored Archer" in reference to the English champion jockey Frederick Archer. Other sportswriters suggested that Archer should instead be referred to as the "white Murphy."

Murphy began racing in 1875 and was one of the first jockeys to pace his mount for a charge down the home-stretch—a technique soon described as the "grandstand finish." He rode upright and urged his mounts on with words and a spur rather than the whip. His win of the Travers Stakes at Saratoga Springs in 1879 catapulted him to national fame. He rode in the Kentucky Derby 11 times and was the first jockey to win successive Derby crowns and the first three-time winner, in 1884, 1890, and 1891. In 1884 he won the first American Derby in Chicago, the most prestigious race of the era. He

Isaac Burns Murphy, c. 1895. Library of Congress, Washington, D.C. (digital file number: cph 3a50336)

won this race again in 1885, 1886, and 1888. He also won a celebrated match race against fellow Hall of Famer Edward ("Snapper") Garrison in 1890. Murphy's career winning percentage of 34.5 has never been equaled.

Even though Murphy rode before jockeys received a share of the winnings, he was the highest-paid athlete in the United States, earning close to $20,000 a year at his peak in the late 1880s. By the mid-1890s, however, his ongoing battles with weight gain and alcoholism had severely curtailed his career.

SERENA WILLIAMS

(b. Sept. 26, 1981, Saginaw, Mich., U.S.)

Serena Williams and her sister Venus revolutionized women's tennis. With her powerful style of play, Serena Williams became one of the game's most dominant athletes in the early 21st century.

Williams learned tennis from her father on the public courts in Los Angeles and turned professional in 1995, one year after Venus. Possessing powerful serves and ground strokes and superb athleticism, the sisters soon attracted much attention. Many predicted Venus would be the first Williams sister to win a grand slam singles title, but it was Serena who accomplished the feat, winning the 1999 U.S. Open.

At the 2000 Olympic Games in Sydney, Serena and Venus won gold medals in the doubles event. After several years of inconsistent play, Serena asserted

Venus and Serena Williams celebrate, having just won a women's doubles match at Wimbledon, June 30, 2003. Phil Cole/Getty Images

herself in 2002 and won the French Open, the U.S. Open, and Wimbledon, defeating Venus in the finals of each tournament. Known for her fierce tenacity, Serena won the Australian Open and Wimbledon the following year, again besting her sister in the finals, and in 2005 she won the Australian Open again. Beset by injury the following year, she rebounded in 2007 to win her third Australian Open. Serena and Venus won their second doubles tennis gold medal at the 2008 Olympic Games in Beijing. Later that year Serena won the U.S. Open for a third time. In 2009 she captured her 10th grand slam singles title by winning the Australian Open; later that year she won her third Wimbledon singles title, once again defeating her sister.

In 2009 her autobiography, *On the Line* (cowritten with Daniel Paisner), was published.

VENUS WILLIAMS

(b. June 17, 1980, Lynwood, Calif., U.S.)

Along with her sister Serena, Venus Williams redefined women's tennis with her strength and superb athleticism.

Like her sister Serena, Venus was introduced to tennis on the public courts in Los Angeles by her father, who early on recognized her talent and oversaw her development. She turned professional in 1994 and soon attracted attention for her powerful serves and ground strokes. In 1997 she became the first unseeded U.S. Open women's finalist in the open era; she lost to Martina Hingis. In 2000 Williams won both Wimbledon and the U.S. Open, and she defended her titles in 2001.

At the 2000 Olympic Games in Sydney, Williams captured the gold medal in the singles competition to go with the one she claimed with Serena in the doubles event. In 2005 Venus captured the Wimbledon championship. She struggled with injuries and competed in only a few tournaments the following year but went on to win her fourth Wimbledon in 2007. In 2008 Venus defeated Serena for a fifth career Wimbledon title, placing her fifth all-time in women's Wimbledon singles championships.

TIGER WOODS

(b. Dec. 30, 1975, Cypress, Calif., U.S.)

Tiger Woods enjoyed one of the greatest amateur careers in the history of golf and became a dominant player on the professional circuit in the late 1990s. In 1997 Woods became the first golfer of either African American or Asian descent to win the Masters Tournament, one of the most prestigious events in the sport. With his victory at the 2001 Masters, Woods became the first player to win consecutively the four major tournaments of golf—the Masters, the United States Open, the British Open, and the Professional Golfers' Association of America (PGA) Championship.

Woods was the child of an African American father and a Thai mother. A naturally gifted player, he took up golfing at a very young age and soon became a prodigy, taking swings on a television program when he was two years old and shooting a 48 over nine holes at age three. In 1991, at age 15, he became the youngest winner of the U.S. Junior Amateur championship; he also captured the 1992 and 1993 Junior Amateur titles. In 1994 he came from six holes behind to win the first of his three consecutive U.S. Amateur championships. He enrolled at Stanford University in 1994 and won the collegiate title in 1996. After claiming his third U.S. Amateur title, Woods left college and turned professional on Aug. 29, 1996. Playing as a pro in eight PGA events in 1996, he won two titles and was named the PGA Tour's outstanding rookie.

Woods was able to generate such club speed that he routinely hit drives of more than 300 yards. His booming long game, coupled with his expert putting and chipping and his reputation for mental toughness, made him an intimidating opponent and a popular player among fans. At the 1997 Masters Tournament in Augusta, Ga., Woods shot a tournament record 270 over 72 holes and finished 12 strokes ahead of the rest of the field in one of the most dominating performances in the history of professional golf. In 1999 he became the first golfer in more than two decades to win eight PGA tournaments in a year. His six consecutive victories (1999–2000) tied Ben Hogan's 1948 streak, the second longest in PGA history; Byron Nelson holds the record with 11 straight wins. In June 2000 Woods again made history with his record-breaking win at the U.S. Open. He became the first player to finish the tournament at 12 under par, tying Jack Nicklaus for the lowest 72-hole score (272), and Woods's 15-stroke victory was the largest winning margin at a major championship. On July 23, 2000, Woods became the fifth player in golf history, and the youngest, to complete the career grand slam of the four major championships by winning the British Open. (In 1930, when Bobby Jones won the only calendar-year grand slam, the four major tournaments were the U.S. and British Open and Amateur championships.) Woods's victory by a comfortable 8 strokes was a record-setting 19 strokes under par. He won back-to-back Masters titles in 2001–02.

In 2005, after a drought of 10 winless major tournaments, Woods won the Masters and the British Open. He dominated the tour the following year, winning nine events, including the British Open and the PGA Championship. In 2007 he defended his title at the latter tournament to claim his 13th major championship. Some two months after undergoing knee surgery in 2008, Woods captured his third U.S. Open title in his first tournament back on the tour, completing his third career grand slam, a feat matched only by Nicklaus. Woods's dramatic U.S. Open victory—which involved an 18-hole play-off round followed by a sudden-death play-off—aggravated the damage to his knee, and the following week he withdrew from the remainder of the 2008 golf season in order to have more-extensive knee surgery. His return to the sport in 2009 featured a number of tournament wins but no major titles for the first time since 2004. Also in 2009, Woods's unprecedented streak of having never lost a major tournament when leading or co-leading after 54 holes was broken at 14 when he lost the PGA Championship after being ahead by two strokes before the final round.

In November 2009 Woods was involved in an early morning one-car accident outside his home in Orlando, Fla. The unusual circumstances of the crash led to a great deal of media scrutiny into his personal life. It was revealed that Woods, who had married Elin Nordegren in 2004, had a number of extramarital affairs, and his infidelity—which clashed with his solid-citizen reputation that had helped him earn hundreds of millions of dollars in endorsements over the years—became national news. The following month, Woods announced that he was taking an indefinite leave from golf in order to spend more time with his family. He returned to the sport in April 2010 at the Masters Tournament.

It is something of a cliché to talk about athletes "giving back to the community," but many of the sports figures presented here have done just that, through support of causes, involvement with benefits, and establishment of foundations. Athletes and teams also "represent" their communities, fostering civic pride and camaraderie in their fans. As has been demonstrated in this chapter, at different times in history African American athletes have played a very special role as symbolic representatives for the black community.

EPILOGUE

"We Shall Overcome," the unofficial anthem of the civil rights movement, was more than a prediction or a prayer for deliverance; it was a promise, a guarantee that with courage, faith, ingenuity, force of will, mutual reliance, and communal action the ideals of the Declaration of Independence and of the Constitution that had promised so much and delivered so little for African Americans, would become as real for them as they were for other Americans. From the perspective of the early 21st century, it can be argued that, through the efforts and achievements of the African Americans profiled in this book and those of countless others like them, much of that promise has been kept. Yet hurdles remain. The United States is a colour-blind society only when seen through rose-tinted glasses, but increasingly Americans have come to embrace and celebrate difference while their respect for one another's common humanity more and more becomes second nature.

This book has examined black achievement and excellence accomplished despite barriers and hardship and in the face of ignorance and intolerance. But it is not only the story of "firsts"; it is also simply the story of human accomplishment, of the triumphs of Americans who happen to be of African descent, triumphs that are not to be marginalized or rarefied but that are at the centre of American history. In his most famous speech Martin Luther King, Jr., said that he had been to the mountaintop and seen the promised land. What if that mountaintop now were, in the fashion of Mount Rushmore, a site where the achievements of African Americans were commemorated in chiseled portraiture? Who would be there? Martin Luther King, Frederick Douglass, Harriet Tubman, Booker T. Washington, W.E.B. Du Bois, Malcolm X, Toni Morrison, Barack Obama? Let the debate begin.

GLOSSARY

aegis Support or sanction.

alderman Representative in a city legislature.

arbitrator A person authorized to make decisions or to mediate conflict.

ascetic Applying strict self-discipline as a means of self-improvement.

bellwether A sign of future trends.

bildungsroman A novel showing the moral and psychological growth during the main character's formative years.

bondman/bondwoman A male or female slave or servant working without pay.

brigadier general A military rank just above that of colonel.

cavalry Military force mounted on horseback, formerly an important element in the armies of all major powers.

cleric Clergyman or clergywoman.

contralto Also known as alto, in vocal music, the second-highest voice in four-part music.

de facto Resulting from situational, as opposed to statutory, factors; in reality.

disfranchisement Denial of the right to vote.

elegiac An elegiac poem is one that laments loss, whether of worldly goods, glory, or human companionship.

epistolary novel A work taking the form of a series of letters written by one or more of the book's characters.

epochal Of great consequence or importance.

eschew To shun something, often as a matter of principle.

forensic Pertaining to argument or rhetoric.

foundry Location where metal is cast.

franchise A constitutionally guaranteed right or privilege, usually in reference to the right to vote. Also, membership in a professional athletic organization or league.

fulcrum Something that supplies capability for action.

graft Money or benefits procured by questionable or unlawful means.

impasto Paint that is so thickly applied to a canvas that it stands out from the surface.

infantry Soldiers who fight on foot.

ironclad An iron- or steel-plated wooden warship.

kinesis Physical response of an organism to a stimulus that causes an alteration in speed or direction of movement, though not necessarily in the direction of the stimulus.

modicum A small or limited amount.

morphology The form and structure of an organism or any of its parts.

nascent Recently born or newly formed.

nonet A musical group comprised of nine instruments or voices.

paean Tribute.

parity Equality.

patrician Pertaining to aristocracy or high social status.

peonage System of servitude in which employers induce or deceive individuals into signing contracts for labour to pay their debts or to avoid fines that might be imposed by the courts.

polemic An aggressive attack on the opinions or principles of another.

polymath A learned person whose knowledge spans a wide variety of subjects.

posthumous Following or occurring after one's death.

pro tempore Latin phrase literally meaning "for the time being." When applied to an office or legislative position, denotes one individual who assumes the responsibilities of another in his or her absence.

protégé An individual whose career or training is guided by the experience or influence of another.

provost A high-ranking university administrator.

pugnacious Prone to argumentation or belligerence.

restrictive covenant An agreement limiting the use of property.

sharecropper A farmer who works the land for an agreed share of the value of the crop minus charges for seeds, tools, living quarters, and food.

shtick Comic routine.

sobriquet Nickname.

solicitor general In the United States, the second highest ranking attorney in the Department of Justice after the Attorney General who is appointed to represent the United States in the Supreme Court.

strafing attack The attack by a low-flying aircraft on ground troops or targets.

suasion A persuasive effort or attempt or the act of doing so.

taxis The physical orientation of an organism in a specific spatial relationship to a stimulus.

BIBLIOGRAPHY

ABOLITIONISM AND ACTIVISM

Biographical and critical works on Frederick Douglass include Nathan Irvin Huggins, *Slave and Citizen: The Life of Frederick Douglass*, ed. by Oscar Handlin (1980); Dickson J. Preston, *Young Frederick Douglass: The Maryland Years* (1980), from his birth to his escape from slavery in 1838; William S. McFeely, *Frederick Douglass* (1991); David W. Blight, *Frederick Douglass' Civil War: Keeping Faith in Jubilee* (1989), tracing his intellectual evolution; and Eric J. Sundquist (ed.), *Frederick Douglass: New Literary and Historical Essays* (1990). Earl Conrad, *Harriet Tubman* (1943, reissued 1969) is a useful study of Harriet Tubman. The life and contributions of Booker T. Washington are considered in Louis R. Harlan, *Booker T. Washington: The Making of a Black Leader, 1856–1901* (1972), and *Booker T. Washington: The Wizard of Tuskegee, 1901–1915* (1983). Biographical and critical works concerning W.E.B. Du Bois include Arnold Rampersad, *The Art and Imagination of W.E.B. Du Bois* (1976, reissued 1990); Jack B. Moore, *W.E.B. Du Bois* (1981); Manning Marable, *W.E.B. Du Bois, Black Radical Democrat* (1986); David Levening Lewis, *W.E.B. DuBois—Biography of a Race, 1868–1919* (1993); Keith E. Byerman, *Seizing the Word: History, Art, and Self in the Work of W.E.B. DuBois* (1994); and Shamoon Zamir, *Dark Voices: W.E.B. DuBois and American Thought, 1888–1903* (1995). Martin Luther King, Jr.'s own writings remain useful starting points for those interested in his life and thought. In addition to articles, he published four major books: *Stride Toward Freedom: The Montgomery Story* (1958), *Strength to Love* (1963), *Why We Can't Wait* (1964), and *Where Do We Go from Here: Chaos or Community?* (1967). Clayborne Carson (ed.), *The Papers of Martin Luther King, Jr.* (1992–), is a multivolume collection that produced important new findings regarding King's family roots, academic studies, and religious development, and his *The Autobiography of Martin Luther King, Jr.* (1998) is a compilation of King's autobiographical writings. David J. Garrow, *Bearing the Cross* (1986, reissued 2004), is meticulously researched; and Taylor Branch, *Parting the Waters* (1988), *Pillar of Fire* (1998), and *At Canaan's Edge* (2006), a trilogy, remains the most comprehensive of the scholarly works on King, covering the years 1954 to 1968. Malcolm X and Alex Haley, *The Autobiography of Malcolm X* (1965, reissued 2001), is the classic work and still the best single source on Malcolm X's life and views. George Breitman (ed.), *Malcolm X Speaks* (1965, reissued 1990), is a collection of speeches from Malcolm's final years, which gives insight into his speaking style and wit.

PROTECT AND SERVE

Jesse Jackson's presidential campaign is discussed in Lucius J. Barker and Ronald

W. Walters (eds.), *Jesse Jackson's 1984 Presidential Campaign* (1989). A biography of Jackson is Marshall Frady, *Jesse: The Life and Pilgrimage of Jesse Jackson* (1996). David Mendell, *Obama: From Promise to Power* (2007), is a comprehensive biography of Barack Obama based on interviews with Obama and with his wife, family, friends, aides, and rivals as well as on the author's experience as a journalist covering Obama's rise. Although written by an ardent supporter and former law student of Obama's, John K. Wilson, *Barack Obama: This Improbable Quest* (2007), provides a useful examination of Obama's policy positions in Illinois. Pete Souza, Barack Obama and Lisa Rogak (ed.), *Barack Obama in His Own Words* (2007), is primarily a collection of speeches by Obama. Biographies and studies of Thurgood Marshall's career include Michael D. Davis and Hunter R. Clark, *Thurgood Marshall: Warrior at the Bar, Rebel at the Bench*, updated and rev. ed. (1994); Carl T. Rowan, *Dream Makers, Dream Breakers: The World of Justice Thurgood Marshall* (1993, reissued 2002); and Howard Ball, *A Life Defiant: Thurgood Marshall and the Persistence of Racism in America* (1998).

EXPLORATION, EDUCATION, EXPERIMENTATION, AND ECUMENISM

George Washington Carver is the subject of Rackham Holt, *George Washington Carver: An American Biography*, rev. ed. (1963); and Linda O. McMurry, *George Washington Carver, Scientist and Symbol* (1981). Mother Divine, *The Peace Mission Movement* (1982), offers an insider's view of the movement. Robert Weisbrot, *Father Divine and the Struggle for Racial Equality* (1983), is an important reconsideration of Father Divine that places him and his movement in the context of the civil rights struggle. Mattias Gardell, *In the Name of Elijah Muhammad: Louis Farrakhan and the Nation of Islam* (1997), is the best and most detailed study of Louis Farrakhan's movement. Arthur J. Magida, *Prophet of Rage: A Life of Louis Farrakhan and His Nation* (1996), is a journalistic biography of Farrakhan's life, based on interviews.

ARTS AND LETTERS

The life and art of Toni Morrison are the subjects of Linden Peach, *Toni Morrison* (1995); and Jan Furman, *Toni Morrison's Fiction* (1996). Biographical and critical works dealing with Langston Hughes include Faith Berry, *Langston Hughes, Before and Beyond Harlem* (1983, reissued 1992); Arnold Rampersad, *The Life of Langston Hughes*, 2 vol. (1986-88); and Richard K. Barksdale, *Langston Hughes* (1977). Biographical and critical works about James Baldwin include James Campbell, *Talking at the Gates: A Life of James Baldwin* (1991); David Leeming, *James Baldwin* (1994); Therman B. O'Daniel (ed.), *James Baldwin: A Critical Evaluation* (1977); and Fred L. Standley and Nancy V. Burt (eds.). Works of biography and criticism about Richard Wright include

Robert Felgar, *Richard Wright* (1980); Addison Gayle, *Richard Wright: Ordeal of a Native Son* (1980); Michel Fabre, *The World of Richard Wright* (1985), and *The Unfinished Quest of Richard Wright*, trans. from French, 2nd ed. (1993); Robert Butler, *Native Son: The Emergence of a New Black Hero* (1991); and Henry Louis Gates, Jr., and K.A. Appiah (eds.), *Richard Wright: Critical Perspectives Past and Present* (1993).

STAGE, SCREEN, AND MUSIC

Biographies of Louis Armstrong include Max Jones and John Chilton, *Louis: The Louis Armstrong Story, 1900–1971* (1971, reprinted 1988); Laurence Bergreen, *Louis Armstrong: An Extravagant Life* (1997); and Gary Giddins, *Satchmo: The Genius of Louis Armstrong* (2001). Biographical and critical works about Duke Ellington include Barry Ulanov, *Duke Ellington* (1946, reprinted 1975); Derek Jewell, *Duke* (1977, reissued 1986); Mercer Ellington with Stanley Dance, *Duke Ellington in Person* (1978, reissued 1988), by his son; and John Edward Hasse, *Beyond Category: The Life and Genius of Duke Ellington* (1993, reissued 1995). James Brown and Bruce Tucker, *James Brown: The Godfather of Soul* (1986, reissued 1997), is his autobiography. Gerri Hirshey, *Nowhere to Run: The Story of Soul Music* (1984, reissued 1994), pp. 54-63, contains information based on interviews with Brown. Aretha Franklin's career is discussed in Peter Guralnick, *Sweet Soul Music: Rhythm and Blues and the Southern Dream of Freedom* (1986, reprinted 1994), pp. 332-352; and Jerry Wexler and David Ritz, *Rhythm and the Blues: A Life in American Music* (1993), pp. 203-216, an overview written by Franklin's main producer, Wexler. Aretha Franklin and David Ritz, *From These Roots* (1999), is an autobiography. David Mills, et al., *George Clinton and P-Funk: An Oral History* (1998), is a definitive collection of viewpoints from Parliament-Funkadelic players themselves. Daniel Wolff et al., *You Send Me: The Life and Times of Sam Cooke* (1995), is an informative biography of Sam Cooke. James S. Haskins, *Spike Lee: By Any Means Necessary* (1997); and Melissa McDaniel, *Spike Lee: On His Own Terms* (1998), consider the life and career of Spike Lee.

SPORTS

Jules Tygiel, *Baseball's Great Experiment: Jackie Robinson and His Legacy* (1983, reissued 1993, expanded ed. 1997); David Falkner, *Great Time Coming: The Life of Jackie Robinson, from Baseball to Birmingham* (1995, reissued 1996); Arnold Rampersad, *Jackie Robinson: A Biography* (1997), study the life and impact of Jackie Robinson. Thomas Hauser, *Muhammad Ali: His Life and Times* (1991), and Mike Marqusee, *Redemption Song: Muhammad Ali and the Spirit of the Sixties* (1999), are biographies of Muhammad Ali. An informative biography of Jesse Owens is William J. Baker, *Jesse Owens: An American Life* (1986).

INDEX

Y